Saʻudi Policies towards Migrants and Refugees
A Sacred Duty

The King Faisal Center for Research and Islamic Studies (KFCRIS)

The KFCRIS is an independent non-governmental institution based in Riyadh, the Kingdom of Saʻudi Arabia. The Center was founded in 1403/1983 by the King Faisal Foundation (KFF) to preserve the legacy of the late King Faisal and to continue his mission of transmitting knowledge between the Kingdom and the world. The Center serves as a platform for research and Islamic Studies, bringing together researchers and research institutions from the Kingdom and across the world through conferences, workshops, and lectures, and through the production and publication of scholarly works, as well as the preservation of Islamic manuscripts.

The Center's Research Department is home to a group of established and promising researchers who endeavor to produce in-depth analyses in various fields, ranging from Socio-Economic, African, Asian, and Yemen Studies. The Center also hosts the Library which preserves invaluable Islamic manuscripts, the Al-Faisal Museum for Arab Islamic Art, the Al-Faisal Institute for Human Resources Development, the Darat Al-Faisal, and the Al-Faisal Cultural Press, which issues the *Al-Faisal* magazine and other key intellectual periodicals. For more information, please visit the Center's website: www.kfcris.com

Sa'udi Policies towards Migrants and Refugees
A Sacred Duty

Joseph A. Kéchichian and Fahad L. Alsharif

Copyright © The King Faisal Center for Research and Islamic Studies (KFCRIS), 2022.

The right of Joseph A. Kéchichian and Fahad L. Alsharif to be identified as Authors of this work has been asserted in accordance with the Copyright, Designs and Patents Act 1988.

2 4 6 8 10 9 7 5 3 1

First published in 2022 in Great Britain by
SUSSEX ACADEMIC PRESS
PO Box 139
Eastbourne BN24 9BP

Distributed in North America by
SUSSEX ACADEMIC PRESS
Independent Publishers Group
814 N. Franklin Street
Chicago, IL 60610

All rights reserved. Except for the quotation of short passages for the purposes of criticism and review, no part of this publication may be reproduced, stored in a retrieval system, or transmitted, in any form or by any means, electronic, mechanical, photocopying, recording or otherwise, without the prior permission of the publisher.

British Library Cataloguing in Publication Data
A CIP catalogue record for this book is available from the British Library.

Library of Congress Cataloging-in-Publication Data
To be applied for.

Hardcover ISBN 978-1-78976-144-3

Typeset & designed by Sussex Academic Press, Brighton & Eastbourne.
Printed by TJ Books Ltd, Padstow, Cornwall.

Contents

Acknowledgments ix
List of Tables and Graphs xi
A Note on Transliteration xiii

Introduction 1
Conflicts, Wars and Refugees 5
The Experiences and Policies of Saʻudi Arabia 10
Definitions 12
Structure of the Book 14

1
A Theoretical Perspective on Migration 19
A Glance at International Migration 20
Theories of International Migration 22
   Migration Theories: A Classification 23
   Analysis of Migration Theories 25
   Neo-classical Theory 26
   The New Economics of Labor Migration (NELM) 27
   Dual Labor Market Theory 28
   Network Theory 29
   Migration System Theory 30
   Institutional Theory 31
   Cumulative Causation Theory 31
The 1951 Refugee Convention and 1967 Protocols 33
International Migration and Globalization 36
Conclusion: Adopting a Multidisciplinary Approach 36

2
Saʻudi Policies towards Refugees 39
Critics of Saʻudi Migration Initiatives 41
Discrimination and Human Rights Violations 43
Gender Discrimination in Saʻudi Arabia's Nationality Law 45
Stateless Communities in Saʻudi Arabia 47
   The Bidun 49

The Rohingya	50
The Palestinians	52
Migration Regulations	53
Conclusion: A Flexible and Dutiful Approach	54

3
Hijrah, *Zakat*, and Refugees: Religious Obligations — 56

Hijrah and Asylum	57
Refugee Convention and Shari'ah Law	61
Alternatives to the 1951 Convention and 1967 Protocol	67
Religious Norms and Obligations	72
The Case of Rashid 'Ali al-Kilani	74
Muslim Brotherhood Refugees	76
Burmese Refugees in Sa'udi Arabia	78
Iraqi Refugees and the Rafhah Camp Experiment	82
Syrian Refugees	85
Conclusion: Obligation as Custodian of the Two Holy Mosques	87

4
The Concept of *Zakat* and Foreign Aid: From Development to Humanitarian Assistance — 89

Zakat and Foreign Aid	91
Sa'udi Foreign Aid: Humanitarian and Economic Assistance	97
Sa'udi Foreign Aid Before and After 1973	101
The Sa'udi Fund for Development	103
King Salman Center for Humanitarian Relief and Works	105
Humanitarian Assistance to Yemen	109
Conclusion: Aid as Religious Obligation	111

5
Pilgrimage and Migration Dilemmas: African Migrants and Sa'udi Arabia — 116

Annual Pilgrimage Dilemmas	118
An Examination of the Methodology and Data Analysis	122
The Migration Processes	124
Smuggling	124
Overstaying an *'Umrah* or *Hajj* Visa	126
Breaking a Work Contract	127
Undocumented 'Migrants' Born in Jiddah	127
African Migrants in Sa'udi Arabia	129
Issues Related to Working Conditions	132
Legal Issues Facing Undocumented Laborers in Sa'udi Arabia	134

Plans for the Future	135
Amnesty Initiatives	138
Nitaqat and Deportation Laws	140
Conclusion: Pilgrimage Dilemmas	142

6
The Kingdom and Yemen: How Neighbors Became Refugees — 145
Contemporary Saʿudi–Yemeni Ties	147
The Free-Flow of Migrants	152
Yemeni Workers in Saʿudi Arabia	154
Undocumented Yemeni Entries and Smuggling Operations	155
Riyadh's Humanitarian Assistance	157
Saʿudi Amnesty Policies vis-à-vis the Yemen	159
Consequences of the Huthi Takeover (2015–2018)	161
Conclusion: De-escalation Efforts	163

7
Syrian Refugees in Saʿudi Arabia: Integration Rather than Confinement — 166
The Making of a Catastrophe: Millions of Refugees	167
The 2011 Uprisings	170
Controversies Over Casualties	173
Demographic Transformations in Lebanon, Jordan, Iraq, and Turkey	174
Syrian Refugees in Lebanon	177
Syrian Refugees in Jordan	178
Syrian Refugees in Iraq	180
Syrian Refugees in Turkey	181
Impact of Regional Refugees on Saʿudi Arabia	183
GCC States and Syrian Refugees	184
Integration of Syrians within the Kingdom	189
Conclusion: Continuing Warfare, Ongoing Assistance	191

8
The Refugee Challenge for Saʿudi Arabia and the Muslim World — 194

Appendices
1. Universal Islamic Declaration of Human Rights (1981)	205
2. African Charter on Human and Peoples' Right (1981)	216
3. Cairo Declaration on Human Rights in Islam (1990)	231

4. Arab Charter on Human Rights (1994) 239
5. Gender Discrimination in Sa'udi Arabia's Nationality Law 248
6. Royal Decree Number 56660, issued on 13/11/1436 259
   [26 September 2015]
7. Combatting Trafficking in Persons in Accordance with 261
   the Principles of Islamic Law [Excerpts]

Notes 272
Bibliography 323
Index 351
About the Authors 360

Acknowledgments

This book germinated in a panel presented at BRISMES in Edinburgh, Scotland, in 2017. Along with two other colleagues, Faisal Abualhassan and Sumayah Fatani, the two authors submitted papers that highlighted the Kingdom's unique religious position as the Custodian of the Two Holy Mosques. The essays discussed how Sa'udi Arabia was burdened with displaced [as well as non-displaced] migrant workers, refugees and, in far more significant numbers, pilgrimage overstayers who entered the country on temporary *Hajj* visas but opted not to return to their homes. The BRISMES conference raised various points that we noted and expanded upon.

Fahad Alsharif's BRISMES paper was developed further and published as a *Dirasat* by the King Faisal Center for Research and Islamic Studies (KFCRIS), and we thank our institution for the authorization to reproduce portions of that paper in Chapter 5. KFCRIS, our institutional home, provides us with the ideal environment to pursue academic interests. We wish, in particular to thank our Chairman, HRH Prince Turki al-Faisal, for his unwavering support. Prince Turki, a thinker and avid reader in his own right, always encourages us to pursue our intellectual investigations and academic endeavors. We also wish to extend our warmest accolades to the former KFCRIS Secretary-General and our colleague, Saud al-Sarhan, whose support we sincerely valued. Several other KFCRIS colleagues must be named as well as they provided us with valuable assistance during the production phase of this book: Turki Alshuwaier, Habbas Alharbi, Yanal Isak, Subhan Ghani, Muhannad Al-Saho and Abdulaziz Alhumaid.

Permission to reproduce key graphs were generously provided by several organizations. The Pew Research Center authorized a reproduction of Graph 3.1 [Religious Sects in Myanmar and Percentages in General Population], which is drawn from *The World of World Religions*. Graphs 4.1 [SDF Projects and Programs, 1975–2018] and 4.2 [Geographical Distribution of SDF Programs, 1975–2018], are reproduced with the kind permission of the Sa'udi Fund for Development, and we thank Abdullah Alsakran, and Abdullah Binmoamar for their consent. Graph 4.3 [Sa'udi Aid Funding, 2009–2020], is reproduced with the approval of the United Nations Office for the Coordination of Humanitarian Affairs-Financial Tracking Services (OCHA-FTS). Graphs 7.1 [Number of Syrian refugees taken in by countries in the Middle East] and 7.2 [Number of Syrians Living in the Gulf States since the Beginning of the Conflict] are duplicated in this book with the generous agreement of IlmFeed.com, which features articles about Islamic History, Muslim personalities, Mosques around the world, inspirational stories and much more. When the IlmFeed.com graphs were *selectively* reproduced in numerous publications around the world, the organization issued a clarification and explained what the actual situation was, which we also present in some detail. Singular accolades to the Sa'udi Press Agency (SPA), especially its President, Fahad bin Hassan Al-'Akran, for the authorization to reproduce the photographs on the book cover. We also wish to acknowledge the vital work of SPA staff members Waleed Al-Harbi and 'Ali Sa'ad R. Al Sa'ad for their most timely responses to our requests.

Finally, we thank Anthony Grahame, our publisher at Sussex Academic Press, who shepherded the book toward publication.

It is critical to note that the views and opinions contained herein are the authors and should not be attributed to any officials affiliated with KFCRIS or the Government of Sa'udi Arabia. The authors are solely responsible for any errors that remain in the study. For practical purposes, and with minor exceptions, the research scope ends on 1 March 2021.

List of Tables and Graphs

Permissions to reproduce some of the tables and graphs are detailed in the Acknowledgments.

Tables
1.1	Migration Theories: Level-Based Analysis	23
1.2	Migration Theories Across Disciplines	24
3.1	Organization of Islamic Cooperation Refugee Convention Signatories.	69
3.2	Religious Sects in Burma/Myanmar and Percentages in General Population	79
4.1	Sa'udi Arabia International Humanitarian Assistance, 2000–2020	95
4.2	Sa'udi Arabia Overseas Development Aid (ODA) Contributions, 2005–2020	95
4.3	International Humanitarian Assistance from Gulf States, 2005–2020	96
4.4	Sa'udi Development Funds (SDF) Programs and Cumulative Co-financing, 1975–2019 (in Sa'udi Riyals)	104
4.5	King Salman Humanitarian Aid and Relief Center Beneficiary Countries, 2015–2020	106
6.1	Migrant Apprehensions by Nationality, 1978–2015	156
6.2	General Statistics about King Salman Relief Projects for Yemen (as of 31 January 2021).	158
6.3	Attitudes towards the Use of Amnesty Initiatives in Sa'udi Arabia by Undocumented Migrant Communities	160
7.1	Refugees of the Syrian Civil War	185

Graphs
3..1	Religious Sects in Myanmar and Percentages in General Population	80
4.1	Sa'udi Fund for Development (SFD) Projects and Programs, 1975–2018	105
4.2	Geographical Distribution of Sa'udi Fund for Development (SFD) Programs, 1975–2018	108

4.3	Sa'udi Aid Funding, 2009–2020	109
7.1	Number of Syrian Refugees taken in by Countries in the Middle East	187
7-2	Number of Syrians Living in Gulf States since the Beginning of the Conflict	187

A Note on Transliteration

This study follows the transliteration methodologies by the Library of Congress (LC) transliteration system. Although rendering Arabic words and names into English is nearly impossible, we relied on LC protocols, along with the style used by the *International Journal of Middle East Studies* (IJMES) to offer solid versions. For practical purposes, all diacritical marks for long vowels and velarized consonants were eliminated, except for the hamza (') and the ayn ('). Moreover, variations in common names, including the commonly rendered Mohammed or Riad in English, were transliterated as Muhammad and Riyadh. Mecca, still used in some sources, was dropped for the more accurate Makkah, which is also the official adaptation. All quotations that referred to specific spellings were not tampered with, including "Sheik" or " Shaikh" instead of the correct transliteration of Shaykh—according to LC and IJMES protocols.

In modern Arabic, even when using standard pronunciation, the feminine -ah is often ignored, with the h usually silent and not recorded. Consequently, we see it as -a, like in fatwa, Shi'a, Shari'a or even 'Ulama. Strangely, however, the h is kept in other circumstances, including Riyadh or Jiddah or even Shaikh when it is not written as Sheikh. Throughout this study, an effort was made to be both consistent and accurate, which is why the h was recorded in all instances, including when it referred to the *ta' marbutah* (fatihah, rahmah), the *alif* (Abhah, Hasah), the *alif maqsurah* (shurah, fatwah), or even the *hamza* ('Ulamah, fuqahah). Thus, all transliterated words that qualified included the silent h, as in fatwah, 'Ulamah, Shari'ah, Shaykh, and Shurah. This may look odd but, at least, the approach is consistent and, hopefully, scholarly.

An effort was made to clarify family names as well. When referring to the proper appellation of ruling families, the Arabic word Al, which means "family," precedes the name of the eponymous founder. In Sa'udi Arabia, the founder imparted his name to the family, thus the Al Sa'ud. A lower case al- often referred to a sub-branch of the ruling family. In this instance Turki al-Faysal is the son of the late King Faysal bin 'Abdul 'Aziz Al Sa'ud. Furthermore, and although the transliteration of 'Abd (servant or slave in Arabic) is rendered as 'Abdul, we are aware that the "ul" (al) is really the article of the succeeding word, as in 'Abd(ul/al) Allah, and that together they mean "servant of God." Yet, we use 'Abdallah rather than 'Abdullah throughout this text because it comes as close as possible to Library of Congress and *International Journal of Middle East Studies* protocols, and it is a more accurate transliteration from the Arabic, instead of from the Urdu used in Pakistan, Afghanistan and elsewhere.

Arabic speakers will know the correct references and while special care was devoted to standardize the spellings of transliterated words, there are—inevitably—a few inconsistencies that, we trust, readers will understand and forgive any linguistic transgressions.

Saʿudi Policies towards Migrants and Refugees
A Sacred Duty

Introduction

One of the most intriguing "discoveries" of the twentieth century was the imposition of travel restrictions across borders, as relatively free circulation across landmasses and sea-lanes became far more difficult, though of course it was seldom easy throughout history. Until 1914, few countries required "entry" documents—visas in contemporary parlance—even if the very idea of independent nation-states, borders, and associated geographical restrictions were all, comparatively speaking, recent creations.[1] Remarkably, at least 77 million international migrant workers crossed borders in 1965, a figure that jumped to 200 million—or an estimated 3 percent of the global population in 2015.[2] Most were economic migrants in search of better lives even if misery accompanied them every step of the way. Dangers loomed as they crossed borders, only to settle in huge barrios in and around large urban zones, often living under abysmal conditions. Lucky migrants were absorbed as farmhands in the countryside, where the quality of life was superior even if the work was demanding, while many more lingered in decaying urban conditions that pretended to absorb this cheap workforce pool. The trend was for more of the same as mankind embarked on its most prosperous century and, according to United Nations figures, climate change effects were expected to further increase migrations that meant additional cross-border movements. Most of these potential migrants were destined for hardships, surviving in alien societies, often dragged down the misery ladder. At least another 250 to 300 million individuals wished to escape starvation and were ready to move from their native lands towards "greener" shores, as an estimated two billion humans, or approximately 18 percent of global populations migrated in search of food and other basic needs in the second decade of the twenty-first century.[3]

To be sure, there were a variety of migrations, including the search for freedom and higher standards of living for the relatively educated whose aims included guaranteed welfare for their offspring. Some of these migrations were tragic as well as problematic, both for donor as well as recipient countries, confronted by impossible choices. For example, while it was abnormal to have more Malawi physicians in Manchester in the United Kingdom than in their native land—where their skills were sorely needed—and while at least 50 million Chinese preferred to live in the United States, Canada, Australia and other Western countries, it was not surprising that most educated migrants hoped to maximize their incomes and optimize their quality of life (QOL).[4] These were lucky migrants eager to assimilate who, more often than not, managed to integrate with relative ease even if few escaped immigration anxieties. Other migrants, whether less educated or unskilled, were fodder for abuse both at their points of origins and/or at their final destinations if and when they made it that far. Scores of African migrants attempting to cross the Mediterranean Sea, for example, drowned because of mediocre travel conditions and those who were rescued lingered in refugee camps for long periods of time if they were not quickly expelled.

An equally important phenomenon of forced migration was that of war refugees, with many escaping conflicts, first to survive man-made calamities and, second, to ensure security and stability for their offspring. Starting with World War II and until the first two decades of the twenty-first century, hundreds of millions were forced to abandon their properties as they fled civil wars or were the victims of organized assaults on account of ethnicity, gender, religion, or sexual orientation. More often than not, many took significant risks as they trekked on land or the high seas in search of welcoming shores.[5]

According to the latest United Nations statistics, nearly 79 million individuals were displaced by war and by violence in their respective homes in 2019—an astronomical figure. The annual *Global Trends* report released by the UN High Commissioner for Refugees counted the number of the world's refugees, asylum-seekers and internally displaced people at the end of 2019, in some cases following decades of living away from home. Ironically, these figures barely touched ongoing debates regarding refugees at the intersection of international law, human rights and domestic politics, especially the movement in some countries, including the United States and leading European countries, against immigrants and refugees.[6] In a poignant coverage of the annual UNHCR document in 2019, it was revealed that an estimated 11 million people were *newly* displaced in 2019 alone; this figure is stunning given that the grand total of global refugees in 2010 was 41 million.[7] According to the report, five countries accounted for more than two-thirds of all global refugees in 2019 (excluding those defined as long-term Palestinian refugees): Syria (13.2 million displaced persons, including 6.6 million refugees outside of the country), Venezuela (4.5 million), Afghanistan (3.2 million), South Sudan (2.2 million), and Myanmar (1.1 million). Interestingly, Turkey hosted the largest number of refugees worldwide, with 3.9 million people, although Lebanon continued to host the largest number of refugees relative to its national population with about a million. In 2020, one in six persons in Lebanon was a refugee, a statistic that partly explained the chaos that has enveloped that hapless country. Beirut estimated that it hosted 1.5 million Syrian refugees, in addition to Palestinian refugees whose numbers oscillated between 300,000 and 500,000 depending on sources, although these figures were impossible to verify.[8]

As this data confirmed, a significant percentage of political migrations occurred in the Arab and Muslim worlds, as several established regimes collapsed, starting with the late-2010/early 2011 Arab Uprisings. In Tunisia, Egypt, Syria, and Yemen, civil wars catapulted millions to flee danger, either into neighboring countries such as Jordan, Lebanon and Turkey or, for those with an eye for permanent exile, farther away in Europe and Asia and even the Americas. As discussed below, the festering Palestine Question which began in 1948 and continued with the 1967, 1973, and 1982 wars, added to the overall refugee misery. Refugee distress was supplemented with the wars for Kuwait in 1991 and Iraq after 2003, all of which added to the total number of migrations that were not fully resolved when the Arab Uprisings gained momentum and more or less permanently altered the entire Middle East region. In all of these instances, the primary absorption burdens fell on neighboring Arab states, even if key European countries witnessed sharp increases in legal as well as illegal migrations. Ironically, and at the height of these latest human waves that raised the ire of fearful ultra-nationalists, a concerted effort was launched by some Western media outlets against wealthy Arab Gulf countries that, presumably, refused to open their doors to receive fellow Arabs.[9] This was inaccurate but, frankly, all too common for countries that went out of their way to welcome refugees or extend very generous financial assistance for those who made it to neighboring countries.

Few commentators understood existing policies and regulations in place in several Arab Gulf states and fewer took into account indigenous norms that motivated these leading Arab societies to embark on long-term initiatives to address refugee conditions. According to the Sa'udi Ministry of the Interior, for example, there were no refugees in the Kingdom of Sa'udi Arabia in a literal sense, because Riyadh was not a signatory of the 1951 United Nations Convention Relating to the Status of Refugees and the 1967 follow-up Protocol. To be sure, Sa'udi Arabia expressed several reservations on the *Arab Convention on Regulating the Status of Refugees in the Arab Countries* (see Appendix 1), though it certainly opened its doors to millions of migrants even if it never classified these migrants as refugees.

Sa'udi Arabia was not the only Arab country that expressed reservations regarding the 1951 UN Convention and the 1967 Protocol. Others, including Egypt, Iraq, Morocco and the Gulf Cooperation Council (GCC) member-states, issued their own concerns at one point or another. In fact, Arab legal experts have held at least two regional meetings to explore solutions and develop mechanisms to help host countries deal with the influx of refugees, and adopted two main documents: (1) the *Declaration on the Protection of Refugees and Displaced Persons in the Arab World* (see Appendix 2); and (2) the Arab Convention cited above, which was adopted by the League of Arab States in 1994. In addition to these regional initiatives, several Arab countries signed but did not ratify the 1951 United Nations Convention Relating to the Status of Refugees (Refugee Convention) and its 1967 Protocol, although Egypt ratified them with reservations.[10] Still, the Kingdom of Sa'udi Arabia welcomed displaced persons from neighboring states and dealt with them humanely, preserved their dignity, and provided facilities for those who required urgent adjustments to their statuses. Over the years, several reports suggested that refugees in Sa'udi Arabia have not been treated on an equal footing as Sa'udi citizens, which was inaccurate. As discussed in Chapter 3, Riyadh categorically refused to create shelter centers or refugee camps inside the country as it drew lessons from the negative experiments with Iraqi refugees that were housed in such facilities in Rafhah, along the Sa'udi–Iraqi border, in 1990–1991.[11] In the aftermath of the 2015 war in Yemen, for example, and instead of creating refugee camps, Sa'udi authorities initiated the King Salman Humanitarian Aid and Relief Center in Yemen to further assist those in need. Moreover, and notwithstanding the war, it welcomed hundreds of thousands of Yemeni refugees and granted them renewable visitor cards valid for 6-month periods and, for those who wished to stay permanently, provided permanent residency cards. Similarly, and as discussed in Chapter 7, Syrian migrants received the same privileges enjoyed by Yemenis, with the ultimate purpose of integrating them into Sa'udi society, offering them job opportunities, exempting them from fees and fines, allowing them to receive medical treatment in government hospitals, and enrolling children in schools at all levels and adults who wished to pursue their education, for free.[12] Furthermore, and aware of even larger numbers of Syrian refugees in Jordan, Lebanon and Turkey, the Sa'udi government rushed sorely needed financial and material assistance to refugees in these countries, often under extraordinary security conditions.[13]

Why these activities were seldom discussed by leading academics and generally well-informed Western media outlets remains a mystery, though the purpose of this study is precisely to elucidate facts and shed light on Riyadh's policies towards refugees.

Conflicts, Wars and Refugees

Although long-standing, troubled relations between leading Western societies and the Islamic World witnessed escalating tensions starting in 2001, which was telling. Several studies attempted to decipher these ills to better understand how these conflictive relationships shaped the way these societies understood each other in different remits, ranging the gamut from politics to culture to religion.[14] Regrettably, the political and military confrontations that gained fresh incentives after the 9/11 tragedies in the United States, followed by a series of terrorist activities in the United Kingdom, Spain and elsewhere, were all channeled into Afghanistan and Iraq. Wars in these two countries starting in 2001 turned into a daily clash within societies, Western and non-Western, many of which found themselves in need to redefine identities, sharpen values and decipher new ways to presumably coexist with the "Other," ostensibly with the least amount of damage to themselves as well as others.

The War for Iraq after 2003, the Arab Spring phenomena after 2010, and the ongoing wars in Syria and in Yemen, have all had the effect of triggering a migration of peoples out of the area, just as millions trekked out of war zones throughout Europe and Asia during and after World War II. In fact, the War for Iraq produced more than two million refugees, while Syria saw nearly seven million people leave their homes since 2011 as both of these highly mediatized cases affected key European countries that were called upon to provide shelter for refugees fleeing war zones. Even if the refugee phenomenon was not new, the Iraqi and Syrian "models" generated acute sympathy, along with serious spillover effects, including various acts of violence. These refugee crises affected both countries, as the Mesopotamian and Levantine power-houses were literally pulverized into largely dysfunctional entities and created extremely negative consequences for the United States, Australia, Canada and even, as the world tragically discovered in March 2019, New Zealand.[15] The Syrian civil war, in particular, illustrated how a seemingly local catastrophe could awaken sharp views in nations that hosted refugees, as the presence of Syrian migrants in Germany, most of whom were initially welcomed with open arms, pitted Berlin against anti-refugee forces.[16] It was not long before divisions surfaced within the European Union regarding the hospitality of refugees, as Chancellor Angela Merkel—whose government welcomed nearly a million Syrian refugees—stood in direct opposition to Prime Minister Victor Orbán in Hungary and President Andrzej Sebastian Duda in Poland.[17] The latter two donned ultra-nationalist garbs, depicted on social media as new "Crusaders" fighting to preserve the Christian faith in Europe, which betrayed the continent's core humanitarian principles. The European Union's fundamental values, which were codified in the 2009 Treaty of Lisbon, and that revolve around respect for human dignity and human rights, freedom, democracy, equality and the rule of law, all came under siege by the increasing influence of populist far-right movements worried about a possible, irreversible 'Islamization' of their respective societies.[18]

It must be emphasized that the post-2011 Syrian refugee crises had another effect besides awakening dormant historical, cultural, and military disputes and confrontations, some of which dated back a millennia. In fact, what these particular cases revealed were the inadequacies of the current international laws for refugees, as elaborated in Article 1A (2) of the 1951 United Nations Convention, which clearly stated that a refugee was a person with a

> "well-founded fear of being persecuted for reasons of race, religion, nationality, membership of a particular social group or political opinion, [was] outside the country of his nationality and [was] unable or, owing to such fear, [was] unwilling to avail himself of the protection of that country; or who, not having a nationality and being outside the country of his former habitual residence as a result of such events, [was] unable or, owing to such fear, [was] unwilling to return to it."[19]

Moreover, Article 3 of the 1951 Convention maintained that "Contracting States shall apply the provisions of this convention to refugees without discrimination as to race, religion or country of origin." The erecting of hard barriers, thereby closing borders in what was supposed to be the free Schengen movement area, by select countries, further complicated matters. Finally, and as Article 16 of the same convention affirmed, "a refugee shall have free access to the courts of law on the territory of all Contracting States" (which seldom occurred); while Article 27 declared that "States shall issue identity papers to any refugee in their territory who [did] not possess a valid travel document" (disbursed at a snail's pace), all of which further created impossible dilemmas for those countries that did uphold the 2009 Treaty of Lisbon and, of course, the 1951 UN Convention.[20]

Indeed, the founding principles of the 1951 UN Convention, which are discussed in Chapter 1, were remarkable, but what was even more significant was the fact that it stood as a very ineffective tool, whenever its regulations were applied to contemporary settings. This *law* and its accompanying 1967 protocol were thought to work in a post-World War II European setting in more or less intact form though, in practical terms, application effectively meant two things: not taking into consideration the resistance to cultural and religious differences by host countries and, equally important, not providing mechanisms for the prevention of similar cases. These were and remain very serious flaws in the law because, as we will see in more detail throughout this study, much is left to interpretation by a state as to what any given government defines who might be a refugee, under what circumstances, and why. In such instances, the very status of refugee can thus be "studied" and, perhaps, be granted after long, difficult, and in certain cases, humiliating processes.

As discussed below, there is an expanding body of literature assessing why states are not signatories to the 1951 Convention, and what systems of protection they either choose to provide or to refuse for forced migrants, though this has not been systematically applied to Sa'udi Arabia. Instead, the country has been vilified for failing to support displaced populations, particularly Syrians and Yemenis, which is the narrative addressed in this work because, regrettably, few studies have tackled this critical issue. Simply stated, the Kingdom's activities did not enter in the regular accounting of international institutional mechanisms, which meant that whatever occurred on the ground was often ignored or simply underestimated. This narrative needs to be addressed for a variety of reasons, including to clarify the record and to properly evaluate the humanitarian assistance that Riyadh provided and continues to disburse.

Equally important, the mass migration of the last twenty years from the Middle East to the West in general and to Europe in particular, created yet another dire consequence that involved a further discussion of the UN 1951 Convention, namely the very idea that the fundamental principles of the Convention were based on ideals and moral values that were the exclusive prerogatives of Western societies. This interpretation generated many misunderstandings during major crises like the Syrian civil war because the world was largely driven by Western customs or interests. Indeed, while the latter included universal values that were immensely useful, equally cherished practices existed throughout the world that, at least in an idealized world, could no longer be overlooked or ignored. Much like Judeo-Christian values, ethics attributed to Muslim, Hindu, and Shinto faiths, among others, existed, as capable Western scholars who crisscrossed the planet, studied developing societies, and shared their knowledge and findings with decision-makers who tolerated diversity, knew quite well. Over the course of decades, especially in the second half of the twentieth century, fresh interpretations originated from the premise that the 1951 Convention—in its instructive approach—assumed that the reasons why human rights were critical prevailed, overlooking or, perhaps, neglecting the human dimension of refugee needs, which stood out in stark contrast to its lofty prose. In other words, it is important to state that while genuine Western concerns about universal rights need to be balanced with how leading powers intervened in various crises in the developing world, ostensibly to right undeniable wrongs, equally valuable cultural norms exist in non-Western societies that needed to be acknowledged and considered in future endeavors. Basic human rights matters were certainly primary preoccupations though other, equally pertinent, subjects existed and they deserve attention. In Middle Eastern cases, human rights issues included religious regulations, age-old traditions, and rich cultural beliefs, all of which were important facets of these civilizations. Moreover, and while Western regulations like the Magna Carta (1215) and the Declaration of the Rights of Man and the Citizen (1879) were formulated by men who were created equal in the light of God, what this approach prevented was to overlook the need for real dialogue on these issues with non Judeo-Christian religious traditions and their practitioners. The result was that out of the fifty-seven members of the Member States of the Organization of Islamic Cooperation (OIC), for example, only thirty-five signed both the 1951 Refugee Convention and the 1967 Optional Protocol, most with specific reservations, which needed careful analysis so as to emend, if possible.[21]

Instead, the OIC supported the signing of different treaties meant to deal with emergencies caused by wars and authoritarian regimes, illustrating the lack of global cooperation with UN bodies that preferred to overlook OIC-backed norms. Indeed, the *Universal Islamic Declaration on Human Rights* (1981), the *African Charter on Human and Peoples' Rights* (1981), the *Cairo Declaration on Human Rights in Islam* (1990), and the *Arab Charter on Human Rights* (1994), all presented alternatives to the 1951 UN Convention and the 1967 Protocol (these are discussed in Chapter 3. See also Appendices 3 through 6). Without a doubt, such preferences were reactions to the fact that concerned authorities in various Middle Eastern countries were seldom allowed to participate in the drafting of the 1951 Convention or, at least, to see their norms incorporated in UN regulations.

While similarities between Western and Islamic traditions are analyzed in this volume, it is critical to mention in this Introduction that what matters is to establish a common ground to engage in a discussion involving the legal and human rights of refugees and asylum seekers. The idea of human dignity is at the core of all religions and philosophies, and it is on this ground that a comprehensive relationship between all nations ought to be held regarding the treatment of refugees. The thought that the moral principles present in Islam could be ignored or disregarded when trying to establish a framework of understanding was, therefore, not realistic. On the contrary, an effort to identify similarities and differences between *Hijrah* [migration], indigenous traditions, as well as the modern laws on asylum and refugees, for example, seems paramount precisely to avoid misunderstandings.[22] Indeed, an examination of the sacred texts of the three main monotheistic religions—Judaism, Christianity and Islam—reveals how in different periods of time believers were forced out of their homelands. Forced displacements, exile, persecution and wars constituted common destinies for these peoples and, at the risk of generalizing, it was useful to state that Moses saved his people from enslavement in Egypt, Jesus was born in a foreign land, and Muhammad sought refuge in Madinah to escape his enemies. It was, thus, inevitable that the very concept of refugee was indeed embedded in all of these traditions. Nevertheless, that concept by itself was insufficient to understand contemporary mobilities, as the very idea of hospitality, and the legal frame in which cordiality was transformed after World War II, differed from the concept of *Hijrah*. As discussed in more detail in Chapter 1, in the 1951 Convention and its 1967 Protocol, the figure of the refugee was open to different interpretations leaving nowadays refugees in a sort of nebula, which ignored their human rights because, according to the Refugee Convention, a person did "not become a refugee because of recognition, but is recognized because he is a refugee."[23] While this statement was about the declarative dimension of refugeehood and thus was not only about ignoring human rights or having a flexible interpretation of the Convention, inflexible definitions failed to assist refugees nor, for that matter, helped host governments that confronted the consequences of welcoming and absorbing—even if temporarily—large numbers of refugees. As the 1951 Convention did not include in its definition the idea of internally displaced person (IDPs), who were not considered refugees by the regulation in the first place, one could only imagine the various difficulties that arose over the years and which added to the confusion of the matter.[24]

As discussed in Chapter 3, *Hijrah*, as part of *Shari'ah* [Islamic] Law, constitutes a valuable alternative for Muslim countries because it recognizes the value of the person, and applies a concept of hospitality embedded in Islamic cultures. It thus proposes itself as a valid alternative to the void created by the legal definition of refugee, as described by the Convention that, it is worth repeating, relied primarily on Western norms though few accepted *Shar'iah* Law since the latter was misunderstood, if not rejected outright, by leading Western authorities.[25] While a painstaking effort, several Muslim scholars, including Ahmed Abou-El-Wafa—who penned a study that was jointly sponsored by the UNHCR and the OIC—added their voices to the debate, if only to enlarge the parameters of various intellectual exchanges. Abou-El-Wafa devised comprehensive comparisons between customary international law and *Shari'ah* Law on this specific aspect.[26] This tentative dialogue presented alternative mechanisms to enrich debate across civilizations and highlighted specific weaknesses within the Western and the Muslim views, when dealing with the realities on the ground. Simultaneously, it displayed the merit of dissipating lingering prejudices about the contributions of Muslim societies to permanent solutions regarding refugee crises, caused by conflicts in different Middle Eastern countries.

The Experiences and Policies of Sa'udi Arabia

The purpose of this book is to contribute to the ongoing scholarly discussion on the fate that befalls millions of refugees, many of whom hail from Muslim societies, sometimes the victims of harsh indigenous regulations. While the focus is on the experiences of the Kingdom Sa'udi Arabia regarding the hospitality granted to refugees, the study aims to enlarge the conversation not only by identifying specific policies in place, but also by linking various assistance programs to alleviate tensions. Although very limited research was undertaken on this critical subject to date, there were extenuating circumstances that partially explain the lack of attention, including a scholarly preference to study Sa'udi Arabia from a political point of view. In fact, the Kingdom was and is classified as an absolute monarchy that seldom accepts or respects universal norms, ranging the gamut from human rights matters to strict religious interpretations that, presumably, place it outside global values. Equally important is Riyadh's traditional preferences, which come across as being secretive of domestic policies that, naturally, add to the overall confusion. Consequently, the Kingdom appears to be a monolithic entity that discourages open research, and that clearly ill-serves its diversified society. It is, therefore, necessary to reverse this trend and to study one of the most complicated policies of the state and one of the most interesting internal developments in recent memory. It is imperative to further dispel the prejudiced idea of a society closed to any kind of external influence, not keen to grant hospitality to refugees, which is the exact opposite of the country's long legacy. Towards that end, this book is thus an original attempt to focus on the various refugee communities currently living in Saʻudi Arabia, some of which migrated due to war, forced displacement, environmental catastrophe, and economic hardship. Remarkably, and in addition to migrants that settled in the Kingdom coming from bordering countries such as Iraq and Yemen, others reached the Arabian Peninsula coming from several African and Asian countries, all of whom were welcomed even if settlement conditions or repatriations and deportations were not always ideal. This volume does not skirt sensitive issues, including several issues that display undeniable gulfs between policies and practices, to better contribute to the ongoing discussion of how to correct specific policy shortcomings.

Moreover, while the volume discusses and analyzes refugee policies and conditions within the country, an effort is also made to cover various assistance planks that Riyadh espouses in providing financial aid to refugees in third countries, which goes beyond routine United Nations appeals for aid. Few appreciate this burden, which is carried out without prejudice and mostly without publicity. Moreover, the current media neglect of the total level of assistance provided by Saʻudi Arabia is addressed and corrected. Of course, the Kingdom of Saʻudi Arabia is an oil-producing state, but it is still a developing country with immense internal needs. As discussed in Chapter 4, the study highlights how foreign aid is justified by religious obligations, as well as on humanitarian grounds, which form a sacred duty to decision-makers who practice what they believe are true obligations.

In the course of the research conducted for this book, it became clear that Saʻudi Arabia confronted specific obstacles which needed to be overcome in order to contribute to informed discussion. The first impediment was to address accusations of violation of human rights by the international community. This involved a discussion on human rights regarding the "Gender Discrimination in Saʻudi Arabia's Nationality Law" as a primary approach to the problem of statelessness experienced by different communities in the Kingdom. It was important to tackle gender discrimination questions because of various issues raised by individuals who were, presumably, denied their rights in a largely segregated society. Dramatic changes were introduced after 2015 to gradually remove existing prejudices, which Saʻudi society recognized required emendation. Statelessness involved dire political choices that needed attention too. Moreover, the Nationality Law was valuable because it set the basis for granting Saʻudi citizenship to foreign nationals, thereby ensuring their integration into society.

The second hindrance revolved around the researchers' abilities to gather reliable data precisely to counteract the prejudices present in academic and non-academic circles regarding the role played by Sa'udi Arabia in welcoming refugees. Chapter 6, on African undocumented migrants, provides primary data from interviews and focus group discussions obtained through detailed investigations, which offer fresh perspectives on the situation of irregular migrants in Sa'udi Arabia that has been written about in only a handful of academic pieces to date. Notwithstanding these findings, it is important to state that the reticent character of Sa'udi authorities in dealing with "illegal immigrants," at least until 2015, raised serious questions that were left unanswered and this aspect is tackled here to clarify what Riyadh envisages for the future.[27]

A third barrier was the dearth of materials that were necessary to embark on a comprehensive historical exploration of key refugee populations that settled in the country. What were the specific policies implemented at different times and were these vetted to ensure social and political repercussions? These questions are all raised to better and comprehensively chart Sa'udi Arabia's responses to refugees and migrants within its borders, and the way in which Sa'udi humanitarian aid has contributed towards assisting refugees and affected communities throughout the world. The contributions to both have generally been either overlooked or dismissed, and the religious foundations of their commitment to displaced populations has been negatively contrasted against what are seen by most governments and international organizations as the firm human-rights based commitments espoused by Western states through institutions such as the United Nations High Commission for Refugees and the 1951 Convention Relating to the Status of Refugees. How Riyadh addressed these involvements deserves attention.

Definitions

Throughout this book, the term refugee is interchangeably used with stateless person, migrant, and asylum seeker. Although this will seem to be an excessively liberal choice, and to avoid both confusion as well as unnecessary categorizations from policy perspectives, it may be useful to briefly sketch these definitions both to highlight subtle differences and, equally important, not to fall into semantic gymnastics. Again, it is worth repeating the reason why this generalization was chosen—notwithstanding differences highlighted below: the aim is to examine concerns from the policy makers' point of view. Because decision-makers often lump refugees, stateless persons, migrants and asylum seekers together, without assigning blame for such a categorization, the focus here is to concentrate on the needs of individuals so designated and the Kingdom's putative responses.

A "stateless person" is one who is born without documentation and who is not considered a national by any state under the operation of its laws (Art. 1, *UN Convention Relating to the Status of Stateless Persons*, 1954). As such, a stateless person lacks those rights attributable to national diplomatic protection of a state, with no inherent right of sojourn in the state of residence, and no right of return in case of travel. In this book, particularly in Chapter 6 on African migrants, the term is equivalent to those migrants born in Sa'udi Arabia with no documents, that is, any child born to one or more undocumented parents, or a Sa'udi national who is married to an undocumented migrant with no official approval from Sa'udi authorities.[28]

A refugee is someone who has been forced to flee his or her country because of persecution, war, or violence.[29] Such an individual has thus a well-founded fear of persecution for reasons of race, religion, nationality, political opinion or membership in a particular social group, all of which weigh on his or her capacity to survive, integrate in his/her adopted society and, if possible, eventually return to his/her native land. Regrettably, such a person can only return home under specific conditions, or is afraid to do so; this scenario presents dilemmas as well as burdens to host countries. Indeed, because wars, ethnic, tribal and religious violence remain the leading causes of refugees fleeing their countries, their fates are, more often than not, directly tied to political settlements or, in the absence of specific state-to-state accords, temporary arrangements that ought to protect refugees but seldom do. In 2021, two-thirds of all refugees worldwide come from just five countries (Syria, Venezuela, Afghanistan, South Sudan, and Myanmar) —countries that were fully immersed in wars, ethnic, tribal, and religious violence, with few alternatives in sight. Scores of Syrians, Venezuelans, Afghanis, Sudanese, and Rohingyas (from Myanmar), and many others, lingered in refugee camps in several countries, desperate to survive and improve their lives, end their misery, and otherwise regain their rights and dignities as human beings. When that was not possible, the refugee became an asylum seeker, namely a person who flees his home country, enters another country and applies for residence, i.e. seeks the right to international protection at his or her destination. An asylum seeker is a type of migrant who may be a refugee or a displaced person, but not an economic migrant.

Finally, a migrant is a person who travels to a different country often in order to find work, to be engaged, or is engaged, or has been engaged in a remunerated activity in a "State" of which he or she is not a national

(Art. 2[1], *International Convention on the Protection of the Rights of All Migrant Workers and Members of Their Families*, 1990). An irregular migrant, an illegal or an undocumented worker is someone who, owing to illegal entry, or the expiry of his or her visa, lacks legal status in a transit or host country. The term applies to migrants who infringe a country's admission rules and any other person not authorized to remain in the host country (such a person may also be called a clandestine/illegal/undocumented migrant or migrant in an irregular situation).

Structure of the Book

To better address the core questions raised in this study, namely to identify and analyze the Kingdom of Sa'udi Arabia's policies towards refugees, an effort is made to anchor the book in a comprehensive theoretical framework. Chapter 1 examines the theories of international migration, including forced migration, and places the discussion of international migration within the larger globalization dilemmas before and after the memorable SARS–CoV-2 [Corona] virus pandemic that dominated 2020 and introduced significant changes at the local, regional and global levels. Chapter 2 provides an assessment of the Kingdom's policies towards refugees, starting with one of the oldest migrant communities in Sa'udi Arabia, the Bidun, followed by the Rohingya and Palestinian refugees who started arriving just as the country declared its independence in 1932, but especially after 1948. The Bidun are a nomad population descendant of nomadic tribes that failed to register for Sa'udi nationality (similar to their conduct in other nascent Arabian states, including Iraq and Kuwait), even before World War II. It is difficult to know if their exclusion from the process was due to their nomadic character, or whether it was the result of a deliberate decision of the emerging state. Whatever the cause, most Bidun remained stateless for many decades, a situation that drew the ire of the international community. It was only in the last few years that the Kingdom sponsored legislation that guaranteed citizenship for the Bidun and, despite all the problems related to its implementation, this became a priority for the Sa'udi government. How to address their conditions and regularize their legal statuses are now under review, and while this process is time consuming, it is finally a long overdue initiative that will, hopefully, resolve a lingering dilemma.[30]

Equally important, the presence of Rohingya (Burmese) refugees was traced back to the 1962 military coup in Myanmar, which toppled the U Ne Win dictatorship. Starting from the 1960s, and up to the tragic

2018 events, the Rohingya arrived into Saʻudi Arabia in significant numbers, which placed their total numbers in 2021 at around 500,000 persons. For many years, Rohingya refugees were classified as "stateless," though Riyadh granted around 190,000 work permits starting in 2010 in a move to legalize their presence in the country. In addition, the government decided to exempt those who failed to renew their documents from incurring fines thereby revealing its desire to regularize their presence. Following the directives of the Article 7 of the 1989 "Convention of the Rights of the Child" that Riyadh acceded to in January 1996, Rohingya children born in Saʻudi Arabia were granted automatic residency, which was a significant step as well.[31]

The chapter further examines the presence of an estimated 287,000 Palestinians living in the Kingdom, whose status remained in limbo for obvious political reasons. In fact, authorities excluded Palestinians from any naturalization processes because, first, Palestinians did not apply for a different status as most believed their stays were temporary and that they would return to Palestine shortly after their expulsion in 1948 when the State of Israel was established. A second powerful reason was the collective Arab consensus not to grant Palestinians nationality, allegedly because doing so would injure their legal quest in "the right to return." Regrettably, the impossibility of going back to Palestine meant that many lived in precarious conditions, even if Saʻudi Arabia—in the pre-oil boom era, it was worth recalling—absorbed the majority by granting Palestinians residency and work permits.[32]

The chapter then tackles these early initiatives and analyzes several royal decrees, including Royal Decree Number 56660 issued on 26 September 2015 [13/11/1436], which stipulated that Syrian refugees and displaced persons should be granted extension of visas, that they should receive documents for temporary stays, be granted employment facilities, allowed registration in schools, and be given access to medical services. These were critical steps that were replicated in the case of Yemenis, as discussed below.

Chapter 3 clarifies the very idea of refugee as embedded in the 1951 United Nations Refugee Convention and how its principles and values may also be found in Islam. The points of convergence and of differences between Western norms and Muslim values are addressed to expose the limits in both. There is a genuine conviction that in order to solve the immense refugee crisis the world faces, and is likely to confront in the decades ahead, that the entire international community must assume various burdens. Clearly, these challenges cannot and will not be solved unless a dialogue is established between East and West, a dialogue that would set aside prejudices, notwithstanding inevitable cultural differences. While western societies may well refuse the religious nature of their Muslim counterparts in general, and those of Sa'udi society in particular, the risks for ignoring calls for such a dialogue are enormous. Indeed, while a secular approach cannot be imposed on those who value religious norms, it behooves decision-makers to dismiss prejudices in order to ensure the success of sorely needed dialogue, thus enabling positive results toward those most in need. This chapter offers many examples of hospitality granted on Sa'udi soil, from the case of Rashid 'Ali R. al-Kilani (former Prime Minister of Iraq), to the Muslim Brotherhood (Sunni Islamists) from Egypt, to the Burmese minority communities, to the Iraqis in the Sa'udi Rafhah refugee camp, and many others. These examples clarify how Sa'udi refugee policies were driven both by humanitarian concerns as well as religious obligations.

The journey into the Islamic values of hospitality is discussed in Chapter 4, which deals with the concept of *Zakat*, as a paradigm of foreign aid. *Zakat*, the giving of alms to the poor and needy, is the third of the Five Pillars of Islam and constitutes a must for every observant Muslim. Since *Zakat* is not charity—meaning a volunteer action that will make the believer feel better—but an obligation based on an acknowledgment that as sons of God we do not own anything because everything belongs to God, its application is important. In fact, the very idea of alms giving is meant to save believers from greed, and to teach them discipline and honesty. It is also a way to create an effective social framework, which allows societies to protect themselves from calamities produced by men or nature. By providing reliable data on Sa'udi Arabia's contributions to international humanitarian organizations in the last few years in different parts of the world, this discussion dispels the idea that the Kingdom is deaf to calls for action in tragic situations but, on the contrary, that it is obedient to core religious obligations that compel the country to provide *Zakat*.

Parallel to this analysis, an effort is made in Chapter 5 to investigate the impact that different policies, including amnesties as well as the revision of deportation laws, have had on the recognition of the rights of minority communities now living in the country. Whether Sa'udi policies meet global requirements towards minority communities living in the Kingdom, political refugees, as well as economic migrants, are all deserving of investigation. How Riyadh handled the significant economic migrant population is also worth a careful vetting. In fact, the undocumented African migrants' presence in the country, which constitutes a complicated case, is one of the major challenges that confront Sa'udi decision-makers and is analyzed in Chapter 6. Somalis, Ethiopians, Eritreans, Sudanese, Chadians, Nigerians, Burkinabees, Cameroonians,

Ghanaians, and others, pose serious social, economic, and security consequences for Sa'udi society due to the diversity of their countries of origins, various languages, cultures, and how their presence is perceived in the Kingdom. Many of these "refugees" have overstayed their pilgrimage visas and a great majority live in legal limbo, often for generations, which by all measures creates specific hardships. Whether they were born in the Kingdom of Sa'udi Arabia and had no rights, or came as children with their parents, most suffered in one way or another. In 2021, there were many undocumented residents who were the grandchildren of migrants who came even before the Sa'udi state was reconstituted in 1932, though the exact figures were nearly impossible to retrieve from official sources, simply because relevant information was not available. Still, the presence of a large migrant population deserves a careful discussion as it forms part and parcel of the Sa'udi approach to the overall refugee dilemma that the government confronts.

Chapter 7 addresses the often-conflictive relationship between Sa'udi Arabia and Yemen, which generated constant waves of refugees since 1932, most recently after the 2011 uprisings. The data gathered and clarified here highlights, unmistakably, how the Kingdom provided and continues to allocate significant humanitarian aid to Yemeni refugees. The country welcomed over one million evacuees who fled the war in Yemen starting in 2015 despite unending criticisms that it bore the primary responsibility for the conflict. Notwithstanding the causes of the war, which are addressed in the chapter, in mid-2021 most of the aid that reached Yemenis originated in Sa'udi Arabia, a fact that the international community has chosen to overlook—save for the relevant humanitarian organizations that reported the truth.

It would have been impossible to write this book without offering a view of the Syrian refugee crisis from the Sa'udi point of view. Chapter 8 thus examines that conflict and focuses on the post-2011 uprisings and civil wars. Remarkably, there were concrete objections to how little—allegedly—Riyadh assumed in terms of the humanitarian burden, often driven by specific prejudices in widely reported neglect—again, erroneously. Many believed, or chose to persuade themselves, that the Arab Gulf countries in general and Sa'udi Arabia in particular, did not accept refugees from Syria into their territories. The purpose of this chapter is thus threefold: first, to describe Riyadh's policies vis-à-vis Syrian refugees who moved to Sa'udi Arabia; second, to evaluate accusations that the conservative Arab Gulf country refused to alleviate the humanitarian crisis towards Syrian (as well as Yemeni and other) asylum-seekers; and third, to analyze Riyadh's integration rather than confinement policies. Before addressing these critical questions, the discussion provides a brief overview of the wars under way in Syria, assesses casualties and offers educated guesses about the total number of refugees that the ongoing conflict created. Addressing the Syrian case is significant because it highlights one of the misunderstandings raised by the sheer application of Western mechanisms of refugee recognition. These allegations, of the lack of commitment variety, neglected to report what the Kingdom, along with several other Muslim countries, embarked upon. They failed to recognize the Sa'udi preferences not to count refugees as such, as the latter were considered to be "brothers and sisters." As a consequence, they were not and are not included in the counting carried out by the international commission for refugees, which is why this chapter sets out reliable data about Syrian refugee movements.

Finally, Chapter 9 deals in detail with the global efforts made by the Kingdom in the provision of humanitarian aid, as Sa'udi Arabia was, and remains, a leading provider of official development assistance to developing countries. Such aid averaged 1.5% of the Kingdom's gross national income for the period between 1973 and 2008, according to a study conducted by the World Bank.[33] Moreover, Riyadh created the *Sa'udi Fund for Development* that donated more than $2 billion for the period between 2000 and 2010 alone. While this and similar contributions are discussed in the chapter, very little of this "donor phenomenon" was reported about in mainstream media sources, or by academics who demonized Riyadh for a variety of reasons. The fact is that the truth about the Kingdom's unprecedented generosity has been carefully shielded for too long. The Kingdom remained one of the top donors in the world and has been so since the 1970s. In fact, and according to United Nations reports, Riyadh was the sixth or seventh largest donor worldwide—again with specific objectives in mind to assist the needy everywhere.

This volume does not aim to simply highlight Sa'udi Arabia's track record in receiving refugees, but to present a coherent argument with respect to multiple issues that decision-makers address in order to substantiate their actions. Moreover, the book only marginally focuses on repudiating the international ostracism of Sa'udi Arabia in discussions about international humanitarian aid and asylum, though it strives to do so in an unbiased and evidence-led way that includes a detailed assessment of how aid principles translate into policies and practices. Islam contains key tenets about supporting those in need, and while this does not automatically mean that Muslim nations like Sa'udi Arabia operate exclusively according to these teachings, dismissing what many believe to be their sacred duty would be both obstructive as well as unbecoming.

CHAPTER 1

A Theoretical Perspective on Migration

International migration has a long and complex history as the phenomenon lived through the Renaissance, commercial revolution, colonialism, agricultural revolutions, the industrial revolution, the rise of free market economies, modern education, and technological innovation, all of which led to the growth of mass movement across borders, both voluntary as well as involuntary. Globalization boosted migration in recent years, owing to revolutionary developments in the post-industrial era, and stretching into the current information technology age. Notwithstanding high-technology imperatives, economic blocs like the European Union have opened the floodgates to international migration, as such are still dependent on cheap labor. Owing to low transportation rates, affordable housing options, online travel plans, and the availability of dependable destinations with low-cost insurance policies, the initial financial costs of migration were significantly reduced, though none of these facilities assisted illegal travelers and those seeking asylum. To be sure, international migrant conferences, relatively stable environments in many parts of the world, the promotion of skilled and technical labor migrations, and modern low-cost communication facilities, have all become significant motivators for international movements, except in those cases that affected refugees whose very presence around the world was perceived by leading governments as an unbearable burden.

Man-made wars, conflicts, and worsening political conditions, all lead to migration too, and while bilateral and multilateral treaties facilitated the free movement of labor among countries in some parts of the world, global migration became a common occurrence because many opted to assume travel risks away from their native lands.[1] Over the past few decades, intellectual interests developed to study the relationships between international migration and workers' remittances[2] and, from a developed countries' point of view, to assess the brain drain aspect of international movements.[3] There was, however, no overarching theory that incorporated all facets of international migration, even if there was and is a universal appreciation that the phenomenon was affected by a variety of disciplines, including economics, sociology, geography, commerce, management, law, political science, demography, and psychology, making theorizing international migration difficult indeed. According to leading analysts,[4] international migration was synonymous with incoherent and disjointed hypotheses, and there was no comprehensible theory relevant to it. Another observer contended that a long-standing and deeply rooted problem in assimilating research on migration theory was inherent in the diverse and fragmented nature of the field that meant, he noted, "reliance on any one single approach [to] likely . . . lead to a highly specific and incomplete view of the complex process affecting an individual's location decision in the space economy."[5] Still another scholar observed that "[f]inding a general theory of migration with universal validity and applicability [was] the perpetual dream of those working on migration research. To the ambitious this has become an obsession; to the more realistic it has remained a fond hope."[6]

The purpose of this chapter is three-fold. First to examine international migration from a global perspective, then delve into a classification of migration theories, including analyses of the neo-classical, the new economics of labor migration approach, the dual labor market theory, networking, and institutional and cumulative causation theories. Discussion then focuses on the United Nations 1951 Refugee Convention and 1967 Protocols, before concluding through a brief assessment of international migration as a globalization impediment.

A Glance at International Migration

Migration is characterized as people's movement from one location to another to live or work.[7] According to the United Nations, international migration has become a global phenomenon, with widely felt complexities and impacts on various societies.[8] Indeed, international migration displayed both advantages and drawbacks when viewed from the perspective of a country's development, and it could easily be argued that migration was a positive force for development because it helped host countries obtain the skills, experiences, and services of accomplished as well as untrained labor they presumably needed. Still, a host country may suffer as a result of unwanted migrants entering as refugees, a growing problem in several countries. On the other hand, and despite receiving remittances, countries that exported migrants stood to experience brain drain that, in the aftermath of large outflows of skilled labor in particular, left undeniable consequuences. It was thus a given that economic and political issues, as well as natural disasters, led to migration, both of the voluntary as well as forced varieties.

Inasmuch as the contemporary international situation reveals that internal and external conflicts necessitate migration, few should anticipate dramatic changes anytime soon. Syrians, for example, experienced massive displacements because of the ongoing wars in that hapless country, along with millions of Rohingyas who were mercilessly removed from Myanmar and who lived through calamities galore. Yet, and in addition to conflicts that led to emigration, unemployment in developing economies have also become motivating factors for large numbers of people to leave their countries. In fact, migration has now become a common factor for developed societies, a phenomenon that increased in momentum in the twenty-first century. Increasingly, people chose to migrate to wealthy countries for relatively more comfortable standards of living and, in the case of those who fled wars, to survive even if temporarily. Migration has now become a critical demographic force in the world.

The total number of migrants in the world was projected to be over 280 million in 2020, accounting for 3.6% of the global population.[9] The most common migrant destinations were Europe, East Asia, and West Asia. In 2020, the United States of America welcomed 51 million international migrants, the highest number ever hosted by a single country. Germany hosted the second largest number of migrants worldwide (around 16 million), followed by Sa'udi Arabia (13 million), the Russian Federation (12 million) and the United Kingdom of Great Britain and Northern Ireland (9 million).[10] According to available statistics, "nearly half of all international migrants resided in the region from which they originated. Europe had the largest share of intra-regional migration, with 70 percent of all migrants born in Europe residing in another European country. Sub-Saharan Africa had the second largest share of intra-regional migration (63 percent). By contrast, Central and Southern Asia had the largest share of its diaspora residing outside the region (78 percent), followed by Northern America (75 per cent) and Latin America and the Caribbean (74 percent)."[11]

Based on the factors that influenced migration, international migration has been divided into various categories, as defined by leading scholars. For Roel Peter Jennissen (2004) there were four different conditions of migration, including (1) labor migration, (2) return migration, (3) chain migration, and (4) asylum migration.[12] Cross-border migration for the purpose of seeking jobs in another country was labor migration, involving high-skilled, semi-skilled, and unskilled migrants. Return migrants were individuals who wished to return to their home countries after living as international migrants in another political entity for at least a year; whereas chain migrants were those who moved from one country to another in order to reunite with family and/or start a new family. Asylum seekers who moved to another country in search of refugee status were referred to as asylum migrants. According to another scholar, migration was divided into two categories: forced and voluntary migrations, which added specific accountability twists especially in the case of refugees.[13] Forced migrants were those who migrated from one country to another as asylum seekers, refugees, or internally displaced persons, while voluntary migrants were those who moved for a variety of reasons, such as to provide labor. Owing to the difficulties they faced in their home countries, the former group had no choice but to relocate to another country, while the latter group journeyed willingly in search of personal benefits. Different terminologies were used to describe different forms of resettlements in addition to the above, with economic migration used most commonly, ostensibly to better one's situation.

This nomenclature was somewhat close to the conventional idea of labor migration, since priority was often given to economic benefits, followed closely by political asylum seekers. The latter, as described in the literature, were individuals who moved from one country to another as a result of civil war and political discrimination, sometimes described as natural migratory movements.[14] Environmental migrants were groups who departed their home countries because of environmental issues such as desertification, rising sea levels, or drought, conditions that rendered living conditions hazardous. In light of the above, it was relatively simple to see how different forms of international migration developed over time, as researchers explored new forms of migration based on push and pull variables. Consequently, migration became a topic that developed in tandem with research relating to changing socioeconomic and geopolitical circumstances; several theories emerged to understand and explain the various permutations.

Theories of International Migration

Global migration is the subject of a variety of propositions in the vast literature that has preoccupied social scientists and decision-makers for decades. Over the years, researchers categorized detailed migration theories alongside various factors such as origin, migration trends, related disciplines, and implementation. This section examines how such classifications were made and the existence of individual theories applied to international migration.

Migration Theories: A Classification

Leading contributors organized the international migration theories under different levels, including the following three major sets: micro-level, macro-level, and meso-level migrations [Table 1.1].[15] Micro-level theories identified migration decisions from an individual's viewpoint, in other words, honed on their preferences and expectations; macro-level theories looked at migration decisions from a broad viewpoint, such as the country's economic structure. Family relations, social networks, and peer groups were placed between the micro- and macro-levels, in a category that came to be known as the meso-level, where resettlement decisions were made in different ways.

Academics in various disciplines such as economics, sociology, geography, and demography performed detailed research on migration with the goal of theorizing the causes and effects of migration.[16] These efforts produced several additional migration theories with a particular emphasis on economic, sociological, cultural, and geographic factors. Table 1.2 provides a snapshot of international migration theories in different disciplines, including each field's general research question, level or unit of analysis, as well as dominant theories within a particular discipline, along with a sample hypothesis for each.[17]

Table 1.1
Migration Theories: Level-Based Analysis

Migration Theories		
Micro-Level	Meso-level	Macro-level
Push & Pull factors	Social Capital Theory	Neoclassical Macro-Migration Migration Theory
Neoclassical Micro-Migration Theory	Institutional Theory	Migration as System
Behavioral Models	Network Theory	Dual Labor Market Theory
Theory of Social System	Cumulative Causation Theory	Mobility Transition
	New Economics of Labor Migration	

Source: Wickramasinghe and Wimalaratana, "International Migration and Migration Theories," *Social Affairs* 1:5, Fall 2016, p.18.

Table 1.2
Migration Theories Across Disciplines

Discipline	Research question	Levels/Unit of Analysis	Dominant Theories	Sample Hypothesis
Anthropology	How does migration affect cultural change and effect ethnic identity?	Micro Individuals, households, groups	Rational or structuralist and transnational	Social networks help maintain the cultural difference
Demography	How does migration affect population?	Macro Population	Rationalist (borrows heavily from economics)	Migration has a major impact on the size, but a small impact on age structure
Economics	What explains the propensity to migrate and its effects?	Micro Individuals	Rationalist: cost-benefit and utility-maximizing behavior	Incorporation varies with the level of human capital of immigrants
Geography	What explains spatial patterns of migration?	Macro, meso, and micro Individuals, households and groups	Relational, structural, and transnational	Incorporation depends on ethnic networks and residential patterns
History	How do we understand immigrant experience?	Micro Individuals and groups	Eschews theory and hypothesis testing	Not applicable
Law	How does the law influence migration?	Macro and micro The political and legal systems	Institutional and rationalist (borrows from all social science)	Rights create incentive structures for migration and incorporation
Political Science	Why do states have difficulty controlling migration?	More macro Political and international systems	Institutional and rationalist	States are often captured by pro-immigrant interests
Sociology	What explains incorporation and exclusion?	Macro Ethnic groups and social class	Structuralist or Institutionalist	Incorporation varies with social and human capital

Source: Adapted from Eliot Dickinson, *Globalization and Migration: A World in Motion*, London: Rowman and Littlefield, 2017, p. 13.

Importantly, and as states continually attempted to filter who can cross international borders, refugee status closed doors to many migrants.[18] In fact, the United Nations High Commissioner for Refugees (UNHCR) insisted that "refugees [we]re not migrants," which fit the UNHCR's mission that, in short, was to protect refugees from restrictive policies."[19] Leading academics concurred though the destinations could be obscure, and in certain instances were not as clear as some intended them to be. Skeptical media sources voiced their opinion too, as they alleged that "migrants" entered a particular country under the label of a "genuine refugee" without legitimate claims to be admitted and protected.[20] For historical and contemporary political reasons, the idea that migrants and refugees were distinct has spread throughout academia. In the late nineteenth and early twentieth centuries, a large wave of transoceanic European immigration to the New World occurred at a time when neither a separate track for refugee admissions nor an international refugee regime existed. As a result, many early migratory movements, such as Russian Jews fleeing pogroms and Irish subjects fleeing the Great Famine, could be described as forced migrations.[21]

Still, because refugee studies is a newer scholarly field with its own research centers, journals, professional associations, and research paradigms dedicated to the concerns of refugees, their advocates and legal scholars honed in on various interpretations and putative distinctions. In particular, British academics shaped the field, starting in the 1980s, by assuming that refugees were fundamentally different from migrants due to the push factors that drove their movements and the states' unique legal obligations to protect refugees in the postwar regime.[22]

Analysis of Migration Theories

Indeed, most research on immigration aimed to investigate its political, economic, and social consequences on countries from where migrants originated along with host societies that welcomed them. In this regard, anthropologists, sociologists, and political economists of globalization have observed that the continued liberalization of world trade, and the movement of goods and capital by which this was measured, have been matched by a spectacular liberalization of the free movement of persons. Consequently, a sharp decline in a nation state's ability to control population movements occurred, just as humanity entered an era that was and is frequently described as being a new "age of migration."[23] Inasmuch as migration theories were helpful because they offered analytical guidelines for understanding people's movements in a larger context, this could well be a product of economic, social, legal, political, cultural, racial, or other factors, all of which elucidated rapidly evolving patterns. In fact, every theory on international migration included empirical information about international migration that exposed systemic and unique regularities in migration and their relationships. It may thus be useful to briefly examine common theories on international migration that can be subsumed under the following categories: the neo-classical theory, the new economics of labor migration theory, the dual labor market theory, the network theory, the migration system theory, the institutional theory and the cumulative causation theory.

Neo-classical Theory

The oldest and best known theory of international migration was the neo-classical theory, according to Joaquín Arango, which described the effect of labor migration on economic growth.[24] The theory and its extensions affirmed that the source of international migration was a regional disparity in labor demand and supply, presumably because job seekers preferred to move to a high-wage country when the labor supply was elastic, even if wages and marginal productivity were low.[25] Indeed, remittances became a strong incentive for labor-sending countries to promote out-migration, something that few countries were willing to acknowledge. Furthermore, as migration fostered productivity in the labor-host country, the remittance-receiving entity minimized income disparities and wage differentials.[26] Still, this theory's implicit assumption was that eliminating wage differentials would stop labor movements and bring migration to a halt, as discussed by its proponents.[27] Advocates stressed that a migrant's decision to embark on a life-changing experience was strongly affected by work prospects and projected income differentials at the outset. Others advanced the notion that the neo-classical explanation was driven by the notion that international labor migration occurred mainly in markets that demanded labor while other conditions played marginal roles.[28] Still others contended that the neo-classical theory suggested that labor market laws and controls governed both originating and host countries' international migration policies.[29] These presumptions appeared to be correct in the twenty-first century, as several regulations standardized labor exports effectively. In other words, microeconomics' neo-classical school maintained that international immigration (for either legal or illegal purposes) was always calculated based on expected benefits. Therefore, neo-classical theory suggested that factors such as geographic proximity, border control, the likelihood and implications of detention, and the ease of illicit jobs, among other things, determined the possibility of unlawful migration. This model further assumed that undocumented migrants, who were usually less educated, contributed to and competed with the host country's unskilled labor and accepted lower wages. Consequently, income disparities between home and destination countries were the primary determinant of international migration.

In two classic papers, three leading authors established the microeconomic theory by conceptualizing migration as a cost–benefit decision, as prospective migrants measured overall future increases in earnings they expected as a result of moving to a higher-paying position, weighted against the likelihood of landing that job and discounted by a factor representing the lower utility of future earnings.[30] The authors deducted the estimated expense from expected benefits when an individual agreed to migrate only if the anticipated advantages surpassed costs. On the other hand, the macro-level in this school of economic thought stressed that the balance of labor supply and demand within regional markets determined wages. If there was a relative shortage of workers in one market and a relative abundance in another, wages would thus be higher in the former and lower in the latter. Migration, therefore, represented an equilibrating mechanism between the two regions, as workers in low-wage areas moved up. Remarkably, asylum seekers adopted these cost-benefit calculations. For example, one postulates that Rashid 'Ali al-Kilani, a high-ranking Iraqi official who fell out of favor in his native Iraq in the early 1940s, sought asylum from 'Abdul 'Aziz bin 'Abdul Rahman and received it, went through the same calculations in certain cases, as discussed in Chapter 5.

The New Economics of Labor Migration (NELM)

The new economics of labor migration, or NELM, arose to challenge many of the assumptions of neo-classical theory, as decisions were made not by isolated factors but by families or households collaborating to maximize expected incomes and minimize risks from home market failures.[31] Moreover, since many less developed areas did not have insurance for crop failures, price protection mechanisms for "futures markets," or government support during lean times, migration emerged as a panacea for several countries with surplus labor. NELM thus challenged the assumptions and conclusions of the neo-classical theory, given its concern with migration from the micro individual level to meso units such as families, households, and other culturally defined components. In other words, a key insight of this new approach was that migration was not merely an individual decision, but a collective resolution within households or families where the goal was to increase income while balancing that objective with a strategy for risk management.[32] When considered as a group, households diversified their economic well-being risks by utilizing labor resources in a variety of ways. For example, family members reduced the risks of job insecurity and income fluctuations, by assigning each individual economic activity in both the country of origin as well as the host society.[33] Migrant remittances could thus compensate for a decline in local income and vice versa.

In comparison to the neo-classical theory, NELM identified several improvements, with noticeable benefits to migrants and refugees. While the former emphasized that wage differentials were outperformed by household roles, NELM called these earlier assumptions into question. Yet, because wage disparities and household decision-making were not mutually exclusive or antagonistic categories, when choosing a work destination for a family member abroad, families were likely to consider wage differentials to be a strong, if not the leading factor in the decision to journey to a new land.

It was possible to argue that NELM challenged the neo-classical approach only because it considered the individual's structural conditions rather than just the labor market. Remittances were part of a mutually beneficial arrangement between the migrant and the traveler's family, according to the conceptual framework built around the role of families and households under NELM.[34] When compared to the individual role played by the migrant in the neo-classical explanation, NELM's emphasis on labor as a pooled resource of a household thus became a critical criterion for consideration.

Dual Labor Market Theory

In a departure from micro-level models, the dual labor market theory was introduced in 1979; it avoided viewing migration as an individual decision. Instead, it argued that international migration resulted from intrinsic labor demands in industrialized societies. According to Michael J. Piore, the permanent demand from industrialized nations was the root cause of international migration, which emphasized that such migration occurred because of pull factors in host countries rather than push factors in originating countries.[35] Push factors included low wages and high unemployment while pull factors stood as essential and unavoidable needs that international workers in host societies were expected to meet. Furthermore, this theory focused on four key characteristics within industrialized countries that explained why labor was drawn in: namely structural inflation, motivational issues, economic dualism, and labor supply demography.[36] While the dual labor market theory encompassed several ideas included in the neo-classical model, it was not diametrically opposed to them since the latter, and even some factors within NELM, differed in the demand-driven nature of international migration. In this instance, the main idea was that businesses needed migrant workers for structural reasons, rather than varying wages or family preferences driving the demand.

Network Theory

A different approach from the economic paradigm was derived from the sociological perspective. The network theory contended that interpersonal ties connected migrants, former migrants, and non-immigrants in origin and destination countries through friendship and kinship relations. Shared community origins increased the likelihood of immigration, and this was certainly the case in many instances. Such networks reduced migration costs, raised benefits, and lessened various risks. In fact, the empirical evidence suggested that networks played significant roles in shaping individual and household migration decisions, and promoted, even guided, immigration flows.

One observer stated that sociological theories of international migration (including refugees) should be able to explain the size, direction, and composition of population movements that crossed state borders.[37] The theory identified additional factors that affected the decision to migrate and the destination chosen, the characteristics of social integration in host countries and, in the final analysis, highlighted re-migration and return phenomena as they took place. Interestingly, such a bold agenda was never attempted in the area of international migration science, as researchers concentrated on particular aspects of immigration, such as the demographic profiles of refugees, their migration decision-making perspectives, any economic and social adaptation features in host societies, or global population patterns as they arose.[38]

According to Karen O'Reilly, migration structures and the network theory were sociological endeavours, which were best understood in the light of an existing framework—the social and economic relationships between countries in different regions—with special attention paid to the roles that family, acquaintances, and other connections that assisted or discouraged migration.[39] Of course, assisting migrants to settle down in host societies and sustain their links to their respective home countries were also valuable features, presumably since government policies encouraged family reunification that strengthened such networks. Once established, such networks became relatively impervious to policy interventions, which is also significant. In this respect, it is critical to note that the Kingdom of Sa'udi Arabia had no such policies, though family reunification planks were vital to refugees.

Of course, labor migration happens for a variety of reasons, including a desire for high individual income, the diversification of household resources, international labor displacements due to market penetration strategies, as well as recruitment programs to meet employer demands for low-wage workers.[40] Even if the factors mentioned above were all present, these are insufficient to explain actual migration patterns. In some instances, geographic proximity, availability of social networks, tested institutions, and cultural and historical factors were all equally important features.[41] What the concept of a "migration network" revealed was a linkage to the concept of social capital, in what was described as a "set of interpersonal ties that connect[ed] migrants with relatives, friends, or fellow countrymen at home who transmit[ed] information, provide[d] financial backups, and facilitate[d] employment opportunities and housing in various supportive ways."[42] These networks lowered the costs and risks of human movement while increasing migration's expected net returns.

Migration System Theory

The world-systems theory states that migration is a natural course following the globalization of market economies. In this sense, "the processes of economic globalization create[d] a pool of mobile workers in developing countries and simultaneously connect[ed] them to labor markets in particular cities where their services [we]re demanded."[43] This theory's central premise was that migration affect both the host and originating countries' economic, social, cultural, and institutional conditions. According to a leading analyst, the network theory and migration system theory are closely related, with the latter focusing on both macro and micro links between places involved in the migration process.[44] Kinship and friendship systems are micro-level factors, whereas macro-level factors include the economy, dominance, political systems, national immigration policies, and cultural and social systems. The migration system theory, unlike other models, emphasizes the mutual relationship between migration and development.[45] Thus, this theory helped develop a framework that considered migration in the context of broader development. Not only did migration help with economic development, but it also assisted with social development, as remittances to family members, for example, changed the social and economic context of labor-sending countries. It was possible to then argue that migration had the potential to influence the socioeconomic development of the country of origin, and encouraged subsequent migration at both the macro and micro levels.

Institutional Theory

With the beginning of international migration, many institutions and organizations were established to take advantage of disparities between employers in labor-hosting countries and potential migrants in labor-sending countries. The large number of people looking for work in industrialized countries, along with the limited number of immigrant visas available in them, created a significant mismatch.[46] Consequently, a slew of for-profit and non-profit organizations sprung up to address both migrants and employers' needs, as most non-profit organizations focused on the humanitarian needs of migrants. In contrast, profit-making organizations and private entrepreneurs facilitated border crossings, counterfeited travel documents, arranged marriages between migrants, and secured legal residencies in destination countries. All of these services were provided at high-interest credits or in exchange for hefty fees. Most not-for-profit organizations provided relief to affected migrants through counseling, social services, legal advice, and awareness of immigration laws, among other things, because profit-seeking organizations frequently engaged in illegal behavior. Institutional theory was particularly important in contemporary settings, ostensibly to create more favorable and more robust policy frameworks for both labor-sending and host societies.

Cumulative Causation Theory

Finally, and as proposed by Gunnar Myrdal in 1956, the cumulative causation theory explains why a migration flow starts and keeps growing.[47] In a nutshell, it describes how the number of outgoing migrants grows over time as the first travelers provide social capital to family, colleagues, and others in their home country, helping them to find employment quickly and to face minimal risk in destination countries.[48] These conditions inspired and influenced more people to move, which meant that the cumulative causation theory was categorized as part of the system theory or even the network theory.

———❖———

All of these theories dealt with the migration phenomenon from a Western-centric perspective, which emphasized employment, working conditions and wages, long before it focused on intrinsic social rights and duties. As long as migration was a relatively well-managed affair for leading societies, chiefly in Europe and the Americas, few were concerned with sociological repercussions, including family unification privileges or legalized statuses. International migration crises gained momentum after World War II but especially after the mid-1970s, when a large number of people travelled to the Arabian Peninsula in the post-oil boom era. Until that time, the only major post-World War II migration, albeit of the forced variety, was the fate that befell Palestinians expelled from Israel who became "refugees" in neighboring countries.[49] Naturally, the Palestinians were refugees and not migrants per se, though the distinction was blurred as host nation-states confronted dramatic surges in their demographic as well as socio-political settings. More recent conflicts throughout the Arab World added to the heavy burden that governments stretching from the Levant to the Arabian Gulf faced, all with significant repercussions.

What emerged in the study of human movements were the relationships between political and economic determinants, as populations driven by uncertainties formed a nexus of forced migration. All of the theories discussed above were applicable to people moving from poorer to wealthier areas, from economically underdeveloped to growing regions or, in the case of professional and highly qualified migrants, in classic brain drain phenomena. New terms were devised, including transience, to refer to such movements.[50] For its part, the United Nations identified a de jure concept for refugee status (Convention Refugee), which stressed "a well-founded fear of persecution," even if it was no longer possible to regard "refugee" movements as fully independent of the state of the global economy.

There are also complex issues of autonomy, perceived interests, international affairs, and ideological considerations.[51] Wars, political unrests and revolutions, terrorism, the expulsion of ethnic minorities, ethno-religious and communal conflicts, population displacements due to technological developments such as the mechanization of agriculture and hydroelectric schemes, land reforms, and the resettlement of millions were among the most common causes of large refugee movements and asylum requests in the twenty-first century that, naturally, preoccupied decision-makers. In fact, economic, social, and political causes were all intertwined in these situations, since competing interests were prevalent across the world, including in the Middle East. It was fair to state that long-term competition, low-intensity conflicts and soft-power quests for domination pitted various powers against each other, with every political entity protecting intrinsic interests. Often, these interests were far more critical than the rights and duties of migrants and refugees, which few could contest.

For our purposes, and as discussed by Aristide R. Zolberg, Astri Suhrke and Sergio Aguayo, refugee movements did not consist of random events but rather were linked to significant political developments, such as the disintegration of former empires, or states.[52] In fact, the dissolution of states and the emergence of new nations were impeded by economic underdevelopment, which meant that even relatively wealthy and powerful countries acted only in accordance with their national interests. Economic migrants could thus be driven by political oppression as well as material needs, as recent populations movements illustrate.[53] Refugee flights from Ethiopia occurred for both political reasons as well as famine, while residents fleeing from El Salvador did so because of generalized violence rather than individual persecution. Affected by such situations, the distinction between "economic" and "political" refugees became entirely futile, though governments around the world made de facto distinctions between "Convention Refugees" and other migrants, as defined by the United Nations Convention that, as discussed in the next section, was interpreted differently in Western and Muslim societies.

The 1951 Refugee Convention and 1967 Protocols

To better understand the implications and the complex relationships and misunderstandings between leading Western societies and the Muslim world, it is necessary to analyze the similarities in views and differences in perceptions, since both sides advanced different interpretations on the status of refugees. What were the main controversial points and is it possible to highlight some of the past and present synergies precisely to anticipate future ones?

As the reference global accord was and still is the 1951 Refugee Convention, what this critical step achieved decades ago was to establish a legal criterion in a document that defined who was/is a refugee, what were his/her rights, and what kind of obligations did nation-states that welcomed them have. A multi-pronged protocol to this law was added in 1967 with the purpose to remove the geographical and temporal restrictions present in the original Convention. While this Convention was considered the cornerstone of refugee laws, it is important to underscore that it was originally signed when a major refugee crisis affected Europe after World War II, which was presumably alleviated by the 1967 protocol.

Among its key articles in defense of refugees' rights, several stood out, including Article 1A (2) of the Convention, which stated that a refugee was a person with a "well-founded fear of being persecuted for reasons of race, religion, nationality, membership of a particular social group or political opinion, [was] outside the country of his nationality and . . . unable or, owing to such fear, . . . unwilling to avail himself of the protection of that country; or who, not having a nationality and being outside the country of his former habitual residence as a result of such events, [was] unable or, owing to such fear, . . . unwilling to return to it." Article 3 maintained that "Contracting States shall apply the provisions of this convention to refugees without discrimination as to race, religion or country of origin." Article 16 affirmed that "a refugee shall have free access to the courts of law on the territory of all Contracting States," while Article 27 declared that "States shall issue identity papers to any refugee in their territory who [did] not possess a valid travel document."[54]

Yet, and in the wake of ongoing global refugee crises, which involved economic migration together with those fleeing wars and seeking asylum in safe heavens, the refugee convention and protocols were somewhat dated as they demonstrated inabilities to meet new challenges due to the fact that the world of the refugees became far more crowded and more difficult to handle. In particular, after the 1998-1999 War in Kosovo, host states were quickly overwhelmed by the challenges posed by human trafficking and the constant movement across borders. Of course, and without denying the strong humanitarian values on which the Convention rested, leading observers and activists believed that countries, in particular European nation-states, had done little and were doing even less to prevent and avoid the recurrence of such dramatic events that shook the continent in the last decade of the twentieth century. What analysts noted, in particular, was the lack of a standard policy at the European Union level on how to deal with the constant flow of refugees that emerged from the Balkan crises.[55]

It was in this context that the 1951 Refugee laws were revised in order to guarantee all refugees their fundamental rights provided for in the original Convention. This concord, and the rights it clearly provided for any refugee, were the cornerstone of similar agreements elsewhere though with predictable complications that weakened some of its stipulations. In fact, during the last few decades, the provisions of the Convention have shown their limits, largely because the very nature of a "refugee" has changed. Cultural, social, ethnic and in some cases religious factors, which the 1951 original Convention or its revised version—the more universal 1967 Protocol—could have foreseen, were not addressed. Lifting the geographical boundaries that limited the 1951 Convention was a big step forward. However, as discussed below, the Protocol failed in its intent when it did not specifically engage with non-Western cultures. In this sense the Protocol maintained the same Euro-centric framework in which it originated—best illustrated in that the secular character of the Convention did not take into account the religious aspect of some refugees. Indeed, the latter caveat supported a universal idea of what a "refugee" was, ignoring his/her human side that, in the case of refugees with deeply held religious beliefs, stood out. Under the circumstances, the NGOs operating on the ground applied the same concepts regarding humanitarian aid in different countries, along with cultural realities that, sometimes, resulted in interventions that were perceived as interferences more than as helpful steps that were required during a crisis.

This misunderstanding was evident during the latest crises, over Syria in particular, which not only showed the limits of the conventions, but also the deep divisions among European countries in dealing with the Syrian crisis. Indeed, the lack of a common agreement on the number of Syrian refugees that each country should accept within its own borders emerged as just one of the many problems associated with established norms. The dramatic exodus of Syrian migrants escaping from the brutal war that devastated their country triggered divisions in Europe which went beyond a mere question of numbers. The religion of potential asylum seekers, Muslims in their majority, raised concerns in several European countries such as Hungary, for example, which refused to welcome refugees on the ground of a professed European Christian identity that was incompatible with the faiths of most of the refugees. Similarly, repeated tragedies in the Mediterranean Sea, which recorded an undetermined number of accidents that cost the lives of thousands, and the subsequent intransigence of leading governments to severely curtail the arrival of survivors, further highlighted how some other European Union countries responded to the refugee crises triggered by the wars in Syria, Libya, and elsewhere and how a common policy was urgently needed to address various concerns.[56]

Notwithstanding inherent political shortcomings, the incapacity to deal with these crises cannot only be blamed on the limits of international law, as one of the most blatant aspects was a lack of dialogue between two very different worlds, and the recrudescence of the old confrontations between West and East, between the Christian world and the Muslim one. Indeed, the events of the last two decades with the War in Iraq and the consequent war on terrorism, and more recently the rise of Islamic extremist groups, all prevented a constructive approach between the two cultures. There were similarities between the Western and Muslim traditions regarding refugees and asylum seekers, and it surely was possible to establish a common ground between the two to engage in a discussion on the legal and human aspects of this important issue.

International Migration and Globalization

Before concluding this chapter, it was necessary to place our discussion of migrations—the legal as well as the illegal, the voluntary along with the involuntary—in the context of globalization, which is often thought of primarily in economic terms. The term itself was defined as "the development of an increasingly integrated global economy marked especially by free trade, free flow of capital, and the tapping of cheaper international labor markets," though much more needs to be added to the definition.[57] Stated in broader but still concise terms, globalization is "the intensification of economic, political, social, and cultural relations across borders," which is closer to understandings that cross cultures and civilizations.[58] According to David Held, Anthony McGrew, David Goldblatt and Jonathan Perraton, globalization is a process (or a set of processes) that involves the following types of change:

- ☐ It stretches social, political, and economic activities across political frontiers, regions, and continents.
- ☐ It intensifies our dependence on each other, as flows of trade, investment, finance, migration, and culture increase.
- ☐ It speeds up the world. New transport systems and communication mean that ideas, goods, information, capital, and people move more quickly.
- ☐ It means that distant events have a deeper impact on our lives. Even the most local developments come to have enormous global consequences.

In other words, the authors advanced the eminently sound notion that boundaries between domestic matters and global affairs became increasingly blurred, something that necessitated dialogue across cultures and civilizations.[59]

Conclusion: Adopting a Multidisciplinary Approach

The fortunes that befell migrants and refugees preoccupied large numbers of decision-makers, scholars, and lay persons alike. All were truly concerned with dramatic developments around the world, both for humanitarian as well as socio-political reasons, even if the phenomenon presented inherent difficulties for all concerned. As discussed above, a variety of migration theories were devised over the years, each of which identified specific aspects that, within the contexts of globalization, provided useful paradigms that facilitated the study of the migration phenomena regardless of type. What was clear was that undocumented migrants, displaced persons, political refugees, and others classified under a variety of definitions, confronted millions of other human beings as they moved across borders, sometimes under duress. It is crucial to connect all of these situations to globalization that, for better or worse, is a reality that defines mankind in the twenty-first century, and while various priorities preoccupy leading governments, humanitarian needs remain a priority for most at a time when the global village is readily accessible to one and all.

Remarkably, none of the theories or approaches used to study the phenomenon of legal or illegal migrations, including economic, social, and religious theories, postulated how to reduce suffering. Each adopted specific preferences, ostensibly to draw useful frameworks, though few ventured into "related" variables as guides to understanding and explaining various types. As discussed in the chapters that follow, the migration phenomenon affected the Kingdom of Sa'udi Arabia too, both of the legal and illegal varieties, raising concrete challenges to decision-makers. How migrants were received in the Kingdom and what kind of policies Riyadh adopted to address encounters with refugees deserves attention. To better assess reactions, it is necessary to compare different theories to prove their suitability for Sa'udi Arabia, a policy option that was certainly new to the Kingdom's decision-makers. By adopting different approaches, gathering contributions from anthropologists, sociologists, political scientists, historians, and geographers, this study aims to highlight diverse and erratic features of the phenomena in order to focus on the intrinsic difficulties involved.[60]

The adoption of a multidisciplinary approach facilitates the use of data without referring to any specific theory to further strengthen the analyses presented herein. Still, the theoretical discussions are uniquely beneficial as the nature of migrations—in the plural—offer useful comparisons especially when contrasted with cases from other societies and cultures. This multidisciplinary approach is validated by qualitative research— admittedly limited but essential for Sa'udi Arabia where such investigations are not frequent—that honed in on various themes, including respondents' narratives regarding daily life challenges.[61]

In the end, what the theories discussed in this chapter confirmed were the conceptualisation of causal processes at different levels of analysis, which evaluated the individual, his or her household, challenges that confronted originating and host nations, and humanitarian institutions called upon to alleviate sufferings within the international community at large. Each theory aimed to explain why an individual or a group of individuals attempted to migrate. In the case of Sa'udi Arabia, the neo-classical human capital theory and the new economics of migration theory seem to be the most applicable, as they elucidate how senior members of the government reach their decisions, as discussed throughout this volume. The opportunity to test the validity of the dual labour market theory and to apply its parameters to cases in the Kingdom further proved their utility. All of these theories needed to be utilized in unison to secure reliable results, draw on local norms, highlight cultural attributes, stress religious values, and seal within the decision-making processes duties and responsibilities.

CHAPTER

2

Sa'udi Policies towards Refugees

On the heels of a diplomatic spat with Canada over a tweet that called for the "immediate release" of human rights activists detained in Sa'udi Arabia, Riyadh confronted the wrath of international media outlets that blamed it for unmitigated abuses, though it was not long before Ottawa found political retaliation. The August 2018 crisis was a good illustration of what passed for public diplomacy during the first two decades of the twentieth century, as highly motivated officials preferred to troll social media outlets to settle disputes and, worse, conducted foreign relations as a secondary feature of domestic grievances. On 3 August 2018, Canada's Minister of Global Affairs Chrystia Freeland wrote a poorly worded *tweet* demanding the "immediate release" of certain detainees. While the Kingdom's Minister of Foreign Affairs, 'Adil al-Jubayr, recognized Ottowa's inherent right to criticize Riyadh about human rights or women's rights, Sa'udi authorities objected to the phrase "immediate release" given that such an action would bypass the country's judicial process.[1] Freeland's patience paid off as she obtained her retribution when Canada granted refugee status to a young Sa'udi woman who renounced her faith and nationality, barricaded herself in a Bangkok airport hotel to avoid being deported after her passport was confiscated, *tweeted* for global assistance, mobilized public opinion, and sought and received United Nations High Commissioner for Refugees (UNHCR) backing that, presumably, requested Ottawa accept the young woman as a refugee to live in Canada. Prime Minister Justin Trudeau acquiesced and declared: "Canada has been unequivocal that we will always stand up for human rights and women's rights around the world. When the UN made a request of us that we grant . . . asylum, we accepted."[2] Foreign Minister Chrystia Freeland was on hand at the Toronto airport to welcome "a very brave new Canadian," wearing a hoodie emblazoned with the word Canada in red, and a blue cap with the logo of the UNHCR.[3]

These diplomatic quarrels did not occur in a void as journalists and academics honed in on the alleged reasons that the Kingdom of Sa'udi Arabia did not honor putative commitments to human rights concerns and that Riyadh did not share the same values with leading global powers when it came to refugee matters. Julie M. Norman, a Research Fellow in Conflict Transformation and Social Justice at Queen's University in Belfast, Northern Ireland, vented her frustrations in September 2015 because "Sa'udi Arabia and other Gulf states have faced increasing criticism, from sources both domestic and international, for failing to open their borders to those displaced by the conflict" in Syria.[4] Norman focused on the Syrian conflict, reporting how world leaders, journalists, social media outlets and others circulated hashtags shaming the Gulf States for their inaction. She referred to political cartoons that depicted Arab Gulf states with condescension. She even lamented that few found acceptable that "Sa'udi Arabia and its conservative allies offered no resettlement opportunities to refugees." Were these criticisms justified and was the Kingdom of Sa'udi Arabia negligent in honoring its international commitments? What were the Kingdom's policies towards refugees in general? Was there an intentional disparagement of Riyadh that, at least on the surface, was inherently crude? Was Sa'udi society so bereft of any values that it could not even impart minimum sympathy to those most in need? Ultimately, were Sa'udi authorities unaware that their reservations would be received poorly if officials frowned upon the very idea of addressing various concerns?

The purpose of this chapter is to address these sensitive questions and identify Sa'udi policies towards refugees. While the conservative environment within which Sa'udis operated—both at the official as well as popular levels—seldom sought "good press," it was eminently clear that such reticence proved to be harmful and damaged the country's interests and, equally important, mobilized denigrators to launch into unending anti-Sa'udi invective. Some of Riyadh's actions, including the 2018 case of the distraught teenager that galvanized Canadian public opinion against the Kingdom, illustrated intrinsic dilemmas that confronted Sa'udi officials. Irrespective of any merits that such a case may have had, to allow an individual example gain so much momentum that pitted two governments against each other and embark on a war of words, was both unnecessary and counterproductive. In fact, an individual case, or several similar examples, negated the serious assistance extended to hundreds of thousands of the needy and distressed, though the negative publicity cancelled any goodwill. As discussed below, the Kingdom faced serious discrimination and human rights violation charges, along with undeniable gender biases, at least until 2018 when dramatic social changes were first introduced. Whatever justification authorities advanced, ranging the gamut from religious obligations to societal norms, the fact of the matter was that any bigotry against citizens and/or residents alike left negative consequences. Indeed, the gravest result of such rationalizations was a clear dismissal of every good deed undertaken by and on behalf of the Sa'udi people. Nowhere was this more evident than in the case of refugees, as the country's gargantuan efforts were dismissed with the stroke of a pen or the utterance of a few highly critical sentences on television, or distributed on social media outlets by politicians and 'experts' alike. How could Sa'udi officials address such media assaults when few were even willing to confront disparagement? Were there no instances that deserved robust rebuttals? Why were Sa'udis unwilling to discuss the significant assistance the Kingdom extended to the Bidun, Rohingya and the Palestinians? Finally, what were the migration regulations introduced in Sa'udi Arabia to address both short- and long-term initiatives towards refugees?[5]

Critics of Sa'udi Migration Initiatives

As the example of Professor Julie M. Norman illustrated, few were willing to believe what Sa'udi Arabia was embarked upon, or was assiduously planning.[6] What Norman declared was the following: First, that Sa'udi Arabia's claims to have received 2.5 million Syrians since the 2011 conflict began appeared to be "unsubstantiated at best and spurious at worst"; and, second, she further professed that Riyadh may have "welcomed between 100,000 and 500,000 Syrians on visas" that, to her, was a "very unclear data [and] just another sign of the fundamental problem: Saudi Arabia and the Gulf states simply don't 'do' refugees."[7] How Norman could reach these two fundamental conclusions without advancing any evidence to back her assertions was astounding but like much else in recent academia passed for scholarship. Of course, Professor Norman was not the only individual who offered such condemnation of Sa'udi Arabia, as equally intrepid anti-Arab and anti-Sa'udi fault-finders filled various pages with alternating degrees of contempt.[8] Adding insult to injury, many affable prognosticators concluded that no Arab Gulf State had bothered to sign the *UN Convention and Protocol Relating to the Status of Refugees*, which meant that they were not obligated to have clear policies or mandates to accept refugees or process asylum seekers. One commentator lamented that applications for entry visas or work permits were "costly and highly restricted in practice," unaware that Riyadh waived all such costs and allocated specific funds to assist

Syrians wishing to travel to the Kingdom.[9] To her credit, Professor Norman presented the Saʻudi arguments that a visa-based model preserved "the dignity of displaced Syrians by allowing them to have proper residency, freedom of movement, and rights to work, education, and health care," but quickly added, what critics claimed, "that the worker status denie[d] . . . financial support, legal protections, and path to potential citizenship afforded to many recognized refugees, making them vulnerable to restrictions or deportation at any time." The message was clear: one could really not trust Saʻudis and other Gulf countries because they practiced policies and methods that were not comparable to the generosity offered to refugees in the rest of the world.

Most judges touched upon the demographic rationale advanced by conservative Arab Gulf monarchies, which was based on the premise that relatively large expatriate populations were already living on the Arabian Peninsula amongst rather small indigenous residents, and could not possibly add to the overall roster without creating insurmountable burdens. Still, Norman quoted Michael Stephens, a Research Fellow for Middle East Studies and Head of the Royal United Services Institute (RUSI) in Doha, Qatar, who opined that Saʻudi Arabia came to see the war in Syria as a "competition between Sunni Gulf Arab interests and Iranian aligned allies," which was not untrue.[10] It was this wicked *fear*, Stephens, Norman and others advanced, that allegedly denied Syrians work permits. Although these *ungodly* steps were apparently taken in 2012, the policy endured in 2015, when scholars and journalists offered these muses, again without any evidence to back their assertions. To her credit, Norman recognized that Saʻudi Arabia had legitimate security concerns, and while many other states expressed similar reservations, what was missing in Riyadh was accountability to provide "minimum protections during refugee crises."[11]

As discussed in detail in Chapter 7, the Kingdom developed sophisticated policies vis-à-vis Syrian refugees that were certainly preoccupying, but it was incorrect to state that Syrian refugees "had a difficult time" to enter the country. One clueless observer wondered whether "a significant reason for Saudi Arabia" rejecting refugees had to do with the "Islamic State and Syrian Sunni Muslims."[12] Katelynn Kenworthy actually wrote that "a majority of the refugees fleeing to Saudi Arabia are from Sunni areas of Syria—areas that play host to the Islamic State. Saudi Arabian forces have bombed these regions and want to know if the refugees are escaping ISIS or the bombings."[13] Why should Sunni Syrians fleeing ISIS not be welcomed? Moreover, were refugees escaping bombings not worthy of assistance, no matter their creed? Naturally, national security was important, but Riyadh supported Sunni Syrians, did not perceive them as a threat, and did not vet refugees based on their beliefs.

Given the plethora of confused pronouncements and prognostications that gained traction after 2011, what were the specific criticisms lodged against Sa'udi authorities, and how could Riyadh address such concerns? To better answer these questions, and before examining the three cases of the Bidun, Rohingya and the Palestinians, it is necessary to assess specific discriminations, including gender inequities, along with human rights violations. Doing so will clarify Riyadh's policy shortcomings, what the authorities proposed to do about them, and how these policy weaknesses contrasted with the country's actual commitment to refugees and asylum seekers.

Discrimination and Human Rights Violations

According to the Institute on Statelessness and Inclusion, the Global Campaign for Equal Nationality Rights and the European Sa'udi Organization for Human Rights, the Kingdom of Sa'udi Arabia discriminated "against women in nationality legislation," and paid little more than lip-service to "the protracted statelessness experienced by certain groups in the country."[14] These concerns allegedly created and prolonged statelessness. They were not in line with Riyadh's ongoing quest to improve human rights matters inside the country nor with the policy aim to explain its positions to the rest of the world in a clear way. What were these putative grievances and how was the Sa'udi Arabian government responding?

These serious questions were repeatedly addressed by the UN Universal Periodic Review (UPR), a mechanism of the Human Rights Council (HRC) that emerged from the 2005 UN reform process, and that periodically examined the human rights records of all 193 UN Member States. It complemented the work of other human rights mechanisms and the Working Group on the UPR, composed of the HRC's 47 Member States and chaired by the HRC President, which conducted country reviews and, both directly and indirectly, provided assessments on refugee questions. A similar effort was made through the Institute on Statelessness and Inclusion, an independent non-profit organization based in Eindhoven, The Netherlands, dedicated to promoting an integrated, human rights-based response to the injustice of statelessness and exclusion. It was established in August 2014 and stood as the first and only global center committed to promoting the human rights of stateless persons as well policy promotion to end statelessness.[15] The Global

Campaign for Equal Nationality Rights, an arm of the Women's Refugee Commission based in New York, mobilized international action for the removal of gender discriminatory provisions from all nationality laws through its coalition of national and international organizations and activists, which was quite meaningful.[16] The European Sa'udi Organization for Human Rights (ESOHR) was an independent and non-profit human rights organization, led by Ali Adubisi [who was originally from the town of al-'Awamiyyah in Sa'udi Arabia], and was founded in August 2013 in response to alleged human rights violations inside Sa'udi Arabia, but operated outside of the Kingdom from its headquarters in the German capital, Berlin, as well as through representatives in London and Beirut. Between 2013 and 2020, the ESOHR translated and commented on the January 2012 list of 23 Eastern Province youths arrested for dissident activities, among other internal clashes that pitted dissidents against Sa'udi authorities. ESOHR described the Sa'udi government's actions in the Eastern Province in 2017 as "a war . . . unlike anything seen in [Sa'udi Arabia's] 80-year history." It warned against the dissident Israa al-Ghomgham's August 2018 death sentence as a "dangerous precedent" that could lead to executions of other Sa'udi political activists, but neglected to inform about the violent activities of Shi'ah dissidents across the Eastern Province. ESOHR also provided extensive coverage of the arrest, imprisonment and trial of Loujain al-Hathloul, a dissident who was sentenced on 28 December 2020 by the Specialized Criminal Court in Riyadh to five years and eight months in prison (with two years and ten months suspended), and championed a variety of other cases.[17] While all of these sources provided critical evaluations of various human rights concerns, it is important to note that they, along with the UN-UPR, overlooked the serious acts of violence that targeted law enforcement officers as well as civilians. This vital matter is discussed below, though it may first be useful to address the UN-UPR's discussion of Sa'udi Arabia in 2018, the last year when a major review was prepared.[18]

According to the 2018 Universal Periodic Review on the Kingdom, no comments on the issue of stateless communities in Sa'udi Arabia were offered in its previous reportage, and no direct discussions that addressed gender discrimination were made either. The authors of the review assumed nevertheless that the nationality law was discriminatory. In the earlier 2013 report, UPR confirmed that Riyadh had made efforts with respect to the situation of children of women married to non-nationals, as described in Paragraph 56, which read:

> "Saudi women married to non-nationals: Pursuant to Cabinet Decision No. 406 of 12 November 2012, approval was given for the

sponsorship of children of Saudi women married to non- nationals to be transferred to their mother if they are resident in the Kingdom. If they are abroad, their mother is entitled to send for them and the State shoulders the cost of their resident permits. They are also permitted to work in the private sector without any transfer of the sponsorship. They receive the same schooling and medical treatment as any Saudi and are included in the Saudization percentages for the private sector. Saudi women married to non-nationals are further permitted to bring their spouse to the Kingdom if he is abroad or, if he is resident in the Kingdom and so wishes, to have his sponsorship transferred to her."[19]

This was a major social development that deserved careful attention, though it was buried deep inside a UN document. And while several countries made general recommendations to Sa'udi Arabia "with regard to the promotion of gender equality and [the] elimination of gender discrimination," no one specifically identified gender discrimination features included in the Nationality Law.

Gender Discrimination in Sa'udi Arabia's Nationality Law

In its 2018 report, the UN-UPR concentrated on the Kingdom's Nationality Law, examined the Sa'udi Arabian Citizenship System, addressed concerns regarding children of Sa'udi fathers who acquired nationality at birth regardless of the child's birthplace, and lamented the fact that Sa'udi women could not transmit their nationalities automatically to their children. It quoted Article 7 of the law, which states that, "Individuals born inside or outside the Kingdom from a Saudi father, or Saudi mother and unknown father, or born inside the Kingdom from unknown parents (foundling) are considered Saudis."[20] Critics perceived various discriminatory features in this description, including placing "children at risk of statelessness when they cannot obtain the nationality of their father, or if their father is also stateless."

Article 8 of the nationality law allowed children of Sa'udi mothers the option of applying for nationality at the age of majority, under certain circumstances. For example, the Article stated that

"Individuals born inside the Kingdom from Non-Saudi father and Saudi mother may be granted Saudi Citizenship by the decision of The Minister of Interior in case of the following conditions.

a—Having a permanent Resident Permit (*Iqama*) when he reaches the legal age;
b—Having good behavior, and never sentenced to criminal judgment or imprisonment for more than six months;
c—Being fluent in Arabic;
d—Applying for the citizenship after one year of reaching the legal age."

Once met, these conditions presumably allowed the option for children of Sa'udi women to become naturalized, which was deemed insufficient for gender equality and child rights. Moreover, the UN-UPR affirmed, Sa'udi women were denied the right to transfer their nationality to non-national spouses, a right reserved for Sa'udi males, according to Article 14 of the Citizenship act. In other words, Sa'udi Arabia's nationality law contained no safeguards against statelessness at birth, even if Article 7 of the 1989 Convention of the Rights of the Child (CRC) obligated states to ensure every child's right to a nationality, particularly if they would otherwise be stateless. The Kingdom of Sa'udi Arabia acceded to the CRC on 26 January 1996 with the *reservation* that the Government of Sa'udi Arabia rejected articles that were in conflict with the provisions of Shari'ah Law.

As Sa'udi Arabia was a party to other treaties that preserved the right to nationality without discrimination, including Article 7 of the CRC mentioned above that enshrined every child's right to be registered immediately after a birth and to acquire a nationality (and thereby avoid the many problems associated with statelessness), and the Convention on the Elimination of All Forms of Discrimination against Women (CEDAW), which stated in Article 9 that: (2) States Parties shall grant women equal rights with men with respect to the nationality of their children, critics lamented various reservations to such provisions even if the practice of placing specific reservations was widespread throughout the world by scores of states. Still, it was important not to push the concern under the proverbial rug, and address potential discriminatory features in various laws precisely to eliminate excessive burdens in the nationality law that removed existing hurdles with respect to statelessness. Riyadh was thus aware of this serious shortcoming in its gender policies, though it remained to be determined whether it was prepared to modify existing regulations, either on religious or humanitarian grounds. Given the many dramatic transformations introduced in 2018 on gender matters, the chances were excellent that Sa'udi authorities would buttress the courage to alter lingering social and cultural burdens that taxed the state and society at large and, not a negligible point, empowered numerous foes to unleash their venom against the conservative population.

Stateless Communities in Saʿudi Arabia

With respect to statelessness, in 2018, Saʿudi Arabia accepted a recommendation from Mexico, to "consider positively the ratification of the conventions on enforced disappearance, the migrant workers, refugees, statelessness and the reduction of cases of statelessness, and the Optional Protocol to CAT [Convention Against Torture]."[21] It was unclear when this recommendation entered into force especially since Riyadh had not ratified the International Covenant on Civil and Political Rights (ICCPR) or the International Covenant on Economic, Social and Cultural Rights (ICESCR) and, as discussed in this study, the 1954 and 1961 UN Statelessness Conventions as well as the 1951 Refugee Convention and its Protocol. Still, the fact that the government of Saʿudi Arabia accepted such a sensitive recommendation indicated that it was cognizant of its international obligations, notwithstanding critics who opined the opposite. As a founding member of the United Nations, the Kingdom was aware of its responsibilities and duties to the Charter of promoting "universal respect for, and observance of, human rights and fundamental freedoms for all without distinction as to race, sex, language, or religion."[22] In fact, Riyadh's commitments were long-standing, anchored in history, though few recalled how the Third Saʿudi Kingdom was reconstituted by 1932 and what kind of policies were adopted by King ʿAbdul ʿAziz bin ʿAbdul Rahman Al Saʿud, even if the record clarified existing preferences, then as now.

The very concept of protection for refugees was a Western import, which originated in 1921 with the appointment of the first High Commissioner for Refugees at the League of Nations. That effort was chiefly motivated by a desire to assist Armenian survivors of the twentieth century's first genocide perpetrated by the Ottoman Empire.[23] In most of the literature on the formation of the Third Saʿudi Monarchy, the terms refugee (*lajiʾ*), displaced (*nazih*), or expelled (*tarhil*) are sometimes used to refer to various tribes that straddled vastly un-demarcated areas of the Arabian Peninsula. In specific instances, the transformative experiences of forced or involuntary migrations could not be denied, even if most authors downplayed "the interconnected nature of political, economic and social factors in motivating people to move."[24] According to one scholar, "the concept of refugee status was brought to Iraq by the British and applied to tribes like the Shammar [in] Najd, based on British assumptions about their supposed political opposition to Ibn Saud and desire for religious freedom from Wahhabism."[25] Irrespective of such machinations, 'Abdul 'Aziz bin 'Abdul Rahman seldom neglected his established ties with several tribes that roamed throughout the area, even if British authorities advanced their interests within the League of Nations ostensibly to present a humane face for Britain as an empire that cared for people living under its mandate authority. What British authorities did in Mesopotamia and elsewhere throughout the Middle East was to meddle in tribal affairs, as they perceived raids by warriors against "refugees" as being *unacceptable*. Of course, 'Abdul 'Aziz identified this interference as entirely insupportable too, and he was not ready to kowtow. The very idea of tribal "refugees," which presupposed the existence of ethnic minorities amongst tribesmen, was an alien concept. What preoccupied the Najdi was the convenience of pastures and water on the one hand, and on the other hand the desire to raid and avoid punishment for raiding—two essential preoccupations in harsh desert conditions that all tribes engaged in to survive.[26] Ironically, and notwithstanding British pressure on the Sa'udi, 'Abdul 'Aziz understood the principle of *political refugee status*, since he himself provided refuge to Ahmad al-Sanussi, asking the British for clemency as the Libyan leader desired to return to his homeland. His successors offered political refugee status or asylum to several Arab and Muslim leaders over the years, including Idi Amin Dada (Uganda), Nawaz Sharif (Pakistan), Zine El Abidine bin Ali (Tunisia), and 'Abd Rabbuh Mansur Hadi (Yemen), both on humanitarian as well as religious grounds even if such justifications were incomprehensible to many who simply concluded that Riyadh favored tyrants and stood by failed leaders who shared interests with the Kingdom.[27]

For our purposes, what mattered was how Sa'udi leaders, especially the founder monarch, perceived various tribal disputes, not how to apply international humanitarian norms to actual displaced populations, which occurred more or less routinely for millennia. 'Abdul 'Aziz bin 'Abdul Rahman was preoccupied with governance over the tribes, and disputes over "refugee" status did not concern him. This is best illustrated with the case of the *bidun*, originally nomads who lived from subsistence and who drove their flocks through vast desert lands in search of pasture lands for a few months each year. Unattached tribesmen worked on date palm plantations or other agricultural farms, bartered in produce, and seldom obeyed rules other than those imposed by nature. 'Abdul 'Aziz understood them far better than British mandarins, a lesson that was passed on to his successors, all of whom considered a plethora of rules and regulations to deal with such cases. One of the best illustrations of the bidun phenomenon was the fate of the 'Anizah confederation members who did not want to choose any nationality, which was why they represented a disproportionate number of the stateless people that lived in the Iraq–Kuwait–Saudi tri-border region.[28]

In addition to the bidun, there were two other principal stateless communities in the Kingdom, which started as "refugee populations" (as identified by the British) before the latest vague of Syrians arrived after 2011: the Rohingya, and the Palestinians. They, as well as the bidun, deserved brief discussions at this stage to further clarify how Riyadh perceived their presence in the country.

The Bidun

Like their counterparts elsewhere throughout the Arabian Peninsula, the bidun were those stateless individuals who held on to their tribal traditions, and literally stayed out of the nascent nation-state systems that emerged around the turn of the twentieth century.[29] According to a semi-official source, Sa'udi Arabia hosted about 250,000, although the UNHCR statistics hover around 70,000 biduns in the Kingdom.[30] According to public sources and as stated above (but worth underscoring because this is such an important point), the bidun in Sa'udi Arabia consisted of descendants of nomadic tribes who *failed* to register for Sa'udi nationality during the first four decades of the twentieth century, as the nation state was being formed. This may have been the result of poor communication—they either did not know of the registration procedure or were deliberately left out of the procedures—or, more likely, few understood the importance of belonging to the nascent state as well as the value one acquired when one carried proper citizenship documents. As few trusted any authority other than their own immediate tribal chiefs, it was nearly impossible to persuade them from accepting the *nationality* that 'Abdul 'Aziz offered, provided they accepted his leadership. Inasmuch as British advisors manipulated tribal subjects to pressure 'Abdul 'Aziz, many bidun fell into sophisticated traps, unaware of their long-term interests that, in hindsight few foresaw and prepared for. As a result of these imprudent choices, the bidun became unlawful residents—and therefore no longer eligible for Sa'udi citizenship—though, in reality, less than 10,000 fit that category. The vast majority were regularized as Riyadh issued them identity documents (known as "black cards") starting in 2009. It is important to note that these credentials were intended as interim papers, akin to "five-year residency permits" in several countries, while candidates legalized their situations. Of course, critics derided these procedures, claiming that the qualification mechanisms to obtain black cards were unclear (which was not correct), their validity allegedly precarious (also untrue), and potential benefits highly doubtful (which was clearly not the case). Many Sa'udi bidun could favorably compare various advantages included in these new regulations with what their brethren received in Kuwait, for example, and knew the many benefits that a black card provided.[31] In reality, Riyadh engaged in a full-fledged program to grant the biduns living in the Kingdom full nationality though it introduced specific procedures to ensure that their rights in the country were fully protected without creating security risks. Towards that end, the Sa'udi Government clarified that the priority of the individual bidun file was to allow each person access to private and government hospitals for treatment, the acceptance of their children in public schools, to ensure free movement across the country, and to regularize the estimated ten thousand marriages that may have occurred without proper registration. According to Dr. Omar Al-Khuli, a legal adviser who specialized in immigration matters, the problem of the bidun was "an old problem that lingered for more than 60 years," which required modern attention. He described how many came from neighboring border countries, especially Kuwait, ditched whatever official documents were in their possessions, and requested new ones from local authorities ostensibly because they belonged to various tribes that lived along the frontier between the Kingdom and the Shaykhdom.[32]

In the event, and given how serious this lingering matter was, the Sa'udi Ministry of the Interior adopted new measures in 2018, and was in the process of issuing proper identification documents for most biduns, though the burden remained on individuals to produce at least one item that could verify claims and expedite existing procedures.[33] Compared to the avalanche of documents that several countries required, including extensive background investigation for security purposes, this request for a single item was neither excessive nor improper. Still, it was a harrowing experience, akin to similar procedures in most nation-states that granted citizenship, sometimes after decades passed, to verify refugee credentials, though mercifully the condition of the stateless bidun in Sa'udi Arabia was now a priority on its way towards resolution.

The Rohingya

Although the plight of the Rohingya, of whom a million lived in Myanmar (formerly Burma), caught international attention after Yangoon (formerly known as Rangoon) expelled an estimated 625,000 refugees from Rakhine Province in 2017 into neighboring Bangladesh, Sa'udi

Arabia hosted a fairly large population of the Rohingya who first arrived in the Kingdom in the early 1960s, mostly after the 1962 military coup d'état that toppled the Government of Prime Minister U Nu.[34] Several Rohingyas were elected to the Constituent Assembly of Burma before the 1947 independence, even if ugly nationalism that favored Hindus stripped most of the Rohingyas of their citizenships by 1982. Remarkably, Yangoon perceived the Rohingya—who were predominantly Muslim though several thousand practiced Hinduism—as a source of threat. The military Junta, long known for its sectarian practices, failed to protect the Rohingya and practiced open discrimination. Since the Rohingya were not considered to be citizens in Burma, this effectively meant that no religious freedoms were allowed, which added fire to the legal and political fuels. Over the years, many Rohingyas were arrested for teaching and practicing their religious beliefs, and military mistreatment of the entire population was rife.[35] Because Myanmar did not recognize the Rohingya as one of the eight national indigenous races that lived in the country, in 2013 the United Nations identified them as one of the most persecuted minorities in the world. Undeniably, and long before the massive 2017 expulsions, the Rohingya faced military crackdowns in 1978, 1991–1992, 2012, 2015 and, of course the ongoing calamities that began in 2016. With few remaining in Myanmar, the majority of the Rohingya were either in Bangladesh as refugees or resettled in countries that would welcome them.[36]

There were at least 500,000 Rohingyas in the Kingdom of Sa'udi Arabia in 2021.[37] Many have been there for decades and their status and protection has improved over the past few years, as Riyadh issued 190,000 permanent residency permits which allowed undeviating custodianship for four years, though all were automatically renewed when documents expired.[38] Aware of their plight, the authorities exempted applicants from fines that resulted from non-renewal of previous residency permits, even if no decisions were reached regarding potential naturalization. A difficult challenge by any stretch of the imagination, the predicament that confronted stateless Rohingya living in Sa'udi Arabia essentially required a royal decision to alter current conditions, which required the Kingdom to grant half-a-million non-Arabs citizenship. Short of such a solution, Riyadh was keenly interested in providing an adequate resolution, at least regarding their legal status, by transforming short-term residency permits into long-term ones. With over half of the Rohingya population in the Kingdom without a clear legal status, new mechanisms were contemplated to ensure full access to all rights and, in the case of Rohingya children born in Sa'udi Arabia, to grant them Sa'udi nationality in accordance with Article 7 of the 1989

Convention of the Rights of the Child that Riyadh acceded to in January 1996.[39] At the time, the authorities expressed their *reservation* that the rejected articles were in conflict with the provisions of Islamic Law, though naturalizing Muslim Rohingyas did not contravene Shari'ah. The sole remaining hurdle was the cultural integration process, which was not an easy task, though those who learned Arabic and assimilated in society stood an excellent chance of eventual citizenship.[40]

The Palestinians

Palestinians in Sa'udi Arabia numbered about 287,000 in 2021. Most lived in the country for decades with only the status of "residence," and were excluded from all naturalization procedures, chiefly for political reasons.[41] This was, of course, first and foremost what Palestinians themselves wanted as the overwhelming majority refused initial naturalization offers made by several Arab states because most believed that they would return to Palestine shortly after their first expulsions from Israel in 1948.[42] Over time, their stay and status in the Kingdom as elsewhere required that they receive adequate sponsorship (*kafalah*), which effectively translated into double jeopardy conditions. Stateless Palestinians lived in limbo, often under volatile conditions, though over time many received adequate public services. Sponsorship costs towards citizenship, including binding economic privileges that were granted to Palestinians was high, and while some risked deportation, especially for political reasons, Palestinian ingenuity meant that those who wished to succeed in Sa'udi Arabia received every opportunity to do so. Others told of hardships, of rejection and, understandably of fear of deportation.[43]

Still, Arab states in general, including Sa'udi Arabia, refused to facilitate the permanent settlement of Palestinians in their respective countries precisely because they wished to keep the fire of return lit. Towards that end, and while Riyadh disbursed generous donations to various United Nations, League of Arab States and the Organization of Islamic Cooperation agencies providing assistance to Palestinians, they nevertheless declined to change their laws to grant citizenship. This was one of the most politically charged issues that confronted Arab states in general, and Saudi Arabia in particular, because billions of dollars were allocated and disbursed to the Palestinians over the past eight decades with few positive results. How Riyadh envisaged to address the right of return preference with basic humanitarian demands hangs like Damocles' Sword over the heads of officials committed to helping resolve the Palestinian quest for statehood.

Migration Regulations

According to an observer of the Kingdom, "the Saudi regulatory framework of migration has been modified over the last decade through the enactment of a new Labor Law and the Anti-Trafficking in Persons Law," which clarified working conditions, though it also granted local sponsors (employers) "control over the migrant's ability to enter and exit the country and seek other employment."[44]

Several recent laws clarified obscure points without, however, resolving pending questions. For example, the 1992 *Basic Law of Governance* granted certain rights and protections to foreign residents of the Kingdom (including the right to file a lawsuit); while the *Saudi Labor Law* amended protections to all workers, foreign and national (excluding domestic workers), banned sponsors from withholding the passports of their employees without their written consent, and identified key professions reserved for Sa'udi nationals. Likewise, in 2009, Riyadh passed the *Anti-Trafficking in Persons Law* that provided specific protection to victims of human trafficking, even if the mechanisms in place were not ideal (since abusive employers resorted to deportation procedures).[45] These were all useful amendments to existing legal provisions that affected migrants, refugees, and other stateless individuals that lived in the Kingdom.

To be sure, the issue of statelessness was particularly vexing, as discussed above. Still, the enactment of various laws that addressed shortcomings was in and of itself a major step forward which recognized that grievances existed and highlighted what more ought to be done. Naturally, and in an ideal situation, specific amendments to the Citizenship Law could usher in a new era. This, however, was a work in progress even if *Vision 2030*, the major makeover plan that was introduced in 2016 to reduce Sa'udi Arabia's dependence on oil and diversify its economy, promised fresh changes too. Towards that end, one of the most discussed concerns was the right of Sa'udi women to transfer their nationalities to their children and spouses without restriction, and on an equal basis to men.

Equally important was the potential citizenship to the bidun in Sa'udi Arabia, including automatic citizenship to children born in the territory of the Kingdom. In fact, Riyadh contemplated appropriate regulations to safeguard against statelessness of any child who was born in Sa'udi Arabia, though this was a painful process that aimed to balance various interests. Similarly, the situations of the Rohingya and the Palestinians was critical too, as these stateless populations were likely to receive various services over the short-term and, in the case of Rohingya and

Palestinian children born in the country, the right to receive automatic Sa'udi nationality in compliance with international norms over the long-term. In the event, the government of Sa'udi Arabia was committed to end discrimination and to protect all children, which was a key step forward, though no final steps were taken by early 2021.

Conclusion: A Flexible and Dutiful Approach

As discussed throughout this chapter, the Kingdom has opened its doors to hundreds of thousands of refugees, though it seldom created camps to house them, save for the tragic case of Iraqis who were kept at Rafhah (see Chapter 3). The preference has always been to welcome political migrants on the basis of brotherly and ethical principles. Critics rejected this approach and repeatedly claimed that Riyadh was "not doing its part" in the global refugee crisis, which was problematic.

The Kingdom is not a party to the main global refugee protection instrument, namely the 1951 Refugee Convention, nor does it have any specific domestic legal framework pertaining to refugee issues. Moreover, and because of the very large expatriate population that call Sa'udi Arabia home [perhaps as many as 10 million for roughly 30 million nationals], granting citizenship poses inherent political problems that can only be handled with utmost care. Still, Riyadh welcomed 250,000 biduns, an estimated 500,000 Rohingyas, about 300,000 Palestinians and, as discussed in Chapter 8, nearly a million Syrians. Most of these migrants were regularized through the *kafalah* system of sponsorship, which meant that every individual required a patron or a financial guarantor that, more often than not, necessitated that the government take responsibility for them. In this sense, even de facto refugees, those who would technically meet the refugee definition set out in the 1951 Convention, were all in the country legally through a system of labor migration. In other words, the *kafalah* system required every foreign national in the country to have a sponsor, usually a Sa'udi citizen or a company, which defined responsibility. Since such individuals could not circulate without their sponsor's authorization, fresh problems were created that necessitated adjustments and that explains some of the legal hurdles that confront authorities. Riyadh regularized many by issuing residency and work permits, though those mechanisms did not qualify as refugee benefits in globally accepted norms. Nevertheless, the mere fact that the *kafalah* mechanism was used with respect to the Bidun, Palestinians, Eritreans, Yemenis and Rohingyas, meant that many able-bodied men and women from these communities found regular employment. In sum, the authorities displayed flexibility and, more important, allowed refugees to earn salaries and thus retain their familial dignity. As discussed above, Rohingyas have since 2005 been able to regularize their residency statuses and obtain work permits, as authorities encouraged companies to recruit them whenever possible. As explored below, this was also the case for Syrian refugees and, to a large degree, for Yemenis.

"Inherent in this approach to those seeking protection is a state of 'permanent temporariness'," as coined by Charlotte Lysa, who recognized that the Saʻudi system of temporarily regularizing the status of certain groups included certain virtues—like "access to economic participation, education and health care"—even if it did not "sufficiently secure international protection as understood by international refugee law."[46] This was certainly something that authorities were amply aware of and determined to address. Moreover, and while Riyadh preferred to reconcile its geo-economic interests with the needs of refugees by integrating as many as possible into their national agendas, Saʻudi Arabia could not do so without solving the legal status of refugees, even if it successfully funded the education, healthcare, employment, and social integration of hundreds of thousands of people. Remarkably, the Kingdom pursued its goals out of a sense of duty and accepted the notion that its efforts were a work in progress.

CHAPTER
3
Hijrah, *Zakat*, and Refugees
Religious Obligations

While global conflicts, including internecine local and regional civil wars, have played troublesome roles in the overall increase of refugees around the world, the phenomenon accelerated in the twentieth century—a bloody era by any stretch of the imagination.[1] As a result of these wars, many have sought out refuge in other states, as desperate migrants left their homelands for numerous reasons, from the search for liberty to economic welfare. Floods, desertification, famine, political persecution, racial discrimination, acute nationalist and religious beliefs, among other reasons, pushed many to seek alternative abodes. These refugees, whose lives and rights were, and often are, at risk in their countries of origin, sought asylum elsewhere, desperate to flee and survive. Naturally, the phenomenon was ancient as history itself, though fresh conflicts around the globe accelerated the pace of refugee "production" in troubled societies where political leaders endured hardships without an inkling as to how they could address core concerns that resulted in trouble for them as well as their subjects. The aftermaths of the two world wars witnessed waves of collective migration throughout Europe. In the Arab World, the recent catastrophic civil war in Syria, for example, has led millions to flee their land, with an estimated two million seeking asylum in Sa'udi Arabia and other neighboring Arab Gulf states. The Damascus regime endured but failed to come to terms with the post-2011 uprisings and, of course, hardly bothered with the fact that a third of Syrians became refugees dispersed among several countries, while another third were internally dispersed in 2020.

As reviewed in Chapter 2, Syrian refugees were not the first asylum seekers in Sa'udi Arabia, as other collective migrations occurred in the 1950s and 1960s from Burma where Muslim Rohingya were persecuted and driven out of their homes because of their religious beliefs. A number of them found refuge in the Kingdom and still more were keen to settle there. Likewise, Palestinians suffered collective migration and became refugees in the aftermath of several Arab–Israeli wars, starting in 1948. Egyptian Muslim Brotherhood members fled Egypt in the 1950s and 1960s to seek shelter in Sa'udi Arabia too. During the first decade of the twenty-first century, the world witnessed massive migrations from Iraq as a result of repeated wars in Mesopotamia, as some exiles sought and received refuge in Sa'udi Arabia as well.

The purpose of this chapter is to clarify existing norms dealing with *hijrah* (migration) within Muslim traditions that, to some extent will explain and clarify some of the reasons why the Kingdom did not sign the 1951 UN Convention for Refugees. This did not, and indeed does not, mean that Riyadh did not and does not comply with obligations toward refugees. Furthermore, not-signing the 1951 Convention did not mean that Sa'udi Arabia deviated from, or violated international humanitarian principles and ethics. On the contrary, a discussion of key features of the refugee Convention and Shari'ah Law, along with an evaluation of religious obligations, will shed light on various cases, which will further highlight how Muslim sacred norms reflected in the Qur'an and in the Sunnah [traditions and practices of the Prophet], motivated and drove Sa'udi policies that, truth be told, was how the Kingdom actually practiced its un-written refugee policies.

Hijrah *and Asylum*

As discussed in Chapter 1, United Nations deliberations in the late 1940s highlighted why delegates from several countries believed that a Eurocentric posture existed in 1951, when the Convention was adopted, and which alienated other cultures by assuming an unconditional, global adhesion to a secular, non-religious society without taking into consideration humanitarian interventions that other nation-states practiced or were compelled to adopt.[2] The case of Lebanon, for example, highlighted this issue pointedly as the Levantine state became burdened with a massive influx of Palestinian refugees after 1948. As discussed in the section on religious norms below, Beirut was compelled to live with waves of refugees for well over half a century, and refused to sign the 1951 UN Convention for legitimate reasons. Similarly, several Arab and Asian states rejected the Euro-centric preferences of the Convention not because they did not want to extend the welcome mat—most did—but because they either relied on alternative methods or wished to determine whether Convention regulations contradicted intrinsic preferences. In other words, the debate over, and the adoption of, the Convention created a collision course with several countries and, in the case Muslim societies, interfered with the quest for legitimacy, which was largely acquired for the latter through their adherences to Islamic laws and traditions.

Still, in the wake of the aggravation of refugee conditions in the Islamic world—chiefly due to wars and despotic regimes—the Organization of Islamic Cooperation (OIC) supported the signing of different treaties, all of which dealt with the problem of refugees in the Islamic world. The *Universal Islamic Declaration on Human Rights* (1981), the *African Charter on Human and Peoples' Rights* (1981), the *Cairo Declaration on Human Rights in Islam* (1990), and the *Arab Charter on Human Rights* (1994), constituted good examples of how the discussion about Human Rights was conducted and, of course, remained at the center of all Islamic legal discussions concerning refugees.[3] Undeniably, a coordinated action in Muslim countries was seriously affected by repeated refugee crises, which left most of the issues open for debates without permanent solutions. In hindsight, it may have been preferable to engage in a dialogue between the two sociological poles concerned with refugee issues—the secularized Western paradigm along the Muslim model—precisely to better understand human rights concerns, look after refugees by adapting to local conditions, and guarantee the security and stability of all affected countries. Finding a common ground for understandings and actions were, therefore, not only essential, but may well have become vital for the welfare of humanity.

In the context of such putative discussions, and as Mashood Baderin noted, "whatever definition or understanding we ascribe to human rights, the bottom line is the protection of human dignity. There is perhaps no civilization or philosophy in today's world that would not subscribe to that notion."[4] Indeed, human rights do not and cannot belong exclusively to a Western tradition, as references to similar concepts can be found in all religious traditions including Islam, Christianity, Confucianism and Buddhism. From a legal point of view its basic principles can be found in Hammurabi's code (1780 BCE) and in Greek and Roman laws with the concept of *jus gentium* (law for all people). This basic concept should constitute the common ground on which one may build the future dialogue between the West and the Islamic World, regarding the application of a universal idea of human rights. Therefore, it is impossible to start a dialogue over refugee conditions between secular Western powers and leading Muslim countries without first recognizing the philosophical concepts and moral principles present in the Islamic heritage and, simultaneously, refer to them in order to establish an Islamic protection framework. To better achieve this goal, it is important to identify the similarities and differences between *hijrah* and the modern laws on asylum and refugees.[5] Starting from Baderin's statement cited above, one is better served to acknowledge the existence of separate traditions which have and uphold at the center of their normative discourses the protection of human dignity. It is thus fair to note that retracing the history of human rights in leading Western societies illustrates how religion influenced this very concept.[6]

Moreover, it is imperative to recognize that in the three main monotheistic religions, Judaism, Christianity and Islam, the concept of asylum stood out as an important moral obligation. All three sacred texts share the fact that at some time in history believers were forced to leave their homelands, and to seek refuge in foreign spaces. Persecution and wars were the main reasons for the multiple forced displacements suffered by their founders and followers. In Judaism, for example, Jews were enslaved by Egyptians, while Jesus Christ was born under Roman occupation in Christianity, and in Islam, Muhammad himself had to seek refuge in the city of Madinah to escape his enemies. Introducing the concepts of *hijrah* and *muhajirun*, Khadija Elmadmad stated that

> "In Islam, asylum is a right, a duty, and a general and comprehensive form of protection. It is religious but it is also territorial and to some extent diplomatic. No modern international instrument stipulates clearly that individuals have the right to grant or to be granted asylum. All modern texts reserve this right for the State which is free to grant or refuse asylum to those who seek it."[7]

This specific definition constituted a major difference between the two approaches, and as discussed by the prominent Moroccan scholar, left gaps of understanding that were difficult to fill on both sides. According to customary international law, refugees had "the right to seek and enjoy in other countries asylum from prosecution." However, it was not guaranteed that such a state would grant them asylum because of the restrictions of the term "refugee," which was open to various interpretations. Consequently, one was required to acknowledge an increase in the arbitrary approaches each state imposed over the years in how it defined the term, when dealing with refugees. For example, Internally Displaced Persons (IDPs) were not included in the international protection frame that most nation-states relied upon, because there were no mandatory international guidelines related specifically to them. In 1998 specific guiding principles on IDPs were released by the United Nations High Commissioner for Refugees, although states were not obligated to follow them.[8]

Again, according to Khadija Elmadmad, the wording of the Convention left a large gap for states to interpret the new guidelines, especially when it underscored that refugees' right to seek asylum "may not be invoked in the case of prosecutions genuinely arising from non-political crimes or from acts contrary to the purposes and principles of the United Nations."[9] Seyla Benhabib advanced similar arguments when she contrasted various interpretations that broadened "the 1951 Convention to the point of indeterminacy, making it impossible for states not to judge and meddle in one another's domestic affairs via an assessment of their respective human rights' violations."[10] She quoted James C. Hathaway and Michelle Foster for conceding that "not all codified human rights are created equal: some rights have long pedigrees, others are of more recent vintage; some rights are nearly universally agreed, others enjoy only minimal support . . . ",[11] and recommended that one option would be to "focus on the most 'basic international human rights standards' which [Hathaway and M. Foster found] embodied not only in the International Covenant on Civil and Political Rights (ICCPR) and the International Covenant on Economic, Social and Cultural Rights (ICESC) but in the Convention of the Elimination of Racial Discrimination (CERD); in the Convention on the Elimination of all Forms of Discrimination Against Women (CEDAW); the Convention on the Rights of the Child (CRC); and the Convention on the Rights of Persons with Disabilities (CRPD), among others."[12] In fact, and from a mere legal point of view, a conclusive classification of "political crime" did not exist, leaving the definition of "refugee" blurred with the consequences that arose during the refugee crisis triggered by the war in Syria. According to the Refugee Convention, a person "does not become a refugee because of recognition, but is recognized because he is a refugee,"[13] a point that is worth repeating. In many cases, this distinction created a void in which most refugees were trapped, since it was now amply clear that refugees and IDPs alike posed huge challenges to international norms, as governments struggled to keep the pace with the changing nature of the problem of refugees around the world. The insistence on the "authority of the State" to deal with any refugee crisis revealed that this was not only an inefficient procedure from the legal point of view, but also in the delivery of humanitarian assistance, as discussed below.

In contrast to this specific dilemma, on the other hand, the *hijrah* tradition was an integral part of Arab and Muslim practices, nestled at the core of the history of the Prophet Muhammad when he sought refuge in Madinah. The application of Shari'ah law in dealing with asylum seekers was thus a natural process in Muslim countries, because it fulfilled the application of a continuous traditional concept of hospitality preached and practiced in the Islamic culture. In support of this perspective, the final statement issued by Arab Parliamentarians on the occasion of the Symposium and Seminar on International and Regional Refugee Laws held in 2008 defied the uniqueness of the 1951 UN Convention by stating that "the rich tradition, customs and reactions involved in Arab and Islamic values served as a firm underpinning for the integrated protection of refugees and respect for their human integrity."[14]

Refugee Convention and Shari'ah Law

To better answer some of the dilemmas that emerged between these two major interpretations, a comprehensive comparison connecting customary international law and the Shari'ah was carried out by Ahmed Abou-El-Wafa in his 2009 study *The Right to Asylum between Islamic Shari'ah and International Refugee Law*. It is out of the scope of this study to analyze all of the results of this effort, though one of the major conclusions in this seminal study is worthy of attention as it provides an alternative definition of refugee to the one offered by customary international law. As stated above, the prevalence of the "state" over the individual favored by international law left many gaps in the concept and in its application on the ground. This, together with a secular approach to the problem, which in some cases neglected the religious tradition of refugees and of the countries hosting them, caused mistrust and became a barrier to any meaningful dialogue.

Since one of the main differences between the two approaches was the identity of the responsible party that classified actual status—the state under international law whereas every refugee was entitled to protection no matter of origin, race, or religion under Shari'ah—it was necessary to revisit the burdens of responsibility if long-lasting solutions were to be advanced. There is an obligation to provide protection and assistance to persons in need under Islamic Law, and there are many examples of this in the Qur'an related to relations with the People of the Book, Jews and Christians, when the Holy Scriptures refer to the earliest Muslim communities.[15] These references were presumably not only meant to keep unity among competing tribes around Makkah and Madinah during the first few years after revelation, but also to emphasize that Islam was confronted by various human challenges. Religious and secular authorities alike grappled with these contests, which forced everyone to remember how fragile human conditions were in a society in which wars and displacements were the norm and where few, if any, structured organization could provide security and stability. This need for protection thus extended from the circle of a believer's tribe to others, with dramatic repercussions that drew of the teachings and experiences of the Prophet, which was why Muslims developed entirely fresh perspectives on refugees. There are several references in the Qur'an to the People of the Book as "the persecuted people,[16] . . . the oppressed in the land,[17] [and] those who have been unjustly driven from their homes,[18] [along with] those that fled their homes or were expelled from them, and those that suffered persecution."[19] In addressing these conditions, Shari'ah attended to specific needs, which included positive as well as negative consequences, precisely to remain true to the scriptures and, in doing so, set a clear course on the behavior of men towards each other. In fact, punishment was foreseen for those who inflicted sufferings on others, with specific penalties meted out not only to impose justice but also, and more importantly, to remain true to the faith. The Qur'an states that " . . . [t]hose who persecute believers, men and women, and never repent shall be rewarded with the scourge of Hell, the scourge of Conflagration."[20] At the same time Islamic Law is quite positive as in the verses that recommend Muslims to " . . . give aid and comfort to each other. If you fail to do [so], there will be disorder in the land and great corruption," the scriptures elucidate.[21] Moreover, and because of the first example of *hijrah*, which occurred in 615 AD when the Prophet Muhammad ordered a group of Muslims to resettle in the Christian Kingdom of Abyssinia in order to escape the persecution they suffered by the Quraysh tribe, the very concept of refuge was enunciated clearly. From these events, the notion of asylum earned a well-defined understanding as it became an obligation, as well as a right that could be withdrawn if the assumptions embedded in the arrangement failed. In other words, if the "host" fails to comply with the obligations imposed on them by the customs of hospitality, their right can be taken away from them. At the same time, the failure of the refugees to follow those rules can also be punished, something that remains difficult to apply to these uprooted and already enduring hardships.[22]

All this revealed the character of reciprocity in Islamic Law regarding the rights and duties of both sides, refugees and host countries alike. Nevertheless, this approach, as well as the one proposed through customary international law that is now applicable throughout most of the world, leaves serious gaps. The major concern is that it does not oblige states to provide automatic asylum for those who request it. As Kirsten Zaat elucidated, "[n]o such reference obliging humanity to provide asylum to forced migrants exists in *The Universal Islamic Declaration of Human Rights (1981)*, which means that while the right to seek asylum is manifest, there is no international agreement amongst Muslim States that the Shariah legally obliges them to accept asylum seekers," which is a genuine disparity.[23] Notwithstanding this observation, the Qur'an clearly states that Muslim communities are obliged to admit into the territories where a refugee has requested asylum, in unambiguous terms: "The men who stayed in their own city (Madinah) and embraced Islam before them loved those who have sought refuge with them. They do not covet what they are given but rather prefer [their brothers and sisters] above themselves although they are in need. Those who preserve themselves from their own greed shall surely prosper."[24]

Based on the previous examples, and despite the clearly articulated privileges that non-Muslims are protected under Shari'ah Law, some observers assert that there is a large difference between the same idea of rights as expressed in the Western perspective and those affirmed in Muslim societies. While Westerners believe in the universality of human rights, the religious character of Shari'ah Law forcibly entails the exclusion of non-Muslims as best described by a leading analyst. According to Musab Hayatli, editor of the Arabic edition of *Forced Migration Review* published by the Refugee Studies Centre at the University of Oxford:

> "Perhaps the most fundamental difference between an Islamic and an internationalist point of view of human rights lies in the concept of rights itself. While the [Universal Declaration of Human Rights] stresses the universality of human rights, Islam recognizes two types of rights: rights that humans are obliged—by virtue of being the creations of God—to fulfil and obey; and rights that they are entitled to expect from their fellow human beings. It is the latter that correspond to what are elsewhere termed 'human rights.' The former are rights that stem from, and are obtained through, belief in God and religion. In this concept only God truly has rights and the rights of humans are understood as their obligation to abide by God's commands. They are, first and foremost, the rights of individuals to abide by and adhere to the laws that God decreed and are only possible through this belief system, thus excluding non-Muslims."[25]

How can one understand the religious character of Shari'ah in this particular remit, precisely to establish a constructive dialogue between parties that seem to harbor irreconcilable positions? To be sure, how religious identities, beliefs and practices are understood "may provide the underpinnings for humanitarian *responses* to forced migration," which would certainly help clarify some of the obscure points in this debate.[26] Increasingly, analysts seem to agree on "a variety of definitions and typologies . . . vis-à-vis the two key terms . . . 'faith communities' and 'faith-based organizations', as the first term . . . broadly refers to 'formally-recognized groups or bodies which profess a belief in a superhuman reality and/or god(s) and which worship this reality and/or god(s)'," while the "term 'community of believers' may also be appropriate in this regard" too.[27] Gradually, and without fail, intercultural and interfaith discussions among people of goodwill everywhere will form the bases for further dialogue opportunities though the process was likely to take a while for political and socio-cultural reasons.[28]

Before concluding this section of the Convention and Shari'ah, two additional aspects must be analyzed, namely existing contradictions and the economic consequences that refugees generate through no fault of their own. Contradictions between Islamic Law and the lack of actual commitment by several Muslim countries regarding the problems of refugees is a proof that Shari'ah is not applied in most cases. In fact, and in addition to the limits explained above, there is another fundamental difference that can constitute an obstacle to a complete understanding of Shari'ah Law in secularized Western societies. Despite provisions for the equal protection of men, women and children in cases of refugees, it is also true that the principle of equality between genders is denied in Islamic Law. For example, according to the Shari'ah, a woman has to be provided for, and this can create problems when the right to compensation has to be applied in case she is the only head of the household. In some Muslim countries women do not have the right to own or to inherit property, they cannot travel alone, and they always have to be accompanied by a male member of the family. While norms constantly evolve, such extreme cases cannot be ignored, which further illustrates how difficult it may be to reach a global consensus on these vital concerns that, truth be told, affect Muslim societies to a far larger proportion than otherwise assumed.

Beyond differences and similarities between international law and the Shari'ah when dealing with refugees, what stands out in any analysis are the limits that exist in the application of both laws. For if international law relies on the state for the recognition of the status of refugee, Shari'ah law does not imply an obligation on the Muslim state to recognize this same status. This leaves potential refugees in a state of limbo, which places them in very difficult conditions. The fact that in both cases there are no coordinated policies to tackle the problems of refugees constitutes a major obstacle to their applications, a challenge that needs to be addressed by global authorities operating within major international organizations. Regrettably, neither approach has provided a credible and efficient answer to the challenges posed in the last twenty years, as various refugee crises affected leading European, Asian, and Muslim countries, at best with very mixed results. How officials responsible for refugee issues tackle these contradictions will shed light on potential solutions though this too might not be as easily settled as many assume because of sociological constraints. Secularized societies and religiously driven peoples will need to agree not just on definitions but also on the best approaches to meet the humanitarian needs of refugees spread across the globe. This does not mean that preferences articulated by secularized societies are wrong or that those enunciated by Muslim societies are better but that worthier options are necessary. Indeed, leading Muslim countries confronted serious challenges, which raised the ante significantly.[29]

In the last decade alone, two major crises have tested the very concepts of hospitality present in Shari'ah law: the war in Syria and the intervention of Da'ish [Al-Dawlah al-Islamiyyah fil- Iraq wal Sham], the so-called Islamic State in Iraq and Syria (ISIS), which is neither Islamic nor a state. These two calamities have triggered one of the largest exodus from a Muslim country to another in the case of the Syrian war, and a sharp increase in the number of refugees and IDPs in the case of Iraq. The way different countries have dealt with these situations were dissimilar and depended heavily on the social and political realities of each one of them. For example, the intervention of Da'ish in Iraq and the forced displacement of ethnic and religious minorities from their traditional homes recorded a rise in the self-awareness of civil and political rights of the different components involved in that hapless country's unending conflicts. With the intervention Da'ish, refugee camps were built around the most important cities, in particular Dohuk, Erbil and Sulaymaniyyah, as the relatively secular nature of the Kurdish Regional Government, together with the comparative independence from the central government enjoyed by the Kurdish Regional Government (KRG), favored the birth and intervention of local and international NGOs that provided humanitarian support to IDPs as well as refugees. Still, never-ending confrontations between the KRG and the central government in Baghdad—for the control of sensitive areas such as the Ninewa Plain, for example—together with the unstable security situation in these areas prevented IDPs from returning to their homes and to claim any compensation for the immense losses suffered under the extremist Caliphate that pretended to incarnate the Islamic State, though it was neither. From a mere legal point of view, IDPs and refugees in hastily erected camps had the rights to leave the premises, to carry a duly issued identification document and to work. Regrettably, such conditions were not always available in Iraq and, even more problematic, there were non-existent in Syria, where it was not uncommon to find Syrian refugees working in different capacities to earn a living and support their neglected families caught between the hammers of extremists and the anvils of illegitimate states.[30]

The second major area of concern are the economic consequences that refugees generate and that preoccupy officials in every host nation. In the last few years, for example, the economy of the Kurdistan Region in Iraq (KRI) has suffered because of the war with ISIS and the deteriorating relationship with the Iraqi government that, for better or worse, was itself held hostage to regional powers anxious to advance their own interests that seldom coincided with those of the Iraqi population at large. Most public employees have seen their salaries dramatically reduced and the private sector struggled to fulfill the demand for employment.[31] The situation deteriorated further after the 25 September 2017 referendum for independence, as a renewed military confrontation occurred between the KRI and the central government for the control of disputed areas in Kirkuk and in the Ninewa plain, which further worsened an already precarious situation with the arrival of a new wave of IDPs.[32] When the central government banned international flights to the region—a decision that smacked of vengeance and a desire to wrestle power away from the autonomous region—economic conditions were damaged even more.[33]

The ongoing economic crisis in Iraq had an official starting date, June 2014, and the advent of ISIS. This war has had strong economic and social consequences for a region with already weak state institutions and which witnessed an influx in the number of refugees after 2014 from Syria too, which dramatically altered the demography of the region and, in particular, of the main cities of Erbil, Dohuk and Sulaymaniyyah. Although the influx of Syrian refugees started in early 2012, the number of Iraqi IDPs increased sharply after 2014, which created unbearable situations that quickly turned into full-blown humanitarian crises. At the beginning of 2015, there were 257,000 Syrian refugees and 1,003,300 Iraqi IDPs in the KRI region alone, at a time when the so-called Islamic State was still engaged in fierce battles that were largely conducted by Kurdish Peshmergas. According to the KRG Ministry of Planning, the growing number of IDPs complicated matters—as the total number of refugees and IDPs added up to 1.5 million in the KRI region in early 2015. Remarkably, this figure represented a 28 percent increase in the KRI's population, and of the total IDPs and refugees, 60 percent were in Dohuk. The large number of Iraqi IDPs and Syrian refugees resided in many of the same host communities, placing strains on the local economy and access to public services.[34] Between 2006 and 2008, the number of Iraqi IDPs reached the figure of 1.6 million, a figure that remained stable until 2020 despite the demise of ISIS.[35]

This situation prompted the need for short- to medium-term responses in order to guarantee the safety and security of refugees and IDPs as well as provide them with a decent life in the camps.[36] Indeed, what may well be required is a close collaboration between NGOs and business sectors to benefit from IDPs' innate skills that will help improve living conditions and eliminate some of the area's dire economic ailments. The construction sector, for example, represented a strong potential for all of the involved communities since they stood to potentially provide solid opportunities to otherwise idle refugees and IDPs. Two construction company representatives interviewed were able to successfully expand their businesses either by selling electrical goods and related maintenance equipment while undertaking re-construction projects in the villages affected by the war, or by expanding into retail opportunities that exploited their geographical position that also supported the birth of new small businesses run by IDPs and refugees.[37] As illustrated by the case of the KRG, a less strict legislation has the effect of favoring a quicker integration of IDPs and refugees into the hosting society, something which business representatives interviewed were also asking the government to facilitate existing procedures to hire Syrian refugees since their skills and education levels constituted important assets.

Alternatives to the 1951 Convention and 1967 Protocol

Notwithstanding specific changes introduced in Syria and Iraq, refugee conditions did not improve in these two countries overall because UNHCR donors—whose significant assistance was sorely needed and much appreciated—adopted different norms from those espoused by regional supporters or host nations. The former preferred secular criteria whereas the latter opted for religious obligations that, at times, skirted immediate needs over long-term settlements. Although both groups meant well and worked hard to assist refugees, fundamental variances lingered, which raised basic questions as to what were some of the alternatives that Arab and Muslim societies could or would implement to meet their sacred obligations? Were the Universal, African, Cairo and Arab protocols mentioned earlier useful alternatives to the 1951 UN Convention and the 1967 Protocol?

As discussed in Chapter 1, it is critical to reassess the limits of the 1967 Protocol with respect to various efforts to internationalize its provisions, and evaluate its impact on Muslim states. Delegates from several Muslim majority states voiced their reservations during the drafting of the 1967

Protocol, which did not always protect and promote declared as well as perceived objectives. Incredibly, the Protocol did not actually include any of the concerns expressed by Muslim majority states. As several Muslim countries were among the countries with the highest presence of refugees in the world, it is important to ask why the international community failed to recognize and evaluate the interventions of Muslim delegates in dealing with refugee matters? An examination of the history of asylum in Muslim societies will best answer these basic questions.

According to statistics published in 2020, out of fifty-seven members of the Member States of the Organization of Islamic Cooperation (OIC), only thirty-five have signed both the 1951 Refugee Convention, as well as the 1967 Optional Protocol (Table 3.1).

This uneasiness to adopt the international law may be due to the lack of inclusion of Muslim countries in the drafting of the Protocol, which resulted in the exclusion of the Islamic world from the wider international community. This was the consequence of the failure of leading Western powers "to enlist the involvement of local peoples and governments as well as to establish resonance with the rich resources of non-Judeo-Christian religious traditions."[38] Political reasons were and probably still are at the core of decisions reached by different Muslim countries not to sign the Convention. In fact, the failure of the international community to help solve the Palestine Question, thus allowing scores of legitimate refugees to return to their lands, has further jeopardized the real and necessary dialogue between leading Western powers and their vital Muslim counterparts.[39] Among the reservations expressed by those present for the deliberations were several valuable concerns. Egypt, for example, recorded reservations in respect of article 12 (1), articles 20 and 22 (1), and articles 23 and 24. It formulated a reservation to article 12 (1) because Cairo believed that it was in contradiction with the internal laws of Egypt, since this article provided that the personal status of a refugee shall be governed by the law of the country of his domicile or, failing this, of his residence. The Egyptian delegate underlined that this formula contradicted article 25 of the Egyptian civil code, which avowed that

> "The judge declares the applicable law in the case of persons without nationality or with more than one nationality at the same time. In the case of persons where there is proof, in accordance with Egypt, of Egyptian nationality, and at the same time in accordance with one or more foreign countries, of nationality of that country, the Egyptian law must be applied."

Table 3.1
Organization of Islamic Cooperation Refugee Convention Signatories

Name of Country	OIC Member Since	1951 Convention Signed	1967 Protocol Signed
AFGHANISTAN	1969	2005	2005
ALBANIA	1992	1992	1992
ALGERIA	1969	1963	1967
AZERBAIJAN	1992	1993	1993
BAHRAIN	1972	–	–
BANGLADESH	1974	–	–
BENIN	1983	1962	1970
BRUNEI-DARUSSALAM	1984	–	–
BURKINA-FASO	1974	1980	1980
CAMEROON	1974	1961	1967
CHAD	1969	1981	1981
COMOROS	1976	–	–
CÔTE D'IVOIRE	2001	1961	1970
DJIBOUTI	1978	1977	1977
EGYPT	1969	1981	1981
GABON	1974	1964	1973
GAMBIA	1974	1966	1967
GUINEA	1969	1965	1968
GUINEA-BISSAU	1974	1976	1976
GUYANA	1998	–	–
INDONESIA	1969	–	–
IRAN	1969	1976	1976
IRAQ	1975	–	–
JORDAN	1969	–	–
KAZAKHSTAN	1995	1999	1999
KUWAIT	1969	–	–
KYRGYZSTAN	1992	1996	1996
LEBANON	1969	–	–
LIBYA	1969	–	–
MALAYSIA	1969	–	–
MALDIVES	1976	–	–
MALI	1969	1973	1973
MAURITANIA	1969	1987	1987
MOROCCO	1969	1956	1971
MOZAMBIQUE	1994	1983	1989
NIGER	1969	1961	1970
NIGERIA	1986	1967	1968
OMAN	1972	–	–
PAKISTAN	1969	–	–
PALESTINE	1969	–	–
QATAR	1972	–	–
SAUDI ARABIA	1969	–	–

Table 3.1 (*continued*)
Organization of Islamic Cooperation Refugee Convention Signatories

Name of Country	OIC Member Since	1951 Convention Signed	1967 Protocol Signed
SENEGAL	1969	1963	1967
SIERRA LEONE	1972	1981	1981
SOMALIA	1969	1978	1978
SUDAN	1969	1974	1974
SURINAME	1996	1978	1978
SYRIAN ARAB REPUBLIC	1972	–	–
TAJIKISTAN	1992	1993	1993
TUNISIA	1969	1957	1968
TURKEY	1969	1962	1968
TURKMENISTAN	1992	1998	1998
TOGO	1997	–	–
UGANDA	1974	1976	1976
UNITED ARAB EMIRATES	1972	–	–
UZBEKISTAN	1996	–	–
YEMEN	1969	1980	1980

Source: UNHCR, States Parties to the 1951 Convention relating to the Status of Refugees and the 1967 Protocol, Geneva: United Nations High Commissioner for Refugees, 2021, at https://www.unhcr.org/en-au/3b73b0d63.pdf

It added that the competent Egyptian authorities were not in a position to amend this article (25) of the civil code, which required separate legislation. Moreover, Egypt expressed reservations about the 1951 Convention's articles 20, 22 (paragraph 1), 23 and 24, "because these articles consider[ed] the refugee as equal to the national" that, the official delegate believed affected "the discretionary authority of Egypt in granting privileges to refugees on a case-by-case basis."[40]

Two other countries tabled reservations that clarified additional points. Iran concluded that in all cases where refugees enjoyed the most favorable treatment accorded to nationals of a foreign state, Tehran retained its sovereign "right not to accord refugees the most favorable treatment accorded to nationals of States with which Iran has concluded regional establishment, customs, economic or political agreements." This was a widely held principle shared by many countries. Moreover, Iran considered the stipulations contained in articles 17, 23, 24 and 26 as being recommendations and not obligations.[41] Turkey, for its part, considered that the term "events occurring before 1 January 1951" were unacceptable since this presumably referred to the Turkish minority in Bulgaria that was still continuing to suffer when the Convention was signed. Ankara wanted the provision of the Convention to also "apply to the Bulgarian refugees of Turkish extraction compelled to leave that country as a result of this pressure and who, being unable to enter Turkey, might seek refuge on the territory of another contracting party after 1 January 1951." Interestingly, the Turkish Government entered additional reservations under article 42 of the Convention as no provision of the Convention, it was persuaded, could be interpreted as granting refugees greater rights than those accorded to Turkish citizens. It added:

> "The Government of the Republic of Turkey is not a party to the Arrangements of 12 May 1926 and of 30 June 1928 mentioned in article 1, paragraph A, of this Convention. Furthermore, the 150 persons affected by the Arrangement of 30 June 1928 having been amnestied under Act No. 3527, the provisions laid down in this Arrangement are no longer valid in the case of Turkey. Consequently, the Government of the Republic of Turkey considers the Convention of 28 July 1951 independently of the aforementioned Arrangements . . . [Furthermore,] the Government of the Republic understands that the action of 're-availment' or 'reacquisition' as referred to in article 1, paragraph C, of the Convention–that is to say: 'If (1) He has voluntarily re-availed himself of the protection of the country of his nationality; or (2) Having lost his nationality, he has voluntarily reacquired it'–does not depend only on the request of the person concerned but also on the consent of the State in question."[42]

Besides the thorny sovereignty issue that each nation-state exercised, which was the primary reason why the United States had not joined the 1951 UN Convention as of early 2021 [Washington was only a party to the 1967 Protocol], the gap over this specific provision lingered all these years with little prospects for dramatic changes in the near- to medium-range future. While Egypt, Iran, and Turkey eventually acceded to the Convention, others baulked. That was the case of Lebanon, for instance, which in 2021 was universally recognized by the international community for its generosity towards refugees [notwithstanding Beirut's abysmal management of this humanitarian disaster] for hosting the highest number of refugees in the world in proportion to its indigenous population size. Beirut steadfastly rejected ratification of the major refugee law instruments, and insisted that it was not a country of asylum since that would literally upset its complicated demographic make-up that supported its consociational mechanism that required the President of the Republic to be a Maronite (Catholic) Christian, the Speaker of Parliament a Shi'ah Muslim, the Prime Minister a Sunni Muslim and the Deputy Prime Minister a Greek Orthodox.[43] While Beirut acknowledged inherent values in the Convention in general, it accurately argued that there were genuine uncertainties regarding the accord. It worried about state obligations, led by the potential to permanently settle Palestinian refugees on its small territory, whereas the real responsibility, all of its leaders—both Christian as well as Muslim—believed, ought to fall on the shoulders of the UNHCR. Still, and over the years, Lebanon has upheld the notion that "good-neighborliness" amongst Arab states prevented it from even using the term "refugee" [*laji'in* plural of *laji'*], which regional norms rejected. Beirut thus informally upheld the provisions of the Convention and Protocol on a voluntary basis, though it lamented the international community's stale support destined to provide minimum assistance to refugee in various camps.[44] It is important to note that Lebanon cared deeply for human rights for all, including refugees, but simply could not accept conditions that threatened its fragile political set-up based on skewed sectarian/demographic balances. It is worth recalling that Charles Malik, the country's Representative to the United Nations, chaired the UN Commission on Human Rights for two consecutive terms (1951–1952) and co-authored with Eleanor Roosevelt the 1948 Universal Declaration of Human Rights, which confirmed the country's commitments as well as contributions to the development of balanced, fair and effective international systems that protected refugees too. Over the years, Lebanese officials painstakingly explained why the country could simply not ratify the Convention and the Protocol, though few understood or respected the advanced rationales.

Religious Norms and Obligations

Notwithstanding these reservations, and because Muslim societies were largely driven by religious obligations that defined who Arabs and Muslims were as human beings, an examination of these values was necessary. Of course, and because of the post-Renaissance separation between "Church and State," along with the adoption of universal secular practices in much of the West (including in Communist states), any discussion or even mention of religious norms were automatically dismissed as being undesirable or even unrealistic approaches to dealing with refugee matters even if such objections were themselves increasingly untenable. The dichotomy between secular and religious norms was unfortunate since much could be gained from the application of value-based regulations that, in turn, would compel hesitant or challenged governments to fulfill their humanitarian obligations in toto under alternative legal frameworks. In fact, a focus on sacred duties, which was no longer an exclusively Muslim-centric preference as a global awakening was underway, promised to be far more effective, desirable, and practical to better meet refugee needs. What were the religious obligations that Muslims espoused and could these be incorporated in advantageous legal paradigms?

As mentioned above but worth repeating to underscore the point, Scriptures [Holy Qur'an] and history books narrate many migrations by believers and prophets, due to their persecution. Muslims, for example, had to migrate from Makkah to Abyssinia following the Prophet Muhammad's instructions, where they enjoyed the protection of a Christian king. The Prophet himself was a refugee, as he and his followers migrated from Makkah in 622 AD to escape persecution, and received sanctuary from non-Muslim communities in the city of Madinah who, for the most part, welcomed the messenger and converted to the faith. Indeed, and as Islam demands that believers help and protect the vulnerable, the Qur'an provides a number of mechanisms to offer the necessary care and support of such individuals, which need to be underscored while drafting fresh regulations dealing with refugee matters.[45] Cynicism aside, Muslims take their religious obligations seriously, which is often derided by secularized analysts who doubt such devotion.[46] Without denying their rights to question the religious motivations that Muslims in general, and Sa'udi Muslims in particular display, one may still wonder why such obtuse perspectives continued to gain traction. One may disagree but one must also be open-minded about what others believe in and practice for productive dialogue among civilizations. Because Shari'ah Law does not provide a comprehensive legal regime for the protection of refugees and internally displaced persons, and because Islamic Law does not provide such protection in line with the current concept of protection, there are no clear-cut commitments by Muslim states, at least in the Shari'ah, to provide asylum. Muslim scholars in general argue that the pursuit of fulfilling the needs of believers and providing assistance with difficulties they may be facing, are ethical issues. Such aid strengthens the virtues of Islam urged by the Shari'ah, and constitutes a step toward righteousness and the piety of Muslims as ordered in the Qur'an. The Almighty said:

مَّن يَشْفَعْ شَفَاعَةً حَسَنَةً يَكُن لَّهُ نَصِيبٌ مِّنْهَا ۖ وَمَن يَشْفَعْ شَفَاعَةً سَيِّئَةً يَكُن لَّهُ كِفْلٌ مِّنْهَا ۗ وَكَانَ اللَّهُ عَلَىٰ كُلِّ شَيْءٍ مُّقِيتًا ۝

(Whoever intercedes for a good cause will have a reward therefrom; and whoever intercedes for an evil cause will have a burden therefrom. And ever is Allah, over all things, a Keeper) [4:85]

Contrary to what Western analysts believe, these principles apply to both Muslims and non-Muslims as they are written in the holy scriptures:

$$\text{وَإِنْ أَحَدٌ مِّنَ الْمُشْرِكِينَ اسْتَجَارَكَ فَأَجِرْهُ حَتَّىٰ يَسْمَعَ كَلَامَ اللَّهِ ثُمَّ أَبْلِغْهُ مَأْمَنَهُ ۚ ذَٰلِكَ بِأَنَّهُمْ قَوْمٌ لَّا يَعْلَمُونَ ۝}$$

(And if any one of the polytheists seeks your protection, then grant him protection so that he may hear the words of Allah. Then deliver him to his place of safety. That is because they are a people who do not know) [9:6]

The quotes from the Qur'an show that Islamic culture is actually in tune with the Charter on the Status of Refugees, which states, inter alia, that it is prohibited for a state to expel or return a person to a place where he or she may be prosecuted. Therefore, and because Sa'udi society firmly upholds Shari'ah Law, it may be possible to state that while Sa'udi Arabia did not become a signatory to the 1951 UN Convention and 1967 Protocol relating to the Status of Refugees, it consistently, and throughout its contemporary history ever since the unification of the country in 1932, behaved according to the spirit of the refuge convention.[47] The following cases illustrate how the Kingdom has applied an unwritten refuge policy.

The case of Rashid 'Ali al-Kilani

The case of Rashid 'Ali al-Kilani during the reign of King 'Abdul 'Aziz is interesting because it took place before the ratification of the 1951 Refugee convention when parts of the Arabian Peninsula and most of the Middle East were still under the control of European powers, in particular the United Kingdom and France.[48] This case was not unique since at that time many Arab men were exiled from their native countries by occupying powers and found refuge in the Kingdom. Yet, the fact that an individual like al-Kilani, who boasted an impeccably checkered background, spoke volumes about the attitude of the founder of the Third Sa'udi Monarchy.

Starting in the 1920s, Rashid al-Kilani had served in a number of official roles, including Minister of Justice, head of the Royal Court, President of the Council of Deputies and as Prime Minister of Iraq on four separate occasions, all before 1941, leading a revolution that aimed to end the British mandate in that country. At loggerheads with Nuri al-Sa'id, then a leading Iraqi politician, al-Kilani accepted the final status agreement on tribal matters negotiated with Saʻudi Arabia, and pledged to uphold its provisions as well as fulfill ʻAbdul ʻAziz bin ʻAbdul Rahman's extradition requests.[49] At the height of World War II, al-Kilani made strong overtures towards Germany but these failed to secure his increasingly shaky position, and he was forced to step down as Prime Minister on 31 January 1941. Within three months, four leading military officers (the so-called *Golden Square*) placed al-Kilani back into power but Britain refused to recognize the new government fearing that he would support Axis powers. Prime Minister Winston Churchill ordered British troops and equipment to redeploy from India to Basra to meet the challenges of the Iraqi uprisings. In the event, RAF units successfully broke the siege laid by anti-British Iraqi forces.[50] By the end of April 1941, and as British forces were bearing down on Baghdad, al-Kilani, along with the military command, slipped over the border at Khanneqin to seek refuge in Iran and from there dispersed to Germany, Italy and Turkey.[51] At the time, Saʻudi Arabia was not a desirable option for refuge, but after Germany surrendered to the Allies in 1945, the intrepid al-Kilani (by now a wanted war criminal in his native Iraq) escaped to France, sailed from Marseille to Beirut and from there overland to Damascus. He used a fake Syrian ID card under the name of Ahmad ʻAbdul Qadir (a sheep-trader from Dayr al-Zur) to travel across the Jordanian-Saʻudi border all the way to Riyadh. In those days, it was common for strangers to attend mosque prayers with the ruler, which was apparently what al-Kilani planned to do in order to meet with ʻAbdul ʻAziz bin ʻAbdul Rahman. According to one source, the following conversation presumably occurred between the two men when they finally met:

> "Mowlay [my Lord] . . . I am Rashid ʻAli al-Kilani [political fugitive from Iraq] . . . and the king relaxed/cooled down . . . . His Majesty said: Oh Rashid . . . I absolutely know what the consequences of this [accepting your refugee will be] . . . it will lead to tensions in our relations with Iraq . . . that may lead to war, but I have no choice once you met me, but to grant you refugee, safety and to protect you."[52]

Al-Kilani offered a different version in 1958. In an interview with Amin Saʻid in Damascus, the fugitive recounted the monarch's confusion when they met face to face, stating: "I spoke with him alone, and there was no one listening to us speak, and I said to him, 'I am Rashid Ali al-Kilani.' And he responded immediately, saying—'Seek refuge in Allah, for there is no might and no power except in Allah'."[53]

Accused of being a war criminal, the Iraqi authorities condemned Al-Kilani to death, and asked King ʻAbdul ʻAziz to hand him over, a request that was made under pressure by the British authorities but which the King rejected, reiterating the impossibility to expel anyone under his protection, who sought his help, or asked for refuge, even in those instances when the ruler did not agree with the individual who made such a request. King 'Abdul 'Aziz formally responded to King Farouk in October 1945 with a letter in which he declared:

> "My brother, I am sure that what worries me also disturbs your majesty, and that those events did not take place by choice or desire. When [I was about to leave Riyadh for Jiddah], it turned out that one of the delegation members, Rashid Ali al-Kilani, was among the disguised delegates that requested to meet me and you know, your Majesty, [we disagree with his political plot against the Iraqi king] . . . as required by the religious virtues [of Islam] and the Arab *shyam* [good manners] [we granted him refuge], [We hope that] . . . His Highness, Prince 'Abdallah, . . . Pardon him . . . Dear brother [King Farouk] . . . kindly write to His Royal Highness Prince 'Abdallah to pardon him . . . "[54]

Upon King Farouk's insistence, 'Abdul 'Aziz replied, "Our position cannot change, because handing the man to the gallows is a shame [that will last forever]", going on to explain that no Saudi would allow his reputation to be tarnished.[55]

This example stands as a perfect illustration how the conduct of international diplomacy with a neighboring state followed core religious rules, something that certainly anticipated the basic concept of the safety of the refugee, which arose just a few years later at the time of the 1951 UN Convention. Thus, the Sa'udi position towards al-Kilani's request for asylum and the monarch's response in the presence of the British envoy, provide valuable insights, perhaps best summarized by his son, then Prince Faysal bin 'Abdul 'Aziz:

> "Know that Rashid 'Ali al-Kilani is a political refugee and we have accepted his asylum and our honor is associated with it. We will never hand him over and whoever wants to take him away from us will only be able do that over our [Al Sa'ud] dead bodies. . . . "[56]

Muslim Brotherhood Refugees

The al-Kilani case was not an isolated episode as the highly controversial Muslim Brotherhood presence in the Kingdom after the 1950s illustrates. Established in 1928 by the Egyptian Muslim scholar Hassan al-Banna, and persecuted in that country at the height of the Nasirist revolution, the Brotherhood left its mark on several Arab countries. Saʻudi Arabia welcomed the first Brothers in 1954, when thousands sought to escape president Jamal ʻAbdul Nasir [Gamal Abdel Nasser] and his suppression policies. This was at a time when the Kingdom hired teachers for its newly established schools and perceived these conservative as well as pious Arab Muslims to be appropriate for its newly created public school system. Starting in the mid-1960s, that is after Heir Apparent Faysal bin ʻAbdul ʻAziz acceded the throne, the ruler championed the creation of public schools across the Kingdom for boys and girls alike, which brought in thousands of Egyptians, Jordanians, Syrians, and Lebanese to fill the newly created posts. At the time, the largely unschooled population—save for those who received religious education—had few qualified teachers, so the government dispatched emissaries abroad, mostly to Egypt and Jordan, to recruit instructors with substantive skills who also were devout Muslims.[57]

It must be reiterated that a hallmark of King Faysal's reign was an effort to create an Islamic alliance in the Middle East to counter the Arab nationalism of Egypt's president. When Nasir, a charismatic strongman and sworn enemy of Saʻudi Arabia, turned against his country's conservative Muslim Brotherhood, King Faysal welcomed those religious conservatives to the Kingdom, as scholars and teachers. But this was a clear humanitarian gesture since he strongly rejected the persecution of fellow Muslims. While King Faysal was probably aware of the Brothers' ideological baggage, he nevertheless expected them to comply with the Kingdom's norms, which rejected extremist tendencies, though he did not suspect that the far more and better organized Brothers would reinforce the fundamentalist hold on the young Ministry of Education, which was founded in 1954 under his predecessor, King Saʻud.[58]

To reiterate, King Faysal encouraged the presence of these Egyptian teachers in his realm not because he shared their ideological goals, but because he abhorred the persecution of fellow Muslims and, for pragmatic reasons, because Saʻudi Arabia needed teachers who were devout Muslims. At no time did the visionary monarch share the extremist Brotherhood's interpretations. Moreover, and based on his support to persecuted members of the Brethren in Egypt, it is safe to argue that King Faysal may well have been a victim of his disproportionate tolerance—to extend a hand when Arab values demanded such behavior. Faysal wanted to help and, in the process, benefit from the skilled Egyptian manpower, but became a casualty of those who entertained an expansionist agenda that intended to overthrow military dictatorships as well as monarchies—as later developments confirmed. In short, the ruler extended the welcome mat to thousands of Egyptian Muslim Brotherhood members, trusting them to espouse common values though this was to naught. Critics interpreted this as naivete though the devout Faysal was not as calculating as many of his foes.[59] In the event, he upheld the Kingdom's values, even when guests turned out to be churlish.

Burmese Refugees in Sa'udi Arabia

As discussed in Chapter 2, and long before the word "Rohingya" became a household name when nearly 600,000 refugees from modern Myanmar reached Bangladesh in 2017, Sa'udi Arabia welcomed thousands of refugees from Burma—as Myanmar was then known—to live in the Kingdom after many were persecuted during the 1960s. It is worth revisiting this issue to further highlight why Riyadh welcomed the Rohingya in the first place.

Burmese Muslims began emigrating to Sa'udi Arabia after the government granted them residence, and while their arrival into the Kingdom was stretched over several years—the first pilgrims reached the holy city of Makkah between 1948 and 1950 during the reign of King 'Abdul 'Aziz—the numbers increased in later years. The second phase was between the early 1950s and 1960s when the majority entered the country via Yemen and Jordan, obtaining Sa'udi nationality, with a third migration occurring between 1963 and 1972, when migrants entered the Kingdom with pilgrimage (*hajj* or *'umrah*) visas and travelled from Pakistan or Bangladesh. The fourth stage, known as the collective migration, ensued after a whole village was demolished in Myanmar in 2018.[60] According to an official publication, Riyadh estimated that nearly 500,000 Rohingya, the original refugees and their descendants, lived in the Kingdom before the latest calamities befell them in Myanmar.[61] Although the Burmese collective migrations came to a halt between 1971 and 2005, individual migrations continued and it is important to underscore that while up to 500,000 Burmese enjoyed the safety of a legal presence, those who escaped Buddhist persecutions continued to make the trek, which meant that the overall numbers were probably higher than those advanced by the government.[62] Consequently, it may well be safe to surmise that the number of Burmese in Sa'udi Arabia who altered their illegal status to legal residency, crossed the quarter million mark, as most blended into Sa'udi society. In fact, the Rohingya were never perceived as an element of instability in the country but, on the contrary, and as the Mayor of Umm al-Salm [Ahmad al-Ma'abdi] neighborhood affirmed:

"The Burmese community is concentrated in the area of Kilo 14, an extension of the old vegetable market to the Ain al-Aziziyah Hosh/yard, many of whom moved to the neighborhoods adjacent to their neighborhood known as the Burmese district. The Burmese lived in this area for many years and many of them dissolved in the Sa'udi society and many of them inter-married with Sa'udis and became part of the social fabric."[63]

Al-Ma'abdi added: "Everyone knows that the state has been working and continues to correct the conditions of the Burmese community that came to the Kingdom decades ago to escape from persecution. The truth is that the Burmese are simple in their dealings and most of them are religious."[64] The plight of this religious minority divided Myanmar's society as its leaders, both military as well as civilian, fueled Islamophobia. The country's demographic imbalances were quite real but adding fuel to the sectarian fire was far more dangerous. As Table 3.2 and Graph 3.1 highlight, Burma/Myanmar was a heterogeneous society, even if anti-Muslim sentiments festered and threatened the entire democratization process. Although predominantly Buddhist, over 20 percent of the entire population practiced other religions that, regrettably, were not valued.

Table 3.2
Religious Sects in Burma/Myanmar and Percentages in General Population

Religion	Percent of Population 1973	Percent of Population 1983	Percent of Population 2014	Percent of Population 2020
Buddhism	88.8	89.4	87.9	79.8
Christianity	4.6	4.9	6.2	7.8
Islam	3.9	3.9	4.3	4.2
Hinduism	0.4	0.5	0.5	1.7
Tribal Religions	2.2	1.2	0.8	5.8
Other Religions	0.1	0.1	0.2	0.2
Not Religious	N/A	N/A	0.1	0.1

Source: Based on the estimated overall population, including both the enumerated and non-enumerated populations of an estimated 53 million, and on the assumption that the non-enumerated population in Rakhine State affiliated with the Muslim faith [where Muslims made up to 35% of the population in 2016). The 2014 data was based on an actual census whereas the 2020 column includes data drawn from official estimates.

It is important to recognize that the need to address living conditions of the Burmese community in Sa'udi Arabia came on the basis of what the Custodian of the Two Holy Mosques' Advisor, Prince Khalid al-Faysal, presented to King 'Abdallah bin 'Abdul 'Aziz in 2012, when a

Graph 3.1
Religious Sects in Myanmar and Percentages in General Population

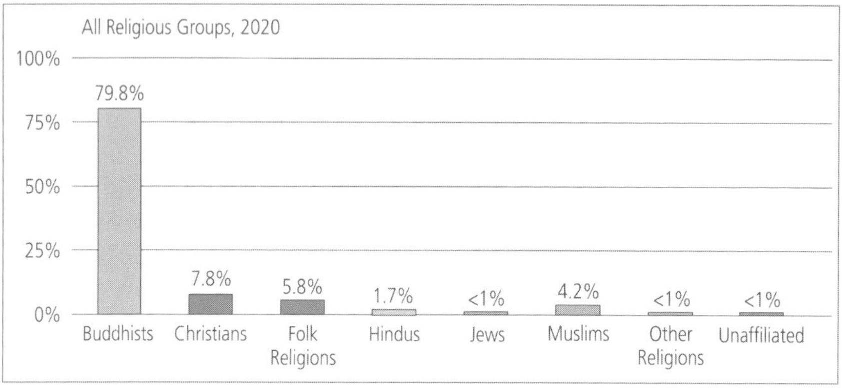

Religious Group	Percentage
Buddhists	79.8%
Christians	7.8%
Folk Religions	5.8%
Hindus	1.7%
Jews	<1%
Muslims	4.2%
Other Religions	<1%
Unaffiliated	<1%

All Religious Groups, 2020

Source: The Future of World Religions: Population Growth Projections, 2010–2050, published by the Pew Research Center, 1615 L Street, NW, Suite 700, Washington, DC 20036; http://www.globalreligiousfutures.org/downloadable/58177.png

decision was reached to ensure that a full-scale development of specific shantytowns be attended to without delay (see below). Despite the fact that the Rohingya were never perceived as being an element of instability in the country, several recent sources denounced some criminal activities of this particular minority, asserting that the percentages were higher than in other instances, which further muddied conditions. Attacks on innocent bystanders, rapes and other criminal activities have of course been committed in the Kingdom as in most societies, and this led to the arrest of a few Rohingyas that tarnished the reputation of the majority. In addition, the public denunciation of the presence of post-2016 Rohingya migrants who engaged in criminal activities, some of whom were held in the Kingdom's notorious Shumaysih detention center, cast a shadow on Sa'udi Arabia's efforts to integrate recent arrivals within its society at large.[65] Regrettably, Rohingyas who were arrested for criminal activities were caught in the country's strict legal web that applied Shari'ah irrespective of nationality or special circumstances.[66] Such arrests have been seen as a reaction to the strict regulation on their employment and movement, and it is now considered one of the main challenges faced by the Kingdom when dealing with the Rohingya.

Myanmar witnessed ethnic wars aimed at cleansing Muslims in the Arakan region of the country, a development that has been ongoing for at least a century. Major efforts by international organizations and states to resolve these disputes failed to achieve justice and democratic coexistence, as suffering, injustice and persecution at all levels prevailed.

Numerous international reports and human rights monitors confirm that the tragedies and plight of the Rohingya Muslims are the result of systematic anti-Muslim practices organized by extremist groups, whose objectives include repression, injustice and ethnic cleansing, all of which have resulted in the displacement of some four million people from their homes. While at least 200,000 were killed under British colonization from 1824 to 1948,[67] Muslims, who accounted for over 4 percent of the population in Myanmar, suffered from the repression of the Burmese government for much of the twentieth century. In fact, successive governments in Yangon (Rangoon), that is all post-1948 regimes, the 1962–2011 military dictatorships, as well as the post 2011 National League for Democracy-led parliament under Prime Minister Aung San Suu Kyi, all engaged in ethnic cleansing and genocide against Muslim Rohingyas in what can only be described as an intended goal for physical removal of this Burmese population from its ancestral lands.[68] What the displacements and dislocations from the homeland meant was little more than a systematic attempt to push a significant portion of the Rohingya population out of the country. Myanmar is an ethnically rich and diverse society with at least 135 distinct groups that consist mainly of Tibeto-Burman peoples, the so-called Bamar that probably make-up an estimated 68% of the population. Rohingya Muslims, estimated at 1.5 to 2 million throughout the world, were about 4 percent of the Myanmar population of the 53 million, representing a very small minority. Most Rohingya have now fled Myanmar, with many refugees living in make-shift camps in neighboring Bangladesh, including 200,000 that settled there in 1978 as a result of the King Dragon operation in Arakan, while another 250,000 left in 1991. An estimated 100,000 fled between 2016 and 2018 in fear of persecution and violence. The total number of Rohingyas in Bangladesh topped the 860,000 in 2020, some of whom were being removed to remote islands. While Riyadh was examining conditions under which it might resettle an undetermined number in the Kingdom, diplomatic disputes with Dacca created significant delays.[69]

As discussed earlier, Sa'udi Arabia welcomed a large number of Rohingyas, nearly half-a-million, and was willing to relocate more from Bangladesh under specific new conditions, including family reunification and proper legal representation. Riyadh extended the welcome mat to this non-Arab population, accepted the Asian nation in its midst, and otherwise upheld its sacred obligations. To be sure, the Rohingya were Muslims, but the criteria to accept large numbers of refugees was never exclusively based on faith. Rather, it was based on extending a hand to those who needed assistance that, in this case, happened to be made up of Muslims. Importantly, most of the young Rohingya who grew up in Sa'udi Arabia adapted fast, with many joining the ranks of teachers given that they knew Arabic. Many preferred to teach in charity schools and Qur'an memorization workshops, or prepared to become imams of mosques after memorizing the holy scriptures. Remarkably, most obtained high school diplomas and countless earned advanced university degrees, while still others opted to work in libraries.[70] Recent studies confirmed that 70 percent of the young in this community concentrated on charities or public schools, or otherwise engaged in the kind of work that fulfilled their religious aspirations. The Kingdom of Sa'udi Arabia regularized their presence in the country, which was why nearly half-a-million called the Kingdom home in 2020, something that often falls below analysts' commentary radars. Riyadh extended significant financial assistance to the Rohingya lingering in refugee camps in Bangladesh too, though most of that aid was channeled through Muslim organizations like the Organization of Islamic Cooperation and the World Muslim League.

Iraqi Refugees and the Rafhah Camp Experiment

An equally important case is that of Iraqi refugees and asylum-seekers, whose numbers increased in the aftermath of the wars that devastated that hapless country even before the 2003 War for Iraq, which saw a number reach the Kingdom of Sa'udi Arabia.[71]

At the beginning of 2021 (the most recent date for which complete statistics are available are from 2018, however), a total of some 500,000 Iraqi refugees were spread across 90 asylum countries around the world, including ones as distant and diverse as South Africa, Sri Lanka, Argentina and Nepal. Of course, the Iraqi diaspora was far larger, with 250,000 Iraqis each in the United Kingdom, Germany, Canada, the United States, 150,000 in Egypt, 130,000 in Jordan, 100,000 in the UAE, and 50,000 in Lebanon.

Nearly 500,000 were settled in Iran, some since the nineteenth century. Of the 500,000 Iraqi refugees that were registered under UNHCR regulations, almost half lived in Western countries while around 70,000 were resettled from their first countries of asylum, usually Syria and Jordan, to Sa'udi Arabia, Turkey, Lebanon as well as Jordan and Syria. In addition, more than 25,000 were resettled from Rafhah, now a closed camp that was specifically set up for Iraqis who fled to the Kingdom at the height of the war; the vast majority of Iraqis who requested asylum in the Kingdom were granted sanctuary.[72] As the Kingdom experimented with a refugee camp in the case of Iraqis after the 1991 war, and vowed to never again embark on such a scheme, it is important to examine this case and draw various lessons from its failures.

In the aftermath of the 1991 War for Kuwait, thousands of Iraqi military personnel surrendered to American, British and other allied forces, most of whom were transferred to Sa'udi Arabia and held in a makeshift camp near the city of 'Artawiyyah. Most of the prisoners were voluntarily repatriated through the International Committee of the Red Cross (ICRC) shortly after the war ended, though those who refused to return to their native country were subsequently deemed to be civilian refugees. Approximately 12,000 captured soldiers were thus *classified* as civilians, and housed at 'Artawiyyah, which was nothing more than a secluded camp in the desert. Regrettably, reclassifying them did not translate into the kind of treatment that civilians receive, which affirmed their isolation that, in time, increased frustrations. Moreover, long resettlement delays into third countries created problems too even before many were transferred to the nearby Camp Rafhah, a facility that welcomed civilians, and which necessitated haphazard construction at first before more permanent facilities were erected. Located about 400 miles northwest of Riyadh, Camp Rafhah welcomed an additional 21,000 civilian Iraqis from the South (mostly from around Basra), who fled their homes during the failed Shi'ah uprising that was brutally put down by forces loyal to Saddam Husayn, in March 1991.[73] The new arrivals included whole families, predominantly Shi'ah Muslims, though many claimed to have been in the armed forces for fear of being turned away by allied authorities. That detail raised suspicions too as post-war operations fueled the extreme caution cauldron. Over the course of several months, and frustrated by their isolation in the camp despite major efforts made by Sa'udi authorities to facilitate their stay, a number of clashes occurred between POWs and Sa'udi military personnel vetting them. Consequently, and under UNHCR guidance, which placed staff members at Rafhah, authorities removed the 12,000 male POWs to a makeshift camp near in nearby al-Tawiyyih in April 1991, hoping that such a measure would reduce tensions. Riyadh allowed representatives of both the International Committee of the Red Cross (ICRC) and the United Nations High Commissioner for Refugees (UNHCR) access to these camps and encouraged repatriation to avoid additional clashes, though that proved to be premature. According to Amnesty International, sharp disagreements emerged between ICRC representatives and the Sa'udis, as the former concluded that all civilian internees were classified under the provisions of the Fourth Geneva Convention Relative to the Protection of Civilian Persons in Time of War (1949), while the Sa'udis deemed them to be only refugees.

In the event, and as repatriations accelerated, the 'Artawiyyah camp was closed down in December 1992 and its remaining population consolidated into the Rafhah camp, which stood at 28,000 in March 1993. By mid-1993, 6,288 of the original 32,000 refugees were resettled in third countries, including Iran, the United States and several Scandinavian countries, while 2,188 reportedly opted to return to Iraq. The number of refugees who remained in Rafhah was estimated at about 23,000 a year later.[74] The drawn-out vetting and resettlement processes created serious obstructions over the course of several years, as reports emerged of arbitrary detention of certain refugees, some of whom were killed in what Amnesty International labelled as extrajudicial executions. In response, Sa'udi authorities made a number of improvements at the camp, and provided additional facilities for its population including air-conditioned pre-fabricated dwellings. In a 1993 brochure titled "Welcome Guests in Saudi Arabia: The Story of Iraqi Refugees," Riyadh affirmed that:

> "The battle of the liberation of Kuwait has led to the departure of tens of thousands of Iraqi people to neighboring countries. These include Saudi Arabia which due to bonds of brotherhood and neighborliness received without undue delay 32,000 Iraqi refugees and provided them promptly with relief supplies to alleviate their plight. . . . As they entered Saudi territory they received from the authorities every care and were given shelter, sustenance, and all humanitarian services needed for their comfort; and with great urgency the Kingdom established two camps to shelter these refugees who had escaped from the oppression of the Baghdad regime."[75]

Amnesty International derided this effort, which it perceived as propaganda, and insisted that Iraqi refugees were neither welcomed nor treated fairly, at least to its own standards. Furthermore, the organization criticized the government of Sa'udi Arabia for its conduct at Rafhah, including the killings of at least nine refugees [ex-POWs] following the riots in March 1993.

Between 1991 and 2005, more than 25,000 Iraqi refugees were resettled from Rafhah to third countries, while slightly over 3,500 were voluntarily repatriated to their troubled homeland. As conditions improved inside Iraq, the remaining refugees returned home under International Red Cross protection.[76] Sa'udi Arabia shut down Camp Rafhah in 2005 and vowed to never embark on such an experiment again. Where serious shortcomings occurred were in mixing POWs with civilians, and while civilian Iraqi refugees were Shi'ah Muslims—who have historically had suspicious, even hostile, relations with the

Kingdom's predominantly Sunni population—Riyadh accepted the refugees when coalition forces completed their hasty withdrawals from southern Iraq.

Syrian Refugees

As discussed in more detail in Chapter 8, the case of Syrian refugees is particularly interesting because it illustrates how difficult it is to overcome sectarian disputes in a humanitarian conflict. Without anticipating the discussion to follow that will highlight how Riyadh and the Sa'udi nation approached the Syrian refugee dilemma, it is essential to underscore a few of the reactions that this situation generated which, at least on the surface, appear to be contradictory. In fact, and given that an overwhelming majority of displaced Syrians were Sunni Muslims—like the Sa'udi population—it is ironic to note that the Royal Sa'udi Air Force, along with coalition units from the United Arab Emirates Air Force and others—participated in the bombings of several areas predominantly inhabited by Sunni Syrians when the civil war in that hapless country was hijacked by extremist forces.[77] In fact, the areas of Syria that were targeted served as bases for the so-called Islamic State of Iraq and Syria (ISIS), which would not have been destroyed if the Kingdom had pursued a sectarian policy to defend and protect fellow Sunnis. Rather, and in what appeared to be an eminent example of Sa'udi opposition to Da'ish, the Arabic acronym for ISIS, Riyadh addressed the problem of state security head-on without neglecting its international commitments. While the Syrian conflict led to scores of refugees fleeing that country, it was important for Sa'udi authorities to understand if the refugees coming from Syria into Sa'udi Arabia were Da'ish victims escaping bombardments, or were simply seeking economic benefits. Authorities did not shy from addressing security concerns and separated the wheat from the chaff. Indeed, Riyadh rejected Da'ish and its violence, even if some of the alleged behavior of the latter was akin to its own conservative/salafi practices (though this was overblown for propaganda purposes by anti-Sa'udi elements). And the fact remains that Sa'udi Arabia accepted hundreds of thousands on its soil without affixing on them the label "refugee"; their acceptance, as discussed in Chapter 8, was dedicated to their plight.

Despite various charges that Riyadh was miserly in welcoming Syrian refugees, Sa'udi Arabia routinely and consistently released the statistics on the number of Syrians present on its territory after 2011, indicating that all enjoyed the freedom to move about, had the right to work and study, as well as having access to free health care. In a speech to the

United Nations on the report of the High Commissioner for Refugees, Nabil Othman, the acting UNHCR regional representative in the Arab Gulf region, confirmed that there were 500,000 Syrians in the Kingdom and that the number of Syrian students receiving free study in the country was more than 141,000, in addition to the 285,000 Yemeni students enjoying the same privilege.[78]

For the purposes of this chapter, suffice it to say that the Sa'udi engagement with the Syrian cause is best summarized in a report entitled "Giving Syrians *Zakat* an Islamic duty," as the Kingdom's Grand Mufti Shaykh 'Abdul 'Aziz Al al-Shaykh called upon Sa'udis to give their annual alms [*Zakat*] to Syrian refugees, to express solidarity with Syrian children suffering in their nation's bloody civil war. According to the Grand Mufti, "Giving *Zakat* to the Syrians is an Islamic duty as it will help save them from poverty and destruction," a message he repeated in a video statement broadcast over the airwaves during a "National Campaign for the Support of Syrians."[79] Ironically, at a time when Riyadh was raising appropriate funds for Syrians, an estimated 100,000 Syrian expatriates already in Sa'udi Arabia were unable to renew their passports because they opposed the regime. Several Syrians told a local newspaper that their country's missions had stopped renewing their passports, with Mohammed al-Turkawi, a member of the Syrian opposition living in Jiddah, emphasizing that this affected approximately 10 percent of the estimated one million Syrians living in the Kingdom. "Syrian expats have to go to neighboring countries to renew their passports," he stated, noting that the "Syrian mission in the Kingdom had previously canceled the passports of some Syrians who were members of the opposition."[80] As most Syrians worked in administrative, medical, and engineering positions in the Kingdom, many were afraid to speak openly at meetings because they feared that "spies" might send reports back to Damascus that, in turn, may lead to negative consequences for their loved ones or extended family members still living in the country. Syrian activists posted tragic stories on various Internet web-pages about the atrocities perpetrated by the regime's military, best clarified by Waleed Abdullah, a Syrian resident in Jiddah: "I use to attack the Syrian government on Twitter. I do not travel to my country because I'm afraid of being arrested the moment I set foot on its soil," he hammered.[81]

These anecdotal declarations cannot be generalized, but they stand as blatant evidence that Syrians in the Kingdom enjoyed specific privileges, which western media sources simply chose to ignore from the beginning of the crisis, neglecting the role that the Gulf countries in general and Sa'udi Arabia in particular played in welcoming refugees from Syria. It is worth repeating that the UNHCR counted refugees by noting only those "persons recognized as refugees under the 1951 UN Convention/1967 Protocol, the 1969 Organization of African Unity Convention, in accordance with the UNHCR Statute, [and] persons granted a complementary form of protection and those granted temporary protection," while Gulf countries defined them as "Arab brothers and sisters in distress." This was the reason why they were not counted into the normal international mechanisms, which added to the misconceptions which lingered that, truth be told, contributed to the distrust between Sa'udi authorities and the international community. Notwithstanding this discrepancy, and as discussed in Chapter 8, Riyadh fulfilled its normative as well as legal obligations to Syrians just like it did to others who sought asylum in the Kingdom.

Conclusion: Obligations as Custodian of the Two Holy Mosques

Sa'udi authorities took their religious obligations seriously in addressing refugee concerns, and while mistakes were committed, especially in the case of Iraqi refugees at Camp Rafhah between 1991 and 2005, Riyadh pledged to fulfill its commitments in toto. There were various differences over the status of refugees and how governments interpreted specific regulations, but these seldom prevented Riyadh from welcoming millions on its soil.

In addition to the religious norms discussed above, Arab honor was at play as well, which motivated the founder monarch 'Abdul 'Aziz bin 'Abdul Rahman and all of his successors to welcome victims and challengers alike. Anyone who sought protection received it though war conditions complicated matters as authorities devised appropriate policies to regularize the presence of refugees in the country. The examples cited in this chapter, from the Iraqi dissident Rashid 'Ali al-Kilani to members of the Egyptian Muslim Brotherhood all to the way to the Rohingyas, Iraqis, Syrians and others, confirm that Sa'udi society, people as well as governments, fulfilled their responsibilities. All drew succor from scriptures that surpassed man-made laws, which were not always well received, when, more often than not, such propositions were simply rejected. This did not mean that Riyadh was deliberately opposed to the UN 1951 Convention and the 1967 Protocol, but rather that it sought alternatives that were adapted to local traditions and norms. In most instances, Sa'udis deemed their reliance on the Holy Qur'an to be far better. This was a difficult proposition for secularized societies to accept, though the Kingdom's pledges and, frankly, commitments, met all contemporary humanitarian protocols. Providing material and financial assistance, as elaborated in the next chapter, drew strengths from religious norms too.

CHAPTER

4

The Concept of *Zakat* and Foreign Aid
From Development to Humanitarian Assistance

Although similarities and differences between the 1951 UN Convention of Refugees and the Muslim concept of hospitality were discussed in earlier chapters, it is important to emphasis and explain existing definition limits on all sides. In their efforts to define what a refugee is, especially in the wake of historical events—spanning a time frame that includes the creation of Armenian refugees after World War I all the way to clashes in Afghanistan, Iraq and Syria—that saw an increase in population movements all around the world, all parties confronted undeniable challenges to uphold the original definition of refugee and to look after those less fortunate who fled their nation-states in search for safety and security. In this sense, the very concept of "refugee" remained a blurred category, since it was difficult to distinguish between refugees, internally displaced peoples [IDPs], and international migrants.

To say that the entire "International Convention of Refugees" debate, along with its following resolutions to adapt to new situations were slow going, would be an understatement. In fact, it might be far more accurate to state that the implementation of carefully reached decisions—to look after refugees after specific calamitous events—was erratic, would not, indeed, could not absolve the international community from its responsibilities as humanity confronted epochal crises throughout the twentieth century and the beginning of the twenty-first. Moreover, the failure to anticipate what became gargantuan refugee crises—which meant that those downtrodden did not fit into the traditional definition of refugee as envisaged in the 1951 Convention and the 1967 Protocol—overwhelmed decision-makers, and constituted an obstacle to the very development of the concept of refugee. This made it difficult to assume the burdens of every humanitarian tragedy that arose, limited public-spirited interventions on the ground, and jeopardized the necessary collaboration within and among different countries. In 2008, António Guterres, the United Nations Secretary-General (2017–) who was then serving as the United Nations High Commissioner for Refugees, stated that:

> "The twenty-first century will be characterized by the mass movement of people being pushed and pulled within and beyond their borders by conflict, calamity, or opportunity. War and human rights violations are already scattering millions across the world in search of safety. Globalization, with its attributes of economic expansion, unresolved poverty, and enduring insecurity, is prompting many people to leave their homes in search of better lives. Climate change and environmental degradation will further exacerbate such trends. At few times in history have so many people been on the move. The extent of human mobility today is blurring the traditional distinctions between refugees, internally displaced people, and international immigrants. Yet attempts by the international community to devise policies to preempt, govern, or direct these movements in a rational manner have been erratic."[1]

Here he identifies the core dilemma that confronted the international community even if few concrete solutions were offered to address the consequences of such large human and geo-political movements. For our purposes, and in this new context, the dilemma took on an even more consequential outcomes since several Muslim countries, including Sa'udi Arabia, were not signatories to the Convention and, therefore, were not bound by its calls for action. Nevertheless, the Kingdom consistently and throughout its post-1932 unification history behaved according to the very spirit of the Convention, which few outsiders were privy to. And this requires elaboration.

The purpose of this chapter is three-fold. First, it is to clarify the concept of *zakat* (alms giving) to those less fortunate as a fundamental driver, which moved believers to fulfill their religious obligations. Second, to document how Riyadh devised various foreign aid programs over the past several decades to further conform to sacred duties, including for economic development as well as humanitarian reasons. Finally, the discussion intends to underscore how the peoples and governments of the Kingdom behaved in the past, driven by profound religious obligations that defined their behavior. These examples explain how Sa'udi society fulfilled the Islamic principles of asylum to refugees in explicit terms.

Zakat and Foreign Aid

Zakat, the obligatory giving of alms to the poor and needy, is the third of Islam's Five Pillars. The others are the profession of faith (*shahadah*), daily prayers (*salat*), fasting during the month of Ramadan (*sawm*), and pilgrimage to Makkah [*hajj*] at least once in a lifetime if possible. *Zakat* is thus obligatory upon every adult Muslim of sound mind and means. The Qur'an says in this respect that the "alms are only for the poor (*fuqara'*), and the needy (*al-Masakin*), and for those employed to collect the funds and "those whose hearts it is necessary to conciliate"—e.g., discordant tribesmen, debtors, volunteers in holy war, as well as pilgrims. According to the Scriptures, *zakat* aims to attract the hearts of those who have been inclined towards the faith; to free captives; assist those in debt; and serve God's "Cause." Moreover, alms must also assist wayfarers (travelers cut off from everything), since this is a duty imposed by God. "And Allah [God] is All-Knower, All-Wise" [9:60], the holy book clarifies. *Zakat* is thus extremely important because it is not conceived as a charity, an act which can make a believer feel good but, instead, is an obligation on every Muslim who must acknowledge that everything which is in his/her possession is God's and that humans do not own any of it. This awareness saves believers from greed, and teaches them discipline, honesty and, above all else, creates a unique social framework that allows societies to be protected and preserved from various calamities.[2]

More precisely, *zakat* is levied on five categories of property—food grains; fruits; camels, cattle, sheep, and goats; gold and silver; and movable goods—and is payable each year after one year's possession. Under the caliphates, the collection and expenditure of *zakat* was a function of the state. In the post-Westphalian nation-state system, it has been left up to the individual to fulfill this obligation, except in the Kingdom of Sa'udi Arabia, where Islamic Law is maintained. Among Twelver Sh'iahs, it is collected and disbursed by scholars (*'ulamah*), who act as representatives for the Hidden Imam. Furthermore, the Scriptures stress that s*adaqah*, or voluntary almsgiving, which, like *zakat*, is intended for the needy, must be applied whenever possible. Twelver Sh'iahs require payment of a one-fifth additional tax, the *khums*, to the Hidden Imam and his deputies, a sum that is intended to be spent for the benefit of the imams in addition to orphans, the poor, and travelers.[3]

According to figures published by the United Nations High Commissioner for Refugees (UNHCR), Muslims made up the majority of refugees around the world in 2020, which prompted the organization to consult with Muslim scholars how to best use *zakat* as a source of aid. In fact, several specialists in Shari'ah confirmed that *zakat* was a viable source of aid provided that it met certain conditions. Because Riyadh applied Shari'ah, UNHCR data for 2008 verified that an estimated $20 billion to $200 billion was donated by Muslim populations annually, including voluntary *sadaqah* and obligatory *zakat*.[4] Of course, these figures included several countries—not just Sa'udi Arabia—and fluctuated year-in and year-out, but they illustrate how seriously believers take their sacred obligations to assist those in need. In the Kingdom, a specific institution known today by the acronym GAZT, was established in 1936 under the name of the Zakat and Income Bureau before it became the Zakat and Income Authority and, ultimately, as The General Authority of Zakat and Tax [Royal Decree No. (A/133) dated 30/7/1437 AH]. It was entrusted with the collection and distribution of alms under the chairmanship of the Minister of Finance. In accordance with its regulations, the Authority was responsible not only for collecting alms but was further empowered to ensure the best performance of its members in carrying out the duties assigned to them. According to GAZT Governor Suhail Abanmi, citizens of Sa'udi Arabia were called upon to fulfill their financial duties, which include *Zakat*, Value Added Tax (VAT), excise and Income Tax via various methods, including electronic declaration. GAZT provided businesses with all the required tools and resources and raised the need to be aware of all obligations and the wider importance of the tax system. In other words, while *zakat* is not an outright taxation system it plays a vital role in the Kingdom's fiscal balance program, diversifying and increasing income for the national budget.[5] In line with recent changes introduced at the behest of the government's *Vision2030* programs, and starting on 1 January 2020, "the direct and indirect investment of oil and hydrocarbon producing companies into Saudi Arabian listed companies and subsidiaries of these listed companies" were subject to *zakat*.[6] Of course, GAZT officials acknowledged that "electronic linkage with competent authorities helped monitor corporate manipulations with financial statements, as some companies were found to be reporting false data to reduce due *zakat* and tax." According to a report published by the *Al-Watan* daily newspaper in Jiddah, manipulations were detected and the authorities promised to impose penalties, among other regulatory measures, "to identify these violations and take the necessary actions against violators."[7]

In a prescient essay entitled "Saudi Arabian Humanitarian Aid in Crises Management Periods," Hassen Altalhi summarized the Kingdom's approach to *zakat* in the following terms:

> "Saudi Arabia is among the first countries in the world to develop global programs for providing humanitarian aid of relief to commu-

nities stricken by natural and manmade disasters or regions severely impacted by catastrophic wars. The government of Saudi Arabia provides such humanitarian aid through the auspices of the United Nations and other official organizations such as the World Bank and nongovernmental organizations (NGOs)."[8]

Indeed, Sa'udi humanitarian support was intended to overcome the distinction between Muslim and non-Muslim, as well as embrace people in need in a wider international context regardless of nationality and cultural differences. Altahi added that "Saudi Arabia [did] not merely provide humanitarian aid for recovery from natural disasters, but also supplie[d] donations in the form of cash or developing projects to developing countries, impacted by critical disasters such as drought and poverty." The Kingdom, he concluded, "perform[ed] or provide[d] free medical assistance for children in various parts of the world and has earned the characterization 'Kingdom of Humanity' due to these initiatives."[9] Although these assessments help clarify various Sa'udi initiatives, Altahi provided answers to four main questions: (1) Was Sa'udi Arabia consistent in providing international humanitarian aid?; (2) Was the Kingdom among the top ten government contributors of international humanitarian assistance?; (3) Was Riyadh providing donations for official development assistance to needy nations? and, (4) How did the monarchy contribute to international humanitarian assistance programs, especially when compared to other donors, including other Arab Gulf States? While what Altahi documented stood out as a unique contribution since it clarified how Sa'udi Arabia acted and continued to assume its responsibilities—all following Muslim principles—it was useful to examine these detailed assessments to answer each of the questions outlined above. What follows therefore are summaries of the points raised by Altahi, whose study incorporated additional details, all of which strengthened the argument that the Kingdom fulfilled its sacred obligations conscientiously.[10]

1. **Sa'udi consistency to provide international humanitarian aid.** Based on the data collected in the course of his investigations, Altahi documented how Sa'udi Arabia, for example, provided sorely needed contributions to the UN humanitarian response in the aftermath of the 2010 earthquake that severely damaged Haiti. Riyadh's donation of US$ 50 million in the Haiti Flash Appeal reflected the country's commitment to help populations foreign to the Islamic religion and culture. In fact, the United Nations Office for the Coordination of Humanitarian Affairs (OCHA) confirmed

that Riyadh stood as the third largest donor to the UN humanitarian response to the earthquake in Haiti, a circumstance that was neither unusual nor a one-off phenomenon.[11] As Table 4.1 illustrates, the Kingdom provided significant financial assistance to those most in need year-in and year-out. This aid was disbursed irrespective of national origins, race, religion, color or creed.

2. **Sa'udi Arabia was among the top ten government contributors of international humanitarian assistance.** In fact, Sa'udi humanitarian assistance in 2020 reached unprecedented levels and while Riyadh made various contributions to fulfill its global commitments, what truly motivated decision-makers was their sacred duties towards fellow human beings. Riyadh was the eighth largest donor worldwide in 2020 in the field of international humanitarian assistance.[12]

3. **Sa'udi Arabia provided donations for official development assistance to needy nations.** Suffice to say, and as Altahi documented, the Kingdom's contributions in terms of donations to countries for developmental initiatives were substantial (Table 4.2), which Iain Watson has confirmed with more recent data.[13]

4. **Compared to other Arab Gulf States, Sa'udi Arabia contributed significant resources, which placed the conservative Arab Gulf monarchies in good light** (Table 4.3, on page 96).

In a careful assessment, Altahi concluded that despite "significant efforts, poverty, deprivation and the need for rehabilitation following natural disasters [could] be reduced but . . . not be eradicated worldwide," which necessitated that humanitarian aid receive "continuous efforts and cooperation from the international community, NGOs, and UN agencies."[14]

In addition to the examples cited by Altahi, there were several equally pertinent cases that illustrate how Riyadh reacted and to what end. In the case of the Indian Ocean earthquake and tsunami that occurred on 26 December 2004 off the west coast of northern Sumatra, Indonesia, hitting the Aceh region hard, the Kingdom moved very fast. At the time, massive waves that grew up to 30 meters (100 ft) high headed inland, devastating numerous communities. An estimated 227,898 people died, with devastation experienced in 14 countries. In addition to the Aceh region, Sri Lanka, the Tamil Nadu region in India, and the Khao Lak area in Thailand recorded direct hits as well. The natural disaster prompted a worldwide humanitarian response, with donations totaling more than US$ 14 billion.[15] The Government of Sa'udi Arabia allocated US$ 30 million in an emergency aid package that included US$5 million worth of food, tents and medicine, to be transported and distributed via

Table 4.1
Sa'udi Arabia International Humanitarian Assistance, 2000–2020

Year	US Dollars ($)
2000	137,677,769
2001	670,425,391
2002	30,294,590
2003	105,779,121
2004	52,716,013
2005	163,764,073
2006	203,640,070
2007	252,564,761
2008	608,348,340
2009	144,567,646
2010	279,678,356
2011	216,681,599
2012	512,925,108
2013	206,553,007
2014	877,663,889
2015	577,732,091
2016	409,793,919
2017	453,302,153
2018	1,652,886,476
2019	1,382,058,734
2020	651,851,681

Source: UN OCHA Financial Tracking Services, at https://fts.unocha.org/donors/

Table 4.2
Sa'udi Arabia ODA Contributions, 2005–2020

Year	US$ (billions)
2005	1.0
2006	2.0
2007	1.6
2008	5.0
2009	3.1
2010	3.5
2011	5.1
2012	1.3
2013	5.7
2014	13.6
2015	6.8
2016	1.6
2017	2.1
2018	4.8
2019	5.9
2020	–

Source: "Saudi Arabia," Development Co-operation Profiles 2020," Paris: OECD, at https://www.oecd-ilibrary.org/sites/b2156c99-en/index.html?itemId=/content/component/b2156c99-en

Table 4.3
International Humanitarian Assistance from Gulf States, 2005–2020 (*US $ Millions*)

Year	Kuwait	Qatar	Saudi Arabia	UAE
2005	23	72	166	179
2006	36	6	178	67
2007	15	0	277	61
2008	106	3	643	126
2009	58	18	161	477
2010	11	2	311	139
2011	14	17	168	203
2012	11	105	500	43
2013	324	109	200	300
2014	351	156	900	375
2015	464	103	600	700
2016	348	44	400	700
2017	205	104	500	300
2018	374	52	1700	2200
2019	175	44	1400	600
2020	132	49	700	400

Source: Development Initiatives based on UN OCHA FTS data. UN OCHA Financial Tracking Services, at https://fts.unocha.org/donors/4849/summary/2020

the Saʻudi Red Crescent, and another US$ 5 million in funds given to several international aid groups such as the Red Cross and the UN High Commissioner for Refugees. After the tsunami, the Saʻudi Charity Campaign donated more than US$ 45 million to Aceh, which included the building of two orphanages, almost 500 houses, a hospital, and restoration of the Baiturrahman Mosque.[16] In the event, an estimated US$ 367 million was allocated by Riyadh to the Aceh disaster, though Antonio Donini acknowledged that the "vast parallel universe of Islamic charities and funds for humanitarian assistance provided by Arab and other Islamic countries, remittances from diasporas and contributions from local entities in crisis countries" were seldom recorded in the official statistics of humanitarian assistance.[17]

The Kingdom even provided humanitarian assistance to the United States in the aftermath of the Category 5 Atlantic hurricane that devasted the city of New Orleans and its surrounding area on 23 August 2005; the event caused over 1,800 deaths and 125 billion dollars' worth of damage. After Hurricane Katrina hit the city, the Houston-based subsidiary of the state oil firm Saudi Aramco donated US$ 5 million to the American Red Cross, along with an additional US$ 250,000 from the Arab Gulf

Program for Development, though Aramco's total aid topped US$ 100 million.[18] When the Kingdom emerged as one of the main contributors to the Haiti Emergency Response Fund in 2010, the United Nations Secretary-General's Special Humanitarian Envoy, Abdulaziz bin Mohamed Arrukban, reported that Sa'udi Arabia stood "ready and prepared to support people in need of humanitarian assistance on the basis of core humanitarian principles and regardless of nationality, race or religion."[19]

These examples highlighted what Altahi's analysis elucidated, while Donini's perceptive exploration confirmed that Riyadh adapted its own foreign aid policies to match those of believers who donated a percentage of their annual incomes in alms to fulfill religious obligations. There was, consequently, a congruence of objectives within Sa'udi Arabian society as rulers and ruled alike applied similar traditions and were bound by identical religious duties. As discussed in more detail in the following section, the very idea of foreign aid—for a country that became relatively wealthy only after the 1974 increases in the price of oil—became ingrained, as the population provided generous assistance to those in need and the government disbursed large sums of financial support through various funds either established solo or with other Arab Gulf countries.

Sa'udi Foreign Aid: Humanitarian and Economic Assistance

As billions of dollars were devoted to refugees around the world every year, it was sometimes difficult to identify the origins of these resources, how they were pledged and, once deposited in specific state or international organization accounts, how they were disbursed. Leading industrialized countries voluntarily transferred significant financial resources to those most in need, often for humanitarian reasons but, equally important, to advance diplomatic agendas, assist allies, and reward recipient countries for a slew of reasons. Often, foreign aid to states or even for refugees included military aid even if certain powers like the United States and Russia feigned incredulity whenever such linkages were made, concentrating on Official Development Assistance (ODA), an Organization for Economic Co-operation and Development (OECD) term developed in 1969 as an indicator of international aid flows.[20] According to the latest available statistics, the 30-members that composed the OECD's Development Cooperation Directorate (DAC) allocated US$153 billion in 2019, up 1.4% in real terms from 2018.

Excluding aid spent on processing and hosting refugees, ODA was stable from 2017 to 2019.[21] Importantly, and as reported by the OECD, the grant-equivalent ODA figure for 2019 was equivalent to 0.30% of the DAC donors' combined gross national income, which was below the target ratio of 0.7% ODA to Gross National Income (GNI) agreed upon in 1970, a target that was re-endorsed at the highest levels at international aid and development conferences ever since. Only five DAC members—Denmark, Luxembourg, Norway, Sweden and the United Kingdom—met or exceeded the 0.7% target in 2019, while non-DAC donors Turkey and the United Arab Emirates, whose ODA was not counted in the DAC total, provided 1.15% and 0.55% respectively of their GNI in development aid.[22]

As discussed in this section, the Kingdom of Sa'udi Arabia was and remained a leading provider of official development assistance to developing countries, averaging 1.5% of its gross national income for the period between 1973 and 2008, according to a study conducted by the World Bank.[23] By the end of 2016, Sa'udi Arabia had provided assistance totaling $139 billion to 95 countries around the world, ranking it fourth among leading donor countries across the globe.[24] As discussed below, these figures increased during the past few years, even if the government reorganized how it disbursed significant donations. In fact, while Riyadh channeled the bulk of its ODA assistance through the Sa'udi Fund for Development (see below) that was established specifically for this purpose, it further donated additional humanitarian assistance for refugees after major disasters struck, which totaled $2.1 billion for the period between 2000 and 2010 and which has grown further in recent years. In 2017 alone, Sa'udi Arabia donated more than $400 million to disaster response operations around the globe, with more "than half of this donations given to organizations on a bilateral basis." Up to July 2018, the Sa'udi government had donated more than $770 million to humanitarian responses with the majority of the donations going towards the Yemen humanitarian response plan.[25]

News reports that concentrated on sensational items regarding the Kingdom, including such allegations that the Sa'udi military deliberately targeted Yemeni hospitals, supported by Médecins Sans Frontières and similar organizations, or discussed arms sales by the United States and other countries that contributed to mayhem in Yemen, seldom broached ODA and humanitarian matters. In the post-2016 period, speculation was rampant about the American sale of up to 153 tanks and other military equipment in a deal worth $1.15 billion, which led a few to opine that Washington contributed to Riyadh's destruction of Yemen, and that the time had come to end these military sales.[26] This was not an isolated incident but part of a pattern of negative coverage related to the War for Yemen, to be discussed in Chapter 7. Of course, the post-2015 war was devastating but failed to take into account several critical factors, including its United Nations mandate, sharp military assaults on the Kingdom itself by Yemeni rebels who cared not about their missile devastation on civilian targets. And despite the human and physical price paid by Sa'udi Arabia, Riyadh's continued allocation of significant humanitarian assistance to Sana'a.

Amid this negative media bonanza, a report that the Kingdom allocated billions in foreign aid during the past four decades (1980–2020) received scant attention, which was not unusual even if unbecoming.[27] There were periodic positive reports on the Kingdom's aid policies, but these were seldom comprehensive.[28] Of course, many countries provided and continue to allocate substantial sums in development assistance to needy nations, but that did not minimize what Sa'udi Arabia, along with other Gulf Cooperation Council states, including Kuwait, Qatar and the United Arab Emirates, have accomplished to date. In fact, efforts to engage in humanitarian assistance and increase the level of social responsibility by distributing foreign aid were nothing new, as all Arab Gulf countries created development funds in the late 1960s and early 1970s for such purposes. What stood out were the linkages made between humanitarian and developmental efforts, especially in terms of religious obligations, with the implication that Arab financial support went to Muslim nations more or less exclusively. This was true to a certain extent not because Sa'udi Arabia and its GCC partners did not disburse aid to non-Muslim countries but because there was so much need in Muslim countries to begin with. Equally important, and though the OECD organization displayed customary generosity, it would be safe to also state that some of their aid was linked to political agendas even if transparency was usually applied.

Still, and amazingly, little of what Sa'udi Arabia offered in terms of humanitarian assistance received coverage in mainstream media outlets. This was, at least in part, a sign of neglect by Riyadh. Indeed, Arab leaders in general and Sa'udi officials in particular, seldom sought the limelight to boast of their generosity, which some misinterpreted and continue to perceive as a sign of weakness or, even worse, that these officials had something to hide or, worse, were not particularly proud of their actions for a variety of reasons. Regrettably, most played defense when winning public relations required offensive moves. Be that as it may, the Kingdom was and is one of the top donors in the world and has been so since the 1970s. In fact, and according to a leading source, Riyadh was the eighth largest donor worldwide in 2020 with US$ 358 million given out.[29] More than 90 countries benefitted from this largesse, including Sri Lanka and India, both of which supplied sorely needed manpower to Sa'udi Arabia that further allowed hundreds of thousands—millions over the years—to earn salaries and support their families back home. Their earnings supported scores of families in their respective countries that, truth be told, was yet another beneficial aspect of the expatriate presence on the Arabian Peninsula even if migrant living and working conditions were not always ideal. As mentioned in the previous section, Sa'udi Arabia provided significant aid to Indonesia in 2004, following the Aceh Province earthquake/tsunami combination that devastated Sumatra. Similar aid was rushed to Pakistan and India after the 2005 Kashmir earthquake and, though most Iranians may have forgotten about it, Riyadh rushed emergency assistance to the victims of the 26 December 2003 Bam earthquake that struck that hapless city and the surrounding Kerman province, which killed over 26,000. At the time, Iranian officials praised the aid provided by the Kingdom of Sa'udi Arabia, noting that the assistance was distinguished both in quality and quantity.[30]

The list of Sa'udi aid is long, and its pledges to assist various Arab countries, ranging from Lebanon—before, during, and after its civil war—to Egypt, speak for themselves. Billions were given to the Palestinian people too as the latter survived and continue to oppose Israeli occupation. Contributions to various UN organizations like the UN Relief and Works Agency that looks after Palestinian refugees and the UNHCR that now devotes attention to Syrian refugees throughout the region, should also be added to the tally. Similar aid was disbursed through the League of Arab States as well as the Organization of Islamic Cooperation. Lest one overlook it, and though few seem to take notice, the Kingdom has welcomed around 2.5 million Syrians since the beginning of the conflict in that hapless country in 2011, discussed in detail in Chapter 8. Yet, because Riyadh chose not to treat them as refugees or place them in refugee camps—and this was important enough to repeat, all were granted the freedom to move about the country, remain in the Kingdom if so they wished, with "legal residency status," or move to third countries like Turkey and Jordan—erroneous accusations were lobbed against it. Negligent reportage concluded that Sa'udi Arabia refused to provide assistance to Syrians. Few took notice that a 2012 royal decree instructed public schools to accept Syrian students gratis, where at least 100,000 were enrolled in 2015–2016.[31]

Given this plethora of assistance, for development projects, humanitarian assistance after natural disasters, and for refugees inside and outside of the Kingdom, it is important to provide an assessment of the billions of dollars in aid that Sa'udi Arabia allocated over the years, aware that world powers engage in organized rivalries with the single goal of advancing each donor state's interests. What follows is first an examination of the country's overall foreign aid before and after 1973, before discussing various funds and mechanisms involved, with appropriate charts of foreign aid [for the 1975 to 2020 periods], which analyze favorite recipients. This section is followed by an evaluation of the obligations that Riyadh identified for itself as the Custodian of the two Holy Mosques, and how it perceives its sacred duty to highlight ODA and humanitarian assistance initiatives.

Sa'udi Foreign Aid Before and After 1973

Although Western sources insisted that Arab foreign aid in general and Sa'udi assistance in particular were negligible before the quadrupling of oil prices in the aftermath of the 1973 October Arab–Israeli War and the 1974 hikes, in reality, generous disbursements began in the early 1960s.[32] Far more important was the establishment of the Organization of the Petroleum Exporting Countries Fund for International Development in 1976, barely 16 years after OPEC was formed in 1960 and about a decade after it moved its headquarters from Baghdad, Iraq, to Geneva, Switzerland, and eventually to Vienna, Austria in 1965. The OPEC Fund played a critical role in extending concrete and effective assistance to needy countries that were affected by the two oil price increases in 1973 and 1974 and, once again, after the outbreak of the Iranian Revolution in 1979. It was at the Algiers Summit of Heads of State and Government in 1975 that OPEC member-states addressed the plight of those developing states and "called for a new era of cooperation in international relations, in the interests of world economic development and stability."[33] The focus was on development assistance to channel large resources that could not possibly be absorbed by Gulf societies that were slowly emerging from the spiritedness of dramatic financial windfalls. Significant aid was also allocated to Palestinian refugees in front-line states.[34]

What occurred after 1973 was nothing if not dramatic as Arab donors—predominantly the Kingdom of Sa'udi Arabia, Kuwait and the United Arab Emirates—became the most generous benefactors in the world, with official development assistance (ODA) averaging 1.5 percent of their combined Gross National Income (GNI) during the period 1973–2008, more than twice the United Nations target of 0.7 percent and five times the average of the OECD–DAC countries. For the 1973–2008 period, Arab ODA accounted for 13 percent of total DAC ODA on average, and nearly three-quarters of non-DAC ODA that, to say the least, was extraordinary. The share of Arab ODA in Arab GNI was exceptionally high in the 1970s and early 1980s, peaking at over 12 percent for the UAE and at about 8.5 percent for Kuwait and Sa'udi Arabia in 1973.[35] Thus, nearly one-third of all ODA during the 1970s was from Arab donors, and while the ratio fell when oil prices collapsed in the mid-1980s, Riyadh and its Arab Gulf allies exceeded on average OECD-DAC member countries in distributing generous global assistance to needy states even during this period. Moreover, and unlike most OECD aid, which was and remained tied to specific expenditures in donor countries, Arab aid was—and generally is—untied. Often, indeed in most instances, Arab aid was and is offered without any conditions or restrictions.

It is important to note that while critics of Arab countries routinely allege that Arab aid was predominantly allocated to Muslim countries, the reach went beyond Arab and Muslim countries in terms of recipient countries. There were, of course, generous grants given to Egypt, Jordan, Lebanon and others, though Arab donors recorded significant firsts with the establishment of several specialized financial institutions that provided development assistance to non-Arab and non-Muslim low-income countries. The assistance that went through these institutions, and which increased substantially, by some estimates over 4.4 percent per year in real terms over the period 1990–2008, was what truly marked Arab aid. These institutional initiatives supplemented government-to-government assistance that was privileged for political reasons though foreign aid was not as politicized as critics assumed.[36]

In addition to the specialized financial institutions stated above, and starting in the 1960s, Arab donors created five regional funds: the Arab Fund for Economic and Social Development (AFESD), the Arab Bank for Economic Development in Africa (BADEA), the Islamic Development Bank (IsDB), the Arab Monetary Fund (AMF), and the OPEC Fund for International Development (OFID). Although the IsDB and OFID included non-Arab members, the largest country that provided the heftiest share of their funding was Sa'udi Arabia. At the United Nations, the Arab Gulf Programme for United Nations Development Organizations (AGFUND) "played a special role in financing technical cooperation and humanitarian assistance through its support for specialized UN agencies" too, which stood as one of the most valuable of such agencies.[37] To their credit, and except for the AGFUND, most of these agencies financed their operations primarily from capital subscriptions and loan reflows.

According to a reliable World Bank report, Sa'udi Arabia ranked as the Arab Gulf donor country "accounting for almost two-thirds of total

Arab ODA. . . . [In fact,] between 1973 and 2008, 64 percent of total Arab ODA was provided" by Riyadh—the majority on highly concessionary terms. It is important to repeat that the Kingdom played a vital role in supporting Arab funds and multilateral development banks by guaranteeing capital increases on a regular basis. It pledged its own resources, and encouraged the leading funds identified above to introduce new facilities such as "private sector development and trade financing windows." In the 1970s, Riyadh provided US$ 66.6 billion (in 2007 prices) in foreign assistance, equivalent to 5.4 percent of GNI. While Sa'udi ODA declined to 2.6 percent of GNI during the 1980s because of a drop in oil prices, total aid volumes reached US$ 74.4 billion. It was only after the costly 1990–1991 War for Kuwait that Sa'udi ODA declined to US$ 11.6 billion, or 0.6 percent of GNI, though substantial increases in oil prices after 2002 recorded jumps in Sa'udi aid in absolute and relative terms as a proportion of national income.[38] In other words, Riyadh practiced its *zakat* (alms giving) obligations rather assiduously, and provided a percentage of its income in assistance, both for development as well as humanitarian needs whenever its income justified it.

Finally, it may be useful to underscore that Arab financial assistance reached a wide range of countries in addition to lower-income Arab states, bearing in mind that there were 57 Muslim-majority countries in the world nestled within the Organization of Islamic Cooperation and 22 Arab countries that are part of the League of Arab States. Indeed, in 2020, OFID had the widest coverage (135 countries), followed by the Kuwait Fund for Arab Economic Development (KFAED) (107), the Sa'udi Fund for Development (SFD) (71), the Islamic Development Bank (IsDB) (56), and the Abu Dhabi Fund for Development (ADFD) (49). The case of IsDB illustrates the growing global reach of Arab financial institutions, having expanded from 22 member countries in 1975, to 57 by 2020.[39] Brief discussions of two organizations will highlight their development and humanitarian assistance over the years. Again, the purpose of these brief sketches is to illustrate the amount of aid that Sa'udi Arabia disburses year-in and year-out, oblivious to most commentators.

The Sa'udi Fund for Development

The Sa'udi Fund for Development (SFD) saw light by virtue of Royal Decree No. M/48, issued on 1 September 1974, and commenced operations on 3 January 1975. As defined by its charter, the Fund's main objectives includes financing development projects in developing countries through loans, technical aids as necessary, and institutional support and financing as well as guaranteeing the national non-crude oil exports of recipients. While the Fund's initial capital of ten billion Sa'udi Riyals (approximately US$ 2.8 billion) was quickly provided by the government, this figure reached SR 31 billion (US$ 8.2 billion) at the end of 2018, a significant jump that the government assumed without fuss. SFD's lending terms were concessional, with an average interest rate of 2 percent, a repayment period of 20–30 years, and a grace period of five to ten years. The grant element of SFD assistance was estimated by SFD itself to be around 60 percent—very generous terms indeed.

As reported by the Fund, from its inception in 1975 and up to the end of 2018, the SDF financed 688 development loans with a total amount of SR 62 billion or about US$ 16.53 billion (see Graph 4.1). A total of 656 development projects and programs were financed in 83 countries worldwide over four decades. In 2019, two additional agreements were signed with the International Development Association for SR 905 m (US$ 241 m), and 714 loan agreements were provided to several countries in Africa and Asia.[40] The SDF's development policy focused on the poorest and least developed countries, concentrating on Africa, where it contributed to the financing of 373 development projects and programs with a total amount of SR 28 billion; and in Asia with 242 projects and programs in 29 countries for a total amount of SR 24 billion. Elsewhere, the Fund contributed to the financing of 20 development projects and programs totaling SR 15 billion in eight countries, as illustrated in Graph 4.2(page 108). It also entered into alliance with other donors to ensure that mega-projects were executed in what were known as "Cumulative Co-financing" initiatives. Until the end of 2017, the total number of such loan agreements stood at 400 accords that were estimated to cost SR 32,952.65 million, representing 59.86% of the total amounts of all signed loan agreements, as illustrated in Table 4.4.

Table 4.4
SDF Programs and Cumulative Co-financing, 1975–2019

Region	Signed Loans No.	Signed Loans Amount (SR)	Co-Financed Loans No.	Co-Financed Loans Amount (SR)	Percentage of Co-Financed Loans Amount of the Total Signed Loans for Each Region
Africa	420	381128	278	19450	50.58
Asia	271	27014	134	14932	55.28
Other Regions	21	1547	8	526	34.01
Total	714	67595	420	34909	51.64

Source: Saudi Fund for Development, Annual Report 2019, p. 52.

Graph 4.1
SDF Projects and Programs, 1975–2018

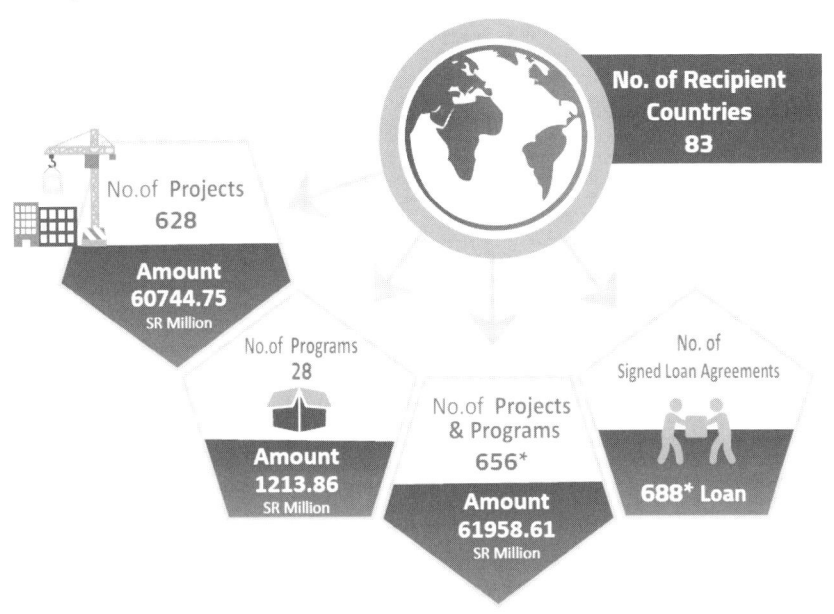

- No. of Recipient Countries: 83
- No. of Projects: 628
- Amount: 60744.75 SR Million
- No. of Programs: 28
- Amount: 1213.86 SR Million
- No. of Projects & Programs: 656*
- Amount: 61958.61 SR Million
- No. of Signed Loan Agreements: 688* Loan

Note: * The reason that the number of signed loan agreements exceeds that of programs and projects is that some projects received more than one loan.
Source: Saudi Fund for Development, at https://www.sfd.gov.sa/en/web/guest/cumulative-activity
See also *Annual Report 2019*, at https://www.sfd.gov.sa/en/web/guest/publications/-/asset_publisher/

In addition to its own donations, SFD administered on behalf of the government various loans and grants to developing countries that totaled US$ 6.7 billion on 1 January 2018, an amount that included US$ 569 million of rescheduled loans and US$ 6.1 billion in grants. Remarkably, the financial assistance provided by the SFD represented a fraction of the total assistance offered by the Government of Sa'udi Arabia, estimated by a recent United Nations report to amount to US$ 90 billion. Approximately one-fifth of this sum was channeled through bilateral funds and Arab multilateral organizations. According to the United Nations Development Program's Millennium Development Goals (MDGs), "Saudi Arabia alone provided over $100 billion [in ODA] to almost 90 countries since the 1970s."[41]

King Salman Center for Humanitarian Relief and Works

Inaugurated in May 2015 under the high patronage of the Custodian of the Two Holy Mosques, King Salman bin 'Abdul 'Aziz, the King Salman

Table 4.5
King Salman Humanitarian Aid and Relief Centre Beneficiary Countries, 2015–2020

Countries	Continent	Number of Projects	Costs (US$)
Yemen	Asia	575	3,465,763,446
Palestine	Asia	94	363,112,732
Syria	Asia	236	304,725,378
Somalia	Africa	57	202,212,059
Multiple Countries	Asia	19	147,169,037
Pakistan	Asia	118	123,436,256
Indonesia	Asia	29	71,672,620
Lebanon	Asia	40	31,789,757
Iraq	Asia	14	30,411,181
Afghanistan	Asia	36	24,240,579
Myanmar	Asia	18	19,402,867
Sudan	Africa	26	15,331,381
Sri Lanka	Asia	8	13,567,525
Tajikistan	Asia	18	11,640,332
Nigeria	Africa	17	11,457,062
Mauritius	Africa	4	10,523,466
Jordan	Asia	14	8,9480,898
Bangladesh	Asia	19	8,310,312
Niger	Africa	11	7,690,945
Mauritania	Africa	13	5,367,686
Burkina Faso	Africa	9	5,274,217
Ethiopia	Africa	11	5,081,534
China	Asia	1	4,978,371
Maldives	Asia	8	4,866,412
Honduras	America	5	4,650,037
Algeria	Africa	5	4,479,205
Djibouti	Africa	12	4,033,227
Nicaragua	America	5	3,622,633
Tanzania	Africa	13	3,506,734
Kazakhstan	Asia	1	3,400,000
Chad	Africa	8	2,665,095
Zambia	Africa	4	2,006,117
Cameroun	Africa	9	1,920,831
Benin	Africa	10	1,324,294
Philippines	Asia	8	1,290,801
Albania	Europe	7	985,101
Thailand	Asia	2	983,125
Senegal	Africa	6	914,015
Kenya	Africa	3	888,853
Kyrgyzstan	Asia	1	805,509
Comoros	Africa	6	607,796
Ghana	Africa	5	529,663
Gambia	Africa	5	529,663

Table 4.5 (*continued*)
King Salman Humanitarian Aid and Relief Centre Beneficiary Countries, 2015–2020

Countries	Continent	Number of Projects	Costs (US$)
Burundi	Africa	2	522,880
Madagascar	Africa	2	482,880
Japan	Asia	1	400,000
Mali	Africa	1	385,000
Morocco	Africa	3	357,525
South Sudan	Africa	2	247,390
Sierra Leone	Africa	1	237,333
Guinea	Africa	1	205,067
India	Asia	1	200,000
Eritrea	Africa	3	177,333
Nepal	Asia	1	108,640
Singapore	Asia	1	107,869
Mozambique	Africa	1	105,333
Congo	Africa	2	100,000
Gabon	Africa	2	100,000
Poland	Europe	1	100,000
Haiti	North America	1	52,800
Total		**1536**	**4,949,538,636**

Source: "General Statistics about KSrelief Projects (completed – ongoing) until 31 January 2021," at The King Salman Humanitarian Aid and Relief Centre (KSRelief) site, https://www.ksrelief.org/Statistics/ProjectStatistics#Countries

Center for Humanitarian Relief and Works (KSRelief) provided humanitarian aid and relief to those in need outside of the Kingdom. Between 2015 and 2020, KSRelief delivered such assistance to more than 59 countries spread over four continents. With international, regional and local partners in place, programs and initiatives that topped US$ 4.9 billion over the course of less than five years allowed millions to benefit from this unprecedented generosity (see Table 4.5). What KSRelief aimed for was to simply "become a leading center for relief and humanitarian activities and to transfer [Sa'udi] values to the world," and "to alleviate the suffering of people all over the world, especially victims of civil wars and natural calamities."

The Center distributed the bulk of all its financial aid with the support of international agencies, which ensured compliance with global norms. Dr. 'Abdallah al-Rabi'ah, an adviser at the royal court and general supervisor of KSRelief, maintained that the organization was instrumental in changing the perception of relief work in coordination with UN agencies, as it worked "to become a model for international relief work," focusing

Graph 4.2
Geographical Distribution of SDF Programs, 1975–2018

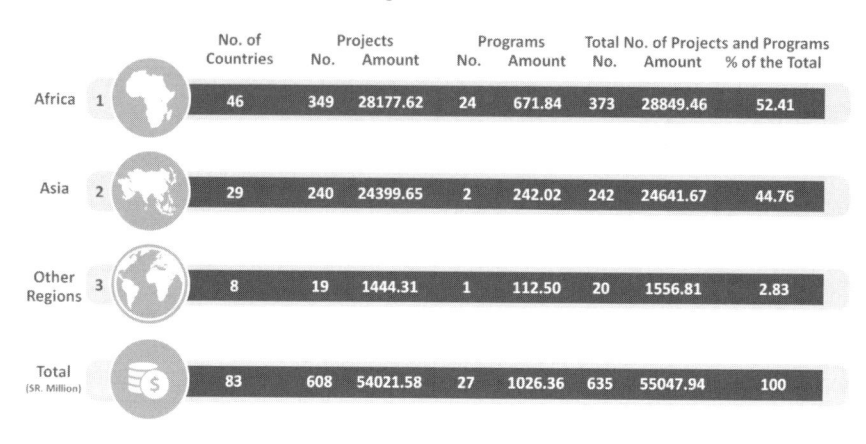

		No. of Countries	Projects No.	Projects Amount	Programs No.	Programs Amount	Total No. of Projects and Programs No.	Total Amount	% of the Total
Africa	1	46	349	28177.62	24	671.84	373	28849.46	52.41
Asia	2	29	240	24399.65	2	242.02	242	24641.67	44.76
Other Regions	3	8	19	1444.31	1	112.50	20	1556.81	2.83
Total (SR. Million)		83	608	54021.58	27	1026.36	635	55047.94	100

Source: Saudi Fund for Development, Annual Report 2017, p. 53.

on the victims of civil wars and natural calamities. What preoccupied the agency was to rush in food security, tent management, shelter, health services, safety, education and environmental protection as quickly as possible after a disaster occurred, though al-Rabi'ah further affirmed that the organization he led extended a helping hand "without any ulterior motives or vested interests" as KSRelief consulted and coordinated with international relief and humanitarian agencies that applied international standards.[42]

In addition to humanitarian assistance disbursed in the aftermath of natural or man-made disasters, KSRelief contributed emergency financial aid groups and individuals caught in the middle of regional crises. In 2018, for example, it allocated one million US$ to the United Nations Relief and Works Agency for Palestine Refugees in the Near East (UNRWA) to help provide urgently needed food assistance to Palestinian refugees in Syria. The UNRWA Commissioner-General, Pierre Krähenbühl, accepted the donation in Riyadh from Dr. Al-Rabi'ah, and expressed his "gratitude to the King Salman Center for Humanitarian Aid and Relief for this generous contribution [that ensured] that Palestine refugees affected by the devastating conflict in Syria feel they are not forgotten."[43] This emergency help came on top of regular Sa'udi assistance to UNRWA, as the Kingdom was the second-largest donor to the critical UN agency. Dr. Al-Rabi'ah confirmed that Riyadh "provided $6 billion in aid to the Palestinian people since 2000", including $263.17 million allocated to renovate or construct "housing units in Palestinian refugee camps in the West Bank, Gaza Strip" and, both the Ayn al-Hilwih as well as Nahr al-Barid camps in Lebanon.[44] In mid-2019, the UN High Commissioner for Refugees (UNHCR) lauded Riyadh for its life-saving refugee aid programs throughout the world. The agency's regional representative to the Gulf Cooperation Council countries, Khaled Khalifa, praised the Kingdom's KSRelief for its useful efforts to help improve conditions for hundreds of thousands of refugees in Yemen, Syria and elsewhere.[45] The acknowledgement was but one example of the type of sustained assistance that the Kingdom delivered to those most in need. On 1 May 2020, an additional one million US$ was allocated to UNRWA to provide emergency equipment for Gaza patients affected by the Covid-19 virus pandemic.[46]

Humanitarian Assistance to Yemen

According to recent United Nations Financial Tracking Service (FTS) data, Sa'udi Arabia was ranked fourth among major world donors of humanitarian aid, including to refugees. In its year-end report for 2020, the FTS provided detailed descriptions of Sa'udi assistance in general and support to refugees with humanitarian relief and development assistance in particular. A total of US$ 651,851,681 funded 271 programs as illustrated in Graph 4.3.

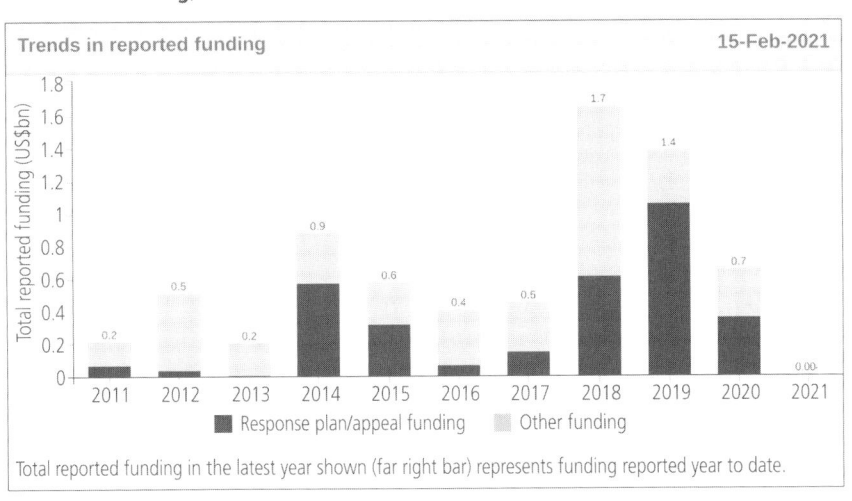

Graph 4.3
Sa'udi Aid Funding, 2009–2020

Source: UN, Financial Tracking Services at https://fts.unocha.org/donors/2998/summary/2020

Speaking at the United Nations in 2018, the assistant general supervisor for planning and development at the King Salman Center for Humanitarian Relief and Works (KSRelief), Dr. Aqeel Al-Ghamdi, declared that the Kingdom provided Rohingya refugees in Bangladesh and Malaysia with assistance amounting to $18.1 million, adding that 13 projects were also implemented for internally displaced persons in Myanmar through the International Organization for Migration (IOM). In addition, Riyadh provided $178.3 million to aid Syrian refugees in Jordan, $88.7 million for those in Turkey, $95.7 million in Lebanon, and another $219.6 million to Syrian refugees in Iraq, Egypt and elsewhere, within 198 humanitarian projects. The data further revealed that Sa'udi Arabia allocated $203.3 million to Jordan to assist Amman as it hosted hundreds of thousands of Syrian refugees.[47] In addition to these sums, the Kingdom provided $500 million to support the UN Humanitarian Response Plan for Yemen in 2018 alone. Of this amount $31 million was allocated to the UNHCR and $23.3 million to the IOM to provide assistance to internally displaced refugees and internally displaced persons. For the years 2019 and 2020, Riyadh allocated US$ 939,113,871 [104 projects] and US$431,964,665 [another 104 projects] in emergency aid, respectively, which were far more than any other donor-country.[48] In fact, the contribution of Sa'udi Arabia to Yemen since the beginning of the crisis in 2015, in humanitarian assistance, development and relief for the Yemeni people, amounted to US$ 11.18 billion in 2018 and US$ 16.92 billion in 2020.[49]

Other recipients included Palestine, for which the Kingdom has been one of the largest donors between 2000 and 2020, providing development, humanitarian and charitable assistance amounting to nearly US$ 6 billion. According to Al-Ghamdi, Somalia received US$ 202 million in assistance, carrying out 57 projects, on top of the US$ 10 million in grants to the UNHCR and IOM to repatriate Somali refugees from Yemen, to help resettle them when they returned. Riyadh allocated a further US$ 11 million for projects in Nigeria, where urgent humanitarian and relief projects were being implemented for displaced people, while in Pakistan, the Kingdom provided assistance amounting to US$ 123 million, implemented for 118 projects, for displaced people affected by floods and earthquakes between 2005 and 2020. Finally, in Afghanistan, Sa'udi Arabia provided assistance to 36 projects for displaced people worth $24 million.[50]

As discussed in Chapter 2, the Kingdom hosted 1.07 million refugees [563,911 of whom were Yemenis, 262,573 Syrians and 249,669 Burmese Rohingyas], representing 5.26 percent of the total number of Sa'udi residents in 2020, a figure seldom reported in global news outlets. It is worth repeating that these refugees exercised the right to residence, mobility and had access to education, health and work, on an equal footing with Saʿudi citizens, notwithstanding occasional mishaps that, unfortunately, made the news that categorized Riyadh as a negligent power when it came to its treatment of refugees. To remedy this missing link, Saʿudi authorities are working on a comprehensive database using internationally recognized standards to record and monitor refugee data within the country, though this effort was still in progress in early 2021. Still, the King Salman Humanitarian Aid and Relief Center's up-to-date bulletins highlight that the Saʿudi relief organization has sponsored numerous projects in cooperation with global, regional, and local partners to assist refugees, including Yemenis, whose fate is discussed in detail in Chapter 7.[51] Notwithstanding the ongoing war's devastation, Riyadh committed significant humanitarian assistance, precisely to relieve human suffering as much as possible, while it also absorbed the consequences of the devastating missile attacks on its own cities.

In addition to the Yemen, attention was also devoted to the Sudan, a country that experienced civil war too. Speaking at a meeting of donors at the UN Office for the Coordination of Humanitarian Affairs (OCHA) in Geneva on 2 May 2019, Dr. Aqeel bin Jumban Al-Ghamdi reiterated that Saʿudi Arabia's multi-billion-dollar relief work reflected the country's commitments to those in need, most recently in the Sudan, which received aid totaling $3 billion, including $500 million provided by the Kingdom and the United Arab Emirates, deposited in the Central Bank of Sudan to strengthen its financial status, reduce pressures on the Sudanese pound and achieve greater stability of the exchange rate.[52] The remaining balance of US$ 2.5 billion was allocated to urgent food, medicine and fuel-derivative needs of the Sudanese people.

Conclusion: Aid as Religious Obligation

Saʿudi Arabia, which was by far the largest non-Western global humanitarian donor, has contributed more humanitarian aid than many established donors over the course of the past few decades. Importantly, the Kingdom ranked between Germany and Switzerland on the United Nations Office for the Coordination of Humanitarian Affairs (OCHA) Financial Tracking Services ranking year-in and year-out, which placed it in good company. Between 2015 and 2020 Riyadh disbursed US$ 1.3 billion for humanitarian aid, of which US$ 500 million went to the World Food Program food crisis appeal, while another US$ 70 million was channeled through the Saudi Red Crescent Society. As discussed in this chapter, generous contributions were made to various refugee communities, along with substantial development assistance that added value where it was needed most in several African and Asian countries.

Sa'udi monarchs take their title "Khadim al-Haramayn al-Sharifyan" [Custodian of the Two Holy Places (Makkah and Madinah)] seriously. This title goes back to the time of Saladin. The Al Sa'ud pay particular attention to their leadership roles both as far as the annual pilgrimage is concerned and the assistance that those entrusted with authority owe to their subjects.[53] In fact, the title specifically refers to a ruler who took his responsibilities to guard and maintain the two holiest mosques in the Muslim World (the Masjid al-Haram [The Great Mosque] in Makkah and the Masjid al-Nabawih [The Prophet's Mosque] in Madinah), with utmost care. The "Amir al-Mu'minin" [Commander of the Faithful], bearer of the title, incurred additional responsibilities, much more than that of a protector (though it should be pointed out that some Muslims used the title in military campaigns). Indeed, the Second Caliph 'Umar ibn al-Khattab (586–644), for example, probably used it as a form of obedience on the basis of the Qur'anic verse: "Obey God and obey the Apostle and those invested with command (*wali al-amr*) among you" [4:59].

Inasmuch as various precedents compelled the Custodian of the Two Holy Mosques with essential duties, such a guardian of the community of believers was also supposed to be just—with all that the term applied—and, in his capacity as the leader of his population, particularly generous. Justice ['*adalah*] and generosity [*takrim*] are critical concepts in Islam and play key roles in Muslim societies as leaders are invited to be ideal paradigms for all believers. Both must be understood in their socio-religious contexts and, for our purposes, justice and generosity were and are fundamental ingredients for those who wish to assist those in need.

Succinctly stated then, justice is a central theme in the Holy Scriptures, dictating a variety of laws and the regulations that were devised over the centuries, as rulers put these norms into practice. Of course, justice must first and foremost be understood as a legal concept, but one must also underscore its divine connotation. With respect to the law, the Holy Qur'an instructs Muslims on how to conduct themselves, especially with respect to intra-communal ties. It states what the various punishments for specific crimes should be, along with the justification behind this reasoning, all in clearly defined narratives. Furthermore, the Qur'an brings across the idea that anyone who propagates the message of justice and acts accordingly will be justly rewarded in heaven. Scholars debate and continue to struggle with the concept of divine justice, and whether different peoples will enjoy the same recompenses. Since the Lord cannot but dispense justice in impeccable fashion, many wondered what might befall non-Muslims, and whether they may also be entitled to divine justice. Naturally, and as recorded in the Holy Qur'an, the Lord would clearly reward the good deeds of all humans [2:62, 5:69, 22:17]. God loves justice for all and calls on believers to be just with each other; this places a special burden on those with earthly responsibilities to do good towards those less fortunate.[54]

Indeed, the call to be generous was not only the result of moral duties towards the Creator, but to also reject treachery, cruelty or corruption. Man is inherently endowed with specific moral standards, which are universal and, in the case of Islam, a fundamental obligation. The Prophet himself taught Muslims to adopt the best of manners and apply high personal characteristics. As God said in the Qur'an:

وَإِنَّكَ لَعَلَىٰ خُلُقٍ عَظِيمٍ ۝

"And indeed, you are of a great moral character" (68:4)

Consequently, generosity was among the countless good qualities of the Prophet, who practiced what he preached. He often reminded his companions that worldly possessions were bounties from God, which ought to be shared. Islam thus encourages generosity—a voluntary inclination to give freely—and embedded the concept as one of its Five Pillars, the obligatory charity known as *zakat* [alms giving]. In Arabic, *zakat* literally means purification of the heart, but in more mundane terminology it also means the payment of a certain percentage of our earnings to charity precisely to provide for all the needy members of a community. As discussed in the first section of this chapter, the other form of generosity in Islam, *sadaqah*, posited that one has to be truthful toward one's Creator, and that anything donated generously with the intention of pleasing God, qualifies. Therefore, it is essential for the just Muslim leader to also be generous, because this was what the Lord intends and guided believers to adhere to.

قُلْ إِنَّ رَبِّي يَبْسُطُ الرِّزْقَ لِمَن يَشَاءُ مِنْ عِبَادِهِ وَيَقْدِرُ لَهُ وَمَا أَنفَقْتُم مِّن شَيْءٍ فَهُوَ يُخْلِفُهُ ۖ وَهُوَ خَيْرُ الرَّازِقِينَ ۝

"Say, Indeed, my Lord extends provision for whom He wills of His servants and restricts [it] for him. But whatever thing you spend [in His cause]—He will compensate it; and He is the best of providers" (34:39)

There are many similar examples that describe acts of justice and generosity that stand as role models in Islam, all of which reinforce duties and responsibilities, and which underline the fundamentals of supporting those in need. It was this outlook that motivated and continues to inspire the Custodian of the Two Holy Mosques as the Kingdom extends its generous hand around the world. Riyadh disbursed modest assistance when circumstances did not allow for larger compensations, but increased its share of assistance when the bounty it harvested permitted it. True believers in the Almighty, the Scriptures advanced, are able to be just and generous because they know that God will reward their just behavior and generosity. Indeed, the Qur'an states:

۞ لَيْسَ عَلَيْكَ هُدَاهُمْ وَلَـٰكِنَّ اللَّهَ يَهْدِى مَن يَشَاءُ
وَمَا تُنفِقُوا مِنْ خَيْرٍ فَلِأَنفُسِكُمْ
وَمَا تُنفِقُونَ إِلَّا ابْتِغَاءَ وَجْهِ اللَّهِ
وَمَا تُنفِقُوا مِنْ خَيْرٍ يُوَفَّ إِلَيْكُمْ وَأَنتُمْ لَا تُظْلَمُونَ ۝

"Not upon you, [O Muhammad], is [responsibility for] their guidance, but Allah [God] guides whom He wills. And whatever good you [believers] spend is for yourselves, and you do not spend except seeking the countenance of Allah. And whatever you spend of good—it will be fully repaid to you, and you will not be wronged" (2:272)

Economic and humanitarian assistance are thus part and parcel of the Sa'udi ethos as individuals assume their fair share of responsibilities through alms giving. For its part, the state, through its designated authorities, were called upon to extend a helping hand to Muslims and non-Muslims alike. Often, these deeds were overlooked, sometimes misunderstood, and, in specific circumstances derided because of misinterpretations and confusing explanations advanced by those who failed to acknowledge how the concepts of justice and generosity marked the norms applied by Sa'udi Arabia. Nevertheless, the record indicates, nevertheless, that the Kingdom of Sa'udi Arabia was motivated by a higher calling to fulfill its religious and socio-economic duties. The record further illustrates that Riyadh disbursed very large sums in foreign assistance to those most in need, be they refugees or those who suffered traumatic events, and did so without any expectation in return. Naturally, a slight preference was displayed towards those who required aid in the

Arab and Muslim worlds, as various examples illustrate but it would be inaccurate to conclude that this generosity only favored Arabs and Muslims. Assistance was given to Africans, Asians and even Europeans and Americans as conditions necessitated. What this altruism displayed was recognition of the roles Saʻudis perceived for themselves, the humanity of their deeds, and the acceptance of their duties towards the nations of the world.

CHAPTER
5
Pilgrimage and Migration Dilemmas
African Migrants and Sa'udi Arabia

As discussed in Chapter 2, specific references documented how the peoples and governments of the Kingdom behaved toward migrant workers and refugees in the past, driven by profound religious obligations that defined their behavior. Indeed, the commitments that Sa'udi Arabia exhibited during the most recent refugee crises on and around the Arabian Peninsula, which constituted the best examples of how the Kingdom fulfilled the Islamic principles of asylum, spoke volumes. Notwithstanding specific instances when some citizens failed to uphold their commitments to expatriate workers, Riyadh welcomed millions on its soil, most of whom earned decent wages and returned to their respective homes significantly enriched. Sa'udis thus remained true to their standards, despite the sudden shifts from a traditional commercial economy to an oil-based one in the 1930s, which dramatically changed the Kingdom as age-old social and economic lives were transformed. In less than two generations, the traditional nomadic society became a modernizing economic powerhouse, which upset those who believed that modernization would ruin intrinsic values.

Of course, while this economic boom led to a dramatic increase in Sa'udi living standards, it simultaneously created fresh needs for skilled and unskilled foreign workers. Migrant populations flocked to the Kingdom but, along with organized labor movements, Riyadh experienced new dilemmas as the numbers of unregulated visitors increased sharply after the mid-1970s. Regrettably, an entire category of illegals emerged, mostly pilgrims who deliberately chose to overstay their *hajj* [pilgrimage that must be performed during a ten-day period, starting on the first and ending on the tenth day of Dhu al-Hijjah, the twelfth and last month of the Islamic calendar] and *'umrah* [a shorter pilgrimage that can be undertaken at any time during the year] visas. In addition to these individuals, the number of illegal visitors increased as migrants were smuggled mostly through Yemen and/or via the Yemen chiefly from African countries. Finally, there were labor migrants who stayed after violating their work contracts, although many of the regulations that determined who worked where and under what circumstances were eased in 2021.

The purpose of this chapter is to examine how Sa'udi Arabia fulfilled its obligations towards migrants under Shari'ah Law. More specifically, it is necessary to investigate how illegals who taxed the system were treated too, which necessitated direct probes of their living conditions. Towards that end, discussion first assesses the dilemmas created by a near-open access to the holy cities of Makkah and Madinah for pilgrimage, which were relatively open cities to all Muslims. Despite strict precautions, and because the country welcomed Muslims on such a large scale, this was an open invitation throughout the year and not just for *hajj*. Indeed, authorities greeted millions of visitors each year, which represented a massive human presence that created logistical nightmares, with its share of incidents. Untold were the fate of a determined number of economic pilgrims who purposefully embarked on *hajj* with the intention of staying in the Kingdom instead of returning to their respective home countries. How did Sa'udi authorities handle violators of *hajj* or *'umrah* visas? Were there any amnesty initiatives to regularize the presence of such self-proclaimed "religious refugees" who took advantage of religion to stay in Sa'udi Arabia? What recourses did such individuals have when they were arrested and deported?

To better answer these questions, this chapter is divided into three distinct parts. First, it offers an assessment of predicaments associated with pilgrimage itself and, second, it delves into an evaluation of specific cases involving African nationals. Discussions of African migrants in Jiddah illustrate various quandaries that confronted decision-makers, though one should not infer that the experiences of a small sample in a single city represent the challenges that others may have faced, or continue to confront, elsewhere. Still, this type of quantitative research was new for the Kingdom and, beyond its rarity, the effort synthesized Sa'udi interests to examine thorny issues, which was also an innovation for social scientists working in the country. Importantly, this research effort confirmed that Riyadh experienced specific challenges with migrants/refugees, even if the phenomenon introduced policy complications while further straining the country's institutional capabilities. In the third part of the chapter, several key policy initiatives are analyzed, including amnesty proposals as well as the *nitaqat* [zoning] and deportation laws, to better identify lessons learned. The chapter closes with a measurement of pilgrimage problems, which Riyadh was entrusted within its capacity as the Custodian of the Two Holy Cities.

The fates that befell migrant workers were distinct from those that confronted refugees. For the purposes of this study, we shall discuss the topic in order to focus on how government officials justified specific policies. Of course, migrant workers were not refugees in the technical sense of the term, but their presence shaped perceptions of responsibility towards "others" in a traditional society with norms driven from religious practices. While the vast majority of migrants were in the country legally, a number took the law into their own hands, which taxed existing institutions. Even if most illegals fended for themselves, many relied on support mechanisms and local charities to survive. Conditions were poor for many who, more often than not, paid a heavy price for their choices. As authorities encountered numerous challenges that necessitated appropriate policies, Riyadh assumed additional burdens without reneging on society's religious obligations. This was easier said than done, though all of the steps conveyed in formulating policies became a learning process—itself a major accomplishment.

Annual Pilgrimage Dilemmas

As millions of pilgrims from around the world visited Makkah and Madinah each year, several critical developments were associated with the rituals that occupied visitors and hosts alike, often with serious socio-economic consequences that required attention. Although figures vary year by year, an estimated 2 to 3 million Muslims visited Sa'udi Arabia each pilgrimage season, even if the total numbers hovered between 4 and 6 million when year-long *'umrah* stays are included in the totals. As in the past, a number of guests chose to stay behind illegally, which was neither a new nor a recent phenomenon, but which saw spikes in the last few decades of the twentieth century. Regrettably, few studies have tackled this critical issue because the visitors did not enter, as clarified earlier, into the regular accounting of international institutional mechanisms, which meant that whatever occurred on the ground was often ignored or simply underestimated.[1]

Sa'udi Arabia in general, and the Jiddah port city in particular, experienced a massive flow of undocumented migrants during the past few decades, as the total number of pilgrims ballooned. This phenomenon was interesting because it involved migrants from different continents and countries, even if twelve communities were disproportionately represented: Africans (Ethiopians, Eritreans, Somalis, Sudanese, Chadians,

Nigerians, Burkinabes, Ghanaians, and Cameroonians), as well as Yemenis, Filipinos and Indonesians. Despite sharing the common experiences of living as undocumented migrants in the Kingdom, their relationships with members of their own communities, along with interactions with others within Saʻudi society at large, were as varied as their backgrounds. Moreover, and because Saʻudi Arabia was where the holy city of Makkah stood, most migrants perceived their presence in and around the city to have religious connotations. Consequently, a significant number of individuals who entered the country for *hajj* or *ʻumrah* purposes opted to stay beyond the period allowed to practice these religious rituals, which created undeniable dilemmas.

According to the fieldwork conducted in the city of Jiddah between 2007 and 2009 (see below), a number of migrants continued to live illegally in the city with no documents, and this necessitated attention.[2] While authorities were aware of their presence, and mainly for humanitarian reasons, many illegal migrants were allowed to stay, though most became a burden on society, taxed existing social institutions that extended a helping hand as required and, in specific instances, joined the criminal underworld. Unfortunately, accurate statistics on the number of pilgrims who have overstayed their visa permits, and the number of people deported during the past few years, proved very difficult to secure. Confidential interviews with senior Saʻudi government officials, along with the interviews conducted in Jiddah—discussed in the next section— provided an estimate of six million undocumented migrants in Saʻudi Arabia, with the greatest number concentrated in Jiddah, Makkah and Madinah. In fact, the number was probably over six million, with most of the undocumented living in the Western Province. Around two million were probably in Jiddah alone, a city considered a paradigm for the whole country. Because of its location and importance as the gateway to the holy cities of Makkah and Madinah, over time Jiddah has become one of the most important cities on the Red Sea with a prosperous port that has engaged in all types of trade activities, including the slave trade. These commercial activities enabled residents to develop the city as a trading hub and, over the course of its long history many merchants from different lands decided to migrate and establish their businesses in this growing city. Simultaneously, countless pilgrims, but also freed slaves, and visitors to the holy cities from different lands, settled in the Hijaz for religious, social, economic, or political reasons.[3]

As analyzed in the fieldwork conducted with a few dozen "religious refugees," several of the interviewees revealed that many of those who entered without documents stayed in Jiddah and that most of them (both female and male) were married to other undocumented migrants. In turn, migrant women gave birth to undocumented children, which further complicated matters even if the assumption seemed to be that these offspring would dissipate in the human melting pot. In fact, the sheer size of this major development over the course of several decades made it nearly impossible for the Sa'udi government to monitor the total number of those who were born in Jiddah or elsewhere throughout the country. While waves of migration made Jiddah's population culturally diverse—now one of the most cosmopolitan cities in the world with a population that included, along with its native Arab tribes, many migrant communities from the Muslim and non-Muslim worlds—the absence of specific laws to hinder the wish of any Muslim to live or settle close to the holy cities in the Hijaz region or to engage in commercial transactions as a laborer or merchant, meant that Riyadh's strict regulations, laws on migration, work permits and the overstaying of visas, were largely ineffective. Estimating the number of undocumented workers in Sa'udi Arabia resembled other cases, including situations in industrialized countries like the United States and the United Kingdom. For example, and as stated in a report published by the British House of Lords, similar concerns were identified rather well:

> "As is the case in most immigration countries, we know very little about the scale of undocumented immigration and undocumented employment of immigrants in the UK. According to Home Office estimates, there were about 430,000 migrants residing undocumented in the UK in 2001. This estimate comes with a number of caveats. Describing the difficulties with measuring undocumented immigration, Professor John Salt of University College London told us that 'no country in the world knows how many people there are who are living or working undocumented, with the probable exception of Australia where they count everybody in and they count everybody out'."[4]

Indeed, the United Kingdom encountered serious "undocumented" migration crises for years, which preoccupied successive governments, with no permanent solution.[5] Similar citations could just as easily be listed, including for the United States that, at last count, was home to an estimated eleven million illegals.[6]

Although not as extensive as leading Western countries, the Sa'udi government faced similar contests, as Riyadh published statistical material on the number of people arrested while attempting to enter the Kingdom; this information was made available to researchers who could then extrapolate from these figures more accurate estimates.[7] Information obtained in the course of several interviews with community leaders of the documented/undocumented migrants, as well as with imams of mosques, individuals who worked in mosques, local *umdas* (plural of *umda* or community leader), and many Sa'udi and some non-Sa'udis who lived or worked in the same districts, confirmed these hypotheses. Several interlocutors estimated that the figures were quite high based on their knowledge of local scenes and experiences within these communities. Senior government officials confirmed various estimates, but as with others involved in this investigation, they insisted on confidentiality and anonymity.

Inasmuch as the collected data, coupled with illegal immigration statistics, highlighted the complexities of the concerns that confronted authorities, the reluctance of the Sa'udi government to accept refugees is understandable. Likewise, Riyadh's commitments to tackle various crises confirmed that the problems caused in the last few decades—by the constant flux of illegal immigrants trying to enter a country with land borders running over thousands of kilometers—would literally overwhelm the authorities. By all accounts, borders on the Arabian Peninsula are extremely difficult to control and, despite the recent introduction of sophisticated security systems, including electrified fences, buried cable and microwave sensors, it was still possible for smugglers to engage in illegal crossings.[8] Interestingly, the data concerning undocumented African migrants in general and those involving Yemenis in particular (especially those who crossed the border from Yemen to Sa'udi Arabia without being apprehended by border guards), reflected a ratio of 1:6, which is high indeed.[9] Available data collected over a twenty-four year period, (i) 1977–1990, (ii) 1994–1997 and (iii) 2002–2007, illustrates both the high numbers of migrants arrested while attempting to smuggle themselves into the Kingdom, as well as their multiple nationalities. Moreover, the identity of different nationalities present in the Kingdom could now be narrowed down more accurately. By extrapolating data from arrested migrants, the number of illegal migrants present in the country could be clarified.

Worldwide, the distinction between illegal migrants and refugees in the twenty-first century is blurred. And Sa'udi Arabia is no exception in its struggle to dealing with waves of immigration. Like most societies, the Sa'udis confronted these dilemmas too, as officers evaluated the best methods or rationales to grant asylum. Just as Western societies calculated economic and/or humanitarian prerogatives, their Muslim counterparts confronted similar challenges, though all faced similar empirical limitations that forced governments to balance local needs with international obligations. Everyone relied on specific measures to cope with local, regional, and global demands and, in the case of Sa'udi Arabia, there was the added responsibility to welcome migrants on religious grounds. The presence of undocumented workers from different countries, coupled with an economy that was increasingly dependent on their skills, made it necessary for the state to intervene, which resulted in the adoption of specific laws intended to decrease various pressures within the society at large. Among these pressures were specific amnesty and deportation measures, which are analyzed below.

An Examination of the Methodology and Data Analysis

Through the testimonies of undocumented African migrants living in Jiddah, in particular Somalis, Ethiopians, Eritreans, Sudanese, Chadians, Nigerians, Burkinabés, Cameroonians and Ghanaians, what follows is an examination of the major social, economic and security consequences of their presence in the Kingdom, which sheds light on official perceptions.[10] To conduct a reliable search for the flow of migrants in and out of Jiddah, several qualitative methods were used, including collection of demographic information, an identification of actual migration processes, an analysis of familial and social ties, an assembly of legal and work issues related to their work in Sa'udi Arabia, and an investigation into the personal plans many of the migrants harbored for the future. A focus group and face-to-face semi-structured anonymous interview questionnaires were distributed with closed and open-ended probing questions too. Data were gathered from migrants while they were neither under arrest nor under any threat of arrest, living and working in the city. In this regard, all interviewees felt comfortable to answer questions without fear because the researcher pledged to treat responses about their real-life experiences in the city as undocumented migrants, in full confidentiality. Using the snowball sampling technique,[11] 61 female and male African labor migrants were interviewed, all living in Jiddah. Interviewees hailed from nine different African countries based on one or more of the following criteria:

1. Subjects entered the country without obtaining an official visa [for example they were smuggled into Sa'udi Arabia by land or by sea];
2. Migrants entered the country legally with *'umrah* or *hajj* visas, but overstayed;
3. Individuals entered the Kingdom legally with an appropriate work permit visa, but left the Sa'udi employers with full consent, and
4. Parties who were born in the city to undocumented parents.

The interviewees agreed to talk in detail about their working conditions as illegal migrants. Each interviewee's confidentiality was protected and careful steps were taken not to break standard norms and rules of professional fieldwork ethics. Moreover, this investigation relied on informants, or gatekeepers, to secure access to undocumented migrants, individuals that were and are trusted and respected members of the different communities. Several were former undocumented migrants themselves who evolved into "advisors and facilitators" in order to establish contact with various communities. To gain better insights into conditions confronted by various migrant communities, the researcher first concentrated on the semi-focus group, before turning to the actual processes of migration, and the methods used to enter the Kingdom.

Approaching the African community as a Sa'udi was not easy and the interviewer had to rely on the collaboration and support of gatekeepers and community leaders to gain this rare access. Due to the importance of the district of *Karantina*, the researcher, with the help of several gatekeepers, was able to organize a focus group in the district. However, during the investigation, the opportunity arose for an unplanned meeting in the house of a Nigerian community leader as well. Many elderly leaders and young men from different communities were present. The older gatekeeper, who was from the Sudan, introduced the investigator to them as someone who is a social science researcher with no government association and who was interested in studying their attitudes, perceptions and views on the city of Jiddah, including the difficulties they faced or continued to confront. There were different African nationalities present in that room. Many spoke clear Arabic with distinctive accents; quite a few had only a moderate ability to communicate in Arabic, but could discuss their concerns through a friend or a relative present in the chamber. At least five of them remained silent, though one could clearly see hardships on their tired faces.

In that unplanned, spontaneous meeting with the undocumented African migrants, the majority seemed relaxed and amused at the fact that a native Sa'udi was curious about important issues that surrounded their near-anonymous lives. The researcher avoided asking personal questions concerning names, addresses and legal statuses, though he was fortunate enough to be able to solicit considerable information about their lives in Jiddah, their plans and their expectations from Sa'udi authorities. All of those present at this gathering were anxious to tell their stories. They spoke of the fact that many of them loved Jiddah either because it was close to the holy cities of Makkah and Madinah, or because they were born in Jiddah, spoke Arabic, and had spent all or most of their lives in the city. Others mentioned that they had no chance of survival in their respective countries of origin, if deported, and complained about the lack of government support in terms of free public health care, schooling for their children, and the constant threat to their daily survival. In this regard, as undocumented migrants who did not have residency permits, or *iqamah*s (plural of *iqamah*), all faced restricted access to medical care and other services and several noted that they had to pay more for medical treatment than Sa'udi citizens. This was because the law restricted access to these services except for people who could show valid identification papers. When the researcher enquired about their young children's' education, they revealed that they had a small unregulated private school in *Karantina* that taught the Qur'an to local youngsters.

Most of those present wished to legalize their statuses. As holders of a valid *iqamah* they would be able to easily access government services, work, drive through the city with their families, and rent homes without violating city laws. This unplanned meeting was important for singling out some of the different themes that the researcher would later develop in the semi-structured interviews with individual immigrants from sixty-one individuals through the interview questionnaire.[12]

The Migration Processes

Historically, the close geographical proximity of Jiddah to the Horn of Africa, and the relatively cheap cost of the journey, almost always constituted a great opportunity for labor migrants. As noted previously, four types of undocumented migrants in Jiddah were identified, to which we turn next. Besides the statistical data this research aimed at reporting the real experiences of the different categories of migrants introduced above. These included:

Smuggling

Out of the 61 respondents from the African communities who were interviewed, 21 (34%) were smuggled into Jiddah, best illustrated by harrowing testimonies. One interviewee, a woman from Ethiopia, noted that the first time she came to Jiddah was with an *'umrah* visa when she was nineteen years old. She worked in Riyadh for four years without documents, was arrested by the *Jawazat* (Sa'udi Office of Passports and Naturalization) and deported to Addis Ababa after spending eight months in jail. Despite the deportation, she decided to return, the second time as a "smuggled" subject. She narrated her experiences in the following terms:

"I woke up at noon on a Friday, put on my clothes and took some food like water and biscuits. I went to a meeting place near a mountain where I met 10 men. There were wild animals, and the men had knives for defense. We walked through the mountains until dawn. We slept in the open all morning until sunset, and then we continued walking. We had a leader from Djibouti to guide us.

We were tired and at times we had short rides on cars and after four days, we reached Djibouti. We arrived there very early in the morning. I wore men's clothing, and I entered the mosque with the other men. My brother and cousin and the other men prayed at the mosque and stayed there until the next morning to avoid thieves. We stayed in a small hotel, and after we ran out of money, we asked our parents to send us some. We paid the money to the captain of a big boat. We were about 170 men and women from different nationalities. After ten hours, we met a huge storm and many drowned, and we stopped on an island.

We stayed two days there without food and water. Two days later, another boat arrived on the island. One hundred and eighty of us went on board. We stayed at sea for 32 hours and reached Yemen. Once we reached the shore everyone left the boat except me because I had problems moving my legs because I had been tied to the boat for many hours in order to avoid falling overboard because of the high waves. My brother and cousin helped me. I almost drowned. We went into a Yemeni farm that had a tent, and we stayed there two days after paying for food and water. Each of us later paid a Yemeni man $100 to drive us to Samta near the Sa'udi border. It was night time when we arrived in Samta; we walked and dragged ourselves on our stomachs on the ground for four hours to avoid border guards. After 4 hours, we met a Sa'udi smuggler who took $160 from each of us to transport us to Jazan. On the road, the Sa'udi man gave me and the other men 'abayas ['abaya is a simple, loose over-garment, a robe-like dress, worn by Sa'udi women] and a niqab (a garment of clothing that covers the face which is worn by conservative Sa'udi women) and gloves to hide ourselves from the police. We arrived in our cousin's flat in Jazan. He is a documented car driver. We stayed there for seven days. We went to a private hospital for medical treatment. My cousin found me a job as a house maid for $267. I stayed in this job for two months."[13]

Another interviewee, this one from Eritrea, was smuggled into Yemen via the Red Sea on a fishing boat with 210 other migrants from different nationalities. Forty were women, and 170 were men. They sailed for

36 hours. Once on the Yemeni seashore, all of them went into different directions. He and two other couples tried to reach the Sa'udi border. He walked for two days without water. He decided to leave the group but lost his way. After two days, he saw two bodies of his earlier companions who had died in the desert. He managed to reach the border and walked all the way to Jiddah.

According to several interviewees, the majority of African undocumented migrants were exploited by security officials who demanded large sums of money once they reached Yemen. Regrettably, migrants had to pay $100 each to police officers after reporting to specific stations, for undetermined fees. This, on top of the amount of money each of them had to pay for the Red Sea crossing. A few women were raped though many female migrants wore men's clothes to hide their gender. Reportedly, their exploitation did not end there, but continued until they reached their destinations in Jiddah. Despite these hardships, and while Sa'udi border authorities have invested in trying to fight undocumented migration, smugglers resorted to creative ways that represented great challenges to all concerned. It should be noted that the length of the land border between Yemen and Sa'udi Arabia posed significant challenges even before the 2015 War started, and included land trails through rough terrain.

In response to the probing question about the cost of smuggling paid by individual interviewees, it seems that "smugglers' fees" varied according to the starting point, but overall, they rose dramatically during recent years. For border crossings such as from the Yemen into the Kingdom of Sa'udi Arabia, Yemeni-Sa'udi smugglers charged an individual migrant between $160 and $533 during the first decade of the twenty-first century. Fees increased more recently simply because all crossings became far more dangerous, amid the chaos of war.[14] Many interviewees noted that the smugglers were knowledgeable about different routes, so they could avoid Sa'udi border guards, though being caught created fresh hardships.

Overstaying an 'Umrah or Hajj Visa

Out of the sixty-one individuals interviewed from various African communities, 23 (38%), overstayed their *hajj* or *'umrah* visas, which was an important category in the migration process. One interviewee from Eritrea told the following story:

> "Twenty-nine years ago, my father came with a *'umrah* visa and later found a *kafil* [guardian employer] who allowed him to bring his wife

[our mother] on a *'umrah* visa and to bring me when I was two years old, together with my older brother and sister. While living in Jiddah, my parents had four more boys and two more girls. My father lost his job and became undocumented. He was arrested and deported 18 years ago. My father lives in Eritrea, he remarried and never tried to come back. My siblings and I were able to attend school in the past because no one asked for documents, but my younger brothers and sisters could not go to school. They all began working at a young age as beggars. When they became older, the males worked in manual jobs and the females, including our mother, worked as housemaids."[15]

An interviewee from Chad said that he came for *hajj* when he was five years old. His parents did not need a visa when they arrived over 50 years ago. He travelled with his family using primitive transportation, a combination of walking and lifts on big trucks directed from Chad to Sudan, Egypt and Jiddah.

Breaking a Work Contract

In the sample, only six (10%) migrants arrived with a work visa and, in the words of an educated undocumented Chadian migrant:

"Most uneducated immigrants from Chad work as car washers or are in some other form of manual labor. Smart and educated Chadians do not smuggle themselves into Jiddah, instead they save or borrow enough money to pay for a *hajj* visa or, if possible, a work visa in order to reach Jiddah. Once in the city, a job as a car washer is a good way to earn money to pay back debts and save money to travel to Paris or the United States."[16]

A Sudanese migrant shared his experiences about breaking a work contract. "I bought a work visa in 1998," he stated, "worked for two years, and left my employer because he was paying me almost nothing. I stayed as an undocumented for three years and I was deported. I came back in 2000 with my wife and my son with a *'umrah* visa and overstayed our visa since that time. We also had two additional children in Jiddah."[17]

Undocumented 'Migrants' Born in Jiddah

Out of the 61 interviewees, 11 (18%) were born in the city with no right to Sa'udi citizenship, or in the possession of proper documents (*iqamahs*) to stay in the city legally. Importantly, these interviewees, who were born in Jiddah from undocumented parents of African origin and, in a few cases, as a result of marriage between an African father or mother and another undocumented person from a non-African nationality, stood out because they did not physically migrate to the city but were born there. Unfortunately, Sa'udi immigration law does not grant automatic citizenship to the children of undocumented migrants, which means that their situations are, in some ways, more difficult than for those of other migrants because their identities and loyalties were presumably divided between a country of origin totally unknown to them and a country that refused to adopt them. Interestingly, the issue of identity proved to be a key factor in how migrants perceived the Kingdom. In the words of Murad, a young man from Nigeria, one was "stuck" in Jiddah on account of one's birth. Murad was one of twenty brothers and sisters who were born in Jiddah from undocumented parents, and had two-step mothers. He noted that he feels a "sort" of loyalty to the city where he was born, and no attachment to his parents' native country, Nigeria.[18] He did not mention the importance of living near the holy cities of Makkah and Madinah, which a few other Africans noted. As far as his future plans were concerned, it seems that he had a limited goal and, after a few probing questions, acknowledged that he dreamt of migrating to Germany or Lebanon to study, because he had relatives there who migrated from Sudan. The dilemma that confronted this young man was the great confusion of having African roots and being born in Sa'udi Arabia without proper documents. Murad was rejected by Sa'udi society and he became a victim of local rules and regulations, which were and often are contradictory and inconsistent. Still, Murad managed to study in private schools but was not able to continue to college and, based on his testimony, planned to marry another undocumented migrant. When he was asked how he could marry an undocumented migrant and raise children, he answered: "Everyone in our community and others has been doing it for years."[19]

Over the last few decades, many undocumented residents who were born in the city, married, had children, and even died as "untouchables." Clearly, there was and is a "generational" dilemma, especially for young undocumented subjects. Based on these facts, and in connection with the data analysis, it is thus possible to suggest that the African community in Jiddah was in search of its identity. In response to the probing question, why they were pulled to the city over other cities in the Gulf region, it was interesting to note that 20 of the interviewees (33%) answered that they had friends and relatives who encouraged them to come to Jiddah by providing financial and other logistical support. Ten (16%) migrants noted it was easier to get an *'umrah*, *hajj*, or work visa for the Kingdom.

Seven (12%) interviewees were attracted by the hope of earning higher wages in Jiddah. Thirteen (21%) noted that the main reason was that it was easy to be smuggled into the city. From these responses, one may also conclude that a combination of macroeconomic plus social networking reasons compelled many African migrants to migrate to Sa'udi Arabia, precisely to ensure better living conditions and to live and work in close proximity to the Muslim holy cities of Makkah and Madinah.

African Migrants in Sa'udi Arabia

Like all migrant workers, Africans were subjected to the Sa'udi *kafalah* (sponsorship) system, which expanded to meet an increasing demand for workers in both the public as well as the private sectors, and that included all types of foreign professional expatriates, ranging the gamut from engineers in the construction field to doctors and nurses for private hospitals and clinics, not to mention, of course, a vast number of semi-skilled and low-skilled workers. *Kafalah* thus sealed the fate of most employees for decades although Riyadh introduced a sharp improvement in early 2021 when it allowed foreign employees to start new jobs without the need for their original employers' sponsor certification. This flexibility changed the nature of working relationships because what workers needed to do was to notify their employers 90 days prior to their departure, which also authorized workers to leave the country "indefinitely" without their employers' permission.[20] This dramatic switch of a system, which had been in place for decades and that locked a worker to his/her sponsor without being able to move to another employer unless the sponsorship was transferred through formal channels, was a first important step. The Sa'udi Ministry of Human Resources and Social Development announced in November 2020 that it would abolish the *kafalah* "sponsorship" system during the first half of 2021.

With *kafala* in place, and the huge import of a very large pool of expatriate workers, unemployment rose among Sa'udi citizens, which led policy makers to adopt "Sa'udization" as a policy to employ nationals in the private sector. Sa'udization aimed to reduce the number of foreign migrants in the country, and while this policy achieved certain goals, it was not the success story many foresaw. Consequently, Riyadh introduced another initiative, the *nitaqat* system, as an effective tool to enforce Sa'udization in June 2011. Both of these policies are analyzed in the last section of this chapter but how Riyadh applied them requires elaboration too. Indeed, the Ministry of Labor teamed up with the Ministry of Interior and employed 1,000 inspectors to enforce the new laws, establish jail terms and fines to Saʻudi citizens who did not comply with them, and promised to deport any foreign guest worker who violated the new policy. As a consequence of this new deportation policy, many undocumented migrants were pressured to go into hiding. From 2012 to 2014, for example, more than one million expatriates were deported under the two new laws. Simultaneously, and parallel to the deportation policy, amnesty policies were adopted to address international human rights concerns regarding the conditions of migrants in Saʻudi Arabia. Interestingly, the standard procedure for the amnesty initiative was to provide migrants with a grace period in order to allow them to rectify their legal status or face a fine, jail time, or outright deportation. Very often, after the deadline passed, authorities would launch raids and round up thousands of undocumented workers: these raids would last from a few weeks to a few months, as different government agencies carried out raids on all types of local markets, restaurants, mini-grocery stores, shopping centers, and residential areas.[21]

Over the years, many migrants fled to Jiddah due to economic, social, political, and environmental reasons. Interestingly, it seems that the domestic realities of the various countries of undocumented migrants were quite similar. For example, civil wars as in the case of Nigeria, or that country's inability to deal with famine and disease, stood out as a main concern. Likewise, Eritrea suffered the worst drought in the late 1990s as tens of thousands of people fled the affected areas.[22] Jiddah became one of their primary destinations, particularly for the poorest sectors of society, while the most educated and wealthy headed to Europe and North America. Chronic political instability and an unsustainable population growth with consequent unemployment, poverty, illiteracy, Islamic radicalization, and, in the case of Somalia, piracy, constituted some of the main reasons for the massive migration from Africa to Saʻudi Arabia.[23] Furthermore, many of these countries were plagued by repeated environmental disasters such as desertification and floods, which made the development of a sustainable agricultural system difficult that, presumably, could have helped more of the population to remain put. All these elements taken together significantly decreased opportunities for the majority to meet their basic needs to sustain rudimentary living conditions in their native countries. These factors contributed to the push factors for labor migrants to leave their homeland in search of a better life.

When African countries were compared to other political entities, it was quite evident that many fell at the bottom of the ladder in terms of economic development. Nigeria was the only exception due to its oil resources that generated significant incomes.[24] In general, African societies boasted larger families—on the average—which put considerable strains on existing natural resources. Among the push factors, therefore, it was evident that the majority of countries under examination have had high unemployment along with very low annual per-capita incomes. The Gross National Income (GNI) in African countries was among the lowest in the world, and varied from $110–$150 in Somalia, to $1,400–$1,600 in Ghana per year, which was quite low. These GNI statistics were much lower than that of Sa'udi Arabia, which stood at $24,310, in 1995 and $49,520 in 2019.[25] No wonder many migrants considered, and many continue to perceive, Sa'udi Arabia as a land of opportunity. Additionally, the geographical proximity of many of these countries to the Kingdom and the economically prosperous Sa'udi economy, worked as contributing pull factors too.

Together with Yemen, the Sudan has been a key transit country for centuries, and was the main route for African pilgrims to reach Makkah for *hajj* and *'umrah*. This religious migration occurred from many African countries like Chad and Cameroon, and even from West African countries such as Burkina Faso, Mauritania and Senegal. After 2013, the Sa'udi campaign against the presence of illegal workers in the Kingdom was strengthened, both for economic as well as security reasons.[26] In fact, the construction of a 1,800-kilometer-long iron fence on the border with Yemen is one of the steps taken by the government to curb the flow of illegal migrants from Yemen, and several African countries.[27] In addition, authorities issued a series of amnesties that allowed the resettlement of five million irregular workers to their countries of origin, all to better resolve the challenges that these migrant populations posed. In 2018, Riyadh was still pursuing its goal of replacing foreign workers with indigenous Sa'udis, in part because of the global economic crisis that has made it difficult to implement job creation programs on a large scale. However, as this discussion demonstrates, all of these measures did not and do not guarantee success in curbing the flow of illegal immigrants coming to Jiddah, or into the country in general.

Furthermore, oil wealth changed the lifestyles of indigenous populations and encouraged the entry of Sa'udi women into the labor market, starting in the 1980s that, in turn, led to an increased demand for domestic laborers such as housekeepers and drivers. These requirements stood as a strong magnet for foreign labor, along with a large market for low-skilled workers. At the same time, the increase in government revenues led to a huge investment in infrastructure projects, which led to significant growth in the need for foreign labor that created indirect employment opportunities for irregular labor migration into the Kingdom. As a result of a perceived reluctance by some Sa'udis to engage in manual work, and the absence of skilled workers for specific skilled jobs, the Sa'udi economy relied on, and heavily depends on, expatriate workers from Europe and America in most areas of development. In this regard, one observer noted that improvement of the country's infrastructure and services inevitably meant an improvement in Sa'udis' everyday lives (and expectations), changing completely the social panorama of the country. This trend provided a unified platform for the implementation of nation-wide social and economic reforms which strengthened the Sa'udi sense of identity.[28]

Issues Related to Working Conditions

The investigation conducted with African migrants in Jiddah identified various challenges that many individuals faced in their everyday lives, ranging from stressful working conditions to security situations. Answers to a series of questions, including whether any had worked in their native countries to how they perceived their work in the Kingdom, highlighted immense difficulties. Responses revealed that a good portion were unemployed before they arrived into Sa'udi Arabia, and that most had diverse employment backgrounds—farmers, carpenters, mechanics, blacksmiths, and other manual jobs. Interestingly, the main reason for the great majority to leave their jobs, if employed, was to seek a better economic life. High local unemployment levels and encouragement by friends or family members who were already in Sa'udi Arabia were major incentives to migrate too. As mentioned above, Jiddah's close geographic proximity to the African continent and the relatively lower cost of being smuggled into the Kingdom, along with the availability of relatives and friends who lived in the city for many years and who were willing to pay for the trip's cost as well as the ease of obtaining a *'umrah* or *hajj* visa, made it relatively easy to overstay in the city. These and many other reasons made Jiddah a better choice for the individual migrant compared to other cities in the Gulf area.

It was a difficult task to list all the types of work that undocumented migrants from the African communities engaged in while living in the Kingdom. One of the reasons, perhaps, was their need to continuously change jobs for a variety of reasons: better pay or to escape arrest and/or deportation. An interviewee from Ghana reported the following about employment during the *hajj* season: "I leave my job as a house maid which pays $400 per month to travel to Makkah where I work as a cook for pilgrims from Africa. This pays around $800 for just 10 days."[29] The number of times an individual interviewee changed his or her job varied from no change to fifty times, a very high rate, whereas 11 (18.0%)

changed their jobs twice, which was the mode. When asked whether it was easy to find a new job when necessary, a large percentage (77.0%) reported that it was indeed difficult to find a new post, whether the same or a different type of employment. Still, the majority admitted that they usually found a job within a few weeks, with 12 (20.0%) stating that they had no problems finding a new post. To the question of how many hours each migrant worked, answers varied according to an individual's type of work. For instance, those involved in begging or the sex trade averaged four to five hours per day while those washing cars, selling nearly-expired goods, and porterage, worked over thirteen hours per day. In terms of income, at the time the interviews were conducted, two individuals were unemployed. The income of the remaining 59 migrants varied from $190 to $4,000 per month depending on the nature or type of job and number of hours worked. In these instances, the total salaries for the 59 African migrants who worked amounted to $31,000 per month combined. This total income of all migrants who worked (including the two women who worked in a brothel and who made $4,000 and $3,200 per month respectively), reflected a $525 mean or average income per month. It should be noted that the two women who worked in a brothel made $7,200 between them. If these two individuals were excluded from the calculation of the average mean of African interviewees, the average mean income stood at $418 per month in the late 2010s. This was close to the calculated mode of $400 per month for this community at the time. In this connection, the amount allocated for rent ranged from paying none (only four interviewees who were living with a friend or parents and, therefore, did not pay for their housing), to $267 per month, with the majority paying between $27 and $53 each month. The southern part of Jiddah is where the poorest districts are located and where accommodation tends to be very poor, sometimes with no running water, electricity or any kind of sewage system. In addition, these accommodations are usually targeted by local authorities, which was the reason why many of the undocumented migrants changed living places so often.[30]

In response to the question regarding the quality of their standard of living compared to that in their native countries, 50 (82.0%) of the interviewees noted that their standard of living had improved since they arrived in Jiddah. The issue of income and salary among undocumented migrants depended on a normal curve of supply and demand. For example, in the case of house cleaners, the supply of female maids from Africa, Indonesia and the Philippines went down, after raids by local authority. Consequently, demand for their services went up and, as a result, increased their average monthly salaries. Another example of wage fluctuations among Africans, Filipino and Indonesian housemaids were difficulties associated with negotiations by their respective countries with the Sa'udi Ministry of Labor regarding contract details, including salary and living conditions in other countries. During these extended periods of labor negotiations, salaries for available undocumented Filipino and Indonesian maids increased due to scarcities within this manpower pool. If the exporting countries refused to send their female expatriates to fulfil the demand of the Sa'udi market for these services, undocumented African females benefitted from such opportunities, and many rushed to fill the gap of such shortages that ensured much higher wages compared to their previous salaries. Decreases in the supply of other female maids made it possible for domestic helpers from the Horn of Africa who lived in the Kingdom not only to find jobs quite easily, but also to demand higher salaries.[31] For example, instead of the usual $214 they could ask up to $533 in 2010, higher more recently. Besides, such fluctuations increased the number of undocumented female migrants to smuggle in from the Horn of Africa to the country. Ironically, many African female housemaids would leave their employers in Jiddah at the time of *hajj* for the opportunity to generate more income by working in Makkah for 10 days, and earn up to $1,334 during the period. This situation made the sex trade a very remunerative activity too, though data on such activities were scarce, and difficult to confirm.

Legal Issues Facing Undocumented Laborers in Sa'udi Arabia

Perhaps as complex as many of the social concerns discussed above, several equally important questions, ranging from deportation to freedom of movement within the country, to dealing with the local authorities, and interacting with the consulates of their countries of origin, raised key legal challenges that deserve attention too. All undocumented migrants faced legal issues related to their statuses. Illegal residents faced arrest and deportation and, like migrants from Asia, the threat of deportation sometimes involved a difficult journey back if they decided to return to Sa'udi Arabia. Because of vast distances, these individuals assumed truly horrendous challenges, especially when compared with the situation of Yemenis, for example, who could travel with relative ease across the long un-demarcated land border between the two countries.[32] Nevertheless, a careful assessment of legal issues raised the following quandaries.

First, a significant percentage of individuals in the case study discussed here (44.3%) claimed that they had problems moving around the city, while an even larger percentage (55.7%)—especially women—indicated they confronted no such difficulties. This was because Sa'udi authorities, following local traditions, seldom stopped cars with women passengers covered in traditional 'abayas. When asked how they protected themselves from constabularies, the typical and consistent answer to this question involved the practice of avoiding, as much as possible, various Sa'udi authority figures presumably to minimize contact and stay away from trouble. For example, fights with Sa'udis and non-Sa'udis including with individuals from their own communities—whether in public or private—represented such dangers. Living in a district where most of the other inhabitants hailed from the same native countries, helped avoid clashes with unfamiliar faces. In the cases of married men with wives in Jiddah, as they travelled as a family the risks were significantly less than for single men moving about in a group. As stated earlier but worth repeating, Sa'udi authorities usually avoided stopping cars where there were women or children, for cultural reasons, as male officers were instructed to avoid contact (*ikhtilat*) with women unrelated to them.

None of the undocumented migrants interviewed considered their respective consulates as a point of reference, as the majority contended that their legations in Jiddah were not supportive, and did not offer assistance when needed. In fact, the engagement of various African missions on issues related to illegal migration is a highly sensitive matter, with most interviewees affirming that their official delegations offered no shelter, while others indicated that they simply did not know of the services available. In short, in addition to persecution by local authorities, all interviewees indicated that they were mostly concerned with the threat of deportation. It was interesting to note that despite all of these difficulties, the great majority (83.6%) affirmed that if they were pressured to leave Jiddah, they would definitely try to come back. Only a small percentage (8.25%) asserted that they would not come back, while an equal percentage declared that they did not know if they would return.

Plans for the Future

Questions related to future hopes and plans were equally revealing, regardless of the difficulties that all of the undocumented migrants in Jiddah faced. A whopping 98.3% affirmed that they preferred their lives in Jiddah, compared to the lives they had or would have in their home countries. When interviewees were asked about their state of mind while living and working with no documents, 78.68% stated that it bothered them living in Jiddah as undocumented workers. Only 21.31% noted that having no documents did not bother them. The majority agreed that the city provided them the opportunities to make a living as well as send money to loved ones back home, but that happiness was not a permanent condition. Again, the majority admitted that harsh work conditions, the long hours spend toiling, and the continuous threat of deportation, did not favor a normal life. Many of the Muslim interviewees added that living close to the two holy cities of Makkah and Madinah, and the possibilities to have a chance to perform *hajj* and *'umrah*, gave them a very pleasant feeling of religious comfort and assisted many to ease difficulties they experienced.

There were other problems, including the impossibility of having a bank account. Even travelling for *'umrah* was a concern, because one could not do such things without a valid *iqamah*. In terms of attitude towards the government's amnesty programs and the possibility of using them, several noted that they would rely on amnesty laws to leave the country, but the overwhelming majority (93.4%) said they had no such plans. Among the justifications offered by interviewees for not using amnesty initiatives to correct their legal statuses in the city, responses varied. A few mentioned the economic incentives that allowed them to avoid paying penalties for violating the *iqamah* requirement. Others were worried about the social factors affecting them. For example, a few were afraid of being separated from their family members and friends, while still others spoke about the threat of being detained, imprisoned or deported for violating the laws of the country if they went to the authorities. In the words of a migrant from Burkina Faso: "I do not know . . . I am happy about being undocumented and not using the amnesty pardon because I am frightened, that they [the Sa'udi authorities] will arrest me or after taking my fingerprints, will deport me, and I will not be able to come back."[33]

Others, who thought along the same lines, reached similar conclusions after heated conversations within their respective communities, including advice received from friends, and other undocumented migrants. From the point of view of most undocumented African maids, amnesty was not a practical mechanism. According to a migrant from Cameroon, "amnesty is not important and it does not affect my life in Jiddah."[34] This individual had been in the city for a long time. Some residents had been there for over 30 years, which explains the intrinsic resilience on display. Naturally, some recalled earlier government amnesty proposals, which aimed to reduce the number of undocumented migrants, and many were first-hand witnesses to earlier programs that, truth be told, achieved limited success. Interestingly, one of the Ethiopians interviewed was able to connect the recent vigor for deportation, to issues related to the Arab Spring. From the interviewees' statements regarding deportation, a few acknowledged that they could avoid being fingerprinted by paying someone who had connections with the immigration police working at the airport *Jawazat* office for a price that ranged between $500 and $1,300, depending on the pressure of the authorities, the availability of corrupt officers, and the legal situation of migrants.[35] An individual could thus leave the country without being fingerprinted.

Indeed, deportation posed serious challenges, since most migrants, especially the women, knew that it would be impossible for them to return. When Sa'udi efforts to deport undocumented migrants through casual raids on particular districts became intense—after the first few weeks immediately following amnesty deadlines—many stopped working and stayed home with their families. Others cautiously stayed with friends or other relatives in districts witnessing much less intensive inspection campaigns. Interviews with local *umdas* (community leaders), and several Sa'udi nationals, along with personal observations gathered in the course of the fieldwork associated with this investigation, revealed that the beginning of the inspection campaign on undocumented migrants led to a noticeable slowdown in the local businesses sector. Notwithstanding denials, the economic and social outcomes that arose immediately after the government initiated its arrests and deportation proceedings, resulted in many shops, grocery stores, restaurants, and small businesses closing down for lack of attainable cheap "undocumented labor to run the businesses" or severely reduced their business turnover.[36] Sa'udi nationals, if available, accepted the low-end jobs, though few filled those posts and, clearly, were not substitutes for undocumented migrants. The average Sa'udi, non-skilled laborer, demanded much higher wages (up to four times more, on average) to perform the same job as the foreign laborer, something that business owners were loath to satisfy. The issue gained traction in the auto repair industry, non-government hospitals, laundries, and slaughterhouses, farm hands, and maids in Sa'udi homes, to name just a few positions. In the case of the latter, with the need for maids especially pronounced, the impact was serious for many families that depended on such assistance. In fact, the average waiting list for a maid from the Philippines stood at six months in 2014, with an average cost of $4,000 recruitment office fees, according to importing labor importing agencies.[37] Some Sa'udi women who lacked the extensive family support base and who held professional positions, juggled schedules between their jobs and home duties to take care of their young children, including taking youngsters to school.

Another legal hurdle was the ability to save money in order to build a small business in their respective countries if and when they left Sa'udi Arabia. For most, this vision was directly associated with their lives in the city, which affected their attachment to their home country. Fieldwork research results revealed that out of all the undocumented African migrants, a greater number of the Sudanese were still strongly attached to their homeland, compared to other African nationalities who, in their majorities, preferred to stay in Jiddah. As an interviewee from the Sudan noted, many of the other African communities "feel hopeless about any future in their respective native countries." An Ethiopian migrant asserted: "I want to save money and go back to see my mother. If my luck is good and I can make a living there, that will be great, otherwise I will buy an airline ticket from Ethiopia to Yemen to avoid the dangerous crossing the Red Sea. Once in Yemen, I will definitely try to be smuggled back to Jiddah. I would love to spend my life here in Jiddah even to die here near Makkah and Madinah."[38] For his part, a Cameroonian stated that he had already bought a small home back in his native country and currently was saving money to buy an *iqamah* by finding a willing *kafil* (sponsor). On the other hand, an older Nigerian announced that he hoped that the Sa'udi government would solve the problem of his childrens' and grandchildrens' residency statuses. "All were born in Jiddah . . . We cannot go back to Nigeria," he confided, and since they never lived in Nigeria, he foresaw eventual difficulties. A Somali migrant asserted:

> "I plan to stay in Jiddah. I have no other place to go to, I have no choice. War and economic problems prevent me from taking my family back to Somalia. I plan to work hard, save money and buy *iqamah* from a Sa'udi for myself and family . . . you should know that there are many Somalis in Jiddah like us. I am not worried about my children in Jiddah. They have food and a place to sleep. If we leave or get deported, it will be a disaster."[39]

As is normal in every migrant community, the attitude towards their conditions seemed to always be ambiguous and problematic, since most were torn between two worlds, with attachments to both.

Amnesty Initiatives

As in most countries, security issues related to undocumented migrants preoccupied decision-makers in the Kingdom. In many cases, amnesty was devised as a policy mechanism to reduce tensions, and diminish uncertainty regrettably generated by the activities of some illegals who resorted to violence. In addition to the examples cited above related to *hajj* and *'umrah* visa violations, there were other concerns regarding the contraventions of the country's laws that indirectly relates to state security. For example, expatriates who entered the country through a contract with a company in the private sector or to work with individuals (for instance, as house cleaners, drivers, etc. . . .), broke their contracts by deciding not to join the sponsor after their arrival in the country.[40]

Parallel to various measures associated with migrants who traveled to the Kingdom during the annual pilgrimage, Sa'udi Arabia confronted the consequences of many who opted to breach their visas issued for *hajj*, staying beyond the allotted time to perform religious duties. Few appreciated the burden that such migrants created for society as a whole. The issue received little publicity on account of the ethos of religious responsibility, which Riyadh took seriously. Over the years, and as the numbers increased, authorities launched several nationwide amnesty programs both to legalize hundreds of thousands of undocumented immigrants in the country in general, and the city of Jiddah in particular, as well as address the socio-economic repercussions of these refugees. The moves, it was always assumed, were designed to assist Sa'udi authorities to better manage the growing population of foreign undocumented workers, meet labor shortages in certain sectors, boost security, and reduce human trafficking from Yemen and African countries. Through the last few decades, the government issued various amnesty initiatives to gain the upper-hand over a spiraling dilemma, as undocumented workers overwhelmed existing welfare institutions in major Sa'udi cities, especially those in the Makkah province.[41]

The standard procedure for the amnesty initiative was to provide migrants a grace period in which to rectify their legal status, or face penalty, jail, and eventual deportation. Very often, after the deadlines passed, Sa'udi authorities embarked on extensive campaigns to round up thousands of undocumented workers; at times, such steps lasted anywhere from a few weeks to a few months. In those instances, different government agencies carried out raids on all types of local markets, restaurants, mini-market stores, shopping centers, and residential areas. When Riyadh issued a blanket amnesty to all undocumented migrants in 1995, an initiative that occurred due to religious pressure from the *'ulamah*, many of those who ended up being deported were not accepted in their original countries because they did not have passports, or were sent to the wrong country, which created fresh quandaries.[42] The situation was so chaotic that a black, disabled Sa'udi citizen was deported in the melee and his family had to go to the African country where he was deported to, in order to bring him back home. Similar anecdotal evidence surfaced and, naturally, drew the ire of senior officials while simultaneously derided by an increasingly wary population that did not approve of mass deportation. In fact, when such news surfaced, Riyadh accelerated its amnesty initiatives, hoping to address core concerns without adding to everyone's woes. Sometimes, the measures proved to be inadequate, which ushered in new measures, like the *nitaqat*.

Nitaqat and Deportation Laws

Nitaqat was a program introduced by the Ministry of Labor in June 2011 that targeted major corporations that employed expatriate workers. The word *nitaqat*, "areas" or "zones" in Arabic, classified all companies into four zones: red, yellow, green, or platinum, according to the percentage of Sa'udis they employed in their respective companies. Each zone, or range, received either privileges or penalties that could lead to their forced closures if they failed to employ a certain percentage of Sa'udis.[43] Alternatively, reward incentives were also included in the program, which essentially granted them a permit to bring in more foreign expatriate workers whenever the percentage of employed Sa'udis increased. *Nitaqat* created a significant change in the country's labor market as most companies were in the red zone, which meant that they did not meet the required percentage and, therefore, needed more Sa'udi workers in order to stay in business. It is worth noting that while the Kingdom has never imposed a minimum wage for both its indigenous as well as expatriate employees, King 'Abdallah bin 'Abdul 'Aziz Al Sa'ud announced precisely such a measure in September 2012. He also issued a decree that set a minimum salary of $800 per month for Sa'udis working in the public sector, while encouraging the private sector to adopt the same measures.[44]

What the *nitaqat* and minimum salary initiatives did was to regulate how Sa'udis dealt with employment questions, which was a concrete step forward as both limited ongoing abuses in the country's burgeoning labor markets. By institutionalizing various issues, Riyadh curtailed inevitable excesses that affected the indigenous population just as much as it affected migrants. It was a long process that shaped part of the country's evolving labor laws, which gained coherence, even if few perceived their gain until very recently. More recent changes aimed to further regularize the creation of jobs and hence, the creation of wealth, fall within *Vision 2030*—the Kingdom's new economic blueprint.[45]

Along with these critical policies, Riyadh applied specific deportation laws. How these evolved, as well as the kind of impact, they left on migrants is important. One of the most widely discussed issues, deportation, touched the lives of many undocumented migrants, sometimes in unsavory ways. Over the course of two short years between 2012 and 2014, more than one million expatriate workers were deported from the Kingdom, after specific new laws were enacted to curtail the overall numbers of illegal residents in the country.[46] Two specific laws required all migrants to work only for their sponsors, which flushed out the undocumented, who were hastily deported. Each and every worker was henceforth required to obtain a work permit for an annual fee of $650, a substantial sum that only companies could afford, and that led individuals in transient situations to criticize the policy change. Fees collected for this purpose filled the coffers of the Saʿudi Human Resources Development Fund, which used the funds to train Saʿudi citizens to enter the labor market. In order to enforce the new laws, the Ministry of Labor teamed up with the Ministry of the Interior, employing 1,000 special inspectors who rounded up illegal workers. Interestingly, the authorities enforced the laws with gusto, imposing jail terms on Saʿudis who did not comply. As a result of these measures, the supply of foreign labor shrank approximately 20 percent by 2015, causing wages to rise and an increase of jobs available to Saʿudi citizens.[47] Still, these tough measures caused many undocumented migrants to go into hiding, in order to avoid deportation.

It is eminently fair to ask whether these strict new laws observed or contravened the principles of hospitality present in Islam. Moreover, it is equally critical to raise concerns over the Islamic world's established traditions, and whether these appeased the international community? As discussed above, Saʿudi Arabia boldly tackled various challenges associated with the very idea of refugee. However, it is equally critical to underscore that Riyadh introduced its own specific mechanisms to make these changes more effective. Two stand out: (1) **Updated pilgrimage mechanisms**, which fixed quotas by country that placed the responsibility onus on states sending pilgrims; regulation of their housing appointments in the Mina area at the height of the annual pilgrimage; inspections during the various religious ceremonies by enhancing the roles of trained volunteers; and the introduction of pardons [amnesty] policies as required. And (2), **the imposition of electronic monitoring devices**, that upset many people. Given the sheer numbers of annual pilgrims who visit the Kingdom, which hovers around the 2 to 3 million mark, the adoption of electronic monitoring devices, like hospital-style bar codes, assign specific residence allocations on a carefully chosen basis for each country. Used on a selective basis, nationals from states prone to sending migrants/refugees would receive screening, both for their own security as well as the application of existing laws. Although such devices raised legitimate privacy concerns, it is obviously necessary to separate economic migrants from genuine pilgrims who visit Saudi Arabia to perform their religious obligations and return to their respective countries.

Conclusion: Pilgrimage Dilemmas

The great majority of migrants in the Kingdom of Sa'udi Arabia lived in legal limbo, very often for generations that, by all measures, created specific hardships. Their fates were, at times, as difficult or even worse than those that affected Yemeni, Iraqi or Syrian refugees who, more often than not, received assistance to manage their affairs either temporarily or permanently. In the *Karantina* district of Jiddah, for example, which was a magnet for most of the newly arrived undocumented migrants into that megapolis, the safe haven for those without official papers proved efficient because government supervision there was rare, and many state agents were reluctant to venture into the area. Yet, most of the residents lived on the margins of city life with no government services and, as one migrant from Burkina Faso confessed, "outside of the law." According to a Sudanese worker, this was the reason why the media depicted them as criminals, a source of disease, and even accused them of providing support to terrorist groups based in the city—all of which were devastating and unfair assessments.[48]

Inasmuch as most African migrants interviewed in the survey were Muslims, it was observed that the great majority attended daily prayers at local mosques, and it seemed that they were devoted regardless of the difficulties they confronted. Remarkably, however, and similar to the Yemeni migrants, most African migrants were "content" with living in Jiddah without documents, for they had no other option.[49] Notwithstanding that the sample of interviewees was relatively small, many demonstrated great awareness of their circumstances and planned accordingly, regardless of their lack of education. This was reflected in anecdotal evidence from the rest of the country in various discussions that the authors held with government officials, concerned citizens and expatriate observers. It is thus safe to conclude that a majority of undocumented migrants, regardless of their nationalities, were stuck in Sa'udi Arabia waiting for something to happen to change their situations, and improve their lives. Few wished to go back to their native countries, especially those who came some time ago, or who were born in the Kingdom, or who were smuggled into it. Overall, many shared the feeling that they were stuck in Jiddah because of their birth, or because of the economic and political circumstances of their respective homelands. Whether they were born in the Kingdom of Sa'udi Arabia and had no rights, or came as children with their parents for *hajj* or *'umrah* only to overstay their visas, most suffered, and often a great deal. It should be noted that there were many undocumented residents in Jiddah who were the grandchildren of migrants who came even before the Sa'udi state was reconstituted in 1932, though reliable figures are impossible to determine from official sources simply because of a lack of accurate data. Quite a few migrants were not aware of, or did not care to get, the Sa'udi national identification card (*bitaqat al-ahwal*) years ago, and for this reason there were several generations of undocumented migrants in the second decade of the twenty-first century. Nevertheless, instability dominated the lives of migrants, with many surviving in a state of continuous anxiety and terror from local authorities and from callous Sa'udis who treated them appallingly. The authorities are aware of these circumstances and continue to invest the necessary resources to address these issues, and if possible to correct them.

Regardless of these identified psychological and social pressures and threats, it is easy to conclude that migrants in the Kingdom worked hard to offer their families the basic life necessities such as food, clothing, and a roof to call their own. These migration challenges were just as serious as most refugee dilemmas and involved similar risks. Young men and women who jeopardized their lives to reach Sa'udi Arabia, vowed to make life meaningful for themselves and their families, and were likely to do everything in their powers to get into the Kingdom (or go elsewhere) to work and make their dreams come true. What stands out is bravery and courage. There was a strong belief among numerous migrants that those who died at sea or in the desert were destined to have their lives end that way. Predestination, in conjunction with the old concept of *hijrah* (migration in Islam), were thus cardinal principles of their beliefs and the efforts they made to get into Sa'udi Arabia. Still, while the chief reason advanced by authorities who initiated deportation procedures of undocumented laborers hovered around the need to create opportunities for Sa'udis, this also stood in direct contradiction of Sa'udi society's religious duties towards fellow human beings.

As discussed throughout this chapter, life in the Kingdom was difficult for most undocumented migrants who were under the constant threat of deportation. Simultaneously, the possibilities of returning to their home countries were even more difficult, because of extremely precarious economic and political situations in their respective homelands. In addition, one could add that it is well known that for hundreds of years African migrants have travelled by foot to Makkah to perform *hajj*. Often, some of these individuals toiled under pressure in alien countries where they were not welcomed, before they even reached the Hijaz. In fact, some families were literally enslaved by landlords on their way to the Holy Cities, while others were forced to sell their children in order to survive harsh trips that, in many cases, lasted fifteen years or more.[50]

Finally, it is important to touch on the *iqamah* (legal residency) concern in this concluding section of the chapter. The issue posed serious challenges for all concerned. Undocumented workers with savvy could secure legal residency and a work permit through bribery or other illegal means, which was telling. Others were condemned to suffer the consequences of living illegally, which was both dangerous as well as impractical in the long run, even if most managed because the migrant community exhibit an extraordinary capacity of care of the other, and assistance in times of need and difficulty was nearly always forthcoming. Deportation efforts initiated by authorities usually involved raids on only one community of undocumented migrants at a time, depending on the particular internal or external circumstances the country was going through. As a result, migrants were always unsure of when they might be rounded up. Moreover, and because consulates seldom assisted their own citizens, wary foreign officials assumed that their nationals were undocumented migrants who did not deserve help given that they were subject to arrest.

As this discussion has highlighted, it is difficult to anticipate any immediate solution to migrants' situations in Sa'udi Arabia in general. Sa'udi policies have proved inadequate and totally oblivious to the realities on the ground. The authorities are aware of the need to address these grave concerns, and the most recent reform initiatives raised expectations. What is sorely required is a complete change in understanding the migrant situation in its global context in order to begin to tackle such problems in more efficient and, especially, more humane ways. Heartedly, Riyadh has pledged to embark upon devising eclectic policies towards migrants and refugees in their nation-state.

CHAPTER

6

The Kingdom and Yemen
How Neighbors Became Refugees

Relations between the Kingdom of Sa'udi Arabia and successive Yemeni states—from the Imamate to the Mutawakkilite Kingdom of Yemen to the separate Yemen Arab Republic and the People's Democratic Republic of Yemen and finally to the reunified Republic of Yemen—were always tense.[1] These neighbors shared much more than many assumed, as southern tribes intermingled and maintained close ties for centuries, even when the area was under Ottoman or British rule—outsiders who intruded and occupied Arab lands. By all accounts, and notwithstanding tribal confrontations over grazing land and water, relatively good relations existed, which were significantly boosted after Riyadh and Sana'a signed a partial border accord in 1934 and renewed their neighborly pledges in 2000.

Over the years, successive governments initiated close cooperation at the economic and military levels, though outside interventions on the Arabian Peninsula—ranging the gamut from Ottoman Empire minions to British colonial incursions, and Egyptian military vagaries—disrupted relatively harmonious ties.[2]

Sa'udi Arabia welcomed millions of Yemenis to live and work in the Kingdom over the past eight decades, and while two recent disruptions took their toll, Riyadh seldom abandoned its brethren. Indeed, despite the 1990 expulsion of nearly one million Yemeni workers from the Kingdom in the aftermath of the Iraqi invasion and occupation of Kuwait—when Yemeni President 'Ali 'Abdallah Salih backed the Iraqi strongman Saddam Husayn [Hussein] against the Arab monarchies—Yemenis continued to have access to Sa'udi Arabia and its lucrative businesses that supported numerous families across the land of the legendary Queen of Shibah. Similarly, and before the outbreak of the 2015 Yemen Civil War, Riyadh and its Arab Gulf partners sought to reconcile Yemenis, meaning 'Ali 'Abdallah Salih and Huthi rebels, though the latter rejected a peaceful political settlement.

Notwithstanding the painful repercussions of the ongoing war, Sa'udi Arabia has provided substantial humanitarian assistance to Yemenis, while the Huthis punished their own nation, rejecting the aid generously extended by Arabs as well as aligning themselves with non-Arab Iran. In fact, the realignments—which were unusual as they pitted Arabs against non-Arabs—of power in the Middle East started before 2011 as extremist forces like al-Qa'idah on the Arabian Peninsula emerged in Yemen, which meant that Riyadh confronted fresh radicalization threats that were both of the indigenous as well as imported varieties. It was this fundamental perception of threat that was fueled by Persian interferences in Arab affairs that led a ten-member military coalition led by Sa'udi Arabia to launch the 2015 war, after, and this is critical to note, all reconciliation offers were rejected by the Huthis. It is also important to note that the coalition launched its military campaign against the Huthis under a United Nations Security Council resolution that explicitly authorized the use of force.[3] Furthermore, and it is necessary to state this as clearly as possible, the coalition was and continued to be logistically backed by leading global powers, including the United States and the United Kingdom, in support of the last elected President of Yemen, 'Abd Rabbuh Mansur al-Hadi.[4] Between 2015 and early 2020, the war recorded nearly 100,000 dead and countless casualties, though the Huthis refused to negotiate, goaded by Iran to resist even as malnutrition and starvation increased.[5] Few wondered where the Huthis acquired the technology to fabricate and launch ballistic missiles on Sa'udi targets, and even fewer raised questions regarding the actual costs of such armoury. In other words, it is eminently fair to ask why the Huthis were determined to spend scarce financial resources on very costly missiles when, for a fraction of the outlay, they could have easily met all of the Yemeni population's nutritional needs. Ironically, and even while continuing their air and naval campaigns, coalition states led by Sa'udi Arabia provided sorely needed humanitarian aid, though Huthis preferred to see Yemenis perish for ideological reasons and, under Iranian dominion, to advance Persian strategic interests rather than defend Arab Yemeni ones.

As discussed below, few wondered why Huthis and their Persian masters opted to tolerate such misery, while continuing to launch ballistic missiles on Sa'udi cities and threatening to bomb civilian airports in Riyadh, Abhah, Jizan, and as far east as Dubai in the United Arab Emirates. This question was seldom raised by academics and policy wonks and routinely ignored by media outlets. Likewise, few examined the significant aid packages allocated to Yemen, including the most recent provisions authorized in the thick of ongoing battles. Yemenis paid a heavy price as Huthi rebels manipulated—and were in turn stage-managed by outside forces—their own population, added to their overall misery, and otherwise accepted horrendous conditions that further sank millions into destitution. How did Yemenis reach such a station and why was Sa'udi Arabia's generosity ignored? What was the size of the financial assistance provided by Riyadh to Sana'a and why did Riyadh continue to disburse large sums both to the Yemeni state as well as various tribal leaders? In the end, how did Riyadh address the fate of Yemeni refugees, at home as well as in the Kingdom for those who lived in, or made it to, Sa'udi Arabia?

The purpose of this chapter is three-fold. First, it is to provide a brief assessment of contemporary Sa'udi-Yemeni ties that witnessed periods of cooperation alongside interludes of serious clashes. A discussion of the free-flow of migrants until 1990–1991 follows to further emphasize how those ties shaped policies in both nations. Second, and to underscore the Yemen's strategic position on the southern tip of the Arabian Peninsula, an effort is made to evaluate how undocumented migrants were smuggled into the Kingdom alongside very porous borders. Third, the chapter provides a summary of the humanitarian assistance extended to Yemenis before and after the Huthi rebels came to power, before closing with an assessment of the Huthi takeover and the war that ensued. Under the circumstances, what is the potential for reconciliation between the two nation-states?

Contemporary Sa'udi–Yemeni Ties

Tribal contacts between the peoples of Sa'udi Arabia and Yemen mean that both were eminently familiar with each other even if the 1818 Ottoman assaults throughout the Arabian Peninsula destroyed the Second Sa'udi monarchy.[6] A few years earlier, around 1803 more precisely, Sa'udi forces relied on several Yemeni tribes to make inroads into territories under the control of the Imamate, specifically in the Tihamah region, which lasted until 1818.[7] More recently, and after 'Abdul 'Aziz bin 'Abdul Rahman restored the Third Sa'udi monarchy in 1932, clashes with the Imam Yahyah of Yemen preoccupied Riyadh, as Sana'a established a protectorate over the Idrisi Sultanate in 'Asir Province, then a disputed territory along the southern border area. 'Abdul 'Aziz captured 'Asir and conquered Jizan, further south, along with most coastal hamlets. At the time, the Imam's forces occupied the Najran oasis inland, though inevitable clashes meant that better trained and equipped Sa'udi troops would eventually regain control over Najran and occupy an additional 100 kilometers of the coastal plain by 1948.[8]

Long before World War II, however, Sa'udi and Yemeni forces clashed intermittently, as King 'Abdul 'Aziz was determined to draw his growing country's borders. The ruler and his savvy advisors loathed the fact that boundaries remained un-mapped and un-demarcated by formal treaties, which Riyadh proposed, in part to meet international requirements imposed by companies anxious to search for oil in clearly defined frontiers. Naturally, the monarch's hands were somewhat tied in the Lower Gulf region as well as the Hijaz on account of the British presence, though by 1932 the powerful King controlled almost all of Arabia, except for the Yemen and key British protectorates along the Arabian Gulf.[9]

What 'Abdul 'Aziz believed could be done along the Southern area was not difficult to understand on account of tribal allegiances, which were severely suppressed by the Ottomans, and which led the Najdi to conclude that Yemenis shared a lot more with their northern neighbors than most assumed. He was confident that he, 'Abdul 'Aziz, and the Imam, could share control over 'Asir and Najran and that minor skirmishes could be set aside when larger benefits were secured for both countries. Regrettably, because the ruler of 'Asir, the Amir Idrissi, was not on the best of terms with his Najdi counterpart since the early 1920s, 'Abdul 'Aziz concluded that the modus vivendi between Hijazi and Yemeni tribesmen would be sufficient, though he underestimated the Imam Yahyah Muhammad Hamid al-Din. What developed next was not surprising, as Idrissi accepted Sa'udi suzerainty in 1926 and, in 1930, joined both lands under his sovereignty and committed the allegiances of most of the tribes into the Kingdom of Najd and Hijaz. The Imam Yahyah was livid as he and key foes—and some rivals in Yemen—perceived this incorporation as a hostile step, which pre-determined clashes between the new Sa'udi Kingdom and Yemen that wished to prevent the provinces of Al Bahah, Jizan and Najran following the same path. This was particularly important for Jizan because that entity was, along with 'Asir, part of the territories controlled by the Amir Idrissi throughout the 1920s. Quarrels gained importance when Idrissi recanted his sworn allegiance to 'Abdul 'Aziz and fled to Yemen to join the Imam Yahyah. Adding fire to the proverbial fuel, a 1931 truce was broken, as Yemeni forces advanced and reached Najran in late 1933. Initial efforts to stop clashes from degenerating to outright warfard failed, and when the Imam Yahyah ordered the arrest of a peace delegation sent by the Sa'udis, allegedly stating: "Who is this bedouin coming to challenge my family's 900-year rule?," the die was cast.[10]

At the start of what escalated into a war in February 1934, the Yemen Government and the British representative in Aden signed a "Treaty of

Friendship," but this only meant that London was now treating both the Sa'udis and the Yemenis on an equal footing since British representatives had secured a similar treaty with 'Abdul 'Aziz. Between March and May 1934, Sa'ud bin 'Abdul 'Aziz led his father's troops as the latter reconquered various Tihamah highland townships, which previously had fallen to the Imam's forces. In May 1934, Sa'udi forces occupied Hudaydah, which controlled trade with the hinterland and that caused shortages in the interior, including Sana'a. The Imam's son fled Sana'a, which was soon threatened by Sa'udi forces but the mountainous region posed significant logistical difficulties. The Sa'udi King demanded the abdication of the Imam and the expulsion from Yemen of the former rulers of 'Asir that, to no one's surprise, fell on deaf ears. In a desperate move, the Yemeni Imam revealed a mysterious plan to advance on Riyadh with 200,000 men, which never took place. Shortly thereafter, peace negotiations began as 'Abdul 'Aziz dropped his demand for the Imam's abdication, and that resulted in the 14 June 1934 Ta'if Treaty that brought the conflict to an end. Riyadh relinquished Hudaydah but incorporated Jizan, 'Asir, and Najran into the Kingdom, and while the 1934 border accord was meant to eliminate such incursions into each others' territories, this was not to be. The very nature of tribal warfare before the middle of the twentieth century meant that grievances would linger. In time, however, the Kingdom of Sa'udi Arabia provided financial aid to the Imam Ahmad, Imam Yahyah's successor, after the latter confronted internal opposition.[11] While few documented the size of these financial donations, the precedent was set, as the Al Sa'ud devised a "Riyal Diplomacy" to tame successive Yemeni forces.

Moreover, and as was customary after such agreements on the Arabian Peninsula, Sa'udis welcomed Yemenis in droves and extended significant assistance, and while much of this aid was conveniently overlooked, the fact remained that Sa'udi Arabia delivered over $10 billion in aid during the past few decades and, as discussed in Chapter 4, continued to allocate sorely needed assistance.[12] Billions more were legitimately earned by Yemeni workers who toiled in the Kingdom on a privileged basis (since most were issued permanent residency papers and were legally employed), and whose transfers to Sana'a allowed Yemen to survive and, in most instances, prosper. In other words, the Al Sa'ud disbursed large sums of money to Yemeni factions and welcomed millions to work as well as to earn a living in the Kingdom, all to contribute to the welfare of their nascent state. Riyadh never considered the few million workers living and toiling in Saudi Arabia as being refugees. In fact, many went from rags to riches, something that was seldom recalled in the second decade of the twenty-first century.[13]

Notwithstanding this largesse, relations were tense for a variety of reasons, though two specific causes in periodic nerve-wracking ties stood out: first, a series of bizarre leadership demands and, second, frequent anti-monarchical discourses that upset traditional tribal contacts. In 1962, for example, the last Yemeni Imam Muhammad al-Badr was unceremoniously deposed by Yemenis anxious to establish a republic. Riding Arab nationalist waves fueled by Egypt's Jamal [Gamal] 'Abdul Nasir, brought 'Abdallah Sallal to power, though Riyadh quickly concluded that an Egyptian-backed revolution was a mortal threat to its well-being. Where Sallal and the so-called Free Officers erred was in assuming that their decision to abrogate the 1934 Ta'if Agreement would be tolerated. Riyadh was furious when Sallal declared that his intention was to re-conquer the three disputed provinces. Even if Sa'udi officials could overlook such objectives, few were could ignore the 70,000 Egyptian soldiers that arrived, ostensibly to support the republic against a guerrilla opposition organized by the pro-Sa'udi Imam Badr and his loyal tribesmen. The Kingdom stood by the Imam Badr through 1968 as the country descended into a bloody civil war that lasted until 1970. An undetermined number of Yemenis flocked to the Kingdom though Riyadh did not treat them as refugees. Rather, it welcomed these survivors, and absorbed them into the workforce, providing them with legal documents that allowed every able-bodied person to earn decent wages. In doing so, Sa'udi authorities remained true to their religious obligations to extend a generous hand to the downtrodden. King Faysal bin 'Abdul 'Aziz recognized the Arab Republic of Yemen (North Yemen) and offered a great deal of financial support, counseled by his Western partners that did not wish to see Russian gains throughout the area, though Riyadh did not need any reminders that the Soviet and Chinese communist threats on the Kingdom's borders were real. Importantly, 'Asir, Najran, and Jizan were safely nestled inside the Kingdom, even if some Yemeni leaders continued to refer to them as Yemeni territory.[14]

Sa'udi Arabia welcomed 'Ali 'Abdallah Salih, the late Yemeni head-of-state who first came to power in July 1978 after Ahmad al-Ghashmi, a leader who was close to the Al Sa'ud ruling family, was assassinated. Often described as a dictator, Salih, ruled over the Yemen Arab Republic (YAR) starting in 1978 and the Republic of Yemen between May 1990—when the two Yemens finally united—and February 2012.[15] Long before unification, Riyadh tolerated Salih's plundering from the poorest Arab country over his two-decade-long rule, and reluctantly welcomed him on and off as circumstances warranted. He was perceived as a unifier though Salih showed his colors in 1990 when he sided with the Iraqi strongman,

Saddam Husayn, instead of backing his long-term Kuwaiti benefactor when the Baghdadi invaded and occupied the Shaykhdom.

Goaded by the War for Kuwait and the inevitable Sa'udi prominence on the Peninsula, Sana'a failed to subdue tribal incursions inside the Kingdom. Once again, Riyadh overlooked Salih's hostile rhetoric, and while it initially objected to the May 1990 union, the Al Sa'ud amended their perceptions in favor of unification. What tipped the balance was the Yemeni's pro-Husayn position at the United Nations. Since Sana'a filled the Arab seat at the Security Council that year, Salih's anti-Arab Gulf votes infuriated King Fahd bin 'Abdul 'Aziz, who ordered the expulsion of nearly a million Yemeni workers from the country.[16] Even if this was a harsh response, what irritated Riyadh was Sana'a's neglect of the Yemeni population, and of Salih's myopic assessments of what would occur on the Arabian Peninsula. Salih bet on Husayn, and probably received generous stipends for his unadulterated devotion, but did not realize that Iraq—and Yemen—could not oppose the will of the international community, including that of its avowed allies in Moscow.[17] In the event, Yemen paid a heavy price for yet another leadership misjudgment, an occurrence that was repeated in 1994, when another civil war started. In the mid-1990s, the contest was between a southern separatist movement and Salih, mostly over poor allocation of the limited resources available to the government.[18]

Riyadh supported the separatist movement to reel Salih in, and showered Sana'a with increased aid after hostilities ended that, truth be told, secured the 2000 Treaty that reconfirmed the borders demarcated by the 1934 Ta'if Accords. Whether allegations that the Kingdom allocated nearly US$4 billion to a variety of Yemeni interests were true are difficult to ascertain. What is not is the fact that senior Yemeni officials, including Salih, benefitted from Sa'udi largesse. In fact, a spike in Sa'udi financial assistance was recorded after the mid-1990s, though how that assistance was distributed was a classic Yemeni mystery.[19]

Coincidentally, it was around this time that the neglected Sa'adah region in Northern Yemen saw anti-Zayidi proselytizing, which was a characteristic Salih tool to rule with his legendary iron fist. Devout Zayidis upheld their traditions and responded to various threats though it was Salih's acquiescence on the border issue that infuriated most. Such consent, many believed, would increase Sa'udi influence over Yemeni domestic politics. Even if Yemeni grievances were legitimately targeted against Sana'a, it was eminently better for Zayidi tribesmen, including one Husayn al-Huthi, to vent against Salih's subservience to Riyadh. Lest we forget, Husayn al-Huthi was killed in 2004 on Salih's orders, as several tribes launched their protracted confrontations against the government and, helter-skelter, against Sa'udi Arabia across the border.[20]

In September 2003, and in an effort by Riyadh to control these Yemeni incursions, the Sa'udis began the construction of a cement-filled pipeline/wall, 10 feet (3 meters) in diameter along their 1934-demarcated border. Following complaints by the Yemeni government that the construction violated the 2000 Treaty, the Sa'udis temporarily stopped work in February 2004, though 47 miles (75 kilometers) of the cement-filled barrier was already up. The remainder of the 1,100-mile (1,800 kilometers) border was left untouched though Riyadh was increasingly concerned with regular incursions that threatened the security of many inhabitants in the area. By 2009, and as Sa'udi authorities understood the consequences of these border incursions, Riyadh sent troops to fight the Huthis, ostensibly to help Salih. The price paid was very high as over 130 Sa'udi soldiers were killed before a cease-fire was reached.[21]

The Free-Flow of Migrants

The wars in Sa'adah after 2004, as well as the southern insurrection since 2007, effectively meant lawlessness along the border region and, for our purposes, a sharp rise in migrants that escaped to Sa'udi Arabia. While an estimated one million Yemenis returned from the Kingdom between 1990 and 1999, at least two million emigrated from Yemen back into the Kingdom.[22] Of course, these movements were not sudden but the result of decades of migration, which witnessed significant demographic alterations. In 1975, for example, of the estimated 1.23 million souls that emigrated from the Yemen Arab Republic (North Yemen), 80 percent went to Sa'udi Arabia. By 1986, data presented by Yemeni authorities stated that 1.17 million went to the Kingdom, while in 1990 alone 1.1 million were apparently living and working in Sa'udi Arabia.[23] Similar figures were registered for the People's Democratic Republic of Yemen (PDRY or South Yemen), which had about 300,000 citizens working abroad in the 1970s, most of whom were in the Kingdom, whose remittances amounted to US$ 33 million in 1973 and US$ 268 million by 1978. Despite this large increase, Riyadh allegedly offered Aden additional assistance, at least $400 million in direct financial aid according to one source.[24] The 1988 PDRY census counted 233,900 laborers abroad, 76 percent of whom were in Sa'udi Arabia and, by 1991, that is the first year after unification, around 12.5 percent of the population of the integrated Yemen lived outside the country, a figure that represented nearly 55 percent of its entire labor force.[25] Yemenis represented the largest national group among foreign migrants in Saʿudi Arabia in 1990–1991, making up 27 percent of all residents.[26]

While this figure was reduced after an estimated one million Yemenis were expelled from the Kingdom in 1990, the drop was temporary since Sana'a depended on remittances from its "emigrants," which meant that compromises were necessary to return most of those who left Saʿudi Arabia involuntarily. Indeed, this was such an urgent matter that Sana'a compromised, as the exodus provoked an unprecedented economic and social crisis that required attention. Remarkably, Yemeni authorities knew exactly how many of their citizens returned: 761,979 in 1991 alone according to the Central Bureau of Statistics in Sana'a, which was a migratory shock as this active labor force imposed a huge burden on the economy.[27] Even if none of these individuals were technically considered to be refugees in Saʿudi Arabia, their economic burden on Yemen transformed them into "reverse-refugees" in their native land. Consequently, unemployment rose to 770,000 Yemenis in 1991 alone, which added to the overall misery experienced by most residents. Poverty increased, since dependable remittances were no longer available, which meant that many households that relied on transfers from migrant workers in the Kingdom suffered severe shortages. It was to remedy such devastating repercussions that President ʿAli ʿAbdallah Salih was forced to alter his foreign policy priorities, even if the hurt was palpable on the Saʿudi side too as most felt betrayed by their Yemeni neighbors who were nurtured over the years and whose loyalties Saʿudis had come to expect as a matter of principle.

In the aftermath of the 2011 uprisings, the revolutionary upheaval reinforced the centrality of remittances for the survival of Yemeni households though the Salih Government demonstrated an intrinsic inability to navigate both the political as well as economic crises that befell the country. Therefore, everything that occurred after 2011 must be viewed through different angles, including a legitimate Saʿudi alarm over Huthi actions. Regrettably, the Huthi capture of Sana'a, their rapid military expansion southward and partial conquest of Aden, along with the ongoing war, all added pressure on migratory movements. Between 2010 and 2019, 188,000 new displacements were recorded in Yemen and 4,066,000 were displaced as a result of the ongoing conflict.[28] Similarly, and while the humanitarian catastrophe associated with the war cannot be underestimated, the Huthis seemed to be further determined to expand the total number of migrants and refugees in the hope of increasing the burden on Saʿudi Arabia. How Riyadh intended to come to terms with this liability was unclear although the country faced a serious demographic challenge with the presence of millions of foreign workers.

Yemeni Workers in Sa'udi Arabia

By early 2020 an estimated 11 million foreign workers were working in Sa'udi Arabia, primarily drawn from Southeast Asia. Although the country is dependent on foreign labor, and while foreign workers retained key technical positions, most were low-skilled employees in the agriculture sector, along with the cleaning and domestic service industries. As discussed above, Yemeni migrants flocked to the Kingdom on account of proximity as well as tribal affinities, which meant that the vast majority was present in the country before the 1973–1974 oil boom that brought in millions from around the world.[29] When oil prices fell in the mid-1980s, and when a number of migrants returned to their respective home countries, the overwhelming majority of Yemenis who mingled with local inhabitants stayed put as they were privileged employees with unmistakable associations with Sa'udis. Most would have remained in 1990 were it not for 'Ali 'Abdallah Salih's political choices to side against the Arab Gulf monarchies, which saw the expulsion of nearly a million Yemenis, including those who carried long-term residency permits.

Of course, Yemenis could enter Sa'udi Arabia with relative ease at any port of entry, receive a visa without difficulty and, unique among all migrant workers, could own and operate businesses without local sponsorship. This went beyond privilege and it remained to be determined why Yemenis would squander such opportunities though regional politics may well have played various roles in preferred options.[30] Undeniable perceptions of security threats colored Sa'udi actions. "Yemeni authorities have also used security issues as bargaining chips in negotiations with regional and western partners alike, alternating between cooperation and turning a blind eye on cross-border trafficking of all kinds–including informal migration, which they have sometimes facilitated."[31] In the aftermath of the 2011 uprisings, and the Huthi takeover of large sections of the country, such perceptions gained traction. Irrespective of the direction that the conflict took, the total number of Yemeni refugees increased that, in turn, preoccupied regional and global actors.

As discussed by Hélène Thiollet, while internal displacement was not a new phenomenon in Yemen, recent political upheavals, including the 2011 occupation of a part of the Abyan governorate by the Islamist Ansar al-Shari'ah group—which renamed the area under its control an "Islamic Caliphate" (or emirate)—meant that Riyadh could no longer stand by and welcome millions of new migrants. Although Yemeni government troops recaptured Abyan in June 2012, "thousands of inhabitants were displaced."[32] Confrontations in the Sa'adah

Governorate engendered a large number of internal refugees too even if the total numbers were guesstimates at best. For example, while in 2012 the government of Yemen advanced the figure of 545,318 refugees, the United Nations Office for the Coordination of Humanitarian Affairs (OCHA) believed 430,000 were made refugees in their own country. For its part, the Office of the United Nations High Commissioner for Refugees (UNHCR) gave a lower figure, 310,000 refugees, and affirmed that it looked after 175,000 of them.[33] What happened to the rest was anyone's guess though war conditions probably meant that UN officials were overwhelmed.

By 2017, displacement induced by political unrest and conflict became much more protracted, as more than two million were forced to flee their homes and an estimated 20 million—out of a pre-war population of 28 million—needed assistance. Starting in December 2016, the UNHCR's country representative, Ayman Gharaibeh, warned that the war was tearing the fabric of Yemen apart, and creating an unprecedented humanitarian catastrophe, though the Huthis seemed reluctant to provide assistance to those under their control.[34] As discussed below, and in addition to the United Nations, the Organization of the Islamic Conference and several Arab Gulf States, including Sa'udi Arabia, provided emergency assistance—though little of these contributions reached their intended destinations on account of the war. In 2019, the number of internally displaced Yemenis had reached 3.6 million people, or about 12 percent of the population, which added to the country's overall misery.[35]

Undocumented Yemeni Entries and Smuggling Operations

Among the many undocumented communities in the Kingdom there were Yemeni communities, a fact often overlooked both by local as well as international representatives. Sa'udi Arabia launched several nationwide amnesty programs during the last three decades to legalize hundreds of thousands of undocumented migrants, but with mixed results. The moves, it was always assumed, were designed to assist Sa'udi authorities to better manage the growing population of foreign undocumented workers, meet labour shortages in certain sectors, boost security, and reduce human trafficking from Yemen and other African countries. Through the last few decades, the Sa'udi Arabian government issued various amnesty initiatives to control the ever-increasing number of the undocumented in most Sa'udi cities, especially in Makkah province, though their numbers did not significantly decrease except in the last few years because of new, and somewhat more effective government reforms and initiatives under *Vision 2030*. One primary reason that contributed to this decrease in numbers was the standard procedure for amnesty initiatives that provided migrants a grace period in which to rectify their legal status or face penalty, jail, and deportation.[36]

The often-conflictive relationship between Sa'udi Arabia and Yemen created a constant exchange of refugees since 1932, until the most recent conflict. The data gathered and explained in Chapter 5 illustrates how Sa'udi Arabia assumed the burden to provide humanitarian aid by receiving a million refugees from the war in Yemen, despite criticisms of its direct involvement in the conflict. Ironically, in early 2021 most of the aid reaching Yemenis originated in Sa'udi Arabia, a fact that the international community failed to acknowledge time and again, opting to concentrate on bombing runs made in retaliation to Huthi attacks on the Kingdom.[37]

Table 6.1
Migrant Apprehensions by Nationality, 1978–2015

Nationality	Apprehended Migrants	Percentage of Migrants
Yemeni	3,419,207	98.688
Eritrean	16,687	0.48
Somali	9,257	0.27
Sudanese	9,014	0.26
Ethiopian	8,723	0.25
Indian	620	0.02
Pakistani	601	0.02
Bangladeshi	316	0.01
Chadian	67	0.002
TOTAL	3,464,176	100

Source: Adopted from the statistics yearbooks of the Ministry of the Interior in Sa'udi Arabia, for the years 1978 to 2015.

Before closing this section, it may be useful to note that the geographic proximity of Yemen and to a certain extent, the Horn of Africa, presents an ideal option to infiltrate Sa'udi Arabia in a clandestine manner. Regardless of advanced technological surveillance equipment that the authorities deployed, the long and very porous border could not be fully monitored. As illustrated in Table 6.1, the magnitude of the high number of clandestine migrants of Yemeni and African origins who were arrested at the Sa'udi land borders over the course of several decades, highlights the immense challenges that Riyadh confronts. These statics illustrate that the number of Yemenis arrested (3,419,207) represented 98.69% of the total, which far exceeded the numbers of any other nationality. African migrants followed with 43,748 or less than one percent. However, the long Sa'udi-Yemeni border is highly porous and offers a great opportunity for Yemenis and Africans to enter clandestinely. In this regard, Yemeni migrants simply crossed the 1,100-mile long border that separated Yemen from Sa'udi Arabia on foot, or by getting a lift from a Yemeni or Sa'udi driver, or paying smugglers to guide them across the border for a fee. In the case of African migrants, they usually went through a dangerous journey by crossing the Red Sea to Yemen first and then were smuggled into Sa'udi Arabia. More recent data confirmed this trend, even if smuggling of African nationals is much reduced on account of the war.[38]

Riyadh's Humanitarian Assistance

Western sources provided detailed statistics on the number of Sa'udi military raids, allegedly based on compilations made by the Yemeni Ministry of Agriculture and Irrigation. Riyadh seldom produced such statistics, or bothered to advance accurate data on the number of Yemeni refugees who fled the war-torn country. One source maintained that from March 2015 until September 2017, "356 Saudi air raids hit farms, 174 targeted marketplaces, and 61 struck food storage sites," while another maintained that "the Saudi-led coalition and Houthi forces have indiscriminately attacked, forcibly disappeared, and blocked food and medicine to Yemeni civilians."[39] According to the Middle East and North Africa director at Human Rights Watch, Sarah Leah Whitson, "governments around the globe can either do nothing while millions sink closer toward famine or use the leverage at their disposal to press the warring parties to end their abuses and impose sanctions on those obstructing aid."[40] This was a fundamental indictment that suggested and clearly implied how Riyadh "weaponized" access to food and ensured Yemen's total reliance on food imports for mere survival. Relying on declarations made by the International Rescue Committee, Martha Mundy, author of *The Strategies of the Coalition in the Yemen War*, maintained that the Sa'udi-led coalition-funded Yemen Comprehensive Humanitarian Operations (YCHO)—which delivered food, medicine, and commercial aid to Yemenis—was engaging in "war tactics," which added insult to injury as it clearly implied that Sa'udi Arabia controlled all of the aid that went to Yemen through key transit and access points.

Apparently, Riyadh gained control over these passageways, which allegedly was its primary objective, rather than address Yemen's immediate humanitarian needs, such as lifting the blockade on Huthi-controlled ports.[41] Beyond these well-intentioned but misplaced concerns, few took note that millions fled the country and sought refuge in the Kingdom of Sa'udi Arabia or in the Sultanate of Oman. An estimated three million Yemenis lived and worked in Sa'udi Arabia in 2019 and at least 600,000 were there as "refugees" according to humanitarian organizations. By January 2021, Sa'udi Arabia had already financed 575 projects in Yemen at a total cost of US$ 3.475 billion dollars, including various relief programs to provide food and drinking water under the auspices of the King Salman Humanitarian Aid and Relief Center (KSRelief).[42]

Table 6.2
General Statistics about KSrelief Projects for Yemen (as of 31 January 2021)

Project sector	Number of projects	Cost (US$)
Food Security	103	1,023,206,277
Health	263	733,126,357
Humanitarian and Emergency relief Coordination	28	669,273,109
Water, Sanitation and Hygiene	30	210,424,274
Camp Coordination	42	161,211,155
Nutrition	11	140,979,999
Multi Cluster	19	124,082,596
Protection	28	121,693,498
Education	21	120,958,108
Early Recovery	22	111,073,024
Logistics	7	42,735,048
Emergency Telecommunication	1	16,000,000
Total	575	3,475,763,446

2021   2 Projects at a total cost of 3,980,000
2020   104 Projects at a total cost of 431,864,665
2019   104 Projects at a total cost 939,113,871
2018   156 Projects at a total cost 1,192,674,572
2017   85 Projects at a total cost 310,255,722
2016   71 Projects at a total cost 366,359,423
2015   53 Projects at a total cost 231,415,192

Source: King Salman Humanitarian Aid and Relief Center at https://www.ksrelief.org/Statistics/CountryDetails/19

As discussed in Chapter 4, the Sa'udi relief programs included the distribution of food baskets and baby milk among a multitude of families in several areas throughout the Yemen, established high quality shelter homes for refugees in coordination with the UN Food Program, rescued scores of Yemenis from war zones to relocate them in safer areas, and provided countless individuals with essential services. The data included in Table 6.2 provides critical details from KSRelief as of 31 January 2021. In addition to the assistance extended by KSRelief, Sa'udi Arabia's total contributions to Yemen between 2015 and 2017 topped US$ 8.27 billion, a figure that rose in 2018 to cross the $14 billion threshold.[43] In addition to the Yemen, Syria, Egypt, Niger and Mauritania, to name just a few recipients, received millions of dollars in assistance too. These were significant contributions that certainly enhanced bilateral ties between Riyadh and scores of nations but, and this needs to be underscored, they also assisted those most in need. To deny the utility of this voluminous assistance to Yemen was obtuse and unbecoming.

Sa'udi Amnesty Policies vis-à-vis the Yemen

Providing financial assistance to meet humanitarian concerns was immensely helpful but also insufficient, especially to those who were uprooted from their homes and nations. All states use the process of regularization as a tool to allow aliens in irregular situations obtain legal status in their new countries; typical practices include granting amnesty, a form of legalization, to aliens who reside in the country for a given length of time but who were otherwise found to be inadmissible. Still, undocumented, illegal or irregular migrants raised concerns regarding state security, undesired cultural influences, economic implications on the local labor force, and humanitarian issues—especially as these individuals were without access to public education or healthcare. Moreover, undocumented migrants, in any geographic location, live in fear of being deported to their home countries, limiting the possibility of movement in and outside of their living environment. This compels them to live in enclosed communities with little social interaction with locals. Despite these handicaps, however, undocumented migrants in Sa'udi Arabia did not take advantage of periodical amnesties that Riyadh offered on several occasions. Table 6.3 provides a comparative snapshot of attitudes towards using or not using amnesty by a number of undocumented migrant communities in the city of Jiddah. Although this particular sample was limited in size and scope, its results highlight core concerns by migrants/refugees who endure significant hardships but still decide to linger in Sa'udi Arabia instead of returning to their home countries. In fact, most undocumented migrants in Jiddah tended to reject amnesty windows initiated by the Sa'udi government, mostly out of fear that they may be deported regardless of any actions taken to regularize their situation. When asked about whether they would take advantage of the most recent amnesty initiative that allowed undocumented migrant safe exit from Sa'udi Arabia to their home countries with no penalties imposed by authorities, 139 out of 146 undocumented migrants interviewed (95%) indicated that they would not use the amnesty, while only seven interviewees (5%) noted that they would. Most declined to state that they would use it for a variety of reasons, including fear of deportation, or because they were born in the Kingdom with no proper documents, or even because the pull factor for economic gain outweighed the risk.

Table 6.3
Attitudes Towards the Use of Amnesty Initiatives in Sa'udi Arabia by Undocumented Migrant Communities

Nationality	Are you going to use the amnesty issued by the Sa'udi government?	
	Yes	No
Africa	0	61
Yemeni	4	25
Filipino	3	23
Indonesian	0	30
Total	7	139

Source: Adopted from Alsharif, *The Good, the Bad and the Ugly*, 2015.

In the case of Yemeni migrants, 25 out of 29 interviewees (86%) said they would not take advantage of government amnesties. A majority of these migrants, especially the males, engaged in circular migration, and noted that they did not need the amnesty to go back to Yemen, as they could smuggle themselves easily between the two countries. Circular migrants, defined as repeat migrants usually of the temporary variety who engaged in repetitive movements between home and host area, exemplifies the Yemeni migrant/refugee conundrum. Many circular migrants honed survival skills and cross-border movements, at least before the start of the War for Yemen in 2015, which presented a unique predicament to Riyadh. In fact, circular migrants represented an established pattern of population mobility, whether across-country, or in rural-urban vectors, which Sa'udi authorities could not ignore. Yemeni migrants, especially the undocumented, while facing the same push factors as their African counterparts, differed greatly in their justifications for not using the amnesty. In this regard, based on the above data and results from a focus group conducted with undocumented Yemeni migrants in Jiddah, the issue of circular migration was frequently raised by officials due to Yemen's geographical proximity to Sa'udi Arabia and the ease of crossing the borders (often through smuggling) between the two countries.[44]

As noted above, concerns about state security are imperative for any country and, in the case of Yemenis residing (legally or illegally) in Sa'udi Arabia, uncertainties were undoubtedly high. The international alliance led by the Kingdom in the War for Yemen that backed the Yemeni government of 'Abid Rabbuh al-Hadi against rebel Huthi forces, as discussed in the next section, clarified various apprehensions. Despite this major quandary, Sa'udi policy-makers failed to initiate policies that curbed the existing population of Yemenis in the Kingdom, or deported undocumented migrants regardless of Sa'udi involvement in the war. Instead, Riyadh ushered in several amnesty initiatives, specifically for Yemenis living in the country, irrespective of their legal statuses, which few noticed.[45] In this regard, Yemeni refugees were treated as welcomed visitors and issued visitor status visas, which allowed them to live and work at will.

Consequences of the Huthi Takeover (2015–2018)

Although the War for Yemen started out as a strictly internal power struggle, various actors quickly dismantled the early, or at least post-2013, signs of democratization that grew out of the national dialogue process. Huthi rebels reopened old wounds and plunged the fragile state into more or less perpetual chaos that, several years later, pushed the hapless country in a quagmire for years if not decades to come. Pro-Republic and pro-Imamate confrontations surfaced on top of lingering North-South disputes, which the 1990 unification program failed to heal, and which the former strongman, 'Ali 'Abdallah Salih, could not bring under his control. If Salih perceived the Huthis as allies in the on-going internal political machinations that Yemenis were well known for, Riyadh did not object to Huthi initiatives—in so far as the objective was to reform the Islah Party.[46] By March 2015, however, Sa'udi authorities concluded that significant Iranian military and financial assistance to Huthis posed an existential threat to the national security interests of the Kingdom.[47] How the war developed, with inevitable damage to civilians, was predictable though few anticipated the proxy war that Tehran waged against Riyadh in the Yemen. In the event, Sa'udi Arabia and its coalition partners responded favorably to the legitimately elected government of Yemen for political as well as military assistance *after* 'Abd Rabbuh Mansur al-Hadi was ousted by Huthi rebels.

Operation Decisive Storm was in compliance with the United Nations Charter (Article 2:4), though two academics raised doubts.[48] The intervention initially consisted of a bombing campaign on Huthi rebel positions and later saw a naval blockade—to deny Iranian resupplies—as well as the deployment of ground forces. The operation was fully backed by the UN Security Council, which acted under Chapter VII of the UN Charter when it passed Resolution 2216 in 2015.[49] Huthi leaders claimed that they took power through a popular revolution, presumably to defend the country from a Western invasion, even if this was not an accurate reading of what transpired. The United States fought extremist groups in the Yemen, especially al-Qa'idah in the Arabian Peninsula [Tanzim al-Qa'idah fi Jazirat al-'Arab], or AQAP, also known as the Ansar al-Shari'ah in Yemen [*Jama'at Ansar al-Shari'ah fil-Yaman*], an extremist militant organization. Washington believed that AQAP was the most dangerous al-Qa'idah group, which was once led by an American citizen, Anwar al-'Awlaki, who was killed in September 2011 after he declared that he planned to establish an Islamic State. Leading Western powers backed Riyadh by providing coalition forces with intelligence and logistical support, including aerial refueling and search-and-rescue missions for downed coalition pilots, all to uphold the legitimate Yemeni government, not necessarily because they approved of or condoned coalition forces to invade and occupy Yemen. In fact, the Security Council's Resolution 2216 expanded the sanctions regime that was imposed earlier through the creation of a targeted arms embargo against the Huthis and authorized states to "take the necessary measures to prevent the direct or indirect supply, sale or transfer to, or for the benefit of Ali Abdullah Saleh, Abdullah Yahya Al Hakim, Abd Al-Khaliq Al-Huthi, and the individuals and entities designated by the Committee established pursuant to paragraph 19 of resolution 2140 (2014)." These measures legitimized the Coalition's lawful support for the rightful government of Yemen though critics opted to overlook the consensus that emerged within the international community. In the event, the Sa'udi-led military coalition announced an end to Operation Decisive Storm on 22 April 2015, shifting the intervention's focus from military operations to a political process.[50] Operation Restoring Hope did not end the war, however, as coalition forces responded to frequent Huthi attacks, including assaults on Sa'udi cities that bore the brunt of long-range Huthi ballistic missile attacks. More recent assaults in 2019 and 2021 amply illustrated that Huthi rebels were determined to continue their aggression, fully backed by Iran.[51]

As stated above, the war received criticisms as it worsened, with a serious humanitarian situation that reached disaster levels, though all blame, at least in Western sources, fell on Saʻudi Arabia. Huthis were seldom identified as bearing any responsibility for the catastrophes under way. Successive United Nations Humanitarian Coordinators for Yemen and Human Rights Watch officials, to cite two sources, placed the bulk of all charges of the war on Riyadh, going so far as to insist that apparent breaches of international law were recorded. Human rights groups repeatedly blamed the Saʻudi-led military coalition for killing civilians and destroying health centers and other infrastructure, which resulted in significant damage and, importantly, in the death of an estimated 131,000 as of December 2020 according to the UN Office for the Coordination of Humanitarian Affairs (OCHA)—out of a total of 233,000 deaths. The Yemen Data Project estimated that 17,729 civilians were killed as of March 2019 though this figure was probably too low.[52] In early 2021, a large portion of the Yemeni population continued to be in urgent need of food, water and medical aid. Remarkably, most of the aid reaching Yemenis originated in Saʻudi Arabia though, once again, little of this made the front pages of leading Western sources. Of course, coalition jets prevented Iranian planes from landing in Sana'a, even if *Reuters*, which reported this news in one instance, failed to cite that Iranian planes carried weapons as well as humanitarian assistance.[53] While no one denied that Yemenis paid a very heavy price for the war, perhaps with more than five million people internally displaced by the fighting, it was also clear that over one million Yemenis found refuge in the Kingdom of Saʻudi Arabia. Riyadh was keenly interested in ending the war and the corollary humanitarian catastrophe that introduced famine and threatened scores of Yemenis without, however, sacrificing its national security interests. Aware that diseases like cholera spread throughout Yemen, Saʻudi Arabia provided sorely needed medical assistance to alleviate the sufferings and prevent their spillovers inside the Kingdom.

Conclusion: De-escalation Efforts

After several attempts to engage warring factions in serious negotiations, the Special Envoy of the United Nations Secretary-General for Yemen, Martin Griffiths, brokered a cease-fire centered on the besieged Red Sea port city of Hudaydah, Yemen's largest port. The 17 December 2018 accord, which convened in Sweden under the auspices of the United Nations, reached a consensus to exchange prisoners, detainees, missing persons, arbitrarily detained and forcibly disappeared persons, and those under house arrest. It ushered in hope that a de-escalation process would finally be possible on the road to a comprehensive peace settlement. The Stockholm talks promised to form a committee to discuss various pending disputes, and while all sides agreed to redeploy their forces outside Hudaydah, this was still a work in progress at the time of writing this chapter. Regrettably, the fighting seldom stopped and while the Stockholm Agreement "provided the Saudi-led coalition with the possibility of gradually extricating itself [from] its intervention in Yemen," Huthi rebels were adamant in their opposition to any settlement.[54] Mercifully, and in response to the ongoing global Corona virus pandemic, a ceasefire was reached in 2020, though this also proved to be short-lived. In the event, Riyadh called for a unilateral ceasefire beginning on 9 April 2020, though the effort failed after several missile attacks were launched on Sa'udi cities.[55] Notwithstanding these setbacks, on 27 September 2020 the United Nations announced that the Iran-backed Huthi rebels and the al-Hadi government agreed to exchange about 1,081 detainees and prisoners related to the conflict, as part of a release plan reached in early 2020. The agreement, which released 681 rebels along with 400 al-Hadi government forces, included fifteen Sa'udis and four Sudanese, and was finalized after a week-long meeting held in Switzerland.[56]

What was comprehensible were the reasons why Huthis were reluctant to relinquish their advanced weaponry, chiefly ballistic missiles, used to attack Sa'udi Arabia, the United Arab Emirates, and maritime shipping. They wanted to win the war but have failed in this endeavour. For now, the prospects for returning to a unified Yemen appear poor, although the priority is not to find a political solution but to stop the ongoing fighting. Whether that is even possible is highly doubtful. As the failures associated with the previous experiment in political gerrymandering—within the 2013 National Dialogue Conference that reached a broad national consensus on a new order that was breached by the Huthis—lingered, there were few prospects in sight, even if every political effort was made by the UN Special Envoy to reach such a settlement. In time, chances are good that some level of normalcy might return to the country, though local players confront grave consequences for their nonchalance. Goaded by Iran to vex Sa'udi Arabia, Yemeni Huthi rebels seem ready to sacrifice more of their population to deny power to a legitimate central government, which implies that Yemen is heading for a more or less permanent dissolution into "competing self-declared autonomous regions" that threaten the unity of the country and impose additional hardships on the Yemeni nation.[57] Many paid the ultimate price; many more were internally displaced; still others received shelter in neighboring countries, while Sana'a continued to believe that Iran would always side with the

Huthis and that they would eventually conquer the Yemen, lock, stock, and barrel. Yet, by perpetuating the war and by rejecting Arab Gulf assistance to reach a political settlement, the Huthis prolonged the war, augmented woes on this hapless population, and ensured additional misery to Yemeni refugees.

Whether the Joe Biden administration, which reversed its predecessor's last-minute designation of Yemeni Huthi rebels as terrorists, might bring in a permanent settlement is too early to know as of this writing in early March 2021. Importantly, Washington named the veteran diplomat Timothy Lenderking as its special envoy to the Yemen, and entrusted him with the authority to negotiate a settlement. This was followed on 4 February 2021 by a presidential announcement that the United States would halt "offensive support" for the Sa'udi-led coalition's war effort in Yemen, including the transfer of precision-guided munitions that, in reality, were suspended several years ago.[58] What remained unclear were the putative ties between the War for Yemen and a potential region-wide conflagration with Iran, given that Washington seems determined to deny Tehran both a nuclear capability as well as continued interferences in Arab affairs. In the end, this was a Yemeni war that produced Yemeni internally displaced persons and refugees, and it behooves Yemenis themselves to end the long struggle for power.

CHAPTER
7

Syrian Refugees in Sa'udi Arabia

Integration Rather than Confinement

Blatant accusations that all Arab Gulf states, led by Sa'udi Arabia, were loath to accept Syrian refugees filled most media sources for the better part of the past several years. Why were Syrians moving to Western countries, some wondered, when they could move to the Gulf region, which was much closer? What prevented Arab States, especially those relatively wealthy Arab Gulf monarchies, to step-up to the plate and assume their responsibilities? Why was there a reluctance to accept fellow Arabs at a time of need and could they not do more to help solve one of the most difficult challenges in the region? Remarkably, poorly informed reportage asserted that beyond a token presence, Arab Gulf monarchies in general and Sa'udi Arabia in particular refused to take Syrian refugees and that, at most, the Kingdom disbursed funds to host governments like Lebanon and Jordan, to simply alleviate some of the misery refugees confronted in those countries. Most praised Germany, for example, for offering to accept nearly a million Syrian refugees and while Berlin deserved heaps of praise for its humanitarian efforts, what were the facts regarding the Arab Gulf monarchies? What were the policies and decisions towards Syrian refugees adopted by the Kingdom of Sa'udi Arabia?[1]

In reality, several Arab Gulf States extended the welcome mat, accepted hundreds of thousands of Syrian refugees in their midst, and went out of their ways to accommodate specific needs as required. Based on a 2015 official Sa'udi Ministry of Foreign Affairs statement, the Kingdom alone received on its soil 2.5 million Syrians between early 2011 and mid-2015, without labelling any of them "refugees." Instead of creating dedicated camps, Riyadh regularized their papers, which transformed them into "legal residents," a status that allowed them to move about the country or travel to other destinations as they wished. Similar efforts were introduced in Kuwait and the United Arab Emirates, while smaller numbers of Syrian refugees were welcomed in Bahrain, Oman and Qatar. At the end of 2020, at least half a million Syrians were still in Sa'udi Arabia, where free medical care and education were available, along with opportunities for those who preferred to thrive in the business world.[2] All Syrian children that were still in the Kingdom with their parents received free schooling and were enrolled alongside their Sa'udi brothers and sisters. Likewise, adults who wished to further their education were enrolled in specialized courses in innovative programs, which aimed to improve their socio-economic standings. Regrettably, few were aware of these measures, and fewer bothered to examine the record before condemning Riyadh for its alleged lack of empathy. Importantly, the opposite of these denunciations was accurate, and as discussed below, Sa'udi officials issued specific directives to look after Syrian refugees in full.

The purpose of this chapter is threefold: first, it is to describe Riyadh's policies vis-à-vis Syrian nationals who moved to Sa'udi Arabia; second, to evaluate accusations that the conservative Arab Gulf country refused to alleviate the humanitarian crisis towards Syrians (as well as Yemeni and other asylum-seekers) in the Kingdom as well as toward Lebanon, Jordan, Iraq and Turkey; and third, to analyze Riyadh's integration rather than confinement policies. Before addressing these critical questions, discussion provides a brief overview of the wars underway in Syria, assesses casualties and offers educated guesses about the total number of refugees that the conflicts created.

The Making of a Catastrophe: Millions of Refugees

Although a comprehensive discussion of the War for Syria or, more accurately, of the wars under way in the Levant, are beyond the scope of this study, it is important to raise a few salient points that preoccupied this hapless country since 2011 to better understand its refugee calamities and how various nations responded to the on-going bloodbath. Indeed, and as the multi-sided armed confrontations gained importance, the country's fate was more or less sealed. What started out as localized internal uprisings against the Ba'ath regime quickly took on regional and global dimensions when a variety of countries, ranging the gamut from Iran to Turkey and from Russia to the United States, positioned themselves on the Levantine checkerboard. Each fought its own battles to advance narrow interests and seldom those of the hapless Syrian people. In late 2020, and despite various prognostications that the wars were about to end, numerous forces that opposed the government, regional foes, and most of the surviving opposition groups from among 1,500 that were still engaged in combat along varying combinations, ensured that the conflicts continued sine die.[3]

Disappointed by the Bashar al-Assad rule, whose early promises for genuine socio-political reforms around the turn of the century raised expectations, the vast majority of Syrians were anxious to free the country from Ba'ath Party rule that combined Arabism with socialism while denigrating both. The result was an outright dictatorship that ruled with an iron first, on Syria, as well as on neighboring Lebanon though the 2005 Cedar Revolution reduced—but has not eliminated—Damascene influence in Beirut. In the whirlwind of the post-2011 Arab Uprisings, the unrest that started in the historical town of Dar'ah, south of Damascus, spread across Syria as angry but unarmed protestors took to the streets to vent their frustrations that, at least initially, mobilized in disorganized opposition movements.[4] It was the Assad regime that escalated what were peaceful protests into armed conflicts, as Damascus rejected calls for change and, emboldened by Iran, struck at Syrians with impunity throughout the land. What followed were systematic suppressions alongside the classic acceleration of the use of unmitigated violence by the state against its own people.[5] Thousands of prisoners were released into fresh militias as the Ba'ath regime fell back on diabolical schemes to terrorize civilians. Poorly trained recruits were empowered to assume guerrilla functions, given that the Syrian Arab Army was more or less exclusively trained to fight land warfare against Israel. Loyal groups of armed militiamen, known as the *Shabihah* (apparitions), and mostly composed of 'Alawite elements that supported the Ba'ath Party led by the al-Assad family, were let loose to further terrorize the population into complete submission.[6]

In time, the uprisings became outright wars, fought by several factions, including the Syrian government, its Iranian and Russian allies, a loose alliance of Sunni Arab revolutionary groups [including the Free Syrian Army that lost most of its momentum by 2014]; the majority-Kurdish Syrian Democratic Forces (SDF); several extremist groups like al-Nusrah Front or Jabhat al-Nusrah that became the Jabhat Fatah al-Sham after July 2016 [sometimes also described as al-Qa'idah in Syria or al-Qa'idah in the Levant]; and the Islamic State of Iraq and the Levant (ISIL) that morphed into the Islamic State of Iraq and Syria (ISIS) before it took on a regional focus as simply the Islamic State (IS)], as well as several Arab and Western powers. According to one observer, more than 1,500 groups fought in Syria at one point or another since 2011.[7]

Over the course of the years, an American-led international coalition was established with the declared purpose of countering ISIS after 2014, but that failed to achieve much of its objectives as it conducted airstrikes against haphazard targets. Iran and Hizballah, the Lebanese militia that operated on Tehran's behalf out of extensive bases in Lebanon, supported the Syrian government militarily with undeniable gains.[8] Still, it was Russia that sustained the Assad regime, and rescued it from imminent fall in September 2015 when it deployed air force assets to Syria and conducted a sustained air campaign against opposition forces.[9] Turkey was also deeply involved from the very beginning but more so after 2016 as Ankara actively supported several opposition groups. Furthermore, Turkish troops occupied large swathes of North-Western Syria, ostensibly to deny both the Yekineyen Parastina Gel (People's Protection Units—a Kurdish Jihadist group better known by the abbreviation YPG) and the Partiya Yekitiya Democrat (the Kurdish Democratic Union Party PYD), from hooking up with the secessionist Partiya Karkeren Kurdistane (the Kurdistan Workers' Party or PKK), a militant and political organization based in Turkey and Iraq that was secessionist in nature and substance, and that threatened both Ankara and Baghdad.[10] In reality, however, Ankara deployed its forces to retain a winning hand in the future of a country with which Turkey shared a long land border—nearly 520 miles or about 825 kilometers—and whose political fate would, most likely, affect its own, especially if it were partitioned.[11]

Irrespective of motivations by local, regional, and international actors, the wars in and for Syria created severe human rights violations and massacres. The conflicts also caused a major refugee crisis that affected bordering states and several European countries. By the end of 2020, an estimated 600,000 Syrians were killed and, perhaps, 15 million became refugees. At no time since Syria gained its independence from France in 1946 was the population in such dire straits. Nothing in the country's dictatorial past compared with the on-going suffering, not the numerous coup d'états that chequered its history before 1963, nor the ironclad Ba'ath rule that gripped the country afterwards. Syria went through several coups and changes in leadership during the 1960s, though it was a 'Alawi officer, Hafiz al-Assad, who ushered in a period of stability after March 1971, when he imposed his tyrannical regime.[12]

On 31 January 1973, Hafiz al-Assad implemented a new constitution, which led to a national crisis, because he insisted that secular Ba'athism ought to prevail over all. Unlike previous constitutions, the 1973 paradigm did not require that the President be a Muslim, which upset conservative elements and lead to fierce demonstrations in Hama, Homs, and Aleppo, largely organized by the activist Muslim Brotherhood organization. Extremist elements labeled Assad the "enemy of God" and called for a jihad [holy war] against his rule. Damascus crushed the Muslim Brotherhood in several battles that culminated in the 1982 Hama massacres when scores were killed.[13] Upon Hafiz al-Assad's death in 2000, his son Bashar al-Assad was selected as President of Syria, raising expectations that the young head-of-state—married to a Sunni Muslim born and educated in Britain—would transform the country into a modernizing entity that, at the very least, would begin to introduce the rule of law. Not surprisingly, and because of entrenched party interests, the Damascus Spring that witnessed some social and political debates lasted less than a year. For all practical purposes, the modernization experiment ended by August 2001, when scores of "dissidents" were arrested because some of them called for *democratic* elections. Then, and ever since, Bashar al-Assad reasserted his view that terrorist groups operating in Syria were manipulated by outside powers. His viewpoint is neither accurate nor pertinent to the simple demands for representation, democratization, and the protection of law.[14]

The 2011 Uprisings

In the whirlwind of major uprisings in Tunisia, Libya, Egypt and Yemen, protests began throughout Syria on 15 March 2011, when thousands marched in Damascus, demanding democratic reforms and the release of political prisoners. Security forces retaliated by opening fire on naive protesters oblivious to the record of the regime. Some were confident that the Ba'ath would quickly fold like other Arab governments, as hundreds of thousands were mobilized by social media connections that created false hope, and raised expectations. In villages across Syria, children drafted brazen graffiti on walls, and scores chanted: "Al Sha'ib Yuriduh Isqat al-Nizam" [The people want the fall of the government]. In Dar'ah, a city with genuine history dating back hundreds of years and that saw French attacks against Druze patriots, a 13-year-old boy, Hamzah al-Khatib, was caught red-handed scribbling anti-state graffiti on a city wall. He was arrested and executed under routine torture. His mutilated body was returned to his parents in what was supposed to be a popular warning that Damascus would not tolerate, even from 13-year-olds, any opposition, which reminded one and all that Syria resembled Stalinist Russia rather than an aspiring Arab republic with traditional norms that valued family life. In the event, on 20 March 2011, protesters burned down a Ba'ath Party office. The regime quickly determined that such actions could not be tolerated if it was to stay in power. The ensuing clashes claimed the lives of police officers and protesters, whose bold and violent responses accelerated as ordinary people shed their fear of the regime, and no longer accepted the state's foreign conspiracy theories to subjugate the masses into full submission and vassalage. By the end of May 2011, 1,000 civilians and 150 soldiers and policemen had been killed and thousands detained; among the arrested were many students, liberal activists and human rights advocates.[15]

Emboldened by Iran and the Hizballah militia, whose troops fought alongside the Syrian Arab Army against Arab Syrian citizens who formed the bulk of the opposition, the Damascus regime relied on chemical weapons to gain the upper-hand, which threatened to involve global powers.[16] On 20 August 2012, President Barack H. Obama issued his renowned "red line" warnings, which asserted that Washington was "very clear to the Assad regime, but also to other players on the ground, that a red line for us is we start seeing a whole bunch of chemical weapons moving around or being utilized." "That would change my calculus," declared Obama, adding: "That would change my equation."[17] Of course, chemical weapons were used in four previous attacks before 2012, though few seemed to have taken any note of their deployment, ostensibly for purely political reasons as the United States, Russia, and other global powers weighed their options. A belated decision was taken on 21 August 2013 when an opposition-controlled area in the suburbs around Damascus, known as the Ghutah (or Ghouta), was attacked with chemical weapons. Several hundred people died [at least 281 and perhaps as many as 1,729] though the timid international community reacted cautiously.[18] A UN fact-finding mission investigated *alleged* chemical weapons attacks while the United States and several European Union states accused the Syrian government of using sarin gas and other chemical weapons.[19]

No retaliatory attacks were launched against the Syrian regime although a confidential August 2016 report by the United Nations and the Organization for the Prohibition of Chemical Weapons (OPCW) explicitly blamed the Syrian military for dropping chlorine bombs on the towns of Talminas (in April 2014) and Sarmin (in March 2015). Remarkably, and to its credit, the OPCW also blamed ISIS elements for using sulfur mustard on the town of Mari'ah in August 2015, which was accurate, though the Netherlands-based organization never elucidated the origins of the chemical weapons in the hands of these extremists.[20] In the event, Barack Obama made a deal with Russia's Vladimir Putin to look the other way, as Sergey Lavrov, the Russian Foreign Minister, secured from the American Secretary of State, John Kerry, a commitment to empower the OPCW to assume responsibility for Syria's chemical weapons. On 9 September 2013, Lavrov announced a Russian proposition whereby Syria would agree to place its chemical weapons under international control and to dismantle them, while the United States agreed not to conduct a military strike on the country—even if, in reality, no strikes were contemplated. What happened to most of these weapons remained a mystery although in 2015 the UN mission disclosed previously undeclared traces of sarin compounds in a "military research site" that, to say the least, raised many fresh questions about the international commitment to peace and security.[21] In fact, the OCPW inspectors asked Syria to hand over its remaining chemical weapons, perhaps unaware that Damascus failed to fulfil its obligations under the Lavrov–Kerry entente, which proved to be ineffective as fresh chemical attacks occurred around the city of Dumah (or Doumah) in 2017.[22]

On 4 April 2017, after a sarin attack at Khan Shaykhun in Idlib Province that left hundreds dead or crippled, President Donald J. Trump apparently told his Secretary of Defense Jim Mattis: "Let's fucking kill" [President Bashar al-Assad] in a telephone call, adding, "Let's go in. Let's kill the fucking lot of them."[23] Beyond Trump's colorful language that, regrettably, was not exclusive to this head-of-state, the United States launched its first attack against Syrian government forces when warships of the US Navy launched 59 Tomahawk missiles at the Syrian government's Shayrat Air Base, which was said the be the source of the chemical attack.[24] A spokesman for Vladimir Putin declared that the Russian President viewed such an American attack as "an act of aggression against a sovereign country violating the norms of international law, and under a trumped-up pretext at that."[25] The United States representative at the United Nations Security Council emergency meeting declared that "the moral stain of the Assad regime could no longer go unanswered," and American forces hit the Syrian military again on 18 May 2017, when a Syrian army convoy advancing in the vicinity of the border town of al-Tanf, which hosted a U.S.-controlled airbase used for training anti-government forces, came under attack by U.S. fighter jets.[26] The wars continued, though Russia, Iran, and Turkey signed an agreement in Astana on 4 May 2017 to create four "de-escalation zones" inside Syria that, instead of helping resolve the conflicts under way, added fuel to the many fires burning in the hapless country because of competing and often contradictory interests.

Between 2018 and 2020, the War for Syria took on additional international features, including a September 2018 deal that was reached by Russian president Vladimir Putin and Turkish president Recep Tayyip Erdoğan, ostensibly to create a buffer zone in Idlib Province. Washington was not thrilled with this development, though President Trump abruptly announced on 19 December 2018 the withdrawal of all American troops from Syria, after which Turkey lowered its tempo. Not to be left out of the regional game, on 25 December 2018, Israel launched yet another attack from or across Lebanese air space, "in response to an anti-aircraft missile launched from Syria" that, conveniently, did not draw a Russian condemnation save for usual diplomatic regrets. Turkey continued its offensives throughout 2019, which necessitated a new accord. Russia escalated its attacks against rebel forces in Idlib on behalf of the Syrian government, and while Washington imposed new sanctions against Syria and Russia, as well as Iran, these threats fell on deaf ears. The year ended with more of the same catastrophes that befell on Syria throughout the past decade.[27]

Controversies Over Casualties

Irrespective of motives, what the wars in Syria recorded more than any other phenomenon were the number of deaths, even if accurate data was nearly impossible to locate. On 2 January 2013, that is less than two years after the initial Spring 2011 uprisings, an official United Nations figure stated that 60,000 had been killed since the civil war began. At the time, the UN High Commissioner for Human Rights, Navi Pillay, claimed that "the number of casualties is much higher than we expected, and is truly shocking."[28] Four months later, the UN's updated figure for the death toll had reached 80,000. On 13 June 2013, the United Nations released an updated figure of people killed since the fighting began, with a new figure standing at exactly 92,901 killed up to the end of April 2013. Navi Pillay stated that "this is most likely a minimum casualty figure" as the real toll was guessed to be over 100,000 in mid-2013.[29] Within a year, a new UN study concluded that at least 191,369 people died in the Syrian conflict, but the 20 August 2014 report was the last published by the world body for reasons that are difficult to comprehend.[30] In fact, the UN stopped collecting statistics after mid-2014, though a study by the Syrian Centre for Policy Research released in February 2016 estimated the death toll to be 470,000, with 1.9 million wounded (reaching a total of 11.5% of the entire population either wounded or killed) by the end of 2015.[31] Casualty figures rose once again in 2016 with Human Rights Watch repeating the 470,000 killed numbers as of February 2016, though Amnesty International opted not to advance any numbers of the dead.[32]

Of course, the number of casualties continued to rise as various groups painstakingly collected available figures on a more or less daily basis. The

Syrian Network for Human Rights, for example, broke down its data in the following way: 222,114 civilians killed between March 2011 and September 2018, which ignored military deaths. Nevertheless, the site listed 27,989 children and 25,179 women killed, along with 14,024 dead due to torture and 118,829 in a category listed as arbitrary arrests.[33] By 2021, the number of civilians killed stood at 227,413, with 29,457 children and 28,458 women killed as well.[34] Again, the Syrian Network for Human Rights did not provide a separate list for military or security force casualties, which is unusual to say the least. For its part, the British-based Syrian Observatory for Human Rights, which was founded in 2006—that is before the 2011 uprisings—by Rami Abdurrahman, a leading Syrian in exile who monitored the war with the assistance of countless in-country informants, stated that at least 511,000 people were killed in the war between March 2011 and the end of 2017.[35] Data from the Syrian Observatory for Human Rights revealed that 593,000 were killed in Syria by early December 2020, including 22,149 children and 13,804 women.[36] No matter how one assesses the figures, the number of Syrians killed is very high, to which one must add an undetermined number of dead from among the following nations that were caught in the melee or were directly or indirectly involved in the fighting: Palestinians, Lebanese, including Hizballah fighters, Turks, Iraqis, Iranians, Russians and several Westerners who trekked to the Syrian killing fields as journalists or observers. The total list is undetermined but records many deaths, which means that it is probably impossible to know exactly how many were killed, how many were wounded, and how many were missing. Survivors of the conflicts became internally displaced persons and those who could escape became refugees in neighboring countries or further afield.

Demographic Transformations in Lebanon, Jordan, Iraq and Turkey

Syrian IDPs and refugees altered the country's demographic composition and, in turn, transformed neighboring countries' population compositions. Thus, and in addition to the numerous casualties that scarred Syria, the conflicts that befell the country caused major refugee crises that involved several nation-states, preoccupying leading powers. Over the course of the decade, and while a number of peace initiatives were launched, the most visible consequence was the large numbers that fled by land or sea. The privileged could escape early on to settle in Arab financial mega-cities like Dubai and Cairo, though the overwhelming majority paid the ultimate price or, if they were lucky, found shelter in neighboring countries like Lebanon, Jordan, Iraq and Turkey.[37] Although leading scholars examined Syria's refugees crises, perhaps the most important development associated with the phenomenon was the fact that the country's demographic set-up was literally and profoundly affected by the movement of millions of individuals. Moreover, and because the overwhelming majority of refugees were Sunni Muslims, the impact of this demographic transformation was significant even if poorly understood.[38]

Estimated at around 23 million inhabitants in 2011, the chief transformation of the Syrian Uprisings was, undoubtedly, the dramatic population changes that will, in all likelihood, alter the status-quo and introduce permanent divisions when peace returns to Syria. In 2018, an independent Syrian media organization, 'Anab Baladih [also spelled Enab Baladi], claimed that the Syrian population stood at 28 million, of which 21 million were living in Syria, while 7 million were made refugees. These were optimistic figures as the number of refugees most probably crossed the 10 million mark and the population that was actually inside the country was nowhere near 21 million. In fact, one source estimated that the population stood at 17,951,639 in 2014 and 18,028,549 in mid-2017, significant declines from 2011 on account of a galloping death rate [4 deaths/1,000 population estimated in July 2017], a noticeable falling birth rate [21.2 births/1,000 population in 2017], and a sharp increase in the net migration rate [-27.82 migrant(s)/1,000 population in 2012].[39]

Few denied that the impact of the on-going wars was serious, as several million refugees huddled in make-shift camps along the Jordanian border, inside Turkey near border villages and cities, and spread throughout Lebanon.[40] Millions were internally displaced, either voluntarily or forced to relocate, to satisfy ethnic cleansing operations. In reality, there was no detailed information about ethnic and religious groups in Syria, which ought to be the base of any contemporary demographic assessment because of the consequences of the post-2011 war(s) that witnessed a sharp hike in sectarian and tribal reassignments. In Latakiyyah, for example, it was nearly impossible to know how many Sunnis were still living in the coastal city, which became an 'Alawite stronghold par excellence.[41] Likewise, and while non-Kurds were visible in Qamishlih and Dayr al-Zur, the north-eastern part of the country was now predominantly inhabited by Kurds. Of course, Arab nationals constituted the overwhelming majority, standing at nearly 85% of the population, though Kurds were the second largest ethnic group, making up around 10% of all residents, with several smaller minority groups, including Yazidis, Turkmens, Assyrians, Circassians, Armenians, as well as even smaller numbers of Albanians, Bosnians, Georgians, Greeks, Pashtuns, Persians, and Russians. In short, whereas Syrians numbered around 23 million in 2011, their actual demographic strength was less than 23 million in 2020, with only 15 to 16 million living in the country. Refugees who lived outside Syria numbered between 4 and 7 million, while an additional 5 to 7 million were internally displaced. All of these people certainly deserved attention, as various countries, including the Kingdom of Sa'udi Arabia, opened their doors to welcome as many refugees as possible. To date, however, and with rare exceptions, the story of Syria's 15 to 16 million refugees remains poorly analyzed although numerous journalistic essays were published to discuss various aspects of the issues that concerned refugees in key countries, some of which are discussed below.[42] In the event, very few essays, journalistic or academic, ventured to assess linkages between Syrian refugees with the Arab Gulf states.

According to the United Nations High Commissioner for Refugees (UNHCR), there were over 5.4 million Syrians registered as refugees in Turkey, Lebanon, Jordan, Iraq and Egypt by the end of 2020, though these figures changed on a more or less daily basis as some refugees returned home while others escaped Syria or even received permanent resettlement offers in foreign countries.[43] By universal acknowledgment, host countries and communities showed exceptional generosity towards refugees, though hundreds of thousands or, perhaps several million, did not even bother to register with the United Nations agency for a variety of reasons, including fear. In some instances, Levantine business acumen meant an unregistered refugee could simply collect hand-outs more often than those who followed prescribed protocols, which was also far more lucrative. Of course, wealthy Syrians were not in need to collect global assistance, which was the reason why in a country like Lebanon, for example, an undetermined number of Syrians simply relied on themselves to rent apartments, or purchase them when possible, which allowed many to run businesses and mingle within society at large.[44]

Syrian refugees in Lebanon, Jordan, Iraq and Turkey were key players in internal, regional and global struggles as Damascus perceived its Sunni citizens in negative terms. Secularized Ba'athists who worshipped Assad and backed the dictatorship reasoned that these were little more than traitors who deserved their fate. Iran, which carried out sophisticated demographic realignments in Syria to encourage Shi'ahs to resettle precisely to redraw various demographic maps, looked on too, as many lingered in misery.[45] For their part, Arab Gulf states extended humanitarian assistance to many groups, while also settling disputes by backing warring factions. Turkey used the pressure of the refugees to "negotiate" with European powers, secure financial support whenever possible and, regrettably, used the downtrodden as fodder in its decades-old political race for relevance within the European Union arena.[46] It was thus important to discuss the position of Syrians in other Middle Eastern countries given their absolute relevance to the arguments developed in this study, especially how the region and the world dealt with them, in comparison with Arab Gulf societies.

Syrian Refugees in Lebanon

Lebanon hosted around two million Syrian refugees although only 875,531 were registered by the UNHCR at the end of 2020, which was still a very high number for a country whose citizen population was less than five million. Often overlooked, this figure was in addition to the estimated 500,000 Palestinian refugees who were also living in Lebanon, although and unlike the Syrians, the overwhelming majority of the latter were confined to twelve camps.[47] In the case of the Syrians, Beirut estimated that the refugee population reached around 25% of all residents living in the country, which suffered from chronically weak services and infrastructure even before the large influx. Yet, estimates by senior Lebanese government officials, leading clerics, and several Non-Government Organizations all agreed that there were at least 1.5 million Syrian refugees in Lebanon.[48] By all accounts, the high percentage of refugees compared to the native or citizen population drastically affected the social and economic situation in the country; the situation made all the worse given Lebanon's failure to recover from its own protracted internal conflicts. Still, and except for Syria, no country was as affected by the wars in that hapless country as Lebanon because local politicians could not agree to set up proper refugee camps (like Jordan and Turkey). Instead, refugees were accommodated throughout the country, in every city, village or hamlet, which meant that the Syrian conflict spilled-over. Host communities, as well as the refugees themselves, suffered from deteriorating living conditions despite United Nations assistance. As an estimated 170,000 Lebanese citizens lived below the poverty line by 2015 (according to figures released by the International Labor Organization), because the high unemployment rate meant that wages were kept low, the influx of even cheaper Syrian manpower increased to the total level of poverty in the country by at least 20%. Although half-a-million Syrians were legally employed in Lebanon before 2011, the addition of economically active refugees added the overall pool for low-skill jobs in the unorganized economy that, naturally, further depressed prices. In short, the presence of Syrian refugees in Lebanon increased the vulnerability of many, both Syrians as well as Lebanese, which further sharpened negative perceptions of the "others" despite the rhetoric of brotherhood between neighboring peoples spread by Levantine spin-doctors.[49]

Across Lebanon, Syrian refugee children were accommodated in local public schools, split into morning and afternoon shifts with their Lebanese counterparts—a unique phenomenon in refugee care. Syrian teachers—themselves in exile—followed their country's education curriculum while many benefitted from UNICEF assistance to look after so many children. Saʿudi Arabia and several Arab Gulf States extended regular and substantive material assistance to Syrian refugees enrolled in hundreds of schools throughout Lebanon, providing them with books and other needs, winter clothing during the season, food packages on a regular basis to ensure that no one went hungry, regular health visitations by local doctors and nurses and, even more important, bestowed parents with monthly stipends that allowed many to purchase essentials. All of this, before, during, and after the post-17 October 2019 Lebanon uprisings that rocked that society and plunged the country into more or less permanent socio-economic (as well as political) catastrophe.

Syrian Refugees in Jordan

Unlike refugees in Lebanon, a portion of the Syrians who crossed the border into Jordan were housed in special camps, although close to 80 percent of registered refugees lived outside of the camps, primarily concentrated in urban and rural areas in the northern governorates of Jordan. According to the UNHCR, and as of 3 March 2021, the total number of registered Syrian refugees in Jordan stood at 664,603.[50] The first camp was set up at Mafraq in 2011 though the largest facility was and remained the nearby Zaatari Camp (±80,000).[51] Smaller facilities were erected at Azraq Camp (±36,000) and the Emirati Jordanian Camp (±7,000). Given Jordan's limitations and severe environmental restrictions, especially the lack of water, the number of Syrian refugees in Jordan strained the country's resources. Of course, and like Lebanon, Jordan housed multiple other refugee populations or "persons of concern," including 65,922 Iraqis, and more than 13,000 from Sudan, Somalia, and Yemen, all of whom topped the hundreds of thousands of Palestinians who flocked to the country after 1948 and especially after the 1967 and 1973 Arab–Israeli wars. There were in total about 1.4 million Syrian refugees in Jordan and, again, only about 20 to 25 percent were concentrated in the camps.[52] Jordanian sources reported that the refugee population increased slightly in 2017 though fewer people lived inside camps compared to the previous year as an undetermined number left the country for European shores.[53] Ironically, and despite some returnees, the actual number of refugees increased slightly, simply because few trusted the regime in Damascus. Naturally, humanitarian aid organizations requested significant assistance from international donors to look after these refugees, whose presence in the Hashemite Kingdom increased pressure on Amman's infrastructure, specifically sanitation facilities, housing, and energy use on top of the provision of water supplies.[54]

Even if unintentional, tensions between Jordanian hosts and Syrian refugees became prevalent in several cities and surrounding areas outside of refugee camps, which challenged Amman to react with utmost care. As Syrian refugees absorbed scarce resources and took certain jobs from locals, some of the refugees came into conflict with Jordanian residents, with the cost of hosting refugees rising sharply. According to a leading news source relying on Jordanian data, the use of electricity and water subsidies cost Amman "around $3,000 per year, per Syrian, as well as half of the Health Ministry's budget for medical care or $350 million." *The Washington Post* reported that "roughly 160,000 jobs have been given to illegal Syrian workers while 20 percent of Jordan's citizens remain[ed] unemployed."[55] To help alleviate these financial burdens, Washington "provided nearly $668 million in support, promising $3 billion over the next three years in general aid to support the Jordanian government."[56] By all accounts, the influx of refugees left an impact on the quantity and quality of services delivered, and generated the need for humanitarian assistance across the board throughout the country to all "persons of interest." In response to this crisis, leading members of the international community and key Arab Gulf States, including the Kingdom of Sa'udi Arabia, worked with Amman to create the Jordan Compact, a groundbreaking "deal that aimed to provide 200,000 work permits for Syrian refugees in exchange for preferential access to the European markets as well as access to conditional financing from the World Bank," even if the record was mixed at best. Simply stated Jordan was not in a position to fulfill all of its obligations, provide adequate housing, look after the education needs of so many children, and otherwise absorb into its fragile health infrastructure hundreds of thousands of refugee cases that necessitated attention, without foreign aid. Again, and lest we forget, both the United Arab Emirates and the Kingdom of Sa'udi Arabia provided assistance to the Jordanian Government precisely to overcome such shortfalls although much more was required.

In early 2018, Amman welcomed more than 300,000 displaced Syrians, with more than 60,000 fleeing south, hoping to find safety in the Hashemite Kingdom. Confronted by yet another wave of refugees,

Amman closed the border and refused to let the newcomers in, insisting that the country could do no more. This was an unpopular position as compassionate Jordanians called the decision shameful and vowed to share whatever they had with the refugees. Some Jordanians matched words with actions, organizing private relief efforts to help those trapped along the border region. This popular reaction pushed the government to rescind its earlier resolution, and allow some refugees to cross the border temporarily, ostensibly for medical assistance but in reality to seek sanctuary. Remarkably, Jordanians expressed their understanding of conditions that befell refugees, and supported them to the best of their abilities.[57]

Syrian Refugees in Iraq

According to the UNHCR, and as of 3 March 2021, Iraq hosted 243,890 Syrian refugees, most of whom (over 95 percent) were in the Kurdistan region. An estimated 58,000 arrived in 2017 when the war in Eastern Syria was in full swing. Several refugee camps were set up for Syrian refugees of ethnic Kurdish origins, although the burden on Baghdad was significant because of the post-2014 conflict that added at least 3.3 million internally displaced Iraqis to the mix.[58] Interestingly, Syrians were seldom granted asylum upon arrival in Iraq but received, instead, a 15-day visa for medical or visit purposes. After an initial security clearance, most were allowed to travel further. Unlike several other neighboring countries, Baghdad based its admissions policies entirely along security considerations, which was eminently understandable given the challenging security situation within the county. Because of Iraq's proximity to the predominantly Kurdish region in Syria, UNHCR observed regular human traffic between the two countries, as an undetermined number of Syrians spontaneously returned to Syria. In contrast, a trickle attempted the same routine with Turkey, which reflected much stricter controls even if smuggling along that border was frequent. UNHCR officers attempted to regulate these crossings, reunifying family members where possible, and monitoring as many border points as feasible to prevent irregular activities.[59]

Two major concerns preoccupied UNHCR officers in Iraq: legal stipulations and potential resettlements. In a country that agonized from acute war conditions, Syrian refugees and asylum seekers who sought legal assistance were not always privileged, although some interactions with key judiciary authorities occurred. As Baghdad reorganized its society, the commitment towards principles of international protection was revived, with positive consequences for an estimated 10,000 Syrians.

Most received civil documentation, residency and labor permits, and otherwise were granted some protection. In cases that involved the legalization of marriage and other civil rights questions, including birth registration, such legal protection proved to be critically important as it allowed many to find relative peace of mind. UNHCR officers assisted refugees with their court representations with the majority of "claims relating to legalization of divorce, marriage, birth, domestic violence, custody and alimony as well as detention over illegal entry," being resolved satisfactorily.[60] What remained a nearly impossible dilemma was resettlement for those who wished to do so, even if practicality imposed itself. After 2017, 775 Syrian refugees who resided in Iraq were submitted to resettlement countries, including the United Kingdom followed by Canada, the United States and Sweden.[61] Unfortunately, interest from resettlement countries was limited, save in the rare family reunification cases. The vast majority of refugees stayed put with few prospects to return to their native land.

Syrian Refugees in Turkey

More than 3.6 million Syrian refugees sought and received sanctuary in Turkey since early 2011. According to a recent study, their "numbers, through births and new arrivals, [were] increasing by approximately 1,000 people per day," as many hoped to join the estimated half a million asylum seekers and refugees from other countries.[62] Whether Turkey's difficult political environment would allow Syrians to survive and prosper was an open question as Turkish civil society underwent its own challenges. Ankara attempted to encourage its international partners to share in the burden, with mixed results, which meant that most of the day-to-day responsibilities to look after so many individuals fell on local authorities. Although specific camps were set-up for Syrians, more than 95 percent settled in urban centers along border towns, ranging from Kilis, which is now a "Syrian" city since the majority living in it are no longer Turks, to Gaziantep.

By 2017, at least 560,000 registered Syrian refugees lived in Istanbul, though those in the capital city tended to belong to privileged classes with relatively independent survival means. Although able to support themselves financially, Turkish authorities perceived the large refugee presence as a source of danger, which was why Ankara removed an estimated 100,000 unregistered Syrians from Istanbul and resettled them elsewhere throughout the country.[63] Along border towns, municipalities adopted innovative methods to look after as many people as possible, "running free language courses, instituting social support programs, permitting a degree of legal flexibility for Syrians opening businesses, and in the case of at least one district, Bağcilar, encouraging Syrians to participate in advisory citizens' councils." According to one source: "The Marmara Municipalities Union, which include[d] nearly 300 local governments in Istanbul and its surrounding regions that collectively represent[ed] more than 20 million residents, house[d] a migration policy center that enable[ed] its constituents to share best practices, coordinate refugee support activities, and develop evidence-based policies to promote integration."[64]

Turkish officials embarked on a full-scale integration effort, though few Syrians accepted the offers, as most hoped their presence in Turkey was temporary. That was the primary reason why the UNHCR and other aid agencies were so active in Turkey, where the vast majority of refugees applied for asylum to European countries. Of course, the preference was to return home and, short of that option, most refugees contemplated European shores instead of permanently settling in Turkey. Despite Ankara's significant efforts to integrate as many Syrians as possible, a large segment of the Turkish public rejected their presence, which was probably the legacy of severe political tensions between the two societies that went back decades or centuries.[65] Most Turks perceived Syrian refugees as a burden and, based on numerous terrorist activities since 2011 that saw Syrians settle scores amongst each other, blamed the latter for the deteriorating security situation.[66] Of course, public services were affected by the presence of such a large foreign population, with spillover effects in the economy as prices increased and unemployment ballooned. Ankara's integration efforts were thus not particularly successful. The situation became even more complicated after Turkey justified its military interventions into northern Syria, ironically alongside the United States and Russia.[67] Comically, Turkish authorities "[began] to remove Arabic shop signs across the country in a bid to soothe popular resentment over the Syrian refugees, which—stoked by Turkey's economic crisis—has raised the political costs for the government." Nationalist Turks perceived the Arabic signs as a reminder of the multifaceted refugee problem, with some even fretting that Turkey [was] "being lost" or "Arabized," something that was deemed insulting and, of course unacceptable.[68]

Notwithstanding Turkish efforts to look after Syrian refugees, large numbers attempted perilous crossings across the Mediterranean to the Greek island of Lesbos, to reach Europe. UNHCR statistics reported that 216,054 arrived during the whole of 2014, 520,000 during the first nine months of 2015, and over 300,000 migrants made the dangerous crossing in 2016. Many were rescued after their makeshift "vessels," courtesy of smugglers who raked-in huge profits, failed. Heartbreaking images of Syrian refugees on the high seas in atrocious conditions filled the airwaves, sometimes with unexpected political consequences, as was the case with the washed-up body of a young Kurdish boy, Aylan Kurdi, on 2 September 2015.[69] The image of the three-year-old's tiny body spoke volumes, which prompted international responses and, at least temporarily, unlocked closed borders. Tragically, and with family members in Canada, Kurdi failed to reach Europe because Ottawa denied repatriation before the ill-fated crossing. Others were luckier as at least a million settled in various European countries.[70] Turkey played a key role in hosting a large number of refugees but it also bargained with their lives with European Union member states, extracting financial concessions to look after them, instead of cooperating with European nations. For years on end, hundreds of thousands transited throughout Europe hoping to reach Germany or the United Kingdom, often with tragic circumstances. Most of those who were left behind planned to return to Syria as soon as they could possibly do so.

Impact of Regional Refugees on Sa'udi Arabia

As discussed above, and at the height of the Syrian crises that enveloped that hapless country in both a particularly violent civil war as well as acute regional and international confrontations, hundreds of thousands fled their homes, a number that grew steadily between 2011 and 2020. At first, most displacements were of the internal variety as residents sought refuge in nearby villages with relatives or acquaintances, though neighboring states quickly became preferred destinations. Jordan to the South, Iraq to the East, Turkey in the North and Lebanon to the West swelled with millions of Syrian refugees before a stream trekked to various European countries, chiefly via Turkey and Lebanon.[71] Most required assistance that created unprecedented humanitarian crises in the four countries discussed above. In fact, the United Nations Office for the Coordination of Humanitarian Affairs in Syria confirmed that an "average of 5.2 million people benefitted from food assistance on a monthly basis" throughout 2020, "8 million people were served through repair, rehabilitation augmentation of water system and almost 2.5 million children and youth were reached through formal and non-formal education services."[72] These sobering figures increased in 2019 with 4.5 million receiving food assistance, 1.9 million receiving agricultural assistance, 7.6 million receiving direct water, sanitation/hygiene kits and assistance, 4.7 million children and teachers benefitting from quality education programs, and 748,439 girls and boys accessing protection services in 2019 alone.[73]

Of the estimated five million Syrians registered with the UNHCR, and to underscore the impact that these mass movements had on neighboring countries, it is worth repeating that Turkey hosted over 3.6 million refugees, Lebanon almost 1.7 million (though the number of unregistered Syrian refugees probably meant that nearly two million moved into the neighboring country), and Jordan welcomed 1.5 million, chiefly within the huge Zaatari Camp that became the second largest city in the Hashemite Kingdom after the capital city of Amman.[74] Germany took in nearly a million as assistance to displaced persons, while several other European countries, including Armenia, Austria, Belgium, Bulgaria, Croatia, Denmark, France, Greece, Hungary, the Netherlands, Norway, Sweden, Switzerland, the United Kingdom and others have taken significant numbers too [see Table 7.1].

In North Africa, Tunisia took in 4,000, Libya, 30,000, Algeria 43,000, and Egypt anywhere between 200,000 and 500,000. The Arab Gulf region welcomed 3,500 Syrian refugees in Bahrain, 40,000 in Qatar, 155,000 in Kuwait, 242,000 in the UAE, and over 500,000 in Sa'udi Arabia. For reasons that are murky at best, otherwise reputable organizations—ranging from Amnesty International to the Brookings Institution, claimed that Sa'udi Arabia and its Gulf Cooperation Council partners have taken in zero refugees—which was both nonsensical as well as wrong. In fact, the Kingdom of Sa'udi Arabia and its Gulf Cooperation Council (GCC) allies responded far better than many assumed, often legalizing the presence of Syrians as residents instead of ramming them into refugee camps.

GCC States and Syrian Refugees

Astonishingly, one particular graphic attributed to Luay Al-Khatteeb, a non-resident fellow at the Brookings Institution in Doha (Qatar), indicated that Sa'udi Arabia, Kuwait, Qatar, and the UAE apparently took in exactly zero Syrian refugees. This egregious claim advanced by a sole Iraqi scholar was naturally cited by nearly every Western media outlet and publication, including *CNN*, *ABC*, *CBS*, *NBC*, *The Washington Post*, and *Foreign Policy*, among others, further reinforcing the untruth (Graph 7.1, page 186).[75] Even worse, and because these media sources were often used as primary sources by scores of counterparts in the rest of the world, this untruth gained unprecedented traction that perpetuated the falsehood.[76] In fact, the dedicated chart with four

Table 7.1
Refugees of the Syrian Civil War

Regions with important populations (over 1,000 refugees)		
Country	2020	2015–2018
Turkey	3,643,700 (registered)	
Lebanon (Settled)	910,256 (registered)	2.2 million
Jordan (Settled)	656,213 (registered)	1,265,000
Germany		879,980 (Dec. 2019)
UAE		100,000 (2015)
Sudan		250,000 (2017)
Iraq (99% in Iraqi Kurdistan)	247,440 (registered)	
Sweden		191,530 (2019)
Egypt	130,074 (registered)	124,534 (UNHCR estimate 2017)
		500,000 (Egypt MFA estimate 2016)
Netherlands		105,440 (2020)
Yemen		100,000 (2015)
Hungary		72,505 (2015)
Canada		62,000+ (applicants to Feb. 2017)
		43,000+ (approved as of Feb. 2017)
		40,081 (resettled as of Feb. 2017)
Croatia		55,000 (2015)
Greece		54,574 (2016)
Qatar		54,000 (2017)
Austria		45,827 (2017)
Algeria		43,000 (2015)
Libya		26,672 (2015)
Armenia		22,000 (2017)
Denmark		19,433 (2015)
Bulgaria		17,527 (2015)
United States		16,218 (2016)
Belgium		16,986 (2016)
Norway		13,993 (2015)
Singapore		13,856 (2015)
Switzerland		12,931 (2016)
Serbia		11,831 (2016)
France		11,694 (2016)
United Kingdom		10,583 (2018)
Brazil		9,000 (2015)
Spain		8,365 (2015)
Russia		7,096 (2016)
Finland		6,232 (2017)
Australia		6,000 (2017)
Malaysia		5,000 (2015)
Tunisia		4,000 (2015)
Cyprus		3,527 (2015)

Table 7.1 (*continued*)
Refugees of the Syrian Civil War

Regions with important populations (over 1,000 refugees)		
Country	2020	2015–2018
Bahrain		3,500 (2015)
Argentina		3,000 (approved)
Montenegro		2,975 (2015)
Italy		2,538 (2015)
Romania		2,525 (2015)
North Macedonia		2,150 (2015)
Malta		1,222 (2015)
Somalia		1,312 (2016)

Source: UNHCR Syria Regional Refugee Response, 2020, available online at: https://en.wikipedia.org/wiki/Refugees_of_the_Syrian_civil_war

prominent zeroes next to or underneath the names of Kuwait, Qatar, the UAE and Sa'udi Arabia was widely reproduced, including in *The Washington Post*, although *ilmfeed.com*, a web source dedicated to publishing informative and inspirational articles about Islam and Muslims, updated the same graphic with more accurate data (see Graph 7.2).

Not surprisingly, numerous non-scholarly assertions were posted online, and in letters to editors on countless web-pages, along with many daily and weekly publications around the world, all to deride the Kingdom and its Gulf partners for doing so little to assist Syrian refugees. The gist of such comments raised a credulity problem for Riyadh that was allegedly overtly sympathetic to the plight of the Syrian people without, critical observers concluded, the desire to welcome refugees into the Kingdom. The observations and questions regarding this unwillingness to accept refugees were meant as a reprimand because it was believed that Riyadh had not taken in any refugees. Sometimes, amateur commentators compared how "Europe and America have taken in many hundreds of thousands of Muslim refugees and not housed them in migrant camps, but in apartments and homes," in contrast to what Muslims and Arabs allegedly did: thrust Syrian refugees in miserable camps. Such commentaries were meant to illustrate Western respect for civil liberties and, simultaneously, Arab disrespect for basic human rights which was gratuitous as well as incorrect.[77]

In fact, the six GCC countries were mistakenly condemned for "keeping their doors to refugees firmly shut," though mainstream western media sources, activists and challenged politicians remained

Graph 7.1
Number of Syrian Refugees taken in by countries in the Middle East

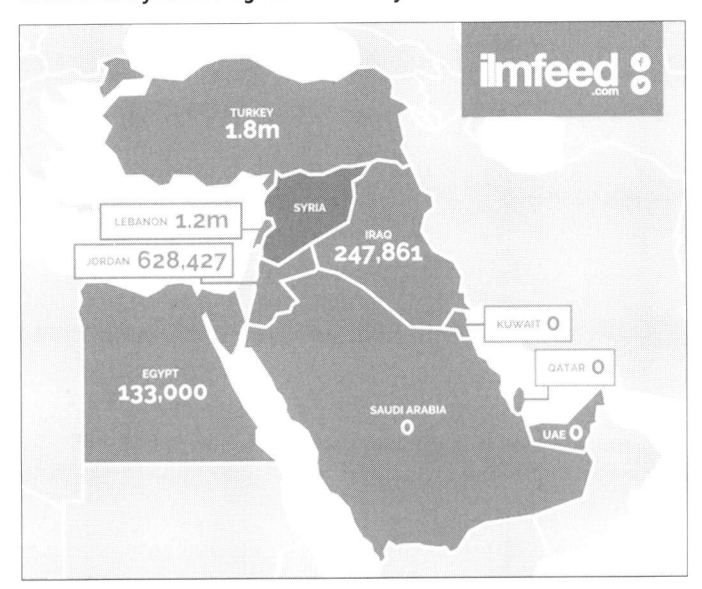

TURKEY 1.8m
LEBANON 1.2m
JORDAN 628,427
IRAQ 247,861
EGYPT 133,000
KUWAIT 0
QATAR 0
SAUDI ARABIA 0
UAE 0

Source: Graphic in Ishaan Tharoor, "The Arab world's wealthiest nations are doing next to nothing for Syria's refugees," *The Washington Post*, 4 September 2015, at https://www.washingtonpost.com/news/worldviews/wp/2015/09/04/the-arab-worlds-wealthiest-nations-are-doing-next-to-nothing-for-syrias-refugees/

Graph 7.2
Number of Syrians Living in Gulf States since the Beginning of the Conflict

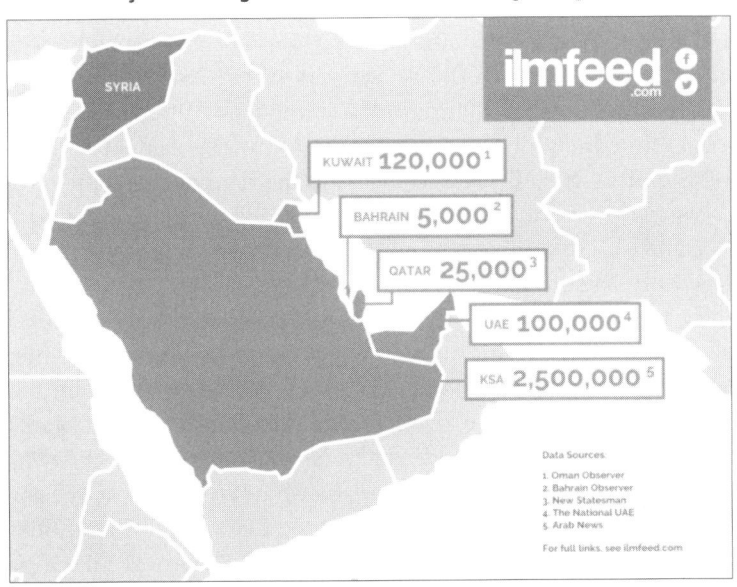

KUWAIT 120,000[1]
BAHRAIN 5,000[2]
QATAR 25,000[3]
UAE 100,000[4]
KSA 2,500,000[5]

Data Sources:
1. Oman Observer
2. Bahrain Observer
3. New Statesman
4. The National UAE
5. Arab News

For full links, see ilmfeed.com

Source: "Did the Gulf States Really Take in Zero Syrians?," *ilmfeed.com*, 30 September 2015, at http://ilmfeed.com/?s=Syrian+Refugees

oblivious to the notion that Arab Gulf states, as non-signatories of the United Nations High Commissioner for Refugees "Convention," did not fit the refugee counting/classification pattern.[78] Most organizations relied on the UNHCR classification though it is asinine to say there were no Syrian refugees, not a single one, in Bahrain, Kuwait, Oman, Qatar, Sa'udi Arabia, and the United Arab Emirates. It is worth repeating that of the nearly three million Syrians in the GCC States, most of whom arrived after the outbreak of the civil war in 2011, not one was considered to be a refugee and not one was classified as such, which explains why they were not part of UNHCR statistics. While it was the business of UN bodies to categorize their constituencies as refugees or persons-of-interest and similar terms, GCC governments relied on a different terminology: Syrians were classed as "Arab brothers and sisters in distress" instead of refugees covered by UN treaties. The UNHCR corrected its initial classification and acknowledged that Sa'udi Arabia welcomed over 500,000 Syrian refugees in September 2015, though by this time the media damage was already done.

For its part, the government of Sa'udi Arabia was slow to react to the spread of the many falsehoods that belittled its reputation, though it did issue an official declaration on 11 September 2015, in which it declared that it granted permanent residency to hundreds of thousands of Syrians.[79] Riyadh was not keen to deal with these individuals as refugees, or to put them in refugee camps but, on the contrary, Sa'udi officials repeatedly declared that Syrians were allowed complete freedom of movement. The government further authorized Syrians to work, allocated free medical care, and ensured that all children received free education. In 2015, over 100,000 Syrian students were being educated in Sa'udi schools, gratis. By 2016, more than 141,000 Syrian children pursued their education free of cost and, by the end of 2020, over 100,000 Syrians were still legal residents in the Kingdom, free to circulate as they wished.[80] Similar efforts were recorded in the UAE and other GCC countries, though such efforts were conveniently ignored by challenged media sources.[81]

Finally, the task now is to offer a preliminary evaluation of accusations that the conservative Arab Gulf country refused to alleviate the humanitarian crisis towards Syrians (as well as Yemenis and other asylum-seekers), even if the record indicated that all GCC States but especially the Kingdom of Sa'udi Arabia *donated more than $2.3 billion by the end of 2015 to various charities to help the downtrodden*. Lest one assume that the amount donated was small compared to the total aid handed over by Western countries, available data affirms otherwise. Indeed, Sa'udi Arabia, the United Arab Emirates, Qatar, and Kuwait were in the top ten countries giving aid to Syrian refugees, much more than Germany, Canada, Japan, Australia, France and Italy combined. Ironically, the $2.3 billion was donated to support the UN refugee agency's efforts in countries neighboring Syria, including UNHCR camps in Jordan and Iraq, where tens of thousands received shelter. Saʻudi Arabia and Qatar allocated significant additional funds for food, shelter and clothing to Syrians in Lebanon and Turkey. They also assisted the Lebanese Government to keep many elementary, primary and secondary schools open from 2 to 8 p.m. to specifically cater to Syrian nationals anxious to continue with their country's educational curriculum. In September 2015, the Saʻudi Press Agency announced that Saʻudi Arabia provided around $700 million to UN aid agencies in Syria and set up clinics at refugee camps.[82] These figures reached US$ 304,725,378 by the end of 2020.[83]

Integration of Syrians Within the Kingdom

In early 2016, a reputable German source lamented that Arab Gulf states have taken in few Syrian refugees, and quoted experts concluding that no one should expect "the oil-rich monarchies to change their course anytime soon even if they needed labor and shared a common language/culture with Syrians."[84] After going through more or less the same ground covered above, the writer concluded that Syrians were not to be trusted, and required "a visa and passport to enter the Gulf monarchies." The report quoted Metin Çorabatir, a former UNHCR spokesperson and later president of the Research Center on Asylum and Migration in Ankara, Turkey, saying that GCC governments "prefer to share their responsibility with financial donations." It further cited a Saʻudi dissident who ran the Institute for Gulf Affairs (IGA) in Washington, D.C., Ali al-Ahmed, who claimed that the "Saudis have invested in the Syrian war; now they must invest in refugees." Beyond such facile and largely erroneous pronouncements, what the *Deutsche Well* author aimed for was to confirm whether Riyadh actually feared Syrians for ethnic, sectarian and political reasons. Ali al-Ahmed apparently persuaded his interviewer that Saʻudi Arabia could easily welcome three million Syrian refugees because it enjoyed the space. Moreover, the IGA advanced an attractive argument to *Deutsche Well*, namely that nearly 10 million expatriate workers—chiefly from the Indian subcontinent—could easily be replaced by Syrians even if most of the latter were unskilled laborers whereas the Levantines were far more educated and filled professional posts as illustrated by the nearly one million that were absorbed in Germany. Berlin opened its doors on humanitarian grounds even if, one further assumed, because it also cherished and welcomed skilled Syrians who filled a noticeable void in the rapidly greying German workforce. Nevertheless, *Deutsche Well* concluded that Saʿudi Arabia and its five partner monarchies within the Gulf Cooperation Council (GCC) rejected Arab laborers because the latter posed security threats.

While there was some truth to this assertion, especially in the wake of the post-2011 Arab Uprisings that witnessed raw sectarian rationales as ʿAlawis fought Sunnis, the logic that Syrians fleeing a republican dictatorship to seek refuge in monarchies threatened conservative Arab societies was an untenable proposition. Moreover, Çorabatir's assertions that GCC States' "political structures and demographics [meant that] they [would] never take in a million refugees" were equally unreasonable. For the Turkish national whose own country was knee-deep in a full-blown refugee crisis and was, furthermore, fighting potential secessionist movements, Syrians were little more than "destabilizing elements."[85] Al-Ahmed confirmed that Syrians harbored "ideas of revolution" that, presumably, was unacceptable to Saʿudi and GCC governments, though welcoming around 2.5 million did not indicate fear or excessive concerns that Syrians were prone to revolution. Furthermore, there was nothing in the report that many Yemenis lived and worked in the Kingdom too, which was evidence that Riyadh welcomed large numbers of migrants and refugees.

Likewise, and as Riyadh provided free access to healthcare and, especially, education, this alleviated lingering concerns that a few mavericks were among the refugees. On the contrary, Saʿudi actions spoke loud and clear and quickly authorized Syrians already in the country to sponsor family members and extended relatives to legally enter the Kingdom. GCC states adopted similar policies, redefining extended family to include distant relatives as well, which meant that these policy preferences highlighted integration within society as the Kingdom rejected the mass movement of peoples who could only be housed in vast camps. It is worth underscoring that the creation and running of very large camps to house hundreds of thousands was something entirely familiar to Saʿudi Arabia on account of proven experiences in welcoming millions to perform the annual pilgrimage (*hajj*) in Makkah. Indeed, yearly arrangements that necessitated extraordinary logistics for the growing number of pilgrims transformed Saʿudi authorities into genuine experts at running such facilities, though the policy for Syrian refugees was quite different. While it was relatively acceptable to house anywhere between one to three million adult pilgrims in tent cities on a temporary basis—as most stayed for less than two weeks in the Mina area near the Holy City—Saʿudis did not believe that it was a satisfactory solution to house, transport, provide sanitation and health for hundreds of thousands of families, many with small children. That, more than any other reason, illustrated Riyadh's preferences even if few outsiders fathomed it. As discussed in Chapter 3, Riyadh rejected this option after its experience in the Rafhah Camp situation in the aftermath of the Gulf War, which it vowed to never repeat.

Conclusion: Continuing Warfare, Ongoing Assistance

Saʿudi ties with Syria reached new lows starting in the Summer of 2011 after Damascus launched vicious attacks against its own people. Riyadh backed opposition forces that aimed to end Iranian control of the Bashar al-Assad regime, which effectively meant that Saʿudi Arabia and Syria were in a Catch-22 situation that, to say the least, placed the two nations on opposite sides of the political spectrum. It was the late Saʿudi monarch, ʿAbdallah bin ʿAbdul ʿAziz Al Saʿud—who went out of his way to reconcile Assad with most of his Arab foes—but who also became the first Arab leader to condemn the Assad government in August 2011 "due to its method to deal with the anti-government" demonstrations.[86] His successor, King Salman bin ʿAbdul ʿAziz, perceived the Syrian head-of-state as a leader unwilling, perhaps even unable, to end the war, or introduce meaningful reforms.[87] In 2015, Foreign minister ʿAdil al-Jubayr maintained there were no circumstances where Bashar al-Assad could remain in power, and anticipated a putative exit either through politics or by force. After the Russian intervention, however, Riyadh recognized that al-Assad was going to stay in power for some time to come. Heir Apparent Muhammad bin Salman reiterated that he "believe[d] that Bashar's interests [we]re not to let the Iranians do whatever they want[ed] to do" in Syria, though this was impossible to know given the incredibly close relationship between Damascus and Tehran.[88] In the event, and despite repeated conclusions that the wars in Syria were on the wane, sporadic confrontations continued in late 2020. What is undeniable, and beyond sharp political differences that require astute attention for decades to come, is that Riyadh welcomed a very large number of Syrians on its territory as permanent residents. Its policy was one of integration rather than confinement into refugee camps. Moreover, and as discussed above, Riyadh provided significant assistance to Syrian refugees in Jordan, Lebanon and elsewhere, especially through the King Salman Humanitarian Aid and Relief Centre.

Notwithstanding this level of assistance to Syrian refugees, the ongoing wars created a slew of frustrating situations that further distressed Arab donors. Remarkably, leading global authorities stood idly by when it was revealed that Turkey and Lebanon were "rounding up hundreds of workers and sending many back to volatile parts" of Syria, often without prior notification. Deportations were preceded by the confiscation of mobile phones, at least in Turkey, which meant that the hapless migrants "were held incommunicado from families or lawyers and forced to sign papers saying they 'voluntarily' agreed to return to war-ravaged" land. Even United Nations officials seemed distressed but that was the level of their irrelevance at a time when Ankara and, to a lesser extent, Beirut, demonstrated their pro-Bashar al-Assad inclinations.[89] Ankara under Recep Tayyip Erdoğan seemed to have grown tired of its 3.6 million Syrian refugee population and, more important, shifted its policies towards Damascus. In 2019, Turkey allied itself with armed opposition groups and no longer pushed for regime change. Meanwhile in Beirut, Prime Minister Sa'ad Hariri, who first backed the armed opposition, changed his mind and became an ally of politicians from all denominations [a fringe Druze community leader, Talal Arslan, the Shi'ah dominated Hizballah, and the predominantly Maronite Free Patriotic Movement (FPM) of President Michel Aoun], "whose fortunes [were] tied to the Assad regime." Hariri paid lip service to Syrian refugees, ostensibly because he was concerned that undocumented migrants were taking jobs that would presumably go to locals, even if the overwhelming majority of Lebanese were too proud to perform menial tasks. In reality, the big lie revolved around the Hizballah–FPM claim that the war in Syria was over, and that conditions were relatively stable to encourage refugees to return. In fact, humanitarian groups denied such groundless assertions, and pointed to ongoing battles in Idlib Province where a Russian and Syrian-led air campaign "killed more than 400 people, including 90 children" during the last week of July 2019 alone. Such assaults continued throughout 2020 with no end in sight as the ongoing crisis in northwest Syria forced thousands of children to flee every day over the last week of January 2020. Sadly, more than 300,000 individuals were displaced in Idlib Province since December 2019, a number that was steady.[90] On 6 April 2020, the UN Security Council published a long overdue report on its investigation into the attacks on humanitarian sites in Syria, where it had examined six sites of attacks and concluded that the airstrikes had been carried out by the "Government of Syria and/or its allies," which was a diplomatically correct reference to Russia.[91] Deadly assaults continued throughout 2020, which produced fresh refugees that trekked to neighboring countries, as both Turkey and

Lebanon—whose governments were in domestic difficulties—preferred to victimize them for narrow and inhuman geopolitical reasons. None of the neighboring countries wished to, or were in a position, to integrate Syrian refugees. The only countries that adopted positive immigration steps were the conservative Arab Gulf monarchies, led by Sa'udi Arabia.

CHAPTER
8
The Refugee Challenge for Saʿudi Arabia and the Muslim World

In the aftermath of the "Arab Uprisings" that literally shook the entire Arab World, and the spillover effects of refugee crises that unsettled regional and global powers, leading Arab countries, led by Saʿudi Arabia, were taken aback by various accusations of indifference and neglect. Commentators and analysts failed to perceive or, more accurately, ignored, what regional governments did to meet the nascent refugee challenge that boomed beyond anyone's expectation as millions fled war zones. As discussed throughout this volume, Riyadh and several Arab Gulf countries welcomed many refugees even if neither the Saʿudi authorities nor officials in neighboring states took to the airwaves to brag about their deeds.[1] Still, all wished to engage in a meaningful discussion with Western, especially European, countries to identify what each party understood to be the main definitions that governed policies towards refugees. Equally important, and certainly related to the quest for expedited and useful assistance to those most in need, Saʿudi Arabia was confronted with excessive denunciations for not doing its fair share. Mainstream media sources conveniently overlooked—in some instances even misled their readers—the Saʿudi humanitarian aid that took place.

This study will, hopefully, set the record straight, contribute to the ongoing discussion, and provide accurate facts and figures to alleviate false allegations. Its key purpose was to answer unilateral charges lobbed by Western academic and journalistic sources that, without providing reliable evidence, reached the conclusion that the Gulf countries did not accept any exiles. In the case of Syrian refugees, whose search for salvation created a major migration challenge to the entire European Community, experts believed that Arab countries failed to open their borders to shelter those fleeing that hapless country's destruction. One example, among many, was the work of Julie M. Norman, a Research

Fellow in Conflict Transformation and Social Justice at Queen's University in Belfast, Northern Ireland, in which she accused Saʻudi Arabia and other Gulf states for failing to open their borders to those displaced by the conflict in Syria.[2] In her widely read essay, Norman doubted that the Kingdom had received 2.5 million Syrians since 2011, as several Saʻudi sources claimed. Most importantly, she concluded that Riyadh did not provide asylum to refugees because it "welcomed between 100,000 and 500,000 Syrians on visas" that, to her, was a "very unclear data [and] just another sign of the fundamental problem." "Saudi Arabia and the Gulf states," she concluded, "simply don't 'do' refugees."[3] Of course, such denunciations made by a single academic would not be enough to undermine the Kingdom' reputation in this specific field, yet, when they become mainstream they run the risk of undercutting possible dialogue and better understanding refugee policy options between Western and Muslim states. As clarified throughout this research effort, nuances existed between how Western and Muslim societies explained their rationales, on the basis of cultural and social variables; false readings skew and reinforce existing prejudices.

In fact, one of the first tasks that this volume tackled was to offer a comparison between the idea of refugee as conveyed by the 1951 United Nations Convention—along with its 1967 Protocol—and the one proposed by Islam. In order to do so, the first preoccupation has been to find common traits between Western and Muslim societies, which can help in setting the ground for further discussion. Drawing from what Mashood Baderin stated, namely that "whatever definition or understanding we ascribe to human rights, the bottom line is the protection of human dignity, [and that] there is perhaps no civilization or philosophy in today's world that would not subscribe to that notion," we embarked on a journey in search of the obvious, and sometimes not so obvious.[4] The study focused on the common religious grounds that exist between the idea of human rights in the West and its counterpart in Islam. The result of this endeavor was that, despite the evident secularization that transformed Western civilizations starting in the eighteenth century, all of the most famous declarations concerning individual rights recognized the notion that all men were equal to the eyes of God.

Remarkably, the 1776 American declaration of independence states: "We hold these truths to be self-evident, that all men are created equal; that they are endowed by their Creator with certain unalienable rights; that among these are life, liberty and the pursuit of happiness," perhaps one of the most eloquent pronouncements on the subject. A few years later, that is with the "Declaration of the Rights of the Citizen" that was ushered in during the French Revolution in 1789, the "Westerner" lost his religious distinctiveness to become a "citizen," which paved the way for a gradual but complete secularization of western societies. Interestingly, and notwithstanding such transformations, there were common roots to Western and Muslim cultures in the legal traditions of the Arab World, where basic principles of human rights existed ever since antiquity in Hammurabi's code (1780 BCE) as well as in Greek and Roman Law, with the concept of *jus gentium* (law for all people).

Supported by the traditional common ground outlined above, our research endeavor opted to further decipher this discussion, until now limited to the past, and to bring it into the contemporary arena, being aware that this almost uncharted territory was destined to generate controversy. The first step was to discover any similarities between the 1951 Refugee Convention (and its 1967 Protocol), with the principles enunciated in Shari'ah Law regarding the treatment of refugees, precisely to understand the strengths and limits of both. What emerged was clear: the Western idea of refugees and rights struggled in adapting to the diversity of new migrants/exiles. Born on the wake of the human crises that were triggered by the horrors of World War II, the Western definition acquired an inherent rigidity in its definition, which stated that the status of refugees did not depend on the objective conditions of the individuals, but on a recognition granted by the state on what were very fluid bases.

Common strengths, as anticipated above, could be found in the desire of guaranteed dignity to those in need of hospitality. However, both interpretations tussled to realize that their principles seemed contradictory, when confronted by real dilemmas. In Western settings, the human aspect of the refugee was somewhat overlooked, which ended up imposing a secular culture on persons in exile that risked isolating him/her from their new environments, while Shari'ah Law was sometimes insufficient in dealing with a humanitarian crisis, which involved the acceptance of non-Muslims, or, in the specific case of Sa'udi Arabia, of people not belonging to their nation. In fact, this latter development was visible in the Kingdom, which hosted various non-Arab communities.

As discussed above but worth reiterating, this approach allowed one to realize that in order to establish dialogue between Western and Muslim societies it was necessary in the case of Sa'udi Arabia to proceed along two roads, which would, at the end, meet in a single route. The first one was a deeper investigation of how the Kingdom and its institutions responded to the waves of immigrants ever since the country was established as an independent entity in 1932. The second was an inquiry into Sa'udi Arabia's international commitments to events that necessitated humanitarian aid. In both cases, the result was really surprising and filled a gap in our knowledge, not only of the Kingdom, but also of other Muslim countries. In both cases the relationships between Saʻudi Arabia and its minority populations, with its neighboring countries, and with the international community, all displayed different shades of experience from the monolithic vision that media sources broadcast ad nausea. Saʻudi society was almost always painted as being almost immobile, somewhat paralyzed and, worse, isolated from the rest of the world as if not part of the planet. Yet, while Saʻudi Arabia faced its own share of internal and external challenges because of specific cultural and legal attributes, it remained fully engaged on the global scene.

Notwithstanding Saʻudi society's particularities, the first community that challenged the uniformity of the Kingdom were the Bidun, nomad tribes who lived on the border with Kuwait and who were not included in the citizenship process during the establishment of the new country, in 1932. Palestinian refugees who arrived after the establishment of Israel in 1948 and the Rohingya from Myanmar who entered the country in different waves starting in the 1960s, were the second and third significant migrant populations that settled in Saʻudi Arabia. In addition, an examination of contemporary immigration patterns into Saʻudi Arabia demonstrated that the Kingdom welcomed people from different continents escaping wars, dictatorships, treacherous economic conditions, and environmental disasters. Naturally, the way the Kingdom dealt with refugees changed over time, as the implementation of different policies such as amnesties, the granting of residence permits and the possibility for children born in the country to acquire citizenships, was enacted. Even if these acts were not sufficient to solve the problem of illegal immigration, they have nevertheless contributed to easing tensions among various communities. Still, most of the time Saʻudi institutions were slow, or lacked the resources, to tackle nascent challenges. For example, the presence in the country of migrants originating in very diverse African communities defied all approaches to fully integrate these individuals into Saʻudi society, which meant that many African "illegal immigrants" lived in constant fear of reprisals and deportation.

An effort was thus made to reach out to these communities in order to gather reliable data and information about their living conditions in the Kingdom. For the first time, and with the help of community leaders, it was possible to talk directly with members of different African communities through individual, semi-structured interviews and focus group exchanges. The outcomes of this effort constituted an intellectual and epistemological capital that countered unsubstantiated opinions uttered by academics whose limited access did not allow for a grasp of the real conditions on the ground. Nevertheless, it is also important to state that the secretive character of Sa'udi authorities in dealing with "illegal immigrants" left little room for objective investigation. What was finally assembled, and presented in this volume, confirmed that Riyadh was both aware of its challenges in this area and displayed specific steps to address serious concerns.

It is important to repeat that investigations within immigrant communities took place alongside analysis of the changes adopted in the legal framework dealing with stateless people, such as in the three communities mentioned above, and which revealed that many changes were introduced in the last decade. For example, the enactment of a new "Labor Law" and the "Anti-Trafficking in Persons Law," which clarified working conditions and granted local sponsors (employers) control over the migrant's ability to enter and exit the country and seek other employment, were concrete steps that aimed at regularizing living conditions. This willingness to change was traced back to 1992 when the "Basic Law of Governance" granted certain rights and protections to foreign residents of the Kingdom (including the right to file a lawsuit), while the "Labor Law" amended protections to all workers, foreign and national (excluding domestic workers), banned sponsors from withholding the passports of their employees without their written consent, and identified key professions reserved for Sa'udi nationals. Likewise, in 2009 Riyadh passed the seminal "Anti-Trafficking in Persons Law" that provided specific protections to victims of human trafficking, even if the mechanisms in place were not ideal, given that abusive employers resorted to deportation procedures to dispose of individuals they wished to dismiss.[5] In 2021, the *kafalah* system was amended as well, which granted an employee the right to changer his/her employer without incurring any penalties.

These were all valuable amendments to existing legal provisions that affected migrants, refugees, and other stateless individuals that lived in the Kingdom. In fact, all of these changes originated from the awareness of difficulties caused by the lack of legislation towards migrant populations, which the authorities addressed with determination, especially after 2017. In particular, the issue of statelessness was markedly serious, though the proposed legislation lacked flexibility. Amendments to the "Citizenship Law," which could really change the way all Sa'udi society deals with the problem, are pending. As of this writing, the issue of citizenship was still very much a work in progress, an issue that was not included in *Vision 2030*, as discussed earlier in the study. Yet, granting nationality to children born from Sa'udi women and non-Sa'udi fathers remains under serious consideration. Nevertheless, the Sa'udi government adopted several recent measures towards the possibility of guaranteed Sa'udi citizenships to children born in the Kingdom, by contemplating the introduction of regulations to clarify the situation. In this way, Riyadh would comply with international norms over the long-term, further removing the canard that the country was not committed to end discrimination and to protect all children.

It was inevitable in this context to investigate how these potential new regulations could actually affect the other illegal communities present in the country. In the course of interviews with dozens of migrants, it became clear that a mere legal intervention could constitute the beginning step toward normalization, even if this was not an ideal solution. Over the past few years the Sa'udi government, with the purpose of easing the situation of immigrants, issued various amnesties that granted residency privileges to illegal immigrants and refugees. Sometimes, these initiatives were not particularly successful for very different pragmatic reasons, with the main difficulty residing in the fact of their furtive conditions. In certain cases, clandestine living lasted for a generation or more, which prevented many migrants from to identifying themselves with the host country. Clearly, better efforts are required to solve the vexing "illegal immigrants" problem. A recent effort is now underway to establish a relationship of trust that may well allow members of these communities to assimilate within Sa'udi society constructively.

The advantage of this kind of investigation is that, perhaps for the first time, it may be possible to provide a fairly reliable database about the communities involved, both to recognize that such a problem exists (which was historical while unknown especially to Western researchers), and to acknowledge that it is possible to include the refugee conundrum facing Sa'udi Arabia and potentially other Arab countries in a wider discussion about refugees and forced migration. This kind of research requires a multi-disciplinary effort in order to study the legal, social and cultural challenges posed in the specific realities in a joint attempt to overcome differences and prejudices that, until now, have jeopardized a constructive dialogue between two different ways to think and to act in the field of human rights. One of the primary outcomes of this investigation was the idea that:

"In Islam, asylum is a right, a duty, and a general and comprehensive form of protection. It is religious but it is also territorial and to some extent diplomatic. No modern international instrument stipulates clearly that individuals have the right to grant or to be granted asylum. All modern texts reserve this right for the State which is free to grant or refuse asylum to those who seek it."[6]

While article 14 of the Universal Declaration of Human Rights states that "Everyone has the right to seek and to enjoy in other countries asylum from persecution," few if any countries grant such privileges automatically. In fact, and to their immense credit, leading advocates struggled to secure asylum from persecution for many who sought such protection—often without success.

Moreover, it is critical to underscore that refugees had the right to ask for asylum in Muslim societies because, according to Islam, every human being has the right to be hosted and protected without depending on rules established by the state. The result of this perspective was clear: a 'person' taken into account by Muslim traditions was a religious individual first and foremost, and this automatically provided for the exclusion of non-Muslims. Yet, this stand—taken together with the fact that Shari'ah Law does not provide for gender equality—stands as another illustration of discord. Of course, when dealing with refugee crises, such views present serious consequences that ought not be overlooked. These differences originate from two different ways to conceive human rights. While Western cultures stress the universality of human rights,

> "Islam recognizes two types of rights: rights that humans are obliged—by virtue of being the creations of God—to fulfill and obey; and rights that they are entitled to expect from their fellow human beings. It is the latter that correspond to what are elsewhere termed 'human rights.' The former are rights that stem from, and are obtained through, belief in God and religion. In this concept, only God truly has rights and the rights of humans are understood as their obligation to abide by God's commands. They are, first and foremost, the rights of individuals to abide by and adhere to the laws that God decreed and are only possible through this belief system, thus excluding non-Muslims."[7]

Consequently, it may be possible to explain why, for example, it is difficult for Muslims to grant refugee status to women who travel without a male member of the family, as this would infringe Shari'ah Law. The latter holds that women depend on men and that men have the duty to provide for their families. As this concept was translated and incorporated into the legal system [Family Law] that, again based on Shari'ah, did not allow women to transfer their own citizenship to their children. Sa'udi authorities struggle to address these legal questions. The failure to clarify and understand this set of rights in Muslim culture has been the source of many misunderstandings and contributes to the idea that Muslim countries fall short when dealing with humanitarian aid.[8]

Critics disparage these explanations and highlight various human rights abuses committed within Saʻudi Arabia against migrants and refugees, including poor detention center conditions, limited access to legal aid and fair trial before deportation, and suspected discrimination against non-Muslim migrants, among other infringements. This study has not skirted such concerns, and did not embark on a one-sided perspective by only identifying positive outcomes in the country, and indeed did not set out to attribute such progressive steps to the government. Moreover, it did not and does not neglect negative policies, and it did not report them in the passive voice to avoid the attribution of responsibility to authorities for perpetuating precarity and human rights abuses. Rather, it has identified specific shortcomings and called on Riyadh to address them without delay, even if it also set out to give credit for actions taken to ameliorate what are extraordinary and difficult conditions. As independent scholars, the authors raised key issues that affected refugees in the Kingdom, acknowledged inadequacies, and recommended specific remedies to improve programs and procedures.

Importantly, this research effort aimed to also engage with, and alleviate the concerns of, those who perceive Saʻudi society in disapproving terms. That is why it was necessary to investigate how *zakat*, one of the Five Pillars of Islam, fit in. As the Holy Qur'an states that "alms are only for the *fuqara'* (the poor), the al-*masakin* (the needy), and those employed to collect the funds," there are specific duties that apply to every Muslim that were pertinent to our discussion. According to Scriptures, *Zakat* aims to attract the hearts of those who have been inclined towards the faith; to free captives; assist those in debt; and serve God's "Cause." Moreover, alms must also assist wayfarers (travelers cut off from their normal way of life), since this is a duty imposed by God. "And Allah [God] is All-Knower, All-Wise" [9:60]. *Zakat* is thus very important because it overcomes the separation between Muslims and non-Muslims when it comes to the provision of aid. With the support of researchers such as Hassen Altahi,[9] and faithful to our purpose to contribute to a constructive dialogue on the idea of human rights coming from Islam, it is critical to answer the following questions:

1. Was Saʻudi Arabia consistent in providing international humanitarian aid?;
2. Was Riyadh among the top ten contributors of international humanitarian assistance?;
3. Was the Kingdom providing donations for official development assistance to needy nations?; and,
4. What was the overall position of Saʻudi Arabia's contributions to

international humanitarian assistance programs, especially when compared to other donors, including among other Arab Gulf States?[10]

Statistics assembled and analyzed by Hassen Altahi and several other scholars have disclosed that Riyadh adapted its own foreign aid policies to match contributions made by individual Muslims, who donated part of their annual incomes in alms to fulfill religious duties. This illustrated the commitment of the country with respect to foreign aid, an undertaking rarely recognized by the international community, and often ignored by global media sources. Remarkably, this occurred despite despite annual World Bank reports that stated what the Kingdom allocated and towards what goal. In fact, Saʻudi Arabia donated $150 billion in foreign aid during the past four decades (1985–2020), an astronomical figure. Along with other Arab Gulf countries, including Kuwait, Qatar and the United Arab Emirates, Saʻudi Arabia created development funds in the late 1960s and early 1970s for such purposes too. What stands out are the linkages made between humanitarian and developmental efforts, especially in terms of religious obligations, with the implication that Arab financial support went to Muslim nations more or less exclusively. Largely true, but the reason for this emphasis was due to the fact that the Middle East was the source and the battleground of the most violent conflicts in the last few decades, which necessitated concerted remedies. Still, and according to the *UN Statistical Report* for 2019, Saʻudi Arabia was the sixth largest donor worldwide and more than 90 countries benefitted from such assistance.

As stated earlier, the Kingdom of Saʻudi Arabia provided significant aid to several countries that suffered devastating natural disasters, including Indonesia, following the Aceh Province earthquake/Tsunami combination that ravaged Sumatra in 2004. Similar aid was rushed to Pakistan and India after the Kashmir Earthquake and to the victims of the 26 December 2003 Bam earthquake that struck that unfortunate city and the surrounding Kerman province, and which killed over 26,000 Iranians. And these are just some examples. It is worth recapitulating that the Kingdom's Development Fund financed 665 loans with a total amount of nearly US$16 billion between 1975 and the end of 2017.

Saʻudi Arabia's disbursements of foreign aid did not stop with the Saʻudi Fund for Development, but were also spread across various other aid programs. In May 2015, for example, Riyadh inaugurated the King Salman Center for Humanitarian Relief and Works, which became "a leading center for relief and humanitarian activities" as it transferred Saʻudi values to the world. Its generous disbursements alleviated the suffering of people all over the world, "especially victims of civil wars and natural calamities." In the short years since its inception, the Center has provided financial support through grants and other mechanisms to NGOs and institutions running different humanitarian aid projects. The mission of this association has been "to become a model for international relief work," focusing on the victims of civil wars and natural calamities. Since its establishment, the center has been working in collaboration with the main UN agencies, including the United Nations Relief and Works Agency for Palestine Refugees in the Near East (UNRWA)—which provides food security, tent management, shelter, health services, safety, education and environmental protection in the immediacy of disasters—especially after the United States ended most of its contributions to UNRWA. In 2018, the Center provided $1 million to alleviate the sufferings of Palestine refugees in Syria. Between 2015 and 2020, the King Salman Humanitarian and Relief Center provided relief to around forty countries, to the tune of nearly US$5 billion.

Finally, it must also be recorded, and as the United Nations Financial Tracking Service (FTS) confirmed, that Sa'udi Arabia was ranked fourth among major world donors of humanitarian aid, including to refugees. The Kingdom hosted over a million refugees in 2019, including 563,911 Yemenis and 262,573 Syrians. It is worth repeating that these refugees exercised the right to residence, mobility and had access to education, health and work, on an equal footing with Sa'udi citizens. As discussed earlier, the authorities were working on a comprehensive database using internationally recognized standards, to record and monitor refugee movements within the country. According to available data for the period 2015–2019 concerning the Yemen and Syria, for example, Sa'udi Arabia supported 579 (for a total of $3,478,489,431) and 236 projects (for a total of $304,725,378), in the two respective war-torn countries. Beyond the numbers, to respond to the polemic that denounced the unwillingness by Sa'udi Arabia and all GCC countries to receive refugees from Syria during the conflict as reported by several Western sources, these figures are important because they illustrate how a constructive collaboration between Western and Muslim societies was possible, despite differences in their respective ways to conceive the idea of human and consequently refugee rights.

In the end, economic and humanitarian assistance was part and parcel of the Sa'udi moral belief as individuals assumed their fair share of responsibilities through alms giving. In turn, the authorities extended a helping hand to Muslims and non-Muslims alike. Often, these deeds were overlooked, sometimes misunderstood, and, in specific circumstances derided because of misinterpretation and confusing explanations advanced by those who failed to acknowledge justice and generosity. Nevertheless, the record indicates that the Kingdom of Sa'udi Arabia was driven by a higher calling to fulfill its religious and socio-economic duties. The record further illustrates that Riyadh disbursed very large sums in foreign aid to those most in need, whether refugees or those who suffered traumatic events, and did so without any expectation in return. Naturally, a slight preference was displayed towards those who required aid in the Arab and Muslim worlds, but it would be inaccurate to conclude that this generosity favored Arabs and Muslims. Assistance was given to Africans, Asians and even Europeans and Americans as conditions necessitated.

Born to answer a controversy raised by the war in Syria and the mass migration the civil war in that country caused, this book provides an opportunity to contribute to a more constructive dialogue between Western and Muslim societies on human rights concerns. We hope to have added value as differences and similarities were highlighted to find common ground. In dealing specifically with the case of Sa'udi Arabia, we trust that the discussion, which was traced back to the history of the presence of refugees in the country, together with the ad hoc legislations introduced by the government since 1932, clarified obscure points. Sa'udi society contributed generously to global humanitarian requirements, especially after the 1970s, and was determined to fulfill its responsibilities towards the international community. It was a *Sacred Duty* that its leaders, as well as members of society, took seriously.

Appendix 1

Universal Islamic Declaration of Human Rights (adopted by the Islamic Council of Europe) 19 September 1981

This is a declaration for mankind, a guidance and instruction to those who fear God.

(Qur'an, Al-Imran 3:138)

Foreword

Islam gave to mankind an ideal code of human rights fourteen centuries ago. These rights aim at conferring honor and dignity on mankind and eliminating exploitation, oppression and injustice. Human rights in Islam are firmly rooted in the belief that God, and God alone, is the Law Giver and the Source of all human rights. Due to their Divine origin, no ruler, government, assembly or authority can curtail or violate in any way the human rights conferred by God, nor can they be surrendered. Human rights in Islam are an integral part of the overall Islamic order and it is obligatory on all Muslim governments and organs of society to implement them in letter and in spirit within the framework of that order.

It is unfortunate that human rights are being trampled upon with impunity in many countries of the world, including some Muslim countries. Such violations are a matter of serious concern and are arousing the conscience of more and more people throughout the world. I sincerely hope that this *Declaration of Human Rights* will give a powerful impetus to the Muslim peoples to stand firm and defend resolutely and courageously the rights conferred on them by God.

This *Declaration of Human Rights* is the second fundamental document proclaimed by the Islamic Council to mark the beginning of the 15th Century of the Islamic era, the first being the *Universal Islamic Declaration* announced at the International Conference on The Prophet Muhammad (peace and blessings be upon him) and his Message, held in London from 12 to 15 April 1980. The *Universal Islamic Declaration of Human Rights* is based on the Qur'an and the Sunnah and has been compiled by eminent Muslim scholars, jurists and representatives of Islamic movements and thought. May God reward them all for their efforts and guide us along the right path.

PARIS
21 Dhul Qaidah 1401
19th September 1981

Salem Azzam
Secretary General

O men! Behold, We have created you all out of a male and a female, and have made you into nations and tribes, so that you might come to know one another. Verily, the noblest of you in the sight of God is the one who is most deeply conscious of Him. Behold, God is all-knowing, all aware.

(Qur'an, Al-Hujurat 49:13)

Preamble
WHEREAS the age-old human aspiration for a just world order wherein people could live, develop and prosper in an environment free from fear, oppression, exploitation and deprivation, remains largely unfulfilled;

WHEREAS the Divine Mercy unto mankind reflected in its having been endowed with super-abundant economic sustenance is being wasted, or unfairly or unjustly withheld from the inhabitants of the earth;

WHEREAS Allah (God) has given mankind through His revelations in the Holy Qur'an and the Sunnah of His Blessed Prophet Muhammad an abiding legal and moral framework within which to establish and regulate human institutions and relationships;

WHEREAS the human rights decreed by the Divine Law aim at conferring dignity and honor on mankind and are designed to eliminate oppression and injustice;

WHEREAS by virtue of their Divine source and sanction these rights can neither be curtailed, abrogated or disregarded by authorities, assemblies or other institutions, nor can they be surrendered or alienated;

Therefore we, as Muslims, who believe
  a) in God, the Beneficent and Merciful, the Creator, the Sustainer, the Sovereign, the sole Guide of mankind and the Source of all Law;
  b) in the Vicegerency (Khilafah) of man who has been created to fulfill the Will of God on earth;

c) in the wisdom of Divine guidance brought by the Prophets, whose mission found its culmination in the final Divine message that was conveyed by the Prophet Muhammad (Peace be upon him) to all mankind;

d) that rationality by itself without the light of revelation from God can neither be a sure guide in the affairs of mankind nor provide spiritual nourishment to the human soul, and, knowing that the teachings of Islam represent the quintessence of Divine guidance in its final and perfect form, feel duty-bound to remind man of the high status and dignity bestowed on him by God;

e) in inviting all mankind to the message of Islam;

f) that by the terms of our primeval covenant with God our duties and obligations have priority over our rights, and that each one of us is under a bounden duty to spread the teachings of Islam by word, deed, and indeed in all gentle ways, and to make them effective not only in our individual lives but also in the society around us;

g) in our obligation to establish an Islamic order:

   i) wherein all human beings shall be equal and none shall enjoy a privilege or suffer a disadvantage or discrimination by reason of race, color, sex, origin or language;

   ii) wherein all human beings are born free;

   iii) wherein slavery and forced labor are abhorred;

   iv) wherein conditions shall be established such that the institution of family shall be preserved, protected and honored as the basis of all social life;

   v) wherein the rulers and the ruled alike are subject to, and equal before, the Law;

   vi) wherein obedience shall be rendered only to those commands that are in consonance with the Law;

   vii) wherein all worldly power shall be considered as a sacred trust, to be exercised within the limits prescribed by the Law and in a manner approved by it, and with due regard for the priorities fixed by it;

   viii) wherein all economic resources shall be treated as Divine blessings bestowed upon mankind, to be enjoyed by all in accordance with the rules and the values set out in the Qur'an and the Sunnah;

   ix) wherein all public affairs shall be determined and conducted, and the authority to administer them shall be exercised after mutual consultation (*Shurah*) between the believers qualified to contribute to a decision which would accord well with the Law and the public good;

x) wherein everyone shall undertake obligations proportionate to his capacity and shall be held responsible pro rata for his deeds;

xi) wherein everyone shall, in case of an infringement of his rights, be assured of appropriate remedial measures in accordance with the Law;

xii) wherein no one shall be deprived of the rights assured to him by the Law except by its authority and to the extent permitted by it;

xiii) wherein every individual shall have the right to bring legal action against anyone who commits a crime against society as a whole or against any of its members;

xiv) wherein every effort shall be made to
(a) secure unto mankind deliverance from every type of exploitation, injustice and oppression,
(b) ensure to everyone security, dignity and liberty in terms set out and by methods approved and within the limits set by the Law;

Do hereby, as servants of Allah and as members of the Universal Brotherhood of Islam, at the beginning of the Fifteenth Century of the Islamic Era, affirm our commitment to uphold the following inviolable and inalienable human rights that we consider are enjoined by Islam.

I. Right to Life

a) Human life is sacred and inviolable and every effort shall be made to protect it. In particular no one shall be exposed to injury or death, except under the authority of the Law.

b) Just as in life, so also after death, the sanctity of a person's body shall be inviolable. It is the obligation of believers to see that a deceased person's body is handled with due solemnity.

II. Right to Freedom

a) Man is born free. No inroads shall be made on his right to liberty except under the authority and in due process of the Law.

b) Every individual and every people has the inalienable right to freedom in all its forms—physical, cultural, economic and political—and shall be entitled to struggle by all available means against any infringement or abrogation of this right; and every oppressed individual or people has a legitimate claim to the support of other individuals and/or peoples in such a struggle.

III. Right to Equality and Prohibition Against Impermissible Discrimination

a) All persons are equal before the Law and are entitled to equal opportunities and protection of the Law.

b) All persons shall be entitled to equal wage for equal work.

c) No person shall be denied the opportunity to work or be discriminated against in any manner or exposed to greater physical risk by reason of religious belief, color, race, origin, sex or language.

IV. Right to Justice

a) Every person has the right to be treated in accordance with the Law, and only in accordance with the Law.

b) Every person has not only the right but also the obligation to protest against injustice; to recourse to remedies provided by the Law in respect of any unwarranted personal injury or loss; to self-defence against any charges that are preferred against him and to obtain fair adjudication before an independent judicial tribunal in any dispute with public authorities or any other person.

c) It is the right and duty of every person to defend the rights of any other person and the community in general (*Hisbah*).

d) No person shall be discriminated against while seeking to defend private and public rights.

e) It is the right and duty of every Muslim to refuse to obey any command which is contrary to the Law, no matter by whom it may be issued.

V. Right to Fair Trial

a) No person shall be adjudged guilty of an offence and made liable to punishment except after proof of his guilt before an independent judicial tribunal.

b) No person shall be adjudged guilty except after a fair trial and after reasonable opportunity for defense has been provided to him.

c) Punishment shall be awarded in accordance with the Law, in proportion to the seriousness of the offence and with due consideration of the circumstances under which it was committed.

d) No act shall be considered a crime unless it is stipulated as such in the clear wording of the Law.

e) Every individual is responsible for his actions. Responsibility for a crime cannot be vicariously extended to other members of his family or group, who are not otherwise directly or indirectly involved in the commission of the crime in question.

VI. Right to Protection Against Abuse of Power
Every person has the right to protection against harassment by official agencies. He is not liable to account for himself except for making a defense to the charges made against him or where he is found in a situation wherein a question regarding suspicion of his involvement in a crime could be *reasonably* raised.

VII. Right to Protection Against Torture
No person shall be subjected to torture in mind or body, or degraded, or threatened with injury either to himself or to anyone related to or held dear by him, or forcibly made to confess to the commission of a crime, or forced to consent to an act which is injurious to his interests.

VIII. Right to Protection of Honor and Reputation
Every person has the right to protect his honor and reputation against calumnies, groundless charges or deliberate attempts at defamation and blackmail.

IX. Right to Asylum
a) Every persecuted or oppressed person has the right to seek refuge and asylum. This right is guaranteed to every human being irrespective of race, religion, color and sex.

b) Al Masjid Al Haram (the sacred house of Allah) in Makkah is a sanctuary for all Muslims.

X. Rights of Minorities
a) The Qur'anic principle "There is no compulsion in religion" shall govern the religious rights of non-Muslim minorities.

b) In a Muslim country, religious minorities shall have the choice to be governed in respect of their civil and personal matters by Islamic Law, or by their own laws.

XI. Right and Obligation to Participate in the Conduct and Management of Public Affairs

a) Subject to the Law, every individual in the community (*Ummah*) is entitled to assume public office.

b) Process of free consultation (*Shurah*) is the basis of the administrative relationship between the government and the people. People also have the right to choose and remove their rulers in accordance with this principle.

XII. Right to Freedom of Belief, Thought and Speech

a) Every person has the right to express his thoughts and beliefs so long as he remains within the limits prescribed by the Law. No one, however, is entitled to disseminate falsehood or to circulate reports which may outrage public decency, or to indulge in slander, innuendo or to cast defamatory aspersions on other persons.

b) Pursuit of knowledge and search after truth is not only a right but a duty of every Muslim.

c) It is the right and duty of every Muslim to protest and strive (within the limits set out by the Law) against oppression even if it involves challenging the highest authority in the state.

d) There shall be no bar on the dissemination of information provided it does not endanger the security of the society or the state and is confined within the limits imposed by the Law.

e) No one shall hold in contempt or ridicule the religious beliefs of others or incite public hostility against them; respect for the religious feelings of others is obligatory on all Muslims.

XIII. Right to Freedom of Religion

Every person has the right to freedom of conscience and worship in accordance with his religious beliefs.

XIV. Right to Free Association

a) Every person is entitled to participate individually and collectively in the religious, social, cultural and political life of his community and to establish institutions and agencies meant to enjoin what is right (*ma'ruf*) and to prevent what is wrong (*munkar*).

b) Every person is entitled to strive for the establishment of institutions whereunder an enjoyment of these rights would be made possible. Collectively, the community is obliged to establish conditions so as to allow its members full development of their personalities.

XV. The Economic Order and the Rights Evolving Therefrom

a) In their economic pursuits, all persons are entitled to the full benefits of nature and all its resources. These are blessings bestowed by God for the benefit of mankind as a whole.

b) All human beings are entitled to earn their living according to the Law.

c) Every person is entitled to own property individually or in association with others. State ownership of certain economic resources in the public interest is legitimate.

d) The poor have the right to a prescribed share in the wealth of the rich, as fixed by Zakah, levied and collected in accordance with the Law.

e) All means of production shall be utilized in the interest of the community (*Ummah*) as a whole, and may not be neglected or misused.

f) In order to promote the development of a balanced economy and to protect society from exploitation, Islamic Law forbids monopolies, unreasonable restrictive trade practices, usury, the use of coercion in the making of contracts and the publication of misleading advertisements.

g) All economic activities are permitted provided they are not detrimental to the interests of the community (*Ummah*) and do not violate Islamic laws and values.

XVI. Right to Protection of Property

No property may be expropriated except in the public interest and on payment of fair and adequate compensation.

XVII. Status and Dignity of Workers

Islam honors work and the worker and enjoins Muslims not only to treat the worker justly but also generously. He is not only to be paid his earned wages promptly, but is also entitled to adequate rest and leisure.

XVIII. Right to Social Security

Every person has the right to food, shelter, clothing, education and medical care consistent with the resources of the community. This obligation of the community extends in particular to all individuals who cannot take care of themselves due to some temporary or permanent disability.

XIX. Right to Found a Family and Related Matters

a) Every person is entitled to marry, to found a family and to bring up children in conformity with his religion, traditions and culture. Every spouse is entitled to such rights and privileges and carries such obligations as are stipulated by the Law.

b) Each of the partners in a marriage is entitled to respect and consideration from the other.

c) Every husband is obligated to maintain his wife and children according to his means.

d) Every child has the right to be maintained and properly brought up by its parents, it being forbidden that children are made to work at an early age or that any burden is put on them which would arrest or harm their natural development.

e) If parents are for some reason unable to discharge their obligations towards a child it becomes the responsibility of the community to fulfill these obligations at public expense.

f) Every person is entitled to material support, as well as care and protection, from his family during his childhood, old age or incapacity. Parents are entitled to material support as well as care and protection from their children.

g) Motherhood is entitled to special respect, care and assistance on the part of the family and the public organs of the community (*Ummah*).

h) Within the family, men and women are to share in their obligations and responsibilities according to their sex, their natural endowments, talents and inclinations, bearing in mind their common responsibilities toward their progeny and their relatives.

i) No person may be married against his or her will, or lose or suffer diminution of legal personality on account of marriage.

XX. Rights of Married Women
Every married woman is entitled to:
a) live in the house in which her husband lives;
b) receive the means necessary for maintaining a standard of living which is not inferior to that of her spouse, and, in the event of divorce, receive during the statutory period of waiting (*'iddah*) means of maintenance commensurate with her husband's resources, for herself as well as for the children she nurses or keeps, irrespective of her own financial status, earnings, or property that she may hold in her own rights;
c) seek and obtain dissolution of marriage (*Khul'ah*) in accordance with the terms of the Law. This right is in addition to her right to seek divorce through the courts.
d) inherit from her husband, her parents, her children and other relatives according to the Law;
e) strict confidentiality from her spouse, or ex-spouse if divorced, with regard to any information that he may have obtained about her, the disclosure of which could prove detrimental to her interests. A similar responsibility rests upon her in respect of her spouse or ex-spouse.

XXI. Right to Education
a) Every person is entitled to receive education in accordance with his natural capabilities.

b) Every person is entitled to a free choice of profession and career and to the opportunity for the full development of his natural endowments.

XXII. Right of Privacy
Every person is entitled to the protection of his privacy.

XXIII. Right to Freedom of Movement and Residence
a) In view of the fact that the World of Islam is veritably *Ummah Islamiyyah*, every Muslim shall have the right to freely move in and out of any Muslim country.

b) No one shall be forced to leave the country of his residence, or be arbitrarily deported therefrom without recourse to due process of Law.

Explanatory Notes
1. In the above formulation of Human Rights, unless the context provides otherwise:
    a) the term "person" refers to both the male and female sexes.
    b) the term "Law" denotes the *Shari'ah*, i.e. the totality of

ordinances derived from the Qur'an and the Sunnah and any other laws that are deduced from these two sources by methods considered valid in Islamic jurisprudence.

2. Each one of the Human Rights enunciated in this declaration carries a corresponding duty.

3. In the exercise and enjoyment of the rights referred to above every person shall be subject only to such limitations as are enjoined by the Law for the purpose of securing the due recognition of, and respect for, the rights and the freedom of others and of meeting the just requirements of morality, public order and the general welfare of the Community (*Ummah*).

The Arabic text of this *Declaration* is the original.

Source: University of Minnesota Human Rights Library, at http://hrlibrary.umn.edu/instree/islamic_declaration_HR.html.

Appendix 2

African Charter on Human and Peoples' Rights (1981)

Preamble

The African States members of the Organization of African Unity, parties to the present convention entitled "African Charter on Human and Peoples' Rights,"

Recalling Decision 115 (XVI) of the Assembly of Heads of State and Government at its Sixteenth Ordinary Session held in Monrovia, Liberia, from 17 to 20 July 1979 on the preparation of a "preliminary draft on an African Charter on Human and Peoples' Rights" providing inter alia for the establishment of bodies to promote and protect human and peoples' rights;

Considering the Charter of the Organization of African Unity, which stipulates that "freedom, equality, justice and dignity are essential objectives for the achievement of the legitimate aspirations of the African peoples";

Reaffirming the pledge they solemnly made in Article 2 of the said Charter to eradicate all forms of colonialism from Africa, to coordinate and intensify their cooperation and efforts to achieve a better life for the peoples of Africa and to promote international cooperation having due regard to the Charter of the United Nations and the Universal Declaration of Human Rights;

Taking into consideration the virtues of their historical tradition and the values of African civilization which should inspire and characterize their reflection on the concept of human and peoples' rights;

Recognizing on the one hand, that fundamental human rights stem from the attributes of human beings which justifies their national and international protection and on the other hand that the reality and respect of people's rights should necessarily guarantee human rights;

Considering that the enjoyment of rights and freedoms also implies the performance of duties on the part of everyone;

Convinced that it is henceforth essential to pay a particular attention to the right to development and that civil and political rights cannot be dissociated from economic, social and cultural rights in their conception as well as universality and that the satisfaction of economic, social and cultural rights is a guarantee for the enjoyment of civil and political rights;

Conscious of their duty to achieve the total liberation of Africa, the peoples of which are still struggling for their dignity and genuine independence, and undertaking to eliminate colonialism, neo-colonialism, apartheid, Zionism and to dismantle aggressive foreign military bases and all forms of discrimination, particularly those based on race, ethnic group, color, sex, language, religion or political opinions;

Reaffirming their adherence to the principles of human and peoples' rights and freedoms contained in the declarations, conventions and other instrument adopted by the Organization of African Unity, the Movement of Non-Aligned Countries and the United Nations;

Firmly convinced of their duty to promote and protect human and peoples' rights and freedoms taking into account the importance traditionally attached to these rights and freedoms in Africa;

Have agreed as follows:

Part I: Rights and Duties

Chapter I: Human and Peoples' Rights
Article 1—The Member States of the Organization of African Unity parties to the present Charter shall recognize the rights, duties and freedoms enshrined in this Chapter and shall undertake to adopt legislative or other measures to give effect to them.

Article 2—Every individual shall be entitled to the enjoyment of the rights and freedoms recognized and guaranteed in the present Charter without distinction of any kind such as race, ethnic group, color, sex, language, religion, political or any other opinion, national and social origin, fortune, birth or other status.

Article 3—Every individual shall be equal before the law. Every individual shall be entitled to equal protection of the law.

Article 4—Human beings are inviolable. Every human being shall be entitled to respect for his life and the integrity of his person. No one may be arbitrarily deprived of this right.

Article 5—Every individual shall have the right to the respect of the dignity inherent in a human being and to the recognition of his legal status. All forms of exploitation and degradation of man particularly slavery, slave trade, torture, cruel, inhuman or degrading punishment and treatment shall be prohibited.

Article 6—Every individual shall have the right to liberty and to the security of his person. No one may be deprived of his freedom except for reasons and conditions previously laid down by law. In particular, no one may be arbitrarily arrested or detained.

Article 7—Every individual shall have the right to have his cause heard. This comprises:
    (a) the right to an appeal to competent national organs against acts of violating his fundamental rights as recognized and guaranteed by conventions, laws, regulations and customs in force;
    (b) the right to be presumed innocent until proved guilty by a competent court or tribunal;
    (c) the right to defense, including the right to be defended by counsel of his choice;
    (d) the right to be tried within a reasonable time by an impartial court or tribunal.

No one may be condemned for an act or omission which did not constitute a legally punishable offence at the time it was committed. No penalty may be inflicted for an offence for which no provision was made at the time it was committed. Punishment is personal and can be imposed only on the offender.

Article 8—Freedom of conscience, the profession and free practice of religion shall be guaranteed. No one may, subject to law and order, be submitted to measures restricting the exercise of these freedoms.

Article 9—Every individual shall have the right to receive information. Every individual shall have the right to express and disseminate his opinions within the law.

Article 10—Every individual shall have the right to free association provided that he abides by the law. Subject to the obligation of solidarity provided for in Article 29 no one may be compelled to join an association.

Article 11—Every individual shall have the right to assemble freely with others. The exercise of this right shall be subject only to necessary restrictions provided for by law in particular those enacted in the interest of national security, the safety, health, ethics and rights and freedoms of others.

Article 12—Every individual shall have the right to freedom of movement and residence within the borders of a State provided he abides by the law.
1. Every individual shall have the right to leave any country including his own, and to return to his country.
2. This right may only be subject to restrictions, provided for by law for the protection of national security, law and order, public health or morality.
3. Every individual shall have the right, when persecuted, to seek and obtain asylum in other countries in accordance with laws of those countries and international conventions.
4. A non-national legally admitted in a territory of a State Party to the present Charter, may only be expelled from it by virtue of a decision taken in accordance with the law.
5. The mass expulsion of non-nationals shall be prohibited. Mass expulsion shall be that which is aimed at national, racial, ethnic or religious groups.

Article 13—Every citizen shall have the right to participate freely in the government of his country, either directly or through freely chosen representatives in accordance with the provisions of the law. Every citizen shall have the right of equal access to the public service of his country. Every individual shall have the right of access to public property and services in strict equality of all persons before the law.

Article 14—The right to property shall be guaranteed. It may only be encroached upon in the interest of public need or in the general interest of the community and in accordance with the provisions of appropriate laws.

Article 15—Every individual shall have the right to work under equitable and satisfactory conditions, and shall receive equal pay for equal work.

Article 16—Every individual shall have the right to enjoy the best attainable state of physical and mental health. States parties to the present Charter shall take the necessary measures to protect the health of their people and to ensure that they receive medical attention when they are sick.

Article 17—Every individual shall have the right to education. Every individual may freely, take part in the cultural life of his community. The promotion and protection of morals and traditional values recognized by the community shall be the duty of the State.

Article 18—The family shall be the natural unit and basis of society.
1. It shall be protected by the State which shall take care of its physical health and moral.
2. The State shall have the duty to assist the family which is the custodian or morals and traditional values recognized by the community.
3. The State shall ensure the elimination of every discrimination against women and also ensure the protection of the rights of the woman and the child as stipulated in international declarations and conventions.
4. The aged and the disabled shall also have the right to special measures of protection in keeping with their physical or moral needs.

Article 19—All peoples shall be equal; they shall enjoy the same respect and shall have the same rights. Nothing shall justify the domination of a people by another.

Article 20—All peoples shall have the right to existence.
1. They shall have the unquestionable and inalienable right to self-determination.
2. They shall freely determine their political status and shall pursue their economic and social development according to the policy they have freely chosen.
3. Colonized or oppressed peoples shall have the right to free themselves from the bonds of domination by resorting to any means recognized by the international community.
4. All peoples shall have the right to the assistance of the States parties to the present Charter in their liberation struggle against foreign domination, be it political, economic or cultural.

Article 21—All peoples shall freely dispose of their wealth and natural resources. This right shall be exercised in the exclusive interest of the people. In no case shall a people be deprived of it. In case of spoliation the dispossessed people shall have the right to the lawful recovery of its property as well as to an adequate compensation.

The free disposal of wealth and natural resources shall be exercised without prejudice to the obligation of promoting international economic cooperation based on mutual respect, equitable exchange and the principles of international law.

States parties to the present Charter shall individually and collectively exercise the right to free disposal of their wealth and natural resources with a view to strengthening African unity and solidarity. States parties to the present Charter shall undertake to eliminate all forms of foreign economic exploitation particularly that practiced by international monopolies so as to enable their peoples to fully benefit from the advantages derived from their national resources.

Article 22—All peoples shall have the right to their economic, social and cultural development with due regard to their freedom and identity and in the equal enjoyment of the common heritage of mankind. States shall have the duty, individually or collectively, to ensure the exercise of the right to development.

Article 23—All peoples shall have the right to national and international peace and security. The principles of solidarity and friendly relations implicitly affirmed by the Charter of the United Nations and reaffirmed by that of the Organization of African Unity shall govern relations between States.

For the purpose of strengthening peace, solidarity and friendly relations, States parties to the present Charter shall ensure that:
  (a) any individual enjoying the right of asylum under 12 of the present Charter shall not engage in subversive activities against his country of origin or any other State party to the present Charter;
  (b) their territories shall not be used as bases for subversive or terrorist activities against the people of any other State party to the present Charter.

Article 24—All peoples shall have the right to a general satisfactory environment favorable to their development.

Article 25—States parties to the present Charter shall have the duty to promote and ensure through teaching, education and publication, the respect of the rights and freedoms contained in the present Charter and to see to it that these freedoms and rights as well as corresponding obligations and duties are understood.

Article 26—States parties to the present Charter shall have the duty to guarantee the independence of the Courts and shall allow the establishment and improvement of appropriate national institutions entrusted with the promotion and protection of the rights and freedoms guaranteed by the present Charter.

Chapter II: Duties
Article 27—Every individual shall have duties towards his family and society, the State and other legally recognized communities and the international community. The rights and freedoms of each individual shall be exercised with due regard to the rights of others, collective security, morality and common interest.

Article 28—Every individual shall have the duty to respect and consider his fellow beings without discrimination, and to maintain relations aimed at promoting, safeguarding and reinforcing mutual respect and tolerance.

Article 29—The individual shall also have the duty:
1. To preserve the harmonious development of the family and to work for the cohesion and respect of the family; to respect his parents at all times, to maintain them in case of need;
2. To serve his national community by placing his physical and intellectual abilities at its service;
3. Not to compromise the security of the State whose national or resident he is;
4. To preserve and strengthen social and national solidarity, particularly when the latter is threatened;
5. To preserve and strengthen the national independence and the territorial integrity of his country and to contribute to its defense in accordance with the law;
6. To work to the best of his abilities and competence, and to pay taxes imposed by law in the interest of the society;
7. To preserve and strengthen positive African cultural values in his relations with other members of the society, in the spirit of tolerance, dialogue and consultation and, in general, to contribute to the promotion of the moral well-being of society;
8. To contribute to the best of his abilities, at all times and at all levels, to the promotion and achievement of African unity.

Part II: Measures of Safeguard

<u>Chapter I: Establishment and Organization of the African Commission on Human and Peoples' Rights</u>

Article 30—An African Commission on Human and Peoples' Rights, hereinafter called "the Commission," shall be established within the Organization of African Unity to promote human and peoples' rights and ensure their protection in Africa.

Article 31—The Commission shall consist of eleven members chosen from amongst African personalities of the highest reputation, known for their high morality, integrity, impartiality and competence in matters of human and peoples' rights; particular consideration being given to persons having legal experience. The members of the Commission shall serve in their personal capacity.

Article 32—The Commission shall not include more than one national of the same state.

Article 33—The members of the Commission shall be elected by secret ballot by the Assembly of Heads of State and Government, from a list of persons nominated by the States parties to the present Charter.

Article 34—Each State party to the present Charter may not nominate more than two candidates. The candidates must have the nationality of one of the States party to the present Charter. When two candidates are nominated by a State, one of them may not be a national of that State.

Article 35—The Secretary General of the Organization of African Unity shall invite States parties to the present Charter at least four months before the elections to nominate candidates; The Secretary General of the Organization of African Unity shall make an alphabetical list of the persons thus nominated and communicate it to the Heads of State and Government at least one month before the elections.

Article 36—The members of the Commission shall be elected for a six-year period and shall be eligible for re-election. However, the term of office of four of the members elected at the first election shall terminate after two years and the term of office of three others, at the end of four years.

Article 37—Immediately after the first election, the Chairman of the

Assembly of Heads of State and Government of the Organization of African Unity shall draw lots to decide the names of those members referred to in Article 36.

Article 38—After their election, the members of the Commission shall make a solemn declaration to discharge their duties impartially and faithfully.

Article 39—In case of death or resignation of a member of the Commission the Chairman of the Commission shall immediately inform the Secretary General of the Organization of African Unity, who shall declare the seat vacant from the date of death or from the date on which the resignation takes effect.

If, in the unanimous opinion of other members of the Commission, a member has stopped discharging his duties for any reason other than a temporary absence, the Chairman of the Commission shall inform the Secretary General of the Organization of African Unity, who shall then declare the seat vacant.

In each of the cases anticipated above, the Assembly of Heads of State and Government shall replace the member whose seat became vacant for the remaining period of his term unless the period is less than six months.

Article 40—Every member of the Commission shall be in office until the date his successor assumes office.

Article 41—The Secretary General of the Organization of African Unity shall appoint the Secretary of the Commission. He shall also provide the staff and services necessary for the effective discharge of the duties of the Commission. The Organization of African Unity shall bear the costs of the staff and services.

Article 42—The Commission shall elect its Chairman and Vice Chairman for a two-year period. They shall be eligible for re-election. The Commission shall lay down its rules of procedure. Seven members shall form the quorum. In case of an equality of votes, the Chairman shall have a casting vote. The Secretary General may attend the meetings of the Commission. He shall not participate in deliberations nor shall he be entitled to vote. The Chairman of the Commission may, however, invite him to speak.

Article 43—In discharging their duties, members of the Commission shall enjoy diplomatic privileges and immunities provided for in the General Convention on the Privileges and Immunities of the Organization of African Unity.

Article 44—Provision shall be made for the emoluments and allowances of the members of the Commission in the Regular Budget of the Organization of African Unity.

Chapter II: Mandate of the Commission
Article 45—The functions of the Commission shall be:
1. To promote Human and Peoples' Rights and in particular:
   (a) To collect documents, undertake studies and researches on African problems in the field of human and peoples' rights, organize seminars, symposia and conferences, disseminate information, encourage national and local institutions concerned with human and peoples' rights, and should the case arise, give its views or make recommendations to Governments.
   (b) To formulate and lay down, principles and rules aimed at solving legal problems relating to human and peoples' rights and fundamental freedoms upon which African Governments may base their legislations.
   (c) Co-operate with other African and international institutions concerned with the promotion and protection of human and peoples' rights.
2. Ensure the protection of human and peoples' rights under conditions laid down by the present Charter.
3. Interpret all the provisions of the present Charter at the request of a State party, an institution of the OAU or an African Organization recognized by the OAU.
4. Perform any other tasks which may be entrusted to it by the Assembly of Heads of State and Government.

Chapter III: Procedure of the Commission
Article 46—The Commission may resort to any appropriate method of investigation; it may hear from the Secretary General of the Organization of African Unity or any other person capable of enlightening it.

Part II: Communication from States

Article 47—If a State party to the present Charter has good reasons to believe that another State party to this Charter has violated the provisions of the Charter, it may draw, by written communication, the attention of that State to the matter. This communication shall also be addressed to the Secretary General of the OAU and to the Chairman of the Commission. Within three months of the receipt of the communication, the State to which the communication is addressed shall give the enquiring State, written explanation or statement elucidating the matter. This should include as much as possible relevant information relating to the laws and rules of procedure applied and applicable, and the redress already given or course of action available.

Article 48—If within three months from the date on which the original communication is received by the State to which it is addressed, the issue is not settled to the satisfaction of the two States involved through bilateral negotiation or by any other peaceful procedure, either State shall have the right to submit the matter to the Commission through the Chairman and shall notify the other States involved.

Article 49—Notwithstanding the provisions of Article 47, if a State party to the present Charter considers that another State party has violated the provisions of the Charter, it may refer the matter directly to the Commission by addressing a communication to the Chairman, to the Secretary General of the Organization of African Unity and the State concerned.

Article 50—The Commission can only deal with a matter submitted to it after making sure that all local remedies, if they exist, have been exhausted, unless it is obvious to the Commission that the procedure of achieving these remedies would be unduly prolonged.

Article 51—The Commission may ask the States concerned to provide it with all relevant information. When the Commission is considering the matter, States concerned may be represented before it and submit written or oral representation.

Article 52—After having obtained from the States concerned and from other sources all the information it deems necessary and after having tried all appropriate means to reach an amicable solution based on the respect of Human and Peoples' Rights, the Commission shall prepare, within a reasonable period of time from the notification referred to in Article 48, a report stating the facts and its findings. This report shall be sent to the States concerned and communicated to the Assembly of Heads of State and Government.

Article 53—While transmitting its report, the Commission may make to the Assembly of Heads of State and Government such recommendations as it deems useful.

Article 54—The Commission shall submit to each ordinary Session of the Assembly of Heads of State and Government a report on its activities.

Article 55—Before each Session, the Secretary of the Commission shall make a list of the communications other than those of States parties to the present Charter and transmit them to the members of the Commission, who shall indicate which communications should be considered by the Commission. A communication shall be considered by the Commission if a simple majority of its members so decide.

Article 56—Communications relating to human and peoples' rights referred to in Article 55 received by the Commission, shall be considered if they:
1. Indicate their authors even if the latter request anonymity'
2. Are compatible with the Charter of the Organization of African Unity or with the present Charter;
3. Are not written in disparaging or insulting language directed against the State concerned and its institutions or to the Organization of African Unity;
4. Are not based exclusively on news discriminated through the mass media;
5. Are sent after exhausting local remedies, if any, unless it is obvious that this procedure is unduly prolonged;
6. Are submitted within a reasonable period from the time local remedies are exhausted or from the date the Commission is seized of the matter; and
7. Do not deal with cases which have been settled by these States involved in accordance with the principles of the Charter of the United Nations, or the Charter of the Organization of African Unity or the provisions of the present Charter.

Article 57—Prior to any substantive consideration, all communications shall be brought to the knowledge of the State concerned by the Chairman of the Commission.

Article 58—When it appears after deliberations of the Commission that one or more communications apparently relate to special cases which reveal the existence of a series of serious or massive violations of human and peoples' rights, the Commission shall draw the attention of the Assembly of Heads of State and Government to these special cases.

The Assembly of Heads of State and Government may then request the Commission to undertake an in-depth study of these cases and make a factual report, accompanied by its findings and recommendations. A case of emergency duly noticed by the Commission shall be submitted by the latter to the Chairman of the Assembly of Heads of State and Government who may request an in-depth study.

Article 59—All measures taken within the provisions of the present Charter shall remain confidential until such a time as the Assembly of Heads of State and Government shall otherwise decide. However, the report shall be published by the Chairman of the Commission upon the decision of the Assembly of Heads of State and Government. The report on the activities of the Commission shall be published by its Chairman after it has been considered by the Assembly of Heads of State and Government.

Chapter IV: Applicable Principles
Article 60—The Commission shall draw inspiration from international law on human and peoples' rights, particularly from the provisions of various African instruments on human and peoples' rights, the Charter of the United Nations, the Charter of the Organization of African Unity, the Universal Declaration of Human Rights, other instruments adopted by the United Nations and by African countries in the field of human and peoples' rights as well as from the provisions of various instruments adopted within the Specialized Agencies of the United Nations of which the parties to the present Charter are members.

Article 61—The Commission shall also take into consideration, as subsidiary measures to determine the principles of law, other general or special international conventions, laying down rules expressly recognized by member states of the Organization of African Unity, African practices consistent with international norms on human and peoples' rights, customs generally accepted as law, general principles of law recognized by African states as well as legal precedents and doctrine.

Article 62—Each state party shall undertake to submit every two years, from the date the present Charter comes into force, a report on the legislative or other measures taken with a view to giving effect to the rights and freedoms recognized and guaranteed by the present Charter.

Article 63—The present Charter shall be open to signature, ratification or adherence of the member states of the Organization of African Unity. The instruments of ratification or adherence to the present Charter shall be deposited with the Secretary General of the Organization of African Unity. The present Charter shall come into force three months after the reception by the Secretary General of the instruments of ratification or adherence of a simple majority of the member states of the Organization of African Unity.

Part III: General Provisions

Article 64—After the coming into force of the present Charter, members of the Commission shall be elected in accordance with the relevant Articles of the present Charter. The Secretary General of the Organization of African Unity shall convene the first meeting of the Commission at the Headquarters of the Organization within three months of the constitution of the Commission. Thereafter, the Commission shall be convened by its Chairman whenever necessary but at least once a year.

Article 65—For each of the States that will ratify or adhere to the present Charter after its coming into force, the Charter shall take effect three months after the date of the deposit by that State of its instrument of ratification or adherence.

Article 66—Special protocols or agreements may, if necessary, supplement the provisions of the present Charter.

Article 67—The Secretary General of the Organization of African Unity shall inform member states of the Organization of the deposit of each instrument of ratification or adherence.

Article 68—The present Charter may be amended if a State party makes a written request to that effect to the Secretary General of the Organization of African Unity. The Assembly of Heads of State and Government may only consider the draft amendment after all the States parties have been duly informed of it and the Commission has given its opinion on it at the request of the sponsoring State. The amendment shall be approved by a simple majority of the States parties. It shall come into force for each State which has accepted it in accordance with its constitutional procedure three months after the Secretary General has received notice of the acceptance.

Note: Adopted by the eighteenth Assembly of Heads of State and Government, Nairobi, Kenya, 27 June 1981, OAU Doc. CAB/LEG/67/3 rev. 5, 21 I.L.M. 58 (1982), entered into force 21 October 1986.

Source: African Commission on Human and Peoples' Rights at https://www.achpr.org/legalinstruments/detail?id=49

Appendix 3

Cairo Declaration on Human Rights in Islam
5 August 1990

The Nineteenth Islamic Conference of Foreign Ministers (Session of Peace, Interdependence and Development), held in Cairo, Arab Republic of Egypt, from 9-14 Muharram 1411H (31 July to 5 August 1990),

Keenly aware of the place of mankind in Islam as vicegerent of Allah on Earth;

Recognizing the importance of issuing a Document on Human Rights in Islam that will serve as a guide for Member states in all aspects of life;

Having examined the stages through which the preparation of this draft Document has so far, passed and the relevant report of the Secretary General;

Having examined the Report of the Meeting of the Committee of Legal Experts held in Tehran from 26 to 28 December 1989;

Agrees to issue the Cairo Declaration on Human Rights in Islam that will serve as a general guidance for Member States in the Field of human rights.

Reaffirming the civilizing and historical role of the Islamic Ummah which Allah made as the best community and which gave humanity a universal and well-balanced civilization, in which harmony is established between hereunder and the hereafter, knowledge is combined with faith, and to fulfill the expectations from this community to guide all humanity which is confused because of different and conflicting beliefs and ideologies and to provide solutions for all chronic problems of this materialistic civilization.

In contribution to the efforts of mankind to assert human rights, to protect man from exploitation and persecution, and to affirm his freedom and right to a dignified life in accordance with the Islamic Shari'ah.

Convinced that mankind which has reached an advanced stage in materialistic science is still, and shall remain, in dire need of faith to support its civilization as well as a self-motivating force to guard its rights;

Believing that fundamental rights and freedoms according to Islam are an integral part of the Islamic religion and that no one shall have the right as a matter of principle to abolish them either in whole or in part or to violate or ignore them in as much as they are binding divine commands, which are contained in the Revealed Books of Allah and which were sent through the last of His Prophets to complete the preceding divine messages and that safeguarding those fundamental rights and freedoms is an act of worship whereas the neglect or violation thereof is an abominable sin, and that the safeguarding of those fundamental rights and freedom is an individual responsibility of every person and a collective responsibility of the entire Ummah;

Do hereby and on the basis of the above-mentioned principles declare as follows:

ARTICLE 1:
(a) All human beings form one family whose members are united by their subordination to Allah and descent from Adam. All men are equal in terms of basic human dignity and basic obligations and responsibilities, without any discrimination on the basis of race, color, language, belief, sex, religion, political affiliation, social status or other considerations. The true religion is the guarantee for enhancing such dignity along the path to human integrity.
(b) All human beings are Allah's subjects, and the most loved by Him are those who are most beneficial to His subjects, and no one has superiority over another except on the basis of piety and good deeds.

ARTICLE 2:
(a) Life is a God-given gift and the right to life is guaranteed to every human being. It is the duty of individuals, societies and states to safeguard this right against any violation, and it is prohibited to take away life except for a Shari'ah prescribed reason.
(b) It is forbidden to resort to any means which could result in the genocidal annihilation of mankind.

(c) The preservation of human life throughout the term of time willed by Allah is a duty prescribed by Shari'ah.
(d) Safety from bodily harm is a guaranteed right. It is the duty of the state to safeguard it, and it is prohibited to breach it without a Shari'ah-prescribed reason.

ARTICLE 3:
(a) In the event of the use of force and in case of armed conflict, it is not permissible to kill non-belligerents such as old men, women and children. The wounded and the sick shall have the right to medical treatment; and prisoners of war shall have the right to be fed, sheltered and clothed. It is prohibited to mutilate or dismember dead bodies. It is required to exchange prisoners of war and to arrange visits or reunions of families separated by circumstances of war.
(b) It is prohibited to cut down trees, to destroy crops or livestock, to destroy the enemy's civilian buildings and installations by shelling, blasting or any other means.

ARTICLE 4:
Every human being is entitled to human sanctity and the protection of one's good name and honor during one's life and after one's death. The state and the society shall protect one's body and burial place from desecration.

ARTICLE 5:
(a) The family is the foundation of society, and marriage is the basis of making a family. Men and women have the right to marriage, and no restrictions stemming from race, color or nationality shall prevent them from exercising this right.
(b) The society and the State shall remove all obstacles to marriage and facilitate it, and shall protect the family and safeguard its welfare.

ARTICLE 6:
(a) Woman is equal to man in human dignity, and has her own rights to enjoy as well as duties to perform, and has her own civil entity and financial independence, and the right to retain her name and lineage.
(b) The husband is responsible for the maintenance and welfare of the family.

ARTICLE 7:
(a) As of the moment of birth, every child has rights due from the parents, the society and the state to be accorded proper nursing,

education and material, hygienic and moral care. Both the fetus and the mother must be safeguarded and accorded special care.

(b) Parents and those in such like capacity have the right to choose the type of education they desire for their children, provided they take into consideration the interest and future of the children in accordance with ethical values and the principles of the Shari'ah.

(c) Both parents are entitled to certain rights from their children, and relatives are entitled to rights from their kin, in accordance with the tenets of the Shari'ah.

ARTICLE 8:

Every human being has the right to enjoy a legitimate eligibility with all its prerogatives and obligations in case such eligibility is lost or impaired, the person shall have the right to be represented by his/her guardian.

ARTICLE 9:

(a) The seeking of knowledge is an obligation and provision of education is the duty of the society and the State. The State shall ensure the availability of ways and means to acquire education and shall guarantee its diversity in the interest of the society so as to enable man to be acquainted with the religion of Islam and uncover the secrets of the Universe for the benefit of mankind.

(b) Every human being has a right to receive both religious and worldly education from the various institutions of teaching, education and guidance, including the family, the school, the university, the media, etc., and in such an integrated and balanced manner that would develop human personality, strengthen man's faith in Allah and promote man's respect to and defense of both rights and obligations.

ARTICLE 10:

Islam is the religion of true unspoiled nature. It is prohibited to exercise any form of pressure on man or to exploit his poverty or ignorance in order to force him to change his religion to another religion or to atheism.

ARTICLE 11:

(a) Human beings are born free, and no one has the right to enslave, humiliate, oppress or exploit them, and there can be no subjugation but to Allah the Almighty.

(b) Colonialism of all types being one of the most evil forms of enslavement is totally prohibited. Peoples suffering from colonialism have the full right to freedom and self-determination. It is the duty of all States peoples to support the struggle of colonized peoples for the liquidation of all forms of and occupation, and all States and peoples have the right to preserve their independent identity and control over their wealth and natural resources.

ARTICLE 12:
Every man shall have the right, within the framework of the Shari'ah, to free movement and to select his place of residence whether within or outside his country and if persecuted, is entitled to seek asylum in another country. The country of refuge shall be obliged to provide protection to the asylum-seeker until his safety has been attained, unless asylum is motivated by committing an act regarded by the Shari'ah as a crime.

ARTICLE 13:
Work is a right guaranteed by the State and the Society for each person with capability to work. Everyone shall be free to choose the work that suits him best and which serves his interests as well as those of the society. The employee shall have the right to enjoy safety and security as well as all other social guarantees. He may not be assigned work beyond his capacity nor shall he be subjected to compulsion or exploited or harmed in any way. He shall be entitled—without any discrimination between males and females—to fair wages for his work without delay, as well as to the holidays allowances and promotions which he deserves. On his part, he shall be required to be dedicated and meticulous in his work. Should workers and employers disagree on any matter, the State shall intervene to settle the dispute and have the grievances redressed, the rights confirmed and justice enforced without bias.

ARTICLE 14:
Everyone shall have the right to earn a legitimate living without monopolization, deceit or causing harm to oneself or to others. Usury (*riba*) is explicitly prohibited.

ARTICLE 15:
(a) Everyone shall have the right to own property acquired in a legitimate way, and shall be entitled to the rights of ownership without prejudice to oneself, others or the society in general. Expropriation is not permissible except for requirements of public interest and upon payment of prompt and fair compensation.
(b) Confiscation and seizure of property is prohibited except for a necessity dictated by law.

ARTICLE 16:
Everyone shall have the right to enjoy the fruits of his scientific, literary, artistic or technical labor of which he is the author; and he shall have the right to the protection of his moral and material interests stemming therefrom, provided it is not contrary to the principles of the Shari'ah.

ARTICLE 17:
(a) Everyone shall have the right to live in a clean environment, away from vice and moral corruption, that would favor a healthy ethical development of his person and it is incumbent upon the State and society in general to afford that right.
(b) Everyone shall have the right to medical and social care, and to all public amenities provided by society and the State within the limits of their available resources.
(c) The States shall ensure the right of the individual to a decent living that may enable him to meet his requirements and those of his dependents, including food, clothing, housing, education, medical care and all other basic needs.

ARTICLE 18:
(a) Everyone shall have the right to live in security for himself, his religion, his dependents, his honor and his property.
(b) Everyone shall have the right to privacy in the conduct of his private affairs, in his home, among his family, with regard to his property and his relationships. It is not permitted to spy on him, to place him under surveillance or to besmirch his good name. The State shall protect him from arbitrary interference.
(c) A private residence is inviolable in all cases. It will not be entered without permission from its inhabitants or in any unlawful manner, nor shall it be demolished or confiscated and its dwellers evicted.

ARTICLE 19:
(a) All individuals are equal before the law, without distinction between the ruler and the ruled.
(b) The right to resort to justice is guaranteed to everyone.
(c) Liability is in essence personal.
(d) There shall be no crime or punishment except as provided for in the Shari'ah.
(e) A defendant is innocent until his guilt is proven in a fast trial in which he shall be given all the guarantees of defense.

ARTICLE 20:
It is not permitted without legitimate reason to arrest an individual, or restrict his freedom, to exile or to punish him. It is not permitted to subject him to physical or psychological torture or to any form of maltreatment, cruelty or indignity. Nor is it permitted to subject an individual to medical or scientific experiments without his consent or at the risk of his health or of his life. Nor is it permitted to promulgate emergency laws that would provide executive authority for such actions.

ARTICLE 21:
Taking hostages under any form or for any purpose is expressly forbidden.

ARTICLE 22:
(a) Everyone shall have the right to express his opinion freely in such manner as would not be contrary to the principles of the Shari'ah.
(b) Everyone shall have the right to advocate what is right, and propagate what is good, and warn against what is wrong and evil according to the norms of Islamic Shari'ah.
(c) Information is a vital necessity to society. It may not be exploited or misused in such a way as may violate sanctities and the dignity of Prophets, undermine moral and ethical Values or disintegrate, corrupt or harm society or weaken its faith.
(d) It is not permitted to excite nationalistic or doctrinal hatred or to do anything that may be an incitement to any form or racial discrimination.

ARTICLE 23:
(a) Authority is a trust; and abuse or malicious exploitation thereof is explicitly prohibited, in order to guarantee fundamental human rights.
(b) Everyone shall have the right to participate, directly or indirectly in the administration of his country's public affairs. He shall also have the right to assume public office in accordance with the provisions of Shari'ah.

ARTICLE 24:
All the rights and freedoms stipulated in this Declaration are subject to the Islamic Shari'ah.

ARTICLE 25:
The Islamic Shari'ah is the only source of reference for the explanation or clarification of any of the articles of this Declaration.

Note: U.N. GAOR, World Conference on Human Rights., 4th Session, Agenda Item 5, U.N. Doc. A/CONF.157/PC/62/Add.18 (1993) [English translation].

Source: University of Minnesota Human Rights Library, at http://hrlibrary.umn.edu/instree/cairodeclaration.html

Appendix 4

Arab Charter on Human Rights (1994)

THE GOVERNMENTS OF:
The Hashemite Kingdom of Jordan
The United Arab Emirates
The State of Bahrain
The Tunisian Republic
The Algerian Democratic People's Republic
The Republic of Djibouti
The Kingdom of Saʻudi Arabia
The Republic of Sudan
The Syrian Arab Republic
The Democratic Republic of Somalia
The Republic of Iraq
The Sultanate of Oman
The State of Palestine
The State of Qatar
The Republic of the Comoros Islamic Union
The State of Kuwait
The Lebanese Republic
The Socialist Libyan People's Arab Jamahiriyyah
The Arab Republic of Egypt
The Kingdom of Morocco
The Islamic Republic of Mauritania
The Republic of Yemen

Preamble
Stemming from the Arab Nation's faith in the dignity of man; from when God favored it by making the Arab nation the cradle of monotheistic religions and the birthplace of civilization; which has reaffirmed [man's] right to a life of dignity based on freedom, justice and peace.

Having achieved the everlasting principles established by the Islamic Shari'ah and the other divine religions enshrined in brotherhood and equality amongst human beings.

Cherishing the humanitarian values and principles which [the Arab Nation] has established throughout its long history, having had a major role in spreading centers of knowledge between East and West, and made it the destination of people from all over the world and of those seeking knowledge, culture and wisdom.

For the Arab World, from one end to the other, has continued to call for preserving its belief, having faith in its unity, struggling for its freedom, defending the right of nations to self-determination and to preserve their wealth, and believing in the Rule of Law, and that mankind's enjoyment of freedom, justice and equal opportunity is the hallmark of the profound essence of any society.

Rejecting racism and Zionism, both of which constitute a violation of human rights and a threat to world peace.

Recognizing the close link between human rights and world peace.

Reaffirming the principles of the United Nations Charter, the Universal Declaration of Human Rights, the provisions of the two United Nations International Covenants, on Civil and Political Rights and on Economic, Social and Cultural Rights, and the Cairo Declaration on Human Rights in Islam.

Affirming all the above, [these governments] agree to the following:

Part One
Article 1
A. All peoples have the right to self-determination and to have control over their wealth and natural resources. By virtue of that right, they have the right to freely determine their political status and to freely pursue their economic, social and cultural development.
B. Racism, Zionism, occupation and foreign control constitute a challenge to human dignity and are a fundamental obstacle to the human rights of peoples. It is a duty to condemn all such practices and to work towards their abolishment.

Part Two
Article 2
Each State party to the present Charter undertakes to ensure that every individual located within its territory and subject to its jurisdiction, shall have the right to enjoy all the rights and freedoms recognized in this [Charter], without distinction on the basis of race, color sex, language, religion, political opinion, national or social origin, wealth, birth or other status, and without any discrimination between men and women.

Article 3
A. There will be no restriction of any basic human right which is recognized or existent in any State party to this Charter, by virtue of law, treaties or custom. Nor may [these rights] be derogated from under the pretext that they have not been recognized in this Charter, or recognized to a lesser degree.

B. No State party to this Charter shall derogate from the basic freedoms contained in [this Charter] and from which the citizens of another state benefit, which affords those freedoms to a lesser degree.

Article 4
A. It is prohibited to impose limitations on the rights and freedoms guaranteed by virtue of this Charter unless where prescribed by law and considered necessary to protect national and economic security, or public order, or public health, or morals, or the rights and freedoms of others.

B. State Parties may, in times of public emergencies which threaten the life of the nation, take measures that exonerate them from their obligations in accordance with this Charter to the extent strictly required by the circumstances.

C. The limitations or derogations shall not affect the prohibition from torture and degrading [treatment], the return to [one's] country, political asylum, trial, the prohibition against retrial of the same act, and the principle of the legality of the crime and punishment.

Article 5
Everyone has the right to life, liberty, and security of person; these rights are protected by law.

Article 6
There can be no crime, or punishment, except for what is stipulated in law. Nor can there be any punishment for any acts committed previous to the enactment of that law. The accused benefits from a subsequent law if it is in his interest.

Article 7
The accused is presumed innocent until proven guilty in a lawful trial where defense rights are guaranteed.

Article 8
Every person has the right to liberty and security of person. No one shall be subjected to arrest or detention or stopped without legal basis and must be brought before the judiciary without delay.

Article 9
Everyone is equal before the judiciary, and the right to judicial recourse is guaranteed for every person, on the territory of a State.

Article 10
Sentence of death will be imposed only for the most serious crimes; every individual sentenced to death has the rights to seek pardon or commutation of the sentence.

Article 11
Under no circumstances may the death sentence be imposed for a political offence.

Article 12
Sentences of death shall not be carried-out on persons below eighteen years of age, or a pregnant woman, until she gives birth, or a nursing mother, until two years have passed from the date of [her child's] birth.

Article 13
A. The State parties shall protect every person in their territory from physical or psychological torture, or from cruel, inhuman, degrading treatment. [The State parties] shall take effective measures to prevent such acts; performing or participating in them shall be considered a crime punished by law.
B. No medical or scientific experimentation shall be carried-out on any person without his free consent.

Article 14
No one shall be imprisoned for proven inability to repay a debt or another civil obligation.

Article 15
Those punished with deprivation of liberty must be treated humanely.

Article 16

No person can be tried twice for the same crime. Anyone against whom such a measure is taken has the right to challenge its legality and request his release. Anyone who is the victim of an illegal arrest or detention has the right to compensation.

Article 17

Private life is sacred, and violation of that sanctity is a crime. Private life includes family privacy, the sanctity of the home, and the secrecy of correspondence and other forms of private communication.

Article 18

The recognition of a person before the law is a character attached to every person.

Article 19

The people are the source of authority. Political capacity is a right for every citizen of a legal age to be exercised in accordance with the law.

Article 20

Everyone residing on the territory of a State shall have freedom of movement and freedom to choose the place of residence in any part of the territory, within the limits of the law.

Article 21

Citizens shall not be arbitrarily or illegally deprived from leaving any Arab country, including their own, or their residency restricted to a particular place, or forced to live in any area of their country.

Article 22

No citizen can be expelled from his own country, or deprived of the right to return to it.

Article 23

Every citizen has the right to seek political asylum in other countries, fleeing persecution. A person who was pursued for a common crime does not benefit from this right. Political refugees shall not be extradited.

Article 24

No citizen shall be arbitrarily denied of his original nationality, nor denied his right to acquire another nationality without legal basis.

Article 25
The right to private ownership is guaranteed to every citizen. Under no circumstances shall a citizen be arbitrarily or illegally deprived of all or part of his property.

Article 26
The freedom of thought, conscience and opinion is guaranteed to everyone.

Article 27
Persons from all religions have the right to practice their faith. They also have the right to manifest their opinions through worship, practice or teaching without jeopardizing the rights of others. No restrictions of the exercise of the freedom of thought, conscience and opinion can be imposed except through what is prescribed by law.

Article 28
Citizens have the freedom of assembly and association in peaceful manner. No restrictions shall be imposed on either of these two freedoms except when it is necessary for national security, or public safety, or the protection of the rights and freedoms of others.

Article 29
The State shall ensure the right to form trade unions and the right to strike within the limits prescribed by law.

Article 30
The State shall ensure every citizen the right to work which guarantees a standard of living that provides the basic life necessities and ensures the rights to a comprehensive social security.

Article 31
The freedom to choose employment is guaranteed, and forced labor is prohibited. Forced labor does not include compelling a person to carry out work in execution a judicial decision.

Article 32
The State shall ensure to citizens equal opportunity in employment, and equal pay for work of equal value.

Article 33
Every citizen has the right to occupy public office in his country.

Article 34
Eradicating illiteracy is a commitment and an obligation. Education is a right for every citizen. Elementary education is compulsory and free. Secondary and university education shall be accessible to all.

Article 35
Citizens have the right to live in an intellectual and cultural atmosphere that reveres Arab nationalism and cherishes human rights. Racial, religious and other forms of discrimination are rejected, while international cooperation and world peace are upheld.

Article 36
Everyone has the right to participate in the cultural life, enjoy literary and artistic production, and be given the chance to advance his artistic thought and creative talent.

Article 37
Minorities shall not be deprived of their right to enjoy their own culture or follow their own religious teachings.

Article 38
A. The family is the fundamental unit of society, and enjoys its protection.
B. The State shall ensure special care and protection for the family, mothers, children and the elderly.

Article 39
The youth has the right to have greater opportunity to develop physical and mental abilities.

Part Three
Article 40
A. The member States of the [Arab] League Council, which are parties to the Charter, shall elect a Committee of human rights experts by secret ballot
B. The Committee shall consist of seven members nominated by State parties to the Charter. The primary elections for the Committee shall take place six months after the Charter enters into force. The Committee shall not include more than one person from the same State.
C. The Secretary-General shall request the State parties to present their nominees two months before the election date.
D. The nominees must have a high level of expertise and financial

capability in the area of Committee work. Experts shall work in their individual capacity, and with total impartiality and integrity.

E. Members shall be elected for a period of three years, three of whose membership may be renewed one time only. The names of the latter shall be randomly drawn from the ballot box, and the principle of rotation will be followed whenever possible.

F. The Committee shall elect its Chairman and will draw up its own internal rules of procedure, outlining how it will function.

G. The Committee shall hold its meetings at the League's General Secretariat headquarters at the invitation of the Secretary-General. The Committee may, with his approval, hold its meetings in another Arab country if the work so requires.

Article 41

1. State parties [to the Charter] shall submit reports to the Expert Human Rights Committee as follows:
    a. An initial report one year from the date the Charter enters into force;
    b. Periodic reports every three years;
    c. Reports that contain the States responses to inquiries by the Committee.
2. The Committee shall study the reports submitted by the State parties to the Charter in accordance with paragraph I of this article.
3. The Committee will distribute a report accompanied by the opinions and comments of the States to the Human Rights Committee of the Arab League.

Part Four
Article 42

A. The Secretary-General of the League of Arab States shall submit this Charter after the League Council approves it to the State parties for signature, ratification or adherence.

B. This Charter takes effect two months after the seventh instrument of ratification or adherence has been deposited at the General Secretariat of the Arab League.

Article 43

This Charter takes effect in each State, after its coming into force, two months from the date of the deposit by that State of its instrument of ratification or adherence to the General Secretariat. The Secretary-General shall notify State parties upon receiving the ratification or adherence instrument.

Appendix 4

Source: League of Arab States, *Arab Charter on Human Rights*, 15 September 1994, available at: https://www.refworld.org/docid/3ae6b38540.html

Appendix 5

Gender Discrimination in Sa'udi Arabia's Nationality Law

Document 1
Sa'udi Arabian Nationality Regulations
Resolution Number 4, 25/1/1374 [25 September 1954]

The Council of Ministers upon reviewing the draft Regulations of the Sa'udi Arabian Nationality Law originally drafted by the Shurah Council, and revised by a committee composed of the legal consultant Ahmad Ibrahim Musah and Husaynn 'Azab, the representative of the Ministry of Interior, and the resolution of the Regulations Committee of the Council of Ministers concerning the said draft, decides by absolute majority the approval of the abovementioned draft as follows:

1. **The Sa'udi Arabian Nationality Regulations**
2. These regulations shall have no retroactive force and shall supplement all resolutions and procedures issued in accordance with earlier regulations that shall remain valid and in full force for all nationalities granted under said regulations if based on correct procedures and true information.
3. The following terms shall in these regulations have the following meanings:
    a. A Sa'udi national is a subject of the Government of His Majesty the King in accordance with the provisions of these Regulations.
    b. A Sa'udi by naturalization is the person who has acquired the Sa'udi nationality in accordance with its special provisions.
    c. An alien is the person who is a non-Sa'udi.
    d. An underage is a child, or an insane individual or a person medically classified as an imbecile.
    e. The age of maturity is that age prescribed by the provisions of Shari'ah.
    f. The Kingdom of Sa'udi Arabia includes the territories, territorial

Appendix 5 **249**

waters and the air space under Saʻudi sovereignty, as well as vessels and airplanes that carry the Saʻudi flag.

4. A Saʻudi national is
   a. Any person who was an Ottoman national on 1332 H., corresponding to 1914, as well as the indigenous peoples of the land.
   b. Ottoman subjects, who were born on the territories of the Kingdom of Saʻudi Arabia and who were residing therein in 1332, corresponding to 1914, and who continued to reside in these territories until 22/3/1345 H [30 September 1026] without acquiring any other nationality before this date.
   c. Any person who was not an Ottoman subject but was residing in the territories of the Kingdom of Saʻudi Arabia on 1332 H and whose residence in these territories extended up to 22/3/1345 H without acquiring any foreign nationality before this date.
5. Provisions of sub section (a) of article 4 shall apply to women, who are indigenous nationals of the Kingdom of Saʻudi Arabia and who apply for the restoration of their Saʻudi nationality following their divorce or the death of their husbands.
6. Applications for Saʻudi nationality shall not be accepted from those who are subject to the provisions of subsections (b) and (c) of article 4, one year after the date on which this provision comes into force; and for these regulations, under aged persons are so defined after one year of the date on which they reach legal age.
7. A Saʻudi is a person who is born in the Kingdom of Saʻudi Arabia or abroad whose father and mother are both Saʻudi nationals, or whose mother is a Saʻudi national and the nationality of his father is unknown or he is without any nationality [amended by Royal Decree Number 20, dated 12/11/1379 H (8 May 1960)—see Document 2 below].
8. Any person born in the Kingdom of Saʻudi Arabia whose parents are foreigners, or any person whose father is a foreigner and his mother is a Saʻudi national shall be regarded as a foreigner. Shall also be regarded a foreigner any person who is born outside the Kingdom of Saʻudi Arabia to a father who is a foreigner with a known nationality and to a mother who is a Saʻudi national; nevertheless, this child shall have the right to become a Saʻudi Arabian national when becomes of legal age if the following conditions are fulfilled:
   a. He shall have made Saʻudi Arabia his permanent residence when he becomes of legal age;
   b. He is of good conduct and sound character and has not been convicted of a crime or imprisoned for a period exceeding six months for an indecent act;
   c. Speaks the Arabic language;

d. Submits an application for Sa'udi nationality within one year after he reaches the age of maturity. An insane or imbecile person will follow the nationality of his father, if his father is still alive. However, if his father is dead, his legal guardian must choose the Sa'udi nationality for him if the above conditions are met [amended by Royal Decree Number M/14, dated 24/5/1405 H (14 February 1985)—see Document 6 below].
9. An alien may be granted Sa'udi nationality if he fulfills the following conditions:
   a. He has reached the age of maturity at the time of submission of application;
   b. He shall not be insane or an imbecile;
   c. At the time of submitting an application:
      A. He shall have been granted permanent residence status in the Kingdom of Sa'udi Arabia by virtue of the special provisions of residence regulations.
      B. He shall be of good conduct.
      C. He must not have been imprisoned for a crime that impugns integrity six months prior to his application;
      D. He must have living resources.
   A person who applies for naturalization shall attach with his application the permanent residence license, his legal passport and any other document, which the authorities considered acting as a legal passport, and any other documents connected with the nationality, which he is going to renounce, and any paper required by the provisions of this act.
10. Saudi nationality is granted by the Prime Minister based on the recommendation of the Minister of Interior. The Minister of Interior, in all cases, may refuse granting Sa'udi nationality to aliens who have fulfilled all the conditions, which are prescribed in article nine.
11. A Sa'udi national is not permitted to acquire foreign nationality without prior permission from the Prime Minister; and any Sa'udi national who acquires a foreign nationality without having this permission in advance is still considered a Sa'udi national, unless the government of his Majesty the King decides to withdraw the nationality of that person in implementation of the provision of article thirteen.
12. When a Sa'udi national acquires a foreign nationality, this will entitle his wife to lose the Sa'udi nationality, if she acquires the nationality of her husband in accordance with the law of that new nationality, unless she decides within one year of the date on which her husband

has acquired the foreign nationality that she intends to keep her Sa'udi nationality.

Underage children, shall loose the Sa'udi nationality if they enter into the new nationality, which their father has acquired by virtue of its law, and they shall have the right to restore the Sa'udi nationality within one year after reaching the age of maturity.

13. Any Sa'udi national may be denaturalized with causative decree in any of the following cases:
    a. If he acquires another nationality, violating the provisions of article (11) of this law.
    b. If he works in the armed forces of a foreign country without prior permission from the government of his Majesty the King.
    c. If he works for the interest of another country, which is in war state with the Kingdom of Sa'udi Arabia.
    d. If he accepts a job in a foreign country or in an international institution and remains in that job despite receiving an order from the government of his Majesty the King to leave that job.

    In all cases, which are prescribed in sub-sections (b), (c) and (d) of this article, the Sa'udi national shall be warned about the consequences of his deed in a proper manner three months at least before issuance of the decree of withdrawal of the Sa'udi nationality. In all cases of denaturalization, in accordance with the provisions of this article, properties of the person who has been denaturalized shall be confiscated in accordance to Real Estate Ownership Law and he may be prevented from residence in the Kingdom of Sa'udi Arabia or to return.

14. If an alien has acquired Sa'udi nationality, his wife shall be a Sa'udi national too, but if she does not decide after one year of the date on which her husband becomes Sa'udi, this would confirm that she intends to keep her original nationality. Underage children, who have not reached the age of maturity, if they are residing in the Kingdom of Sa'udi Arabia, are considered Sa'udi nationals, and they have the right to select the original nationality of their father within one year after reaching the age of maturity. If their residence is outside Sa'udi Arabia, they are considered aliens, and they have the right to select the nationality of their father, the Sa'udi nationality, within one year after reaching age the of maturity.

15. The naturalized person may submit a separate application for acquiring Sa'udi nationality for any of the women who are under his legal guardianship, by virtue of a legal document.

16. An alien woman who marries a Sa'udi national shall acquire his Sa'udi nationality [amended by Royal Decree Number 32 dated 25/6/1380 H (14 December 1960), see Document 4 below]

17. Pursuant to what has been prescribed in the two articles (132) and (133) of the Law of Procedure Before Shari'ah Courts, a Sa'udi woman shall not lose her nationality if she marries an alien unless she has received a permission to leave the Kingdom of Sa'udi Arabia with her husband (in accordance with his special law), and she decides and announces that she will join the nationality of her husband and has actually entered that nationality by virtue of the law of that nationality.
18. A Sa'udi woman who has married an alien may restore her Sa'udi nationality after the end of marriage and her return to reside in the Kingdom.
19. The following provisions shall be applicable on the wives and children of those who have lost Sa'udi nationality:
    a. A wife of a Sa'udi whose nationality has been withdrawn in accordance with article thirteen shall have the right to select the new nationality of her husband or to remain in her Sa'udi nationality. If she selects her husband's nationality, she may restore her Sa'udi nationality if the marriage bond ceases to subsist. Underage children have the right, if they are not residing in the Kingdom of Sa'udi Arabia, to select the Sa'udi nationality, without any restrictions, when they reach the maturity age and they are entitled to all rights of Sa'udi citizens without exception.
    b. Withdrawal of Sa'udi nationality in accordance of article eleven from a person does not entitle the withdrawal of that nationality from his wife or children or from any of his family who have such nationality.
20. Any person who leaves the Kingdom of Sa'udi Arabia with the passport of his original country after residing for the required period for obtaining Sa'udi nationality, and has submitted his application for naturalization, will lose this period if he stays abroad for more than one year; and any person who leaves Sa'udi Arabia after completing the required period and has not applied for naturalization will lose his right to apply for naturalization if he stays outside Sa'udi Arabia for more than the period of his return visa, which is considered six months maximum.
21. Saudi Arabian nationality may be withdrawn by a causative decree based on the request of the Minister of Interior from any person who has acquired that nationality by naturalization under the provisions of articles (8), (9), and (10) of this law, within the first five years of his acquisition in the two following cases:
    a. If he has been punished for a criminal offence or for a crime, which impugns integrity with imprisonment for a period exceeding one year.

Appendix 5 **253**

    b. If it is proved that he has committed or participated in any action, which disturbs public security, or if it is proved that he has committed what makes his stay undesirable in the country.
22. Saudi nationality may be withdrawn, by a decree based on the recommendation of the Minister of Interior and the approval of the Council of Ministers, from any person who has acquired that nationality by naturalization, at any time, if it is proved that he has obtained that nationality based on false statements or by way of deception or by fault or by forgery or by counterfeiting witnesses or documents or data, which he has submitted for obtaining nationality [amended by Royal Decree Number M/4, dated 4/6/1389 H (17 August 1969)].
23. Withdrawal of Sa'udi nationality from a person who has acquired it by naturalization, entitles the withdrawal of that nationality from the person and from those who have acquired nationality through him. If the person who has acquired nationality by belonging is proved to be of good conduct and there are no reasons preventing granting him nationality, he shall be granted nationality and the previous period is calculated. The Ministry of Interior is the entity that has true jurisdiction of implementing this law. All declarations, announcements, papers and applications, referred to in this law, shall be addressed to the Minister of Interior through official notice or by receipt to the concerned officer in the department in the residential location of the applicant or abroad to the legations of the government of his Majesty the King, or to the counselors or to any other officer authorized by a resolution from the Minister of Interior to receive these declarations, announcements, applications and papers.
24. All decrees and resolutions connected with the acquisition, withdrawal, denaturalization and restoration of Sa'udi nationality are deemed valid and enter into force on the date of its publication in the Official Gazette.
25. Notwithstanding any other more severe punishment, any person who presents false statements or untrue documents to the concerned authorities in order to acquire or refute for himself or for others, Sa'udi nationality, shall be punished by imprisonment for a period not exceeding two years or by a fine not exceeding One Thousand SAR. Approval of withdrawal decisions shall be issued by the Minister of Interior.
26. The Minister of Interior shall pass the necessary decisions to implement this law.
27. This law supersedes the Law of Sa'udi nationality issued with Royal Decree Number 7/10/47 dated 13 Shawal 1357 (5 December 1938),

and all prior laws concerned with Hijazi nationality or Najdi nationality, and it also supersedes other provisions of laws, which are contradicting to its provisions.

28. No one, except his Majesty the King, has the right to grant nationality to a person who does not fulfill the conditions prescribed in article Number nine or to withdraw nationality from any Sa'udi national except in accordance with the provisions of article thirteen herein.

THE PRIME MINISTER
Raised to the Chamber of his Highness with Number 566 dated 25/1/1374 (23 September 1954).

Document 2
Amendments concerning the Law
In the Name of Allah the Most Gracious the Most Merciful
Number 20
Date: 12/11/1379 H [8 May 1960]
With the Help of Allah,
We, Sa'ud bin 'Abdul 'Aziz Al Sa'ud,
The King of the Kingdom of Sa'udi Arabia

Upon reviewing the resolution of the Council of Ministers Number 210 dated 7/11/1379 H (3 May 1960), and based on the representation of the Prime Minister,

Declare the following:
First: Article Seven of the Sa'udi Arabian Nationality Law, issued in 1374 H shall be amended with the following text: "A Sa'udi is the person who is born inside or outside the Kingdom of Sa'udi Arabia and whose father is a Sa'udi national; or whose mother is a Sa'udi national and his father of unknown nationality, or without nationality; or who is born inside the Kingdom of Sa'udi Arabia and his parents are unknown—a foundling is considered born in Sa'udi Arabia unless otherwise proved."
Second: The Prime Minister shall implement this law.

Document 3
In the Name of Allah the Most Gracious the Most Merciful
Resolution Number 210 dated 7/11/1379 H (3 May 1960)

The Council of Ministers, upon reviewing the attached transaction, received from the Presidency Chamber with Number 11343 dated

Appendix 5

29/5/79 H (30 November 1959), consisting of an application from Tahsin Ba'ashin requesting an official certificate to be given to the foundling whom he named "Walid" for the purpose of providing him with a Sa'udi ID; and which has been dealt with in the Shurah Council with its resolution Number 49 dated 16/5/79 H (17 November 1959),

Declare the following:
First: Approval of the amendment of article (7) of the Sa'udi Arabian Nationality Law issued in 1374 H with the following text: "A Sa'udi is the person who is born inside or outside the Kingdom of Sa'udi Arabia whose father is a Sa'udi national; or whose mother is a Sa'udi national and father of unknown nationality or without nationality; or who is born inside the Kingdom of Sa'udi Arabia and his parents are unknown—a foundling is considered born in Sa'udi Arabia unless otherwise proved."
Second: A draft of a Royal Decree has been prepared for this purpose—A copy is attached.

PRIME MINISTER

Document 4
In the Name of Allah the Most Gracious the Most Merciful
Number 32
Date: 25/6/1380 H (14 December 1960).

With the Help of Allah,
We, Sa'ud bin 'Abdul 'Aziz Al Sa'ud,
The King of the Kingdom of Sa'udi Arabia

Upon reviewing the two articles (19) and (20) of the Council of Ministers Law, and based on the resolution of the Council of Ministers Number 227 dated 2/6/1380 H (21 November 1960), and based on the representation of the Prime Minister,

Declare the following:
First: Article No (16) of the Sa'udi Arabian Nationality Law, issued on 22/2/1374 H (20 October 1954) shall be amended as follows: "An alien woman who marries a Sa'udi national shall acquire his Sa'udi nationality if she renounces her previous nationality and has announced her intention to acquire a Sa'udi Arabian nationality."
Second: The Prime Minister and the Minister of Interior shall implement this decree on the date of its publication.

Document 5
In the Name of Allah the Most Gracious the Most Merciful
Resolution Number 227 dated 2/6/1380 H (21 November 1960)

THE COUNCIL OF MINISTERS,
Upon reviewing the attached transaction, received from the Presidency Chamber with Number 7044 dated 29/3/1380 H (20 September 1960), and Number 10032 dated 4/5/1380 H (24 October 1960) consisting of nationality of foreign woman after her marriage to a Sa'udi national, and the procedures which shall be followed to add her name in the ID and passport of her husband;
And upon reviewing the resolution of the resolution of the Shurah Council Number 27 dated 16/3/1380 H (7 September 1960);
And upon reviewing the resolution of Laws Commission Number 72 dated 27/5/1380 H (16 November 1960),

Declare the following:
First: The amendment of article (16) of the Sa'udi Arabian Nationality Law issued on 22/2/1374 H (20 October 1954) which reads: "with the following text: An alien woman who marries a Sa'udi national shall acquire his Sa'udi nationality," shall be replaced with the following text: "An alien woman who marries a Sa'udi national shall acquire his Sa'udi nationality if she renounces her previous nationality and has announced her intention to acquire the Sa'udi nationality."
Second: A draft of Royal Decree has been prepared for this purpose—A copy is attached.
PRIME MINISTER

Document 6
In the Name of Allah the Most Gracious the Most Merciful
Number M/14, Date: 24/5/1405 (14 February 1985)

With the help of Allah the Almighty,
We, 'Abdallah bin 'Abdul 'Aziz Al Sa'ud
Deputy King of the Kingdom of Sa'udi Arabia,

Upon reviewing article 20 of the Council of Ministers Law issued by the Royal Decree Number (38) dated 22/10/1377 H (11 May 1958),
And upon reviewing the Sa'udi Arabian Nationality Law issued by the Royal Edict Number 8/20/5604 dated 22/2/1377 H (17 September 1957);

And upon reviewing the resolution of the Council of Ministers Number (86) dated 7/5/1405 H (28 January 1985);

Declare the following:
First: Amendment of article (8) of the Sa'udi Arabian Nationality Law, issued by the Royal Edict Number 8/22/5604 dated 22/2/1377 H, to be read as following:
"(Sa'udi Arabian Nationality may be granted to any person who is born inside the Kingdom of Sa'udi Arabia of an alien father and a Sa'udi mother if the following conditions are fulfilled:
- A. He makes Sa'udi Arabia his permanent residence when he reaches the age of maturity.
- B. He is of good conduct and has not been punished on a penal crime or was imprisoned for a period exceeding six months for a crime that impugned integrity.
- C. He knows the Arabic language well.
- D. He shall submit an application for Sa'udi nationality within one year after he reaches the age of maturity.)

Article (8) with its text before amendment continues to be applicable for beneficiaries of that article, who have applied under that article for selecting Sa'udi Nationality before issuance of this decree.

His Royal Highness the deputy Prime Minister and the Ministers, each in his capacity, shall implement this decree.

Document 7
In the Name of Allah the Most Gracious the Most Merciful
Resolution Number 86 dated 7/5/1405 H (28 January 1985).

THE COUNCIL OF MINISTERS,
Upon reviewing the attached transaction, received from the Presidency Chamber with Number 6/15171/D, dated 13/8/1404 H (14 May 1984) consisting of the letter of His Royal Highness the Minister of Interior Number 3/26514, dated 17/5/1404 H (18 February 1984), concerning his request for amendment of article (8) of the nationality law, issued in 1374 H, which gives those who are born in the Kingdom of foreign fathers the right to apply for the Sa'udi nationality with very simple conditions, and considering the change of circumstances on which that article has been formulated when the number of foreigners who were residing in Sa'udi Arabia and benefiting of the article was limited, and they had links with Sa'udi Arabia more that the material links,

And upon reviewing the report prepared by the Department of Experts with collaboration with the Ministry of Interior,

And upon reviewing the recommendation of the General Commission of the Council of Ministers Number (11) dated 14/1/1405 H (9 October 1984), and its memorandum Number (56) dated 28/2/1405 H (21 November 1984).

Declare the following:
1. Amendment of article (8) of the Sa'udi Arabian Nationality Law issued by Royal Decree Number 8/20/5604 dated 22/2/1374 (20 October 1954) to be read as following:
    "(Sa'udi Arabian Nationality may be granted by a decision of the Minister of Interior for any person born inside the Kingdom of Sa'udi Arabia of foreign father and Sa'udi mother if the following conditions are fulfilled:
    A. He makes Sa'udi Arabia his permanent residence when he reaches the age of maturity.
    B. He is of good conduct and has not been punished for criminal offense or with imprisonment for a period exceeding six months for a crime that impugns integrity.
    C. He knows the Arabic language well.
    D. He shall submit an application to be granted the Sa'udi Nationality on the second year after reaching the age of maturity.
2. Article (8) with its text before amendment continues to be applicable for beneficiaries of that article, who have applied under that article for selecting Sa'udi Nationality before issuance of this decree.
3. A draft of Royal Decree has been prepared for that purpose, which text is attached herewith.

PRIME MINISTER

Source: Saudi Arabian Nationality Regulations 1374 H (1954), at https://www.ecoi.net/en/file/local/1098597/1504_1217587365_saudi-arabian-nationality-regulations.pdf

Appendix 6

Royal Decree Number 56660 issued on 13/11/1436 H (26 September 2015)

Telegram   "Confidential and urgent"

His Excellency Minister of Foreign Affairs
Copy to Ministry of Interior (MoI)
Copy to Ministry of Education (MoE)
Copy to Ministry of Labor (MoL)
Copy to the General Secretariat of the Council of Ministers
Copy to the Presidency of the General Intelligence

Peace and Mercy be Upon You:

We refer to "telegram number 213290," dated 18/7/1436 H (7 May 2015), based on the request of the regional representative of the General Commission of the United Nations High Commissioner for Refugees (UNHCR) in the Gulf Cooperation Council (GCC), in order to consider the possibility of:
- *Extending visas for Syrian refugees and displaced persons who lived in Yemen and were able to enter the Kingdom;*
- *Providing them with the necessary facilities in terms of employment under a 15-day temporary visa;*
- *Enabling their registration in schools;*
- *Providing access to medical services.*

We also refer to telegram of the Ministry of Interior (MoI) Number 163675, dated 16/9/1436 H (6 April 2015), in regard to the telegram of the Presidency of the General Intelligence Number 28671, dated 14/10/1436 H (31 July 2015), and contains the opinion of the Presidency on:
- *Extending temporary visas granted to Syrians and those who need assistance from them;*
- *Enabling their children to register in schools;*

- ☐ *Directing them, if necessary, to employment and craft-work, including guidance to companies and institutions;*
- ☐ *Issuing documents of temporary stay to them.*

We examined the minutes of the Council of Political and Security Affairs Number 671, dated 4/11/1436 H (1 February 2015), which includes the opinion of the Council to approve the views of the Presidency of the General Intelligence in this regard.

We, hereby, inform you of our agreement to what the Council has concluded. Complete what is required.

Muhammad bin Nayif bin 'Abdul 'Aziz Al Sa'ud
DEPUTY PRIME MINISTER

Source: Office of the Deputy Prime Minister, Riyadh.

Appendix 7

Combatting Trafficking in Persons in Accordance with the Principles of Islamic Law
[Excerpts]

. . .

2.1 Characteristics of Islamic Law and its Main Sources
The definition of law in Islam is different than that of "positive laws" in other legal systems. While in many predominantly Muslim countries positive laws have been enacted on the model of European civil law systems, Islamic jurisprudence still governs the law in such realms as rules of marriage, divorce, child custody and inheritance, laws that are relevant in the context of a discussion of trafficking in persons. It is thus important to delineate the major differences with positive legal traditions.

The major distinction between Islamic Law and the civil and common law systems is in the divine origin of Islamic law. As such, Islamic Law is not the product of court decisions, as in the Anglo-American legal system, nor in statutes, as in the civil law system. Rather, Islamic Law is of a divine nature. Islam is an Arabic word which means "submission" or "surrender" to the will of God. Several titles have been used to refer to the law of Muslims, one of which is *Shari'ah* [Islamic Law], an Arabic word meaning the "way to be followed."

. . .

SECTION III
SUBSTANTIVE LAW: PROHIBITIONS OF ELEMENTS OF TRAFFICKING IN PERSONS AS A FORM OF SLAVERY UNDER INTERNATIONAL AND ISLAMIC LAW

. . .

Significantly, Islamic Law is very clear on the prohibition of the institution of slavery, and it is important to devote some attention to this fact, as this prohibition in itself creates the foundation in Islam for a prohibition of trafficking in persons. . . .

3.3 The Gradual Elimination of the Institution of Slavery in Islamic Law

Not unlike international law, Islamic Law has much to say regarding the institution of slavery, setting out a foundation for the prohibition of trafficking in persons at a minimum for such a purpose. It may then be argued that such a prohibition by extension applies to trafficking in persons as a whole, especially when taken in conjunction with other Islamic prohibitions on certain acts, means and purposes that constitute the definition of trafficking in persons.

Slavery was common in pre-Islamic societies and the prevailing view is that Islam did not abolish slavery at the outset, "[L]ike the Hebrew Bible and the New Testament, the previously revealed texts of the Abrahamic faiths, the Qur'an accepted the institution of slavery as an established part of the lives of believers. At the outset, it thus sought to humanize and regulate the practice of slavery rather than seek its outright and immediate abolition" [...]. In fact, some have argued that instead Islam institutionalized and authorized slavery, citing verses of the Qur'an to support the view that Islam allowed sex slavery, such as " . . . if you fear that (in your marital obligations) you will not be able to observe justice among them, then content yourself with only one, or the captives that your right hand possesses" (Qur'an 4:3); "And (also forbidden to you are) all married women, save those (captives) whom your right hands possess (and whose ties with their husbands have been practically cut off) (Qur'an 4:24); "And Allah has made some of you excel others in the means of subsistence, so those who are made to excel do not give away their sustenance to those whom their right hands possess so that they should be equal therein; is it then the favor of Allah which they deny?" (Qur'an 16:71); "Allah sets forth a parable: (consider) a slave, the property of another, (who) has no power over anything, and one whom We have granted from Ourselves a goodly sustenance so he spends from it secretly and openly; are the two alike? (All) praise is due to Allah! Nay, most of them do not know" (Qur'an 16:75); "Prophet, we have made lawful to you the wives to whom you have granted dowries and the slave girls whom God has given you as booty" (Qur'an 33:50); [W]ho abstain from sex, except with those joined to them in the marriage bond, or (the captives) whom their right hands possess . . . except with their wives and slave girls, for these are lawful to them" (Qur'an 23:5–6); and "Prosperous are the believers who in their prayers are humble, and from idle talk turn away, and at alms giving are active, and guard their private parts, save from their wives and what their night hands own, them not being blameworthy" (*Sunnah* 23 [al-Mu'minum], verses 1–5).

However, the view that slavery is an intrinsic part of Islam has been disputed . . . For example, the Qur'an refers to "what their right hands own" as a "temporary" institution that existed at the time and was allowed in early Islamic society. In fact, Islam called for the freeing of sex slaves, making sex permitted only inside the institution of marriage. More generally, freeing a slave was encouraged as a way of expiating of wrongdoings and shortcomings.

Additionally, nowhere in the Qur'an is a Muslim allowed to make a new slave, and the Qur'an makes freeing a slave a good deed that makes up for a wrongdoing. For example, "Those who put away their wives (by saying they are as their mothers) and afterward would go back on that which they have said, (the penalty) in that case (is) the freeing of a slave before they touch one another. Unto this ye are exhorted; and Allah is aware of what ye do" (Qur'an 58:3); "God will not take you to task for a slip in your oaths, but He will take you to task for such bonds as you have made by oaths, when of the expiation is to feed ten poor persons with the average of the food you serve to your families, or to clothe them, or to set free a slave" (Qur'an 5:89).

. . .

SECTION IV
THE PRINCIPLE OF PROHIBITION OF EXPLOITATION IN ISLAMIC LAW

. . .

Islamic law outlines a general prohibition of exploitation, and likewise prohibits certain specific types of exploitation, which include, similarly to the UN Protocol on Trafficking, that of a prohibition of labor exploitation, a prohibition of exploitation of the prostitution of others, and the trafficking of organs. In addition to the practices specifically covered by the UN Protocol on Trafficking, Islamic law likewise condemns additional forms of exploitation, such as those that may arise out of illegitimate adoption practices and forced marriage.

. . .

4.3 The Sponsorship Rule: A Violation of the Islamic Principle of Freedom
Closely related to labor exploitation specifically is the practice of the sponsorship rule: a rule that provides an employer sponsoring a worker with a variety of rights that may infringe on the rights of the employee. This type of practice, however, is in contradiction with the Islamic principles of freedom.

Many countries of the Middle East adopt the sponsorship rule [*kafalah*], a rule that is often argued to contain elements of control and exploitation. Under the rule, foreign workers' travel documents are withheld by employers and an employee may not leave his employer and seek another employment without approval, restricting the workers' freedom of movement; nor is the employee allowed to leave the country for any reason without first obtaining the approval of the employer.

. . .

The sponsorship system nowadays produced visas market, leaving tens of workers living in sub-human conditions, as a large number of laborers are accommodated in small areas. It is really a shame and also it is against the Islamic principles which call for respecting human rights.

Earlier, the Sa'udi Arabian Grand Mufti, the highest Islamic authority in the country, issued a *fatwah* on 3 September 2002, against abuse of foreign labor by Sa'udi employers, stating that "blackmailing and threatening [foreign] laborers with deportation if they refuse the employers' terms, which breach the contract, is not allowed." A recent Sa'udi Council of Ministers' Decree explicitly provides that an alien employee is entitled to keep his travel documents and the travel documents of his family. The employee also has a right to travel anywhere in the Kingdom of Sa'udi Arabia without showing documentation, as previously required.

. . .

SECTION V
PROTECTION OF VICTIMS OF TRAFFICKING IN PERSONS UNDER INTERNATIONAL LAW AND ISLAMIC LAW
As with the various acts, means and purposes of trafficking in persons, Islamic tradition and Islamic Law can provide us with important procedural guidelines that support international law's approach to preventing the crime of trafficking, punishing traffickers and protecting victims of trafficking as mandated by the UN Protocol. For example, Islamic Law places a strong emphasis on prevention, and thus addresses what in international anti-trafficking law is referred to as "the concept of the vulnerable victim." Similarly, Islamic Law takes into account the special needs of children and members of vulnerable communities, such as of refugee populations. In terms of punishment of offenders, Islamic Law provides guidelines that allow us to classify trafficking in persons as a serious crime, as mandated by the UN Protocol, and in terms of the protection of victims of trafficking, Islamic law provides for a variety of

victims' rights, such as the right of privacy and the right to compensation for any harm inflicted.

. . .

5.2 Violence Against Women and Islamic Law
Trafficking in persons may be classified as a form of violence, especially violence against women, who are often physically and psychologically abused, especially when exploited in the sex industry and as domestic servants. More generally, women are among the most frequent victims of trafficking in persons, often as a result of patriarchal social structures and consequent lack of opportunity. These are important considerations when looking at the prohibition of trafficking from an Islamic perspective—we can look at how Islamic tradition approaches violence against women in drawing out the comprehensive Islamic framework of combating trafficking in persons. In doing so, we will first turn to the issue of equality between women and men in the Islamic tradition. A clear understanding of where Islam stands on these issues is crucial to combating trafficking, especially in seeking to ameliorate those conditions that may be contributing to the trafficking infrastructure, as called upon by the UN Protocol on Trafficking.

. . .

5.5 Rights of Victims of Trafficking
According to international law, victims of trafficking should be provided access to a variety of protective services. Article 6 of the UN Protocol addresses comprehensively the elements of assistance to and protection of victims of trafficking. The most critical of these, grounded in international standards of human rights protection, may be identified as follows: *the right to safety; the right to privacy; the right to information; the right to legal representation; the right to be heard in court; the right to compensation for damages; the right to assistance; the right to seek residence; and the right to return.* These are fundamental rights that entitle victims of trafficking to benefits that should be granted irrespective of their immigration status or their willingness to testify in court.

Victims of trafficking should be entitled to the right to safety. If the country requires the victim of trafficking to testify against the traffickers, then the victim should be provided with witness protection as a prerequisite to coming forward and testifying.

Victims of trafficking should be entitled to the right to assistance, in the form of medical, psychological, legal, and social aid. In this regard, the

UN Protocol states: "[E]ach State Party shall consider implementing measures to provide for the physical, psychological and social recovery of victims of trafficking in persons." The U.N. Protocol further explains that victims have the right to be granted: "(a) Appropriate housing; (b) Counseling and information, in particular as regards their legal rights, in a language that the victims of trafficking in persons can understand; (c) Medical, psychological and material assistance; and (d) Employment, educational and training opportunities" (Article 6(3)).

Respect for individual human rights under Islamic Law is crucial to addressing trafficking in persons, a crime which constitutes a violation of human rights. This becomes particularly important since international law calls on States to recognize victims of trafficking as persons entitled to basic human rights.

Respect for the individual is the central precept of Islam—the warning against persecution of individuals is repeated 299 times in the Qur'an and the phrase "justice and equality" appears at least sixteen times. It may also be argued that equal protection is likewise a basic premise in Islamic legal theory. For example, the Prophet Muhammad declared in the Great Pilgrimage that "[a]ll Moslems are brothers unto one another," and that "[t]here is no superiority of an Arab over a non-Arab except as his devotion is concerned."

Islamic Law and legal tradition both provide for many of the rights enumerated above to which victims of trafficking are entitled. As . . . already discussed, Islam recognizes the right to refuge, *asylum and migration* [emphasis added], which is applicable to both the victim's right to safety (since Islam emphasizes the injunction to provide protection to those in distress) and the victim's right to residence, by providing that one whose life is threatened by persecution has the right to seek refuge in another place. As victims of trafficking often face reprisals and possible persecution by their traffickers in their countries of origin, the countries of destination should thus consider providing refuge to victims who are identified and rescued on their territory. The provision of a safe and secure environment to victims of trafficking would thus follow in the tradition of the Prophet who was himself provided refuge after fleeing persecution.

Likewise, the right to privacy is provided for in Islamic Law. It is explicitly provided for in the Qur'an, and applies both to residential privacy: "Enter not houses other than yours until ye have asked permission and saluted those in them. If ye find no one is in the house, enter it not until permission is given to you. If ye are asked to go back, go back" and communication privacy: "and spy not on each other behind their backs". These mandates to respect privacy may be applied to victims of trafficking, for whom the breach of confidentiality can be dangerous. Islamic Law also recognizes the right of a victim of a crime to compensation in accordance with the Islamic tradition of the Prophet, *la darar wa la dirar*, or "no injury and no inflicting of injury." According to this tradition, he who causes harm should repair such harm—the basis for providing compensation for damages. As stated in the *Majallah-el Ahkam-i-Adliya* "a person who does an act shall be held responsible if such act causes harm to another. The purpose of the principle of no injury or repaired harm is to achieve justice, a basic principle under Islamic Law." The right to assistance is likewise covered by the Islamic principles of assistance to those in distress and those in need—victims of trafficking certainly find themselves often psychologically and physically traumatized and do require medical and psychological aid.

In Islam, free men are equal before the law and are entitled to equal protection from the law. "No Arab is superior to a non-Arab except in devotion" runs the *Hadith*. The right of the accused to be presented by counsel is recognized based on the Islamic theory of "protected interests" which guarantees an individual: freedom of religion, right to self-representation, freedom of thought and experience and knowledge, right to procreation, and the right to property. These rights would likewise be applicable to victims of trafficking, providing them with the right to legal representation and to be heard in court.

. . .

SECTION VII
CONTEMPORARY LEGISLATIVE ENACTMENTS PROHIBITING TRAFFICKING IN THE MUSLIM WORLD
That Islamic Law is in harmony with the international law on trafficking in persons is supported by the fact that a number of international and regional human rights documents adopted in the Muslim world, as well as some Muslim constitutions and national legislation have all condemned and prohibited trafficking in persons and/or related crimes.

. . .

7.1 International and Regional Human Rights Documents Propagated in the Muslim World Prohibiting Trafficking in Persons and Related Crimes
Recent international human rights documents promulgated in the

Muslim world have attempted to address the issue of trafficking more explicitly and based on Islamic doctrine. For example, Article 13 of the Cairo Declaration on Human Rights in Islam of 1990 states that an employee "may neither be assigned work beyond his capacity nor be subjected to compulsion or harmed in any way."

Likewise, since prostitution is prohibited under Islamic Law, not only trafficking for the purpose of exploitation of the prostitution of others, but trafficking for the purpose of prostitution is prohibited under the Arab Charter of Human Rights. Article 10 of the Charter makes this distinction, prohibiting "trafficking in human beings for the purposes of prostitution" and "the exploitation of the prostitution of others or any other form of exploitation."

More specifically, Article 10 of the Arab Charter on Human Rights provides that:
All forms of slavery and trafficking in human beings are prohibited and punishable by law. No one shall be held in slavery and servitude under any circumstances.

Forced labor, trafficking in human beings for the purposes of prostitution or sexual exploitation, the exploitation of the prostitution of others or any other form of exploitation or the exploitation of children in armed conflict are prohibited.

Additionally, the Arab Charter also prohibited organ trafficking, stating in Article 9 that "no one shall be subjected to medical or scientific experimentation or to the use of his organs without his free consent and full awareness of the consequences and provided that ethical, humanitarian and professional rules are followed and medical procedures are observed to ensure his personal safety pursuant to the relevant domestic laws in force in each State party. Trafficking in human organs is prohibited in all circumstances".
. . .

CONCLUSION
Trafficking in persons is a problem that affects the Muslim world and an Islamic approach, one complementary to and supportive of the international legal framework confronting the problem can become a valuable asset. Addressing the position of Islam on the various issues of trafficking in persons is imperative if we want to educate Muslims about the magnitude of the problem and in developing ways to confront it. Muslim

scholars should issue *fatwahs* against harmful and illegal acts that constitute trafficking in persons, whether they are manifested as arranged marriages that may take place in the absence of any consent on the part of the woman, mistreatment of domestic workers, or any other forms of labor or sexual exploitation, whether or men, women, or children, in violation of basic principles of Islam. Moreover, Islamic legislation, based upon the two textual sources, the Qur'an and the traditions of the Prophet, provides for general principles, including no injury and no inflicting of injury, enjoining the good and forbidding the evil, and a prohibition of exploitation that should be interpreted through the process of *ijtihad* to establish a general theory of the protection of victims of a crime, including victims of trafficking.

In doing so, . . . [and] on the basis of Islamic texts and supported by a process of interpretation, [an effort was made] to develop a comprehensive Islamic framework that addresses the problem of trafficking in persons in its entirety. In doing so, the paper has presented the international human rights legal framework for punishing the crime of trafficking and protecting victims of trafficking, and provided an overview of the Islamic legal doctrine. Further, the paper traced the evolution of the international legal approach to combating trafficking in persons from the original prohibition of traditional slavery to a more modern concept of trafficking in persons as a crime of exploitation. Having set out these foundational pillars, the paper discussed both the Islamic gradual elimination of the institution of slavery, as well as its prohibition of exploitation, whether labor or sexual exploitation, as applicable to trafficking in persons. Further, the paper attempted to draw a distinction between harmful and illegal acts that constitute customary practices, such as forced and temporary marriage, which contravene principles of Islamic Law, which, in turn, prohibits such practices. Finally, the paper analyzed how Islamic Law classifies the crime of trafficking in persons, and the strict punishment that it invokes for such a crime. Trafficking in persons may be classified as a *ta'zir* crime that every Muslim state should declare as a serious offense which warrants a serious penalty. In the meantime, such a penalty should only be imposed in compliance with Islamic substantive and procedural safeguards that protect the accused. Islamic Law also affords various protective measures to victims of trafficking, especially women, children, refugees, internally displaced persons, and migrants. Qur'anic legislation is explicit in exempting a victim of prostitution from liability if she is forced to perform this act. The tradition of the Prophet further abolishes the statute of limitations, a rule that should apply to violent crimes, including trafficking in persons.

The Islamic prohibition of trafficking in persons is therefore based on a comprehensive set of principles solidly grounded in the Islamic legal tradition that, taken together, not only criminalize the act of human trafficking, but also prevent such an act, and protect victims of this crime. In summary, these principles include: a prohibition of the institution of slavery, a prohibition of all forms of exploitation including prostitution or prostitution-related activities, domestic servitude and other forms of forced labor or services, begging, or trade in human organs, a prohibition against bribery, a denunciation of hardship, rejection of all forms of oppression, recognition of a person's right to privacy, residency and legal representation, a prohibition of injury or harm, provision for compensation of victims, a general duty to enjoin the good and prohibit the evil, and the exultation to non-discrimination, equality and justice.

This approach supports the view that it is not sufficient to simply conceptualize trafficking in persons in the Muslim world as a form of slavery, especially because slavery, at least in the traditional sense, has been outlawed throughout the Muslim world. The essence of trafficking in persons is exploitation, many forms of which still exist in the Muslim world in clear violation of Islamic principles. Trade in human beings, buying and selling them should be condemned, as well as any case of control, undue influence, or exploitation of human beings.

It is encouraging that the Arab Charter of Human Rights of 2004, the latest regional human rights document promulgated in the Muslim world has created a reporting mechanism whereby Arab countries will report on the status of human rights in their countries, including the status of human trafficking in accordance with Article 10 and human organs, in accordance with Article 9. This mechanism should be fully and effectively implemented.

In conclusion, it thus becomes clear that rules of international law and the principles of Islamic law are complementary to each other in effectively and comprehensively combating trafficking in persons.

Source: Mohamed Y. Mattar, Research Professor of Law and Executive Director of The Protection Project at The Johns Hopkins University School of Advanced International Studies (SAIS). Published by the United Nations Office on Drugs and Crime (UNODC) and the Naif Arab University of Security Sciences (NAUSS) in cooperation with The Protection Project at The Johns Hopkins University, School of Advanced

International Studies, in Washington, D.C. Riyadh: Naif Arab University for Security Sciences, 2009.

Notes

Introduction

1 Olivier Zajec, *Frontières: Des Confins d'autrefois aux murs d'aujourd'hui*, Dourdan, France: Éditions Chronique, 2017.
2 Catherine Wihtol de Wenden, *Atlas Mondial des Migrations*, Paris: Autrement, 2009, p. 1.
3 United Nations Development Programme, *Climate Change Vulnerability Index, 2017*, at https://reliefweb.int/report/world/climate-change-vulnerability-index-2017.
4 The International Bank for Reconstruction and Development, *Global Monitoring Report 2005: Millennium Development Goals—From Consensus to Momentum*, Washington D.C.: The World Bank, 2005, p. 85.
5 The migration literature is rich and includes many useful studies that cover various facets of the phenomenon. See, for example, Steve J. Gold and Stephanie J. Nawyn, eds., *Routledge International Handbook of Migration Studies*, 2nd ed., Abingdon and New York: Routledge, 2020; Anna Triandafyllidou, *Routledge Handbook of Immigration and Refugee Studies*, 2nd ed., Abingdon and New York: Routledge, 2019: Tiziana Caponio, Peter Scholten and Ricard Zapata-Barrero, eds., *The Routledge Handbook of the Governance of Migration and Diversity in Cities*, Abingdon and New York: Routledge, 2020; and Tanja Bastia and Ronald Skelton, *Routledge Handbook of Migration and Development*, Abingdon and New York: Routledge, 2020.
6 United Nations High Commissioner for Refugees, *Global Trends: Forced Displacement 2019*, Geneva: UNHCR, 2020, pp. 2–3, at https://www.unhcr.org/5ee200e37.pdf.
7 UNHCR, Global Trends 2019, *op. cit.*, p. 8. See also Rebecca Ratcliffe, "More than 70 million People Now Fleeing Conflict and Oppression Worldwide: One in every 108 people were displaced in 2018, yet offers of resettlement were half level of previous year," *The Guardian*, 19 June 2019, at https://www.theguardian.com/global-development/2019/jun/19/more-than-70-million-people-fleeing-conflict-oppression-worldwide; and "Over 80 Million People Displaced, a 'Bleak Milestone': UN," *The Straits Times* (Singapore), 9 December 2020, at https://www.straitstimes.com/world/europe/over-80-million-people-displaced-a-bleak-milestone-un.
8 "Lebanon: There are More than 1.7 million Refugees in Lebanon. Most

struggle to make ends meet," *Anera* (American Near East Refugee Aid), at https://www.anera.org/where-we-work/lebanon/. See also Kelly Kimball, Robbie Gramer and Jack Detsch, "Beirut Explosion Imperils Lebanon's Refugee Population—and Aid Routes to Syria," *Foreign Policy*, 11 August 2020, at https://foreignpolicy.com/2020/08/11/lebanon-syria-refugee-population-beirut-explosion/.

9   Ishaan Tharoor, "The Arab World's Wealthiest Nations are Doing Next to Nothing for Syria's Refugees," *The Washington Post*, 4 September 2015, at https://www.washingtonpost.com/news/worldviews/wp/2015/09/04/the-arab-worlds-wealthiest-nations-are-doing-next-to-nothing-for-syrias-refugees/. See also Chase Winter, "Arab Monarchies Turn Down Syrian Refugees Over Security Threat," *DW* [Deutsche Welle], 25 January 2016, at https://www.dw.com/en/arab-monarchies-turn-down-syrian-refugees-over-security-threat/a-19002873.

10 See, *Legal Status of Refugees: Egypt, Jordan, Lebanon, and Iraq*, Washington, D.C.: The Law Library of Congress, Global Legal Research Center, December 2013, at https://www.loc.gov/law/help/refugees/2014-010156%20RPT.pdf; and Konrad Adenauer Stiftung, *The Arab Refugee Paradox: An Overview of Refugee Legislations in the Arab Middle East*, Baghdad: Al Nahrain Center for Strategic Studies, 2016, at https://www.kas.de/c/document_library/get_file?uuid=554c5e8e-7c06-a5a5-a73d-06023be2bd88&groupId=252038.

11 Human Rights Watch, *Iraqi Refugees, Asylum Seekers, and Displaced Persons: Current Conditions and Concerns in the Event of War*, Briefing Paper, New York: HRW, February, 2003 at https://www.hrw.org/legacy/backg rounder/mena/iraq021203/iraq-bck021203.pdf.

12 Sari Hanafi, "Gulf Response to the Syrian Refugee Crisis," *Sociology of Islam* 5, 2017, pp. 112–137.

13 Ayman Saleh, Serdar Aydin and Orhan Kocak, "A Comparative Study of Syrian Refugees in Turkey, Lebanon, and Jordan: Healthcare Access and Delivery," *International Journal of Society Systems Science*, 8:14, April 2018, at https://dergipark.org.tr/tr/download/article-file/454654. See also Satoru Nakamura, "Saudi Arabian Diplomacy during the Syrian Humanitarian Crisis: Domestic Pressure, Multilateralism, and Regional Rivalry for an Islamic State," Tokyo: IDE-JETRO [Institute of Developing Economics at the Japan External Trade Organization], 2013, at https://www.ide.go.jp/library/Japanese/Publish/Download/Seisaku/ pdf/201307_mide_13.pdf.

14 Dawn Chatty, *Displacement and Disposession in the Modern Middle East*, Cambridge: Cambridge University Press, 2010. See also Elena Fiddian-Qasmiyeh, Gil Loescher, Katy Long, Nando Sigona, eds., *The Oxford Handbook of Refugee and Forced Migration Studies*, Oxford: Oxford University Press, 2014.

15 "Studies Examine Effects of Iraq War on US and UK," *DW* [Deutsche Welle], 15 March 2013, at https://www.dw.com/en/studies-examine-

effects-of-iraq-war-on-us-and-uk/a-16676385. See also Rick Fawn, "No Consensus with the Commonwealth, No Consensus with Itself? Canada and the Iraq War," *The Round Table* 97:397, 2008, pp. 519-533; Martin Harrow, "The Effect of the Iraq War on Islamist Terrorism in the West," *Cooperation and Conflict* 45:3, September 2010, pp. 274–293, at https://www.jstor.org/stable/45084609; and Tina Besley & Michael A. Peters, "Terrorism, Trauma, Tolerance: Bearing Witness to White Supremacist Attack on Muslims in Christchurch, New Zealand," *Educational Philosophy and Theory* 52:2, 2020, pp. 109-119.

16 Lily Hindy, *Germany's Syrian Refugee Integration Experiment*, New York: The Century Foundation, 6 September 2018, at https://production-tcf.imgix.net/app/uploads/2018/09/03160422/germanys-syrian-refugee-integration-experiment.pdf. See also Hosam al-Jablawi, "Syrian Refugees' Struggle with Temporary Status in Germany," *The Atlantic Council*, 26 February 2019, at https://www.atlanticcouncil.org/blogs/syriasource/syrian-refugees-struggle-with-temporary-status-in-germany/.

17 Angela Merkel visits Poland in bid to thaw chilly relations," *DW* [Deutsche Welle], 19 March 2018, at https://www.dw.com/en/angela-merkel-visits-poland-in-bid-to-thaw-chilly-relations/a-43039203.

18 Elzbieta M. Gozdziak and Peter Marton, "Where the Wild Things Are: Fear of Islam and the Anti-Refugee Rhetoric in Hungary and in Poland," *Central and Eastern European Migration Review* 7:2, June 2018, pp. 1–27, at http://www.ceemr.uw.edu.pl/vol-7-no-2-2018/special-section/where-wild-things-are-fear-islam-and-anti-refugee-rhetoric-hungary.
See also Ivan Kalmar, "Islamophobia in the East of the European Union: An Introduction," *Patterns of Prejudice* 52:5, 2018, pp. 389—95.

19 United Nations High Commissioner for Refugees, *The 1951 Refugee Convention and 1967 Protocols*, Geneva: United Nations, 2010, at https://www.unhcr.org/3b66c2aa10.

20 *Ibid.*

21 Johannes van der Klaauw, "Refugee Rights in Times of Mixed Migration: Evolving Status and Protection Issues," *Refugee Survey Quarterly* 28:4, 2009, pp. 59–86. See also "List of OIC Member States Parties to the 1951 Convention Relating to the Status of Refugees and the 1967 Protocol," *Refugee Survey Quarterly* 27:2, 2008, p. 94.

22 The concepts of *Hijrah*, which can mean migration or forced migration, and the consequent *Muhajirun* (migrants/refugees), are analyzed in Chapter 3 too.

23 *Handbook on Procedures and Criteria for Determining Refugee Status under the 1951 Convention and the 1967 Protocol Relating to the status of Refugees*, HCR/IP/4/Eng/REV.1, Geneva: United Nations High Commissioner for Refugees, 1992, p. 7.

24 Ashraf Haidari, "Need to End Discrepancy Between Refugees and IDPs," *Raisina Debates*, Delhi: Observer Research Foundation, 5 November 2016, at

https://www.orfonline.org/expert-speak/end-discrepancy-between-refugees-and-idps/.

25 The literature on this topic is rich and seldom minces words. See, for example, Christopher van der Krogt, "Analysis: How Does Sharia Law Fit with Western Law?," *Special Broadcasting Service (SBS) News*, 23 October 2014, at https://www.sbs.com.au/news/analysis-how-does-sharia-law-fit-with-western-law. See also Jaan Islam, *True Islam, Jihad, & Terrorism: Science of Islamic Foreign Policy*, New York: Nova Science Publishers, 2016; Jaan Islam, "No, Shari'ah Law Is Not Compatible With Western Values," *Forbes*, 6 October 2016, at
https://www.forbes.com/sites/realspin/2016/10/06/no-shariah-law-is-not-compatible-with-western-values/?sh=4e0471f65eb3; Rafat Y. Alwazna, "Islamic Law: Its Sources, Interpretation and the Translation of It into Laws Written in English," *International Journal for the Semiotics of Law* 29, June 2916, pp. 251–260; Maurits S. Berger, "Understanding Sharia in the West," *Journal of Law, Religion and State* 6, 2018, pp. 236–273.

26 Ahmed Abou-El-Wafa, *The Right to Asylum between Islamic Shari'ah and International Refugee Law: A Comparative Study*, Riyadh: Naif Arab University for Security Sciences, 2009, at
https://www.unhcr.org/4a9645646.pdf.

27 Fahad L. Alghalib Alsharif, "Kafala Reforms in Saudi Arabia: Converging Toward International Labor Standards," Riyadh: King Faisal Center for Research and Islamic Studies, February 2021, at
https://kfcris.com/pdf/130efbcff5567391146fc2bc9002efa4603b6b
4891667.pdf; and Fahad Alsharif, "Undocumented Migrants in Saudi Arabia: COVID 19 and Amnesty Reforms," *International Migration*, 19 March 2021, at
https://onlinelibrary.wiley.com/doi/epdf/10.1111/imig.12838. As discussed in Chapter 5, the data originally collected in 2008-2009, has been updated in 2020 through 15 interviews with gatekeepers covering the communities under investigation.

28 In the words of the sociologist Eric Thompson, children of migrants born and raised in the Arab Gulf States can be termed as "foreign-born natives," a description that is valuable though Sa'udi authorities have not adopted it. See Pardis Mahdavi, *Crossing the Gulf: Love and Family in Migrant Lives*, Stanford, California: Stanford University Press, 2016, pp. 23 and 186.

29 "Refugee facts: What is a Refugee," Washington, D.C.: USA for UNHCR, at https://www.unrefugees.org/refugee-facts/what-is-a-refugee/.

30 Abbas Shiblak, "The Lost Tribes of Arabia," *Forced Migration Review*, April 2009, at https://core.ac.uk/download/pdf/27063823.pdf. See also "The 'Bidoon' of Saudi Arabia: Generations of Discrimination," *Saudi Gazette*, 29 August 2014, at https://saudigazette.com.sa/article/95488; and "Joint Submission to the Human Rights Council at the 31st Session of the Universal Periodic Review: Saudi Arabia," Geneva: Universal Periodic Review, United Nations Human Rights Council [Institute on Statelessness

and Inclusion, the Global Campaign for Equal Nationality Rights and the European Saudi Organization for Human Rights], 29 March 2018, at https://files.institutesi.org/UPR31_SaudiArabia.pdf.
31 Wael Mahdi, "The Rohingya's Lives in Limbo," *The National*, 9 June 2009, at https://www.thenationalnews.com/world/mena/the-rohingya-s-lives-in-limbo-1.490350.
32 "Palestine and Saudi Arabia: Residence Status of Stateless Palestinians, including access to employment, education, health care and other services, and the ability to travel in and out of the country; requirements and procedures to renew residence status, including whether stateless Palestinians whose permits have expired face deportation and detention (2015– November 2017)," Ottawa, Canada: Immigration and Refugee Board of Canada, 14 November 2017, at
https://www.refworld.org/docid/5afadfd94.html. See also Tianshe Chen, "Palestinian Refugees in Arab Countries and Their Impacts," *Journal of Middle Eastern and Islamic Studies (in Asia)* 3:3, 2009, pp. 42–56; and Joseph Kostiner, "Saudi Arabia and the Arab–Israeli Peace Process: The Fluctuation of Regional Coordination," *British Journal of Middle Eastern Studies* 36:4, December 2009, pp. 417–429.
33 Issam M. Saliba, "Regulation of Foreign Aid: Saudi Arabia," Washington. D.C.: The Library of Congress, October 2011, at
https://www.loc.gov/law/help/foreign-aid/saudiarabia.php.

1 A Theoretical Perspective on Migration

1 Jeffrey Scott Rosen, *Remittances, Investment, and Portfolio Allocations: An Analysis of Remittance Usage and Risk-Tolerance*, doctoral dissertation, Ohio State University, 2007, at
https://etd.ohiolink.edu/apexprod/rws_etd/send_file/send?accession=osu1172936345&disposition=inline.
2 Lisa Arrehag, Orjan Sjoberg and Mirja Sjoblom, "Cross-Border Migration and Remittances in a Post-Communist Society: Return Flows of Money and Goods in the Korçë District, Albania," *South-Eastern Europe Journal of Economics* 3:1, 2005, pp. 9–40.
3 Yvonne Stolz and Joerg Baten, "Brain Drain in the Age of Mass Migration: Does Relative Inequality Explain Migrant Selectivity?," *Explorations in Economic History* 49:2, 2012, pp. 205–220.
4 Douglas S. Massey, Joaquín Arango, Graeme Hugo, Ali Kouaouci, Adela Pellegrino and J. Edward Taylor, "Theories of International Migration: A Review and Appraisal," *Population and Development Review* 19:3, September 1993, pp. 431–466.
5 Ian Molho, "Theories of Migration: A Review," *Scottish Journal of Political Economy* 60:5, November 2013, pp. 526–556.
6 Tuck Hoong Paul Chan, "A Review of Micro Migration Research in the Third World Context," in Gordon F. De Jong and Robert W. Gardner, eds,

Migration Decision Making: Multidisciplinary Approaches to Microlevel Studies in Developed and Developing Countries, New York: Pergamon, 1981, pp. 303–328 [the quotation is on page 305].
7   Katalin Huzdik, Migration Potential and Affecting Factors in Hungary in the First Decade of the 21st Century, Godollo, Hungary: Szent István University Doctoral School of Management and Business Administration, 2014, at https://szie.hu/file/tti/archivum/Huzdik_ Katalin_thesis.pdf.
8   United Nations, *International Migration 2020*, at https://www.un.org/development/desa/pd/news/international-migration-2020.
9   United Nations, *International Migration 2020 Highlights*, at https://www.un.org/development/desa/pd/sites/www.un.org.development.desa.pd/files/international_migration_2020_highlights_ten_key_messages.pdf.
10 *Ibid.*
11 *Ibid.*
12 Roel Peter Wilhelmina Jennissen, *Macro-Economic Determinants of International Migration in Europe*, Amsterdam, Holland: Rozenberg Publishers, 2004, pp. 93–116.
13 Roger Zetter, *Protection in Crisis: Forced Migration and Protection in a Global Era*, Brussels, Belgium: Transatlantic Council on Migration and Migration Policy Institute, March 2015, at https://www.migrationpolicy.org/research/protection-crisis-forced-migration-and-protection-global-era.
14 Frank Laczko and Christine Aghazarm, eds., *Migration, Environment and Climate Change: Assessing the Evidence*, Geneva: International Organization for Migration, 2009, at https://environmentalmigration.iom.int/migration-environment-and-climate-change-assessing-evidence.
15 Tomas Hammar, Grete Brochmann, Kristof Tamas, and Thomas Faist, "International Migration, Immobility and Development: Multidisciplinary Perspectives," Abingdon, Oxon., 1997, as cited in A.A.I.N. Wickramasinghe and Wijitapure Wimalaratana, "International Migration and Migration Theories," *Social Affairs* 1:5, Fall 2016, pp. 13–32 [the quotation is on page 18].
16 Nilesh Prakash, *The Development Impact of Workers' Remittances in Fiji*, a thesis presented in partial fulfilment of the requirements for the degree of Master of Arts at Massey University, Palmerston North, New Zealand, 2009, at https://mro.massey.ac.nz/xmlui/bitstream/handle/10179/1281/02whole.pdf?sequence=1&isAllowed=y.
17 Eliot Dickinson, *Globalization and Migration: A World in Motion*, London: Rowman and Littlefield, 2017, p. 13. It should be noted that for others, the subject should only be based on macro and micro levels of analysis. According to one researcher, theories of international migration can be divided into two categories based on their level of analysis: macro and micro, with the latter category comprising groups that considered migration dynamics, categorizing migratory flows and describing them based on their

overall demographic, economic, and social properties. The macro approach included all theories when viewed from a structural or cultural point of view, as sociological factors differed among those who migrated and those who did not, which altered decision-making, satisfaction, and identification features. Such an approach may be thought out from an individual as well as a societal perspective. See Anthony H. Richmond, "Sociological Theories of International Migration: The Case of Refugees," *Current Sociology* 36:2, June 1988, pp. 7–25.

18 Andrew E. Shacknove, "Who is a Refugee?," *Ethics* 95:2, January 1985, pp. 274–284.
19 Erika Feller, "Refugees are Not Migrants," *Refugee Survey Quarterly* 24:4, December 2005, pp. 27–35. See also Alexander Betts and Paul Collier, "Refuge: Transforming a Broken Refugee System," *International Journal of Refugee Law* 30:1, March 2018, pp. 173–178.
20 Heaven Crawley and Dimitris Skleparis, "Refugees, Migrants, Neither, Both: Categorical Fetishism and the Politics of Bounding in Europe's 'Migration Crisis'," *Journal of Ethnic and Migration Studies* 44:1, 2018, pp. 48–64.
21 Aristide R. Zolberg, Astri Suhrke and Sergio Aguayo, *Escape from Violence: Conflict and the Refugee Crisis in the Developing World*, Oxford: Oxford University Press, 1989, pp. 5–6.
22 Richard Black, "Fifty Years of Refugee Studies: From Theory to Policy," *International Migration Review* 35:1, March 2001, pp. 57–78. See also Richmond, Sociological Theories of International Migration, *op. cit.*; and Nicholas Van Hear, "Forcing the Issue: Migration Crises and the Uneasy Dialogue Between Refugee Research and Policy," *Journal of Refugee Studies* 25:1, March 2011, pp. 2–24.
23 For details, see "Euro-African Dialogue on Migration and Development (Rabat Process)," *International Organization for Migration*, at https://www.iom.int/euro-african-dialogue-migration-and-development-rabat-process.
24 Joaquín Arango, "Explaining Migration: A Critical View," *International Social Science Journal* 52:165, September 2000, pp. 283–296.
25 Massey, Arango, Hugo, Kouaouci, Pellegrino and Taylor, *op. cit.*, pp. 431–466.
26 Prakash, *op. cit.*
27 John R. Harris and Michael P. Todaro, "Migration, Unemployment and Development: A Two-Sector Analysis," *The American Economic Review* 60:1, 1970, pp. 126–142.
28 *Ibid.*
29 Douglas S. Massey, Jorge Durand, Nolan J. Malone, "Principles of Operation: Theories of International Migration," in Carola Suarez-Orozco, Marcelo Suarez-Orozco, Desiree Baolian Qin-Hilliard, eds., *The New Immigration: An Interdisciplinary Reader*, New York: Routledge, 2004, pp. 21–33.

30 Larry Sjaastad, "The Costs and Returns of Human Migration," *Journal of Political Economy* 70:5, Part 2: Investment in Human Beings, October 1962, pp. 80–93. See also John R. Harris and Michael P. Todaro, "Migration, Unemployment and Development: A Two-Sector Analysis," *American Economic Review* 60:1, March 1970, pp. 126–142.

31 Massey, Durand and Malone, *Principles of Operation, op. cit.*

32 Edward J. Taylor, "The New Economics of Labour Migration and the Role of Remittances in the Migration Process," *International Migration* 37:1, March 1999, pp. 63–88.

33 Massey, Durand and Malone, *Principles of Operation, op. cit.*

34 Robert E. B. Lucas and Oded Stark, "Motivations to Remit: Evidence from Botswana," *Journal of Political Economy* 93:5, October 1985, pp. 901–918.

35 Michael, J. Piore, *Birds of Passage: Migrant Labor and Industrial Societies*, Cambridge: Cambridge University Press, 1979, pp. 2–4.

36 Massey, Durand and Malone, *Principles of Operation, op. cit.*, p. 21.

37 Richmond, *Sociological Theories of International Migration, op. cit.*, p. 7.

38 *Ibid.*, p. 25.

39 Karen O'Reilly, *International Migration and Social Theory*, New York: Palgrave Macmillan, 2012.

40 Massey, Durand and Malone, *Principles of Operation, op. cit.*, p. 33.

41 Hein De Haas, "Migration and Development: A Theoretical Perspective," *International Migration Review*, 44:1, Spring 2010, pp. 227–264.

42 Joaquín Arango, *op. cit.*, pp. 283–296.

43 Douglas S. Massey, Joaquín Arango, Graeme Hugo, Ali Kouaouci, Adela Pellegrino, Edward Taylor, "Theories of International Migration: A Review and Appraisal," *Population and Development Review* 19:3, September 1993, pp. 431–466.

44 Hein De Haas, "The Internal Dynamics of Migration Processes: A Theoretical Inquiry," *Journal of Ethnic and Migration Studies* 36:10, 2010, pp. 1587–1617. See also Mary M. Kritz, Lin Lean Lim, Hania Zlotnik, *International Migration Systems: A Global Approach*, Oxford: Oxford Clarendon Press, 1992.

45 Lucia Kurekova, "Theories of Migration: Conceptual Review and Empirical Testing in the Context of the EU East-West Flows," Paper prepared for the Interdisciplinary Conference on Migration: Economic Change, Social Challenge, April 6–9, 2011, at University College London, pp. 8–9, at https://www.researchgate.net/profile/Lucia-Mytna-Kurekova-2/publication/268393052_Theories_of_migration_Conceptual_review_and_empirical_testing_in_the_context_of_the_EU_East-_West_flows/links/ 54f5c4e40cf2ca5efefd2442/Theories-of-migration-Conceptual-review-and-empirical-testing-in-the-context-of-the-EU-East-West-flows.pdf.

46 Eytan Meyers, "Theories of International Immigration Policy: A Comparative Analysis," *International Migration Review* 34:4, December 2000, pp. 1262–1263, at

https://www.jstor.org/stable/2675981?read-now=1&refreqid=excelsior%3Afa41998e6c807f812550dcdfe2e85c11&seq=18#page_scan_tab_contents.

47 Circular cumulative causation was a theory developed by Swedish economist Gunnar Myrdal, whose approach concentrated on core variables and linkages, in which a change in one form of an institution will lead to successive changes in other institutions. See Nanako Fujita, *Gunnar Myrdal's Theory of Cumulative Causation Revisited*, Nagoya, Japan: Nagoya University, Economic Research Center Discussion Paper, Number 147, April 2004, at http://133.6.182.153/wp-content/uploads/2016/04/paper147.pdf. See also Elizabeth Fussell and Douglas S. Massey, "The Limits to Cumulative Causation: International Migration from Mexican Urban Areas," *Demography* 41:1, February 2004, pp. 151–171.

48 Fujita, *op. cit.*, pp. 12–13.

49 Tom Segev, *1949: The First Israelis*, New York: The Free Press, 2018. See also Tom Segev, *One Palestine, Complete*, New York: Henry Holt and Company, 2001.

50 James Morrissey, "Environmental Change and Forced Migration: A State of the Art Review," Refugee Studies Centre, Oxford Department of International Development, Queen Elizabeth House, University of Oxford, January 2009, at https://www.rsc.ox.ac.uk/files/files-1/dp-environmental-change-forced-migration-2009.pdf.

51 Myron Weiner, "On International Migration and International Relations," *Population and Development Review* 11:3, September 1985, pp. 441–455.

52 Aristide R. Zolberg, Astri Suhrke and Sergio Aguayo, "International Factors in the Formation of Refugee Movements," *International Migration Review* 20:2, June 1986, pp. 151–169.

53 According to one observer, such movements counted as two turns in this game, with each turn represented by two points in the win-loss record. See Alan Dowty, *Closed Borders: The Contemporary Assault on Freedom of Movement*, New Haven and London: Yale University Press, 1987.

54 United Nations High Commissioner for Refugees, *The 1951 Refugee Convention and 1967 Protocols*, Geneva: United Nations, 2010, at https://www.unhcr.org/3b66c2aa10.

55 Senada Selo Sabic, "The Impact of the Refugee Crisis in the Balkans: A Drift Towards Security," *Journal of Regional Security*, 12:1, 2017, pp. 51–74. See also Claudio Minca, Danica Šanti, and Dragan Umek, "Managing the 'Refugee Crisis' Along the Balkan Route: Field Notes from Serbia," in Cecilia Menjívar, Marie Ruiz, and Immanuel Ness, eds., *The Oxford Handbook of Migration Crises*, Oxford: Oxford University Press 2019, pp. 445–464; and Roland Bank, "Forced Migration in Europe," in Eleba Fiddian-Qasmiyeh, Gil Loescher, Katy Long and Nando Sigona, eds., *The Oxford Handbook of Refugee and Forced Migration Studies*, Oxford: Oxford University Press, 2014, pp. 690–702.

56 United Nations High Commissioner for Refugees, *Desperate Journeys: Refugees and Migrants Arriving in Europe and at Europe's Borders (January–December 2018)*, Geneva: United Nations, January 2019, at https://www.unhcr.org/desperatejourneys/#.
57 Merriam Webster Dictionary, "Globalization," at http://www.merriamwebster.com/dictionary/globalization.
58 Hans-henrik Holm and Georg Sorenson, eds., *Whose World Order? Uneven Globalization and the End of the Cold War*, Boulder: Westview Press, 1995, p. 1.
59 David Held, Anthony McGrew, David Goldblatt and Jonathan Perraton, "Globalization," *Global Governance* 5:4, October–December 1999, pp. 483–496.
60 For additional details on this multi-pronged approach, see Caroline B. Brettell and James F. Hollifield, eds., *Migration Theory: Talking Across Disciplines*, New York and Abingdon, Oxon.: Routledge, 2015.
61 David Collier and Colin Elman, "Qualitative and Multimethod Research: Organizations, Publication, and Reflections on Integration," in Janet M. Box-Steffensmeier, Henry E. Brady, and David Collier, eds., *The Oxford Handbook of Political Methodology*, Oxford: Oxford University Press, 2008, pp. 779–795.

2 Sa'udi Policies towards Refugees

1 Robin Wright, "Saudi Arabia's Crown Prince Picks a Very Strange Fight with Canada," *The New Yorker*, 8 August 2018, at https://www.newyorker.com/news/news-desk/saudi-arabias-crown-prince-picks-a-very-strange-fight-with-canada. See also "We're not a Banana Republic, Saudi FM Tells Canada," *Arab News*, 27 September 2018, at http://www.arabnews.com/node/1378551/saudi-arabia.
2 Kim Mackrael and James Hookway, "Canada Grants Refugee Status to Saudi Teen: Woman had barricaded herself in a hotel room and posted about her situation on Twitter," *The Wall Street Journal*, 11 January 2019, at https://www.wsj.com/articles/canada-grant-refugee-status-to-saudi-teen-who-fled-family-11547232542. See also "Rahaf al-Qunun: Saudi teen granted asylum in Canada," *BBC News*, 11 January 2019, at https://www.bbc.com/news/world-asia-46844431.
3 Chris Helgren, "Saudi Teen Who Fled Family Welcomed as 'Brave New Canadian' in Toronto," *Reuters*, 12 January 2019, at https://www.reuters.com/article/us-thailand-saudi/saudi-teen-who-fled-family-welcomed-as-brave-new-canadian-in-toronto-idUSKCN1P60IE.
4 Julie M. Norman, "Saudi Arabia Doesn't 'Do' Refugees—It's Time to Change That," *The Conversation*, 23 September 2015, at http://theconversation.com/saudi-arabia-doesnt-do-refugees-its-time-to-change-that-47307.
5 No effort was made in this short review of Sa'udi policies towards refugees

to provide a systematic and chronological review of migration, including an examination of the period before the 1973 Arab–Israeli War, followed by the October 1973 War to the 1990-1991 War for Kuwait period, and from the 1991 rout to the present. The preference was to concentrate on the three major populations that migrated to the Kingdom and either became refugees or asylum seekers. In fact, few Arabs sought such a status before or after 1973. Iraqi refugees who crossed into Sa'udi Arabia after the 1991 War for Kuwait are discussed in Chapter 3 while the fate that befell African migrants are analyzed in Chapter 6. Similarly, Yemenis and Syrians, perhaps the two communities with the largest refugee populations on the Arabian Peninsula, are discussed in Chapters 7 and 8. Therefore, providing a chronological review of migration into the Kingdom would simply be redundant. The authors evaluated such an option but concluded that a chronological discussion was not as relevant for Sa'udi Arabia as, perhaps, for other countries. Moreover, the objective here is to assess relevant policies and to address excessively harsh criticisms by outsiders determined to pigeon hole Sa'udi Arabia into the "bad-country" category.

6 Needless to say that Julie M. Norman was fully entitled to offer her analysis as others were allowed to refute any erroneous claims.
7 Norman, *op. cit.*
8 See, for example, Michael Stephens, "Migrant Crisis: Why the Gulf States are not Letting Syrians in," *Royal United Services Institute* (RUSI), Doha, 7 September 2015, at https://www.bbc.com/news/world-middle-east-34173139. See also "Saudi Arabia Says Criticism of Syria Refugee Response 'False and Misleading'," *The Guardian*, 12 September 2015, at https://www.theguardian.com/world/2015/sep/12/saudi-arabia-says-reports-of-its-syrian-refugee-response-false-and-misleading; "Why Aren't Rich Gulf States Welcoming Syrian Refugees . . . or are they?," *Euro News*, 30 September 2015, at https://www.euronews.com/2015/09/30/why-aren-t-rich-gulf-states-welcoming-syrian-refugeesor-are-they; and Chase Winter, "Arab Monarchies Turn Down Syrian Refugees Over Security Threat," *DW* [Deutsche Welle], 25 January 2016, at https://www.dw.com/en/arab-monarchies-turn-down-syrian-refugees-over-security-threat/a-19002873
9 Norman, *op. cit.*
10 Michael Stephens, "Migrant Crisis: Why the Gulf States Are Not Letting Syrians In," *BBC News*, 7 September 2015, at https://www.bbc.com/news/world-middle-east-34173139 .
11 Norman, *op. cit.*
12 Katelynn Kenworthy, "10 Important Facts About Refugees in Saudi Arabia," *The Borgen Project*, 15 June 2017, at https://borgenproject.org/refugees-in-saudi-arabia/.
13 *Ibid.*
14 "Saudi Arabia," Joint Submission to the Human Rights Council at the 31st Session of the United Nations Universal Periodic Review, New York: United Nations, 29 March 2018, at

http://www.institutesi.org/UPR31_SaudiArabia.pdf.
15. For additional details on the Institute on Statelessness and Inclusion, see its dedicated web-page at http://www.institutesi.org.
16. For additional details on the Global Campaign for Equal Nationality Rights, see its dedicated web-page at https://equalnationalityrights.org.
17. See, for example, "Saudi Arabia Sentences Loujain al-Hathloul to Prison: Human Rights Advocacy is not a Crime," Berlin: The European Saudi Organization for Human Rights (ESOHR), 29 December 2020, at https://www.esohr.org/en/?p=3195.
18. To date, there have been three major reviews undertaken by the UN-UPR team, in February 2009, October 2013 and in November 2018. The next UN-UPR evaluations for Saudi Arabia are scheduled for November 2023.
19. "National Report Submitted in Accordance with Paragraph 5 of the Annex to Human Rights Council Resolution 16/21—Saudi Arabia," Human Rights Council, Working Group on the Universal Periodic Review Seventeenth session, Geneva: United Nations General Assembly, 21 October–1 November 2013, A/HRC/WG.6/17/SAU/1, pp. 14–15, at https://www.upr-info.org/sites/default/files/document/saudi_arabia/session_17_-_october_2013/a_hrc_wg.6_17_sau_1_e.pdf.
20. Kingdom of Sa'udi Arabia, "Saudi Arabia Citizenship System," Riyadh: Ministry of the Interior, available at http://www.refworld.org/pdfid/3fb9eb6d2.pdf.
21. https://www.upr-info.org/database/index.php?limit=0&f_SUR=149&f_SMR=All&order=&orderDir=ASC&orderP=true&f_Issue=All&searchReco=&resultMax=300&response=&action_type=&session=&SuRRgrp=&SuROrg=&SMRRgrp=&SMROrg=&pledges=RecoOnly.
22. Charter of the United Nations, "Chapter IX: International Economic and Social Co-Operation, Article 55c," San Francisco: United Nations, 26 June 1945, at https://www.un.org/en/sections/un-charter/chapter-ix/index.html.
23. Claudena Skran, *Refugees in Inter-War Europe: The Emergence of a Regime*, Oxford: Clarendon Press, 1995. See also Peter Gatrell, *The Making of the Modern Refugee*, Oxford: Oxford University Press, 2015; and Joseph A. Kéchichian, *Power and Succession in Arab Monarchies*, Boulder, Colorado: Lynne Rienner Publishers, 2008, pp. 37–41.
24. This insight was drawn from Joshue Yaphe, *Saudi–Iraqi Relations, 1921–1958*, Doctoral Dissertation, Washington, D.C.: American University, 2021, p. 12. See also Dawn Chatty, *Displacement and Dispossession in the Modern Middle East*, Cambridge: Cambridge University Press, 2010.
25. Yaphe, *ibid.*, pp. 12–13.
26. For insights on tribal affairs on the Arabian Peninsula, see Badriyyah al-Bashar, *Najd Qabla al-Naft: Dirasah Susyilujiyyah Tahliliyyah lil-Hikayat al-Sha'biyyah* [Najd Before Oil: Sociological and Analytical Studies of Popular Stories], Beirut: Jadawel, 2013. See also the three volumes by Khayr al-Din al-Zirikli, *Shibh al-Jazirah fi 'Ahd al-Malik 'Abdul-'Aziz* [The Peninsula in the Era of King 'Abdul 'Aziz], Beirut: 1970.

27 Lest one conclude that the Kingdom welcomed only dictators, 52 countries have hosted at least one strongman, and the leading exile destinations in a major study that examined all exiles after 1946, were the United States, the United Kingdom, Russia, Argentina, and France, "each of which has hosted at least 5 exiled rulers since 1946." See Daniel Krcmaric and Abel Escribà-Folch, "Where do Ousted Dictators Go? Fewer Countries Now Offer a Warm Welcome," *The Washington Post*, 30 January 2017, at https://www.washingtonpost.com/news/monkey-cage/wp/2017/01/30/where-do-ousted-dictators-go-fewer-countries-now-offer-a-warm-welcome/; and Daniel Krcmaric and Abel Escribà-Folch, "Dictators in Exile: Explaining the Destinations of Ex-Rulers," *The Journal of Politics* 79:2, April 2017, pp. 560–575.

28 For a discussion of the Zubayr tribe within the larger ʻAnizah confederation, see Yusuf Hamad al-Bissam, *Al-Zubayr Qabla Khamsin ʻAman maʻ Nubdhah Tarikhiyyah ʻan Najd wal-Kuwayt* [Zubayr Fifty Years Ago with a Historical Portion about Najd and Kuwait], London: Dar Al-Hikmah, 1971.

29 Bidun, sometimes written as bidoon [Egyptian-English], is a literal translation from the Arabic that means "without." Although Kuwaiti biduns are vocal and demand representation during most parliamentary elections [without success], elsewhere their presence is quite limited, notwithstanding efforts to naturalize as many as possible in the United Arab Emirates and Qatar.

30 Najlah al-Harbi, "Bitakat bi-Salahiyat Awsaʻ lil-Bidun [License Cards with Larger Benefits for the Bidun], *Al-Watan* (Saudi Arabia), 22 November 2015, at https://www.alwatan.com.sa/article/281070/.

31 See European Saudi Organization for Human Rights, *Deprivation of Nationality in Saudi Arabia: A Quarter of a Million People, and A Suffering for Nearly Half A Century*, Berlin: ESOHR, April 2016, at https://www.esohr.org/en/wp-content/uploads/2016/03/Deprivation-of-nationality-in-Saudi-Arabia.pdf. See also "Saudi Arabia: Situation of Bidoons, including ability to obtain a passport; whether a person born to a Saudi mother and Bidoon father can obtain Saudi citizenship, and would be issued a Saudi passport as a minor (2014–June 2016)," Ottawa, Canada: Immigration and Refugee Board of Canada, 6 June 2016, at https://www.refworld.org/docid/584406344.html; and "Bidoon: Generations of Discrimination," *Saudi Gazette*, 30 August 2014, at http://saudigazette.com.sa/article/95488/Bidoon-Generations-of-discrimination.

32 Najlah al-Harbi, *op. cit.*

33 Saʻad al-Maniʻ, "Dama al-Bidun wa Hamilik al-Bitaqat wa-Jawazat Muhadadat al-Mudat li-Nisb al-Tawtin fi al-Khas" [Include Bidun and Holders of Fixed-Term (Residency) Cards and Passports for the Special [private sector] Settlement Rates], *Al-Madinah* [Daily], 12 January 2014, at https://www.al-madina.com/article/278693/ . . . See also Ahmed Ibrahim, "Shurut Tajnis al-Qabaʼil al-Nazihat fil-Saʻudiyyah, 1442" [Conditions for

Naturalization of Displaced Tribes in Saudi Arabia 1442 (2021)], *Al-Badil*, 31 January 2021, at https://www.badil.cc . . . /.

34 Nehginpao Kipgen, "Political Change in Burma: Transition from Democracy to Military Dictatorship (1948–62)," *Economic and Political Weekly* 46:20, 14–20 May 2011, pp. 48–55. See also Aye Chan, "The Development of a Muslim Enclave in Arakan (Rakhine) State of Burma (Myanmar)," *SOAS Bulletin of Burma Research* 3:2, Autumn 2005, at https://www.soas.ac.uk/sbbr/editions/file64388.pdf.

35 For additional background materials, see Engy Abdelkader, "The Rohingya Muslims in Myanmar: Past, Present, Future," *Oregon Review of International Law* 15:3, 2013, pp. 393–411.

36 "Three years after exodus, Rohingya refugees 'more vulnerable than ever'," UN News, 25 August 2020, at https://news.un.org/en/story/2020/08/1070962. See also Mohammad Tanzimuddin Khan and Saima Ahmed, "Dealing with the Rohingya Crisis: The Relevance of the General Assembly and R2P," *Asian Journal of Comparative Politics* 5:2, 2020, pp. 121–143.

37 "Myanmar Rohingya: What You Need to Know About the Crisis," *BBC News*, 23 January 2020, at https://www.bbc.com/news/world-asia-41566561.

38 "190,000 Myanmar Nationals Get Residency Relief in Saudi Arabia," *Al Arabiya*, 25 January 2017, at http://english.alarabiya.net/en/News/gulf/2017/01/25/Over-190-000-Myanmar-nationals-granted-Saudi-residency.html. See also Asma Shakir Khawaja, Asma Hussain Khan and Adnan Jamil, "An Insight Into Rohingya the Unwanted People," *Margalla Papers 2018*, Islamabad, Pakistan: National Defence University, 2018, pp. 53–62, at https://ndu.edu.pk/margalla-papers/doc/Margalla-Papers-2018.pdf.

39 Hanan Fawzih, "Shurut al-Husul alal-Jinsiyyah al-Sa'udiyyah" [Conditions to Obtain Sa'udi Nationality], *Muhtawahat*, 27 February 2020, at https://mhtwyat.com/ . . . See also See also 'Abdul Wahab al-Shaqhah, "Hukuk al-Tifl fil Mamlakah al-'Arabiyyah al Sa'udiyyah [The Rights of Children in the Kingdom of Sa'udi Arabia," *Al Jazirah* [Daily] 2 March 2007, at https://www.al-jazirah.com/2007/20070302/ar11.htm.

40 Morad Alsahafi, "When Homeland Remains a Distant Dream: Language Attitudes and Heritage Language Maintenance Among Rohingya Refugees in Saudi Arabia," *International Journal of Bilingual Education and Bilingualism*, April 2020, pp. 1–12.

41 Abbas Shiblak, "Stateless Palestinians," *Forced Migration Review* 26, August 2006, pp. 8–9, at http://www.fmreview.org/sites/fmr/files/FMRdownloads/en/palestine/shiblak.pdf.

42 Samih K. Farsoun, "Palestinian Diaspora," In: Melvin Ember, Carol R. Ember, and Ian Skoggard, eds, *Encyclopedia of Diasporas*, Boston: Springer, 2005, at https://link.springer.com/referenceworkentry/10.1007%2F978-0-387-29904-4_23#howtocite.

43 Sarah Aziza, "A Palestinian Refugee in Saudi Arabia: 50 Years of Lost Dreams," *Middle East Eye*, 29 February 2016, at http://www.middleeasteye.net/columns/palestinian-refugee-saudi-arabia-civic-immobility-and-lost-dreams-344102002.
44 Maysa Zahra, "Saudi Arabia's Legal Framework of Migration," Explanatory Note No. 4/2013, Gulf Labour Markets and Migration, European University Institute (EUI) and Gulf Research Center (GRC), 2013, available at http://www.gulfmigration.eu. See also Maysa Zahra, "Saudi Arabia's Legal Framework of Migration," Explanatory Note No. 3/2018, Gulf Labour Markets and Migration, European University Institute (EUI) and Gulf Research Center (GRC), 2018, available at http://www.gulfmigration.eu.
45 Rashid Hassan and Sharif M. Taha, "Saudi Arabia's Fees on Expats' Dependents Draw Mixed Reactions," *Arab News*, 6 July 2017, at http://www.arabnews.com/node/1125051/saudi-arabia. See also "Saudi Arabia: Tier 2 Watch List," in *Trafficking in Persons Report*, Washington, D.C.: United States Department of State, June 2018, pp. 369–372, at https://www.state.gov/documents/organization/282798.pdf.
46 Charlotte Lysa, "A Recent History of Refugees in Saudi Arabia," *Ref-Arab Project*, 12 November 2020, at http://refugeehistory.org/blog/2020/11/12/a-recent-history-of-refugees-in-saudi-arabia.

3 *Hijrah, Zakat*, and Refugees: Religious Obligations

1 For interesting data on the twentieth-century wars, see Niall Ferguson, *The War of the World: Twentieth-Century Conflict and the Descent of the West*, New York: Penguin Press, 2006. For details on global refugees, see Peter Byers, *Rethinking Refugees: Beyond State of Emergency*, Abingdon, Oxon.: Routledge, 2013.
2 Irial Glynn, "The Genesis and Development of Article 1 of the 1951 Refugee Convention," *Journal of Refugee Studies* 25:1, March 2012, pp. 134–148.
3 Malin Delling, *Islam and Human Rights*, Goteborg University, Sweden, Department of Law, School of Economics and Commercial Law, 2004, at https://core.ac.uk/download/pdf/16310495.pdf. See also, Abdul Azeez Maruf Olayemi, Abdul Majeed Hamzah Alabi, Ahmad Hidayah Buang, "Islamic Human Rights Law: A Critical Evaluation of UIDHR & CDHRI in Context of UDHR," *Journal of Islam, Law and Judiciary* 1:3, 2015, pp. 27–36; and Khaled Abou El Fadl, "Islamic Ethics, Human Rights and Migration," in Ray Jureidini and Said Fares Hassan, eds., *Migration and Islamic Ethics: Issues of Residence, Naturalisation and Citizenship*, Leiden and London: Brill, 2020, pp. 13-27.
4 Mashood A. Baderin, *International Human Rights and Islamic Law*, Oxford: Oxford University Press, 2005, p. 29.
5 The concepts of *hijrah*, which translates as migration or forced migration

Notes to Chapter 3

and *muhajirun* (migrant/refugees) will be mentioned frequently in this study.
6. The same concept of equality derives from the idea that each human being is equal in front of God.
7. Khadija Elmadmad, "Asylum in Islam and in Modern Refugee Law," *Refugee Survey Quarterly* 27:2, January 2008, pp. 51–63.
8. Seyla Benhabib, "The End of the 1951 Refugee Convention? Dilemmas of Sovereignty, Territoriality, and Human Rights," *Jus Cogens*, 2, July 2020, pp. 75–100.
9. Elmadmad, *op. cit.*, p. 53.
10. Benhabib., *op. cit.*, p. 85.
11. James C. Hathaway and Michelle Foster, *The Law of Refugee Status*, Cambridge: Cambridge University Press, 2014, p. 200.
12. Benhabib., *op. cit.*, p. 85.
13. *Handbook on Procedures and Criteria for Determining Refugee Status under the 1951 Convention and the 1967 Protocol Relating to the Status of Refugees*, HCR/IP/4/Eng/REV.1, Geneva: United Nations High Commissioner for Refugees, 1992, p. 7.
14. The Law Library of Congress, Global Legal Research Center, *Legal Status of Refugees: Egypt, Jordan, Lebanon, and Iraq*, December 2013, at https://www.loc.gov/law/help/refugees/2014-010156%20RPT.pdf.
15. Kirsten Zaat, "The Protection of Forced Migrants in Islamic Law," Research Paper Number 146, Geneva: United Nations High Commissioner for Refugees, December 2007, at https://www.unhcr.org/research/working/476652cb2/protection-forced-migrants-islamic-law-kirsten-zaat.html.
16. Qur'an 7:137.
17. Qur'an 4:97, Qur'an 7:127.
18. Qur'an 22:39, Qur'an 2:246, Qur'an 17:76, Qur'an 60:90.
19. Qur'an 3:195.
20. Qur'an 85:10.
21. Qur'an 8:73.
22. For background on these issues, see Ernest Alfred Wallis Budge, *A History of Ethiopia: Volume I—Nubia and Abyssinia*, New York: Routledge Revivals, 2014 [Originally published in 1928]; Muhammad El Fasi and Ivan Hrbek, *Africa from the Seventh to the Eleventh Century*, Berkeley and Los Angeles: University of California Press, 1988; and William Montgomery Watt, *Muhammad: Prophet and Statesman*, New York: Oxford University Press, 1961.
23. Zaat, *op. cit.*, p. 19.
24. Qur'an 59:9.
25. Musab Hayatli, "Islam, International Law and the Protection of Refugees and IDPs," *Forced Migration Review*, June 2012, at https://www.fmreview.org/sites/fmr/files/FMRdownloads/en/FMRpdfs/Human-Rights/human-rights.pdf.

26 Elena Fiddian-Qasmiyeh, "Introduction: Faith-Based Humanitarianism in Contexts of Forced Displacement," *Journal of Refugee Studies* 24:3, September 2011, pp. 429–439.

27 *Ibid.*, p. 430.

28 There are various examples of humanitarian aid provided by faith organizations both in Islam and Christianity. A comparison between the two approaches could actually contribute positively to a constructive dialogue on the concept of human rights and their application on the ground through an inter-faith encounter.

29 For a sample of Western and Muslim perceptions of refugee conditions, see Leen d'Haenens, Willem Joris, François Heinderyckx, eds., *Images of Immigrants and Refugees in Western Europe: Media Representations, Public Opinion and Refugees' Experiences*, Leuven, Belgium: Leuven University Press, 2019. See also, B. S. Chimni, "The Geopolitics of Refugee Studies: A View from the South," *Journal of Refugee Studies* 11:4, 1998, pp. 350–374; Serena Parekh, "Reframing the Refugee Crisis: From Rescue to Interconnection," *Ethics and Global Politics* 13, 2020, pp. 21–32; Tobias Müller, "Constructing Cultural Borders: Depictions of Muslim Refugees in British and German Media," *Zeitschrift für Vergleichende Politikwissenschaft* [Comparative Governance and Politics] 12, March 2018, pp. 263–277; and Madeline-Sophie Abbas, "Conflating the Muslim Refugee and the Terror Suspect: Responses to the Syrian Refugee 'Crisis' in Brexit Britain," *Ethnic and Racial Studies* 42:14, 2019, pp. 2450–2469.

30 While Syria is discussed in detail in Chapter 8, the following background material on Iraq provide reliable information on refugee conditions in Mesopotamia. Human Rights Watch Briefing Paper, "Iraqi Refugees, Asylum Seekers, and Displaced Persons: Current Conditions and Concerns in the Event of War," New York: Human Rights Watch, February 2003, at https://www.hrw.org/legacy/backgrounder/mena/iraq021203/iraq-bck021203.pdf. See also "Kurdistan Region of Iraq: Refugees' Movements Restricted—2 Miscarriages From Lack of Hospital Access," New York: Human Rights Watch, 27 November 2019, at https://www.hrw.org/news/2019/11/27/kurdistan-region-iraq-refugees-movements-restricted; Erlend Paasche, "Elites and Emulators: The Evolution of Iraqi Kurdish Asylum Migration to Europe," *Migration Studies* 8:2, 2020, pp. 189–208, at https://watermark.silverchair.com/mny036.pdf; and Michiel Leezenberg, "Iraqi Kurdistan: A Porous Political Space," *Anatoli* 8, 2017, pp. 107–131.

31 *The Kurdistan Region of Iraq: Assessing the Economic and Social Impact of the Syrian conflict and ISIS*, The World Bank Group, 2015.

32 Interview with Nawzad Pols Hakim, Soraya Organization, Erbil, 20 December 2017.

33 *Baghdad's Flight Embargo on KRI's Airports has Direly Affected Millions of People Across Kurdistan Region and Iraq*, Joint Crises Coordination Center, KRG, at http://jcc.gov.krd/en/article/read/146.

34 The refugee and IDP numbers are obtained from the KRG Ministry of Planning; and from the KRG and United Nations' *Immediate Response Plan Phase II (IRP2) for Internally Displaced People in the Kurdistan Region of Iraq.*

35 Hewa Haji Khedir, "IDPs in the Kurdistan Region of Iraq (KRI): Intractable Return and Absence of Social Integration Policy," *International Migration*, 2020, pp. 1–17, at https://onlinelibrary.wiley.com/doi/epdf/10.1111/imig.12716.

36 See *The Kurdistan Region of Iraq: Assessing the Economic and Social Impact of the Syrian Conflict and ISIS*, Washington, D.C.: World Bank, 2015, at http://documents.worldbank.org/curated/en/574421468253845198/pdf/940320REVISED0000Box391428BIQ0FINAL.pdf.

37 Interviews with business representatives in the KRG held in Erbil in December 2017.

38 Larry Minear, and Thomas Weiss, "Do International Ethics Matter? Humanitarian Politics in the Sudan," in Larry Minear, *Humanitarianism Under Siege: A Critical Review of Operation Lifeline Sudan*, Trenton, New Jersey: Red Sea Press, 1991.

39 Paragraph 11 of the United Nations General Assembly Resolution 194 (III) of 11 December 1949 clearly called for the right of return or compensation for Palestinian refugees. The failure of the implementation of this Paragraph did not help the case for the signing of the Convention by several Muslim countries.

40 "Convention Relating to the Status of Refugees, Geneva, 28 July 1951", United Nations, *Treaty Series* 189:2, p. 7, at https://www.unhcr.org/5d9ed32b4.

41 *Ibid.*, pp. 8–9.

42 *Ibid.*, p. 12.

43 See, for example, Joseph G. Jabbra and Nancy W. Jabbra, "Consociational Democracy in Lebanon: A Flawed System of Governance," *Journal of Developing Societies* 17:2, January 2001, pp. 71–89. See also Imad Salamey, "Failing Consociationalism in Lebanon and Integrative Options," *International Journal of Peace Studies* 14:2, Autum/Winter 2009, pp. 83–105, at https://www.jstor.org/stable/41852994.

44 Maja Janmyr, "No Country of Asylum: 'Legitimizing' Lebanon's Rejection of the 1951 Refugee Convention," *International Journal of Refugee Law* 29:3, 2017, pp. 438–465.

45 Amal Qutub, Nazir Khan, and Mahdi Qasqas, "Islam and Social Justice," in Norma Jean Profitt and Cyndy Baskin, eds., *Spirituality and Social Justice: Spirit in the Political Quest for a Just World*, Toronto: Canadian Scholars' Press, 2019, pp. 131–152.

46 This is a loaded subject and the intention is not to add fuel to the fire. Rather, it is to point out that the time was long overdue to reassess prejudices that prevented people of goodwill in the West to work in unison with their Muslim counterparts to address core concerns that refugees required. For a discussion of expert derisions, see, for example, Joyce Dalsheim, "On

Demonized Muslims and Vilified Jews: Between Theory and Politics," *Comparative Studies in Society and History* 52:3, July 2010, pp. 581–603; and Dustin J. Byrd, *Islam in a Post-Secular Society: Religion, Secularity and the Antagonism of Recalcitrant Faith*, Leiden and Boston: Brill, 2016, especially pp. 202–281 and 282–314.

47 United Nations Treaty Collection, *Chapter V Refugees and Stateless Persons*, at https://treaties.un.org/doc/Publication/MTDSG/Volume%20I/Chapter%20V/V-2.en.pdf.

48 'Abdul 'Aziz bin 'Abdul Rahman became king of the Hijaz and Sultan of Najd and its Dependencies in 1926, before he assumed the title of King of Sa'udi Arabia in 1932.

49 Nuri al-Sa'id (December 1888–15 July 1958) was an Iraqi politician who held various cabinet positions and served fourteen terms as Prime Minister of Iraq too. In 1930, he signed the Anglo-Iraqi Treaty, which granted London unlimited rights to station military units in Iraq along with very generous transit terms. Equally important, the treaty granted Britain control of the country's oil industry that, in time, drew the ire of Iraqi nationalists. Britain's mandate ended in 1932, though the anglophile Nuri al-Sa'id (who stood by London against the wishes of the overwhelming majority of Iraqis), was caught by surprise by the popular anti-colonial mood. A day after the Iraqi monarchy was toppled on 14 July 1958, Nuri al-Sa'id attempted to flee the country disguised as a woman but was captured and killed. See Charles Tripp, *A History of Iraq*, 3rd ed., Cambridge: Cambridge University Press, 2007, pp. 122–142.

50 Tripp, *ibid.*, pp. 96–103.

51 'Uthman Kamal Haddad, *Harakat Rashid 'Ali al-Kaylani Sanat 1941* [The Movement of Rashid 'Ali al-Kaylani in 1941], Sidon, Lebanon: Al-Maktabah al-'Asriyyah, ca. 1947–50, pp. 129, 132–33 [this section draws materials from Joshua Yaphe, Saudi–Iraqi Relations, 1921–1958, Doctoral Dissertation, Washington, D.C.: American University, 2021, pp. 219–222]. See also Farouk Al-Umar, *Rashid al-kilani's Refuge to King Abdul-Aziz Between Arabic Tradition and Diplomacy: World Conference Researches on King Abdulaziz History*, Riyadh: King Faisal Center for Research and Islamic Studies, 1985.

52 Ahmad Fawzi, *Twelve Prime Ministers*, Baghdad, n.p, 1984, p. 134, in Farouk Al-Umar, *op. cit.*, p. 5.

53 Quoted in Yaphe, *op. cit.*, p. 221.

54 As reported by Salih Muhammad al-Jasir, "Mithl Zubnat Rashid" [Like Rashid's Patron], *Al-Iqtisadiyyah*, 25 January 2011, at http://www.aleqt.com/2011/01/25/article_495851.html.

55 The British and Iraqi Governments lodged several complaints, but 'Abdul 'Aziz very generously built al-Kilani a comfortable house and provided stipends to his children. Shortly after the ruler passed away in 1953, al-Kilani was asked to leave the Kingdom, and he moved to Egypt. After the 1958 revolution in Iraq, he believed that it was safe for him to return home, only

to be arrested on his arrival. He received a three-year imprisonment sentence, allegedly for fomenting an elaborate plot, to overthrow the government. See Uriel Dann, *Iraq under Qassem: A Political History, 1958–1963*, New York: Praeger, 1969, pp. 128–35.

56 Mit'ab bin Salih al-Farzan, "Min Shawahid al-Tamyiz Lada al-Malik 'Abdul 'Aziz!!" [Evidence of Excellence in King 'Abdul 'Aziz !!," *Al-Jazirah Daily* [Riyadh], 8 May 2011, at
http://www.al-jazirah.com/2011/20110508/wo1.htm.

57 Ahmad Ibrahim Shukri, *Education Manpower Needs and Socio-Economic Development in Saudi Arabia*, Doctoral Dissertation, University of London, United Kingdom, 1972, pp. 43–70.

58 For additional details on Faysal's education policies, see Joseph A. Kéchichian, *'Iffat Al Thunayan: An Arabian Queen*, Brighton, Chicago, Toronto: Sussex Academic Press, 2015, pp. 108–160.

59 Mohamed Mokhtar Qandil, *The Muslim Brotherhood and Saudi Arabia: From Then to Now*, Washington, D.C.: The Washington Institute for Near East Policy, 18 May 2018, at https://www.washingtoninstitute.org/policy-analysis/muslim-brotherhood-and-saudi-arabia-then-now. See also Andrew Lipp, *The Muslim Brotherhood: Exploring divergent views in Saudi Arabia and Qatar*, Masters Thesis, Ames, Iowa: Iowa State University, 2019, at https://lib.dr.iastate.edu/cgi/viewcontent.cgi?article=8048&context=etd.

60 For a glimpse on the atrocities and the plight of the refugees, see *'Bangladesh Is Not My Country:' The Plight of Rohingya Refugees*, New York: Human Rights Watch, 5 August 2018, at
https://www.hrw.org/sites/default/files/report_pdf/bangladesh0818_web2.pdf.

61 King Salman Humanitarian and Relief Center, "Saudi Arabia Support to Rohingya Muslims," Rome, Italy: The Royal Embassy of Saudi Arabia in Rome, 2018, at
http://www.arabia-saudita.it/files/news/2018/07/rohingya_brochure_rev.pdf. See also "Myanmar Rohingya: What You Need to Know About the Crisis," *BBC News*, 23 January 2020, *at* https://www.bbc.com/news/world-asia-41566561.

62 Lily Myat, "The Rohingya Refugee Crisis: Social, Economic and Environmental Implications for the Local Community in Bangladesh," Masters Thesis, College of Humanities, Arts and Social Sciences, Adelaide, Australia: Flinders University, 2018, p. 38, at
https://flex.flinders.edu.au/file/20455f70-482e-480d-843e-288609037d12/1/thesis%20myat%202018.pdf.

63 Nasir Almaghamsi, "Al Barmawiyyah: Ma Hiya Hikayatuhum wa Tafasil Hayatahum? wa Min Ja'u? wa Ma Hakikat Ma Ta'aradu Lahu fi Biladihim" [The Burmese: What is their Story and the Details of their Lives . . . Where did they Come From? And What is the Truth about what they Experienced in their Country?], *Mazmaz*, 12 May 2015, at https://mz-mz.net/478555/.

64 *Ibid.*

65 C.J. Werleman, "We Would Rather Die Now than be Kept in Here Forever: Life Inside a Saudi Detention Centre for Rohingya Refugees," *ByLine Times*, 9 July 2019, at https://bylinetimes.com/2019/07/09/we-would-rather-die-now-than-be-kept-in-here-forever-life-inside-a-saudi-detention-centre-for-rohingya-refugees/.

66 For further details, see Muhammad Ahmad al-Hassani, "Qadiyyat al-Burmawiyyun Tatafaqam Duna Hal" [The Case of the Bermese is Worsening without A Solution], *Okaz*, 6 August 2011, at https://www.okaz.com.sa/article/673034. See also 'Abdallah Bajubayr, "Wa Ma Adruq Ma al-Burmawiyyah" [I Do Not Know What is the Burmawiyyah (Rohingya)], *Al-Iqtisadiyyah*, 1 May 2009, at http://www.aleqt.com/2009/05/01/article_10547.html; and "Mufadiyyat al-Laji'in: Al-Tajribat al-Sa'udiyyah fi Tas-hih Awda' al-Burmawiyyun 'Ra'idat'," [The Office of the Refugees: The Sa'udi Experience in Correcting Conditions of the Burmese is a 'Pioneering' (Step)], *Okaz*, 31 March 2019, at https://www.okaz.com.sa/article/1716071.

67 Anagha Neelakantan, *New Attacks on Muslim Villagers in Myanmar's Rakhine State*, Brussels: International Crisis Group, 26 January 2014, at https://www.crisisgroup.org/asia/south-east-asia/myanmar/new-attacks-muslim-villagers-myanmar-s-rakhine-state. See also Kassandra Neranjan and Sakshi Shetty, "From Encounter to Exodus: The Rohingya Muslims of Myanmar," Research Paper, 2018, at https://www.researchgate.net/publication/326922106_From_Encounter_to_Exodus_History_of_the_Rohingya_Muslims; and Amy Doffegnies and Tamas Wells, "The Vernacularization of Human Rights Discourse in Myanmar: Rejection, Hybridization and Strategic Avoidance," *Journal of Contemporary Asia* 51:2, 2021, at https://www.tandfonline.com/doi/full/10.1080/00472336.2020.1865432?src=.

68 On 1 February 2021, a military coup d'état toppled Prime Minister Aung San Suu Kyi, with few clues as to which direction the new government projected to advance. See Alice Cuddy, "Myanmar coup: What is happening and why?," *BBC News*, 5 February 2021, at https://www.bbc.com/news/world-asia-55902070.

69 David Mathieson, *Perilous Plight: Burma's Rohingya Take to the Seas*, New York: Human Rights Watch 2009, p. 3, at https://www.hrw.org/report/2009/05/26/perilous-plight/burmas-rohingya-take-seas#. See also Peter Ford, "Why Deadly Race Riots Could Rattle Myanmar's Fledgling Reforms: Myanmar's president warned of a threat to stability and democratization as Buddhist and Muslim minorities clash over longstanding grievances," *The Christian Science Monitor*, 12 June 2012, at https://www.csmonitor.com/World/Asia-Pacific/2012/0612/Why-deadly-race-riots-could-rattle-Myanmar-s-fledgling-reforms; "Bangladesh: Halt Rohingya Relocations to Remote Island—Transfers Need Independent Assessment, Refugees' Informed Consent," New York: Human Rights Watch, 3 December 2020, at

https://www.hrw.org/news/2020/12/03/bangladesh-halt-rohingya-relocations-remote-island; and Zobaer Ahmed, "Rohingya: Why Bangladesh is in a Diplomatic Fix over Saudi Repatriation," *DW* [Deutsche Welle], 15 January 2021, at https://www.dw.com/en/rohingya-why-bangladesh-is-in-a-diplomatic-fix-over-saudi-repatriation/a-56240710.

70 Fahad Alsharif, *The Good, the Bad and the Ugly: Undocumented Labour in Saudi Arabia: The case of Jeddah*. Unpublished Doctoral Thesis, Exeter University, United Kingdom, 2015.

71 Yusuf Salih, *Al-Laji'un al-'Iraqiyyun fil-Sa'udiyyah* [Iraqi Refugees in Saudi Arabia], Riyadh: Maktabat al-'Arabi al-Hadith, 1993, pp. 14–15, 17–20, 32, 39–41, 43–46, 48–50, 55–60, 74–77, 80–81.

72 The statistics gathered here are from various UNHCR documents. For one of the more recent such reports, see General Assembly, "Report of the United Nations High Commissioner for Refugees—Covering the period 1 July 2019—30 June 2020," A/75/12, New York: United Nations, at https://www.unhcr.org/excom/bgares/5f69c6ca4/report-united-nations-high-commissioner-refugees-covering-period-1-july.html.

73 For additional details on the wars and refugees, see Ben Sanders and Merrill Smith, "The Iraqi Refugee Disaster," *World Policy Journal* 24:3, Fall 2007), pp. 23–28; and Kathleen Newland, *The Iraqi Refugee Crisis: The Need for Action*, Washington, D.C.: Migration Policy Institute, January 2008, at https://www.migrationpolicy.org/research/iraqi-refugee-crisis-need-action.

74 Sarah Kershaw, "A Nation at War: Iraqi Exiles; In Saudi Desert, '91 Iraqi Refugees Long to Return," *The New York Times*, 11 April 2003, at https://www.nytimes.com/2003/04/11/world/a-nation-at-war-iraqi-exiles-in-saudi-desert-91-iraqi-refugees-long-to-return.html.

75 As cited in "Saudi Arabia: Unwelcome 'Guests': The Plight of Iraqi Refugees," New York: Amnesty International, Index number: MDE 23/001/1994, 9 May 1994, at
https://www.amnesty.org/download/Documents/184000/mde 230011994en.pdf.

76 Peter Kessler, "Iraqis Prepare to Leave Remote Desert Camp," *UNHCR News*, 28 July 2003, at
https://www.unhcr.org/news/latest/2003/7/3f2560974/iraqis-prepare-leave-remote-desert-camp.html.

77 Angus McDowall and Amena Bakr, "Saudi Arabia Confirms Role in Strikes Against Islamic State in Syria," *Reuters*, 23 September 2014, at https://www.reuters.com/article/us-syria-crisis-saudi/saudi-arabia-confirms-role-in-strikes-against-islamic-state-in-syria-idUSKCN0HI1Y12 0140923.

78 Leonid Bershidsky, "Why Don't Gulf States Accept More Refugees?," *Bloomberg*, 4 September 2015, at https://www.bloomberg.com/opinion/articles/2015-09-04/why-don-t-gulf-states-accept-more-refugees-.

79 "Grand Mufti: Giving Syrians Zakat an Islamic duty," *Arab News*,

26 February 2014, available at http://www.arabnews.com/news/531556.
80 *Ibid.*
81 *Ibid.*

4 The Concept of *Zakat* and Foreign Aid From Development to Humanitarian Assistance

1 António Guterres, "Millions Uprooted: Saving Refugees and the Displaced," *Foreign Affairs* 5:87, September/October 2008, pp. 90–99 (the quotation is on page 99).
2 F. Kahan Bodur, *The Book of Alms: A Guide to Understanding Zakat and Wealth*, CreateSpace Independent Publishing Platform, 2020. See also Abdalhaqq Bewley and Amal Abdalhakim Douglas, *Zakat: Raising a Fallen Pillar*, Dammam, Saʻudi Arabia: Diwan Press, 2020; and Shaykh Muhammad Hisham Burhani, translated by Amjad Mahmood, *A Believer's Guide To Zakat: A Treatise on its Rulings and Etiquette in the Hanafi School*, Heritage Press, 2014.
3 Jonathan Benthall, *Islamic Charities and Islamic Humanism in Troubled Times*, Manchester, UK: Manchester University Press, 2016. See also Habibu Umar Gado, *Al-Zakat: L'aumône*, Bassin, Mauritius: Éditions Notre Savoir, 2020; Badr-Edin El Hmidi, *Waqf and Zakat Institutions: The Socioeconomic Dimensions of Financial Accountability in Islam: A Theoretical and Practical Study*, Riga, Latvia: Noor [Shams] Publishing, 2019.
4 Musa Furber, *UNHCR Zakat Collection And Distribution Report*, Abu Dhabi: Tabah Foundation, May 2017, p. 2, at https://unhcrzakatfatwa.com/wp-content/uploads/2017/06/TR-1-UNHCR-Zakat-Collection-And-Distribution-English.pdf.
5 "The Governor's Message," Riyadh: The General Authority of Zakat and Tax, at https://gazt.gov.sa/en/AboutUs/Pages/Message.aspx.
6 "Saudi Arabia: Amendment to the Income Tax & Zakat Regulations and Amnesty Extension," 8 October 2020, at https://www.pwc.com/m1/en/services/tax/me-tax-legal-news/2020/saudi-arabia-amendment-income-tax-zakat-regulations-amnesty-extension.html.
7 As reported in "Zakat and Tax Authority Highlights Manipulation of Financial Statements," *Arab News*, 4 January 2021, at https://www.arab-news.com/node/1787071/business-economy.
8 Hassen Altalhi, "Saudi Arabian Humanitarian Aid in Crises Management Periods," *Open Journal of Political Science* 7, 2017, pp. 380–393, at https://doi.org/10.4236/ojps.2017.73031.
9 *Ibid.*
10 In addition to Altahi, the United Nations UN Office for the Coordination of Humanitarian Affairs (OCHA), Financial Tracking Services, as discussed below, provide useful updates on its web-page at https://fts.unocha.org/donors/.
11 Altahi, *op. cit.*, pp. 387–388.

12 Statista, "Largest Donors of Humanitarian Aid Worldwide in 2020 (in million U.S. dollars), by country," January 2021, at https://www.statista.com/statistics/275597/largers-donor-countries-of-aid-worldwide/.
13 Iain Watson, "Asian ODA, Assessing Emerging Donors in the Asian Region," in *Foreign Aid and Emerging Powers: Asian Perspectives on Official Development Assistance*, Abingdon and New York: Routledge, 2014, pp. 152–185.
14 Altahi, *op. cit.*, p. 391.
15 Sisira Jayasuriya and Peter McCawley, *The Asian Tsunami: Aid and Reconstruction after a Disaster*, Cheltenham, UK: Edward Edgar Publishing, 2010.
16 Krithika Varagur, "Conservative Aceh Shows Limits of Saudi Investment in Indonesia," *Voice of America*, 13 September 2017, at https://www.voanews.com/east-asia-pacific/conservative-aceh-shows-limits-saudi-investment-indonesia. See also John Telford and John Cosgrave, "The International Humanitarian System and the 2004 Indian Ocean Earthquake and Tsunamis," *Disasters* 31:1, 2007, pp. 1–28.
17 Antonio Donini, "Western Aid Agencies don't have a Humanitarian Monopoly," *Humanitarian Affairs Review*, Autumn 2004, pp.12–15, at http://www.humanitarian-review.org/upload/pdf/DoniniEnglishFinal.pdf.
18 Stephanie Strom, "Qatar Grants Millions in Aid to New Orleans," *The New York Times*, 2 May 2006, at https://www.nytimes.com/2006/05/02/us/02charity.html.
19 United Nations Office for the Coordination of Humanitarian Affairs, "Saudi Arabia Joins Top Donors To The Haiti Appeal," *News and Press Release*, 28 January 2010, at https://reliefweb.int/report/haiti/saudi-arabia-joins-top-donors-haiti-appeal.
20 The full definition of ODA is: "Flows of official financing administered with the promotion of the economic development and welfare of developing countries as the main objective, and which are concessional in character with a grant element of at least 25 percent (using a fixed 10 percent rate of discount). By convention, ODA flows comprise contributions of donor government agencies, at all levels, to developing countries ("bilateral ODA") and to multilateral institutions. ODA receipts comprise disbursements by bilateral donors and multilateral institutions." See, International Monetary Fund, *External Debt Statistics: Guide for Compilers and Users—Appendix III, Glossary*, Washington, D.C.: IMF, 28 August 2003, at https://stats.oecd.org/glossary/detail.asp?ID=6043.
21 "Aid by DAC Members Increases in 2019 with More Aid to the Poorest Countries," Paris: Organization for Economic Co-operation and Development, 16 April 2020, at https://www.oecd.org/dac/financing-sustainable-development/development-finance-data/ODA-2019-detailed-summary.pdf.
22 *Ibid.* For the latest data, see "Official Development Assistance (ODA)," at

http://www.oecd.org/dac/financing-sustainable-development/development-finance-standards/official-development-assistance.htm.

23. Issam M. Saliba, "Regulation of Foreign Aid: Saudi Arabia," Washington. D.C.: The Library of Congress, October 2011, at https://www.loc.gov/law/help/foreign-aid/saudiarabia.php.

24. The People's Republic of China, "The Humanitarian Aid Industry in Saudi Arabia Has Developed Rapidly," Beijing: Ministry of Commerce, 2 December 2016, available at: http://www.mofcom.gov.cn/article/i/jyjl/k/201612/201612021 58397.shtml, as cited in Yi Li, "Saudi Arabia's Economic Diplomacy through Foreign Aid: Dynamics, Objectives and Mode," *Asian Journal of Middle Eastern and Islamic Studies* 13:1, March 2019, pp. 110–122.

25. "Sa'udi Arabia," United Nations Office for the Coordination of Humanitarian Affairs, at https://www.unocha.org/middle-east-and-north-africa-romena/saudi-arabia.

26. *Agence France-Presse*, "Saudi Arabia Close to Deal to Buy $1.15bn Worth of Military Equipment from US," *The Guardian*, 10 August 2016, at https://www.theguardian.com/world/2016/aug/10/saudi-arabia-close-to-deal-to-buy-115bn-worth-of-military-equipment-from-us.

27. Sherine El Taraboulsi-McCarthy, *A Kingdom of Humanity? Saudi Arabia's Values, Systems and Interests in Humanitarian Action*, Humanitarian Policy Group Working Paper, London: Overseas Development Institute, September 2017, pp. 13–14.

28. UN-OCHA, "Saudi Arabia Donates an Additional USD $500 Million to Yemen Humanitarian Response Plan," *News and Press Release*, 26 February 2019, at https://reliefweb.int/report/yemen/saudi-arabia-donates-additional-usd-500-million-yemen-humanitarian-response. See also Hannah Cooper, et al., *Funding The Humanitarian Response In Yemen: Are Donors Doing Their Fair Share?*, London: Oxfam, October 2020, at https://reliefweb.int/sites/reliefweb.int/files/resources/bn-funding-humanitarian-response-yemen-271020-en.pdf.

29. Statista, "Largest Donors of Humanitarian Aid Worldwide in 2020 (in million U.S. dollars), by country," January 2021, at https://www.statista.com/statistics/275597/largers-donor-countries-of-aid-worldwide/.

30. UN-OCHA Services, "Five Saudi Relief Planes Reach Iran," *News and Press Release*, 27 December 2003, at https://reliefweb.int/report/iran-islamic-republic/five-saudi-relief-planes-reach-iran. See also Saleh Dabbakeh, "Iran: Saudi Airlift Vital Part of Bam Response," Geneva: *International Federation of Red Cross And Red Crescent Societies*, 23 January 2004, at https://reliefweb.int/report/iran-islamic-republic/iran-saudi-airlift-vital-part-bam-response.

31. "Saudi Official: We received 2.5 mln Syrians," *Al Arabiya News*, 12 September 2015, at https://english.alarabiya.net/News/middle-east/2015/09/12/Saudi-official-we-received-2-5-mln-Syrians-since-conflict.

32. Pierre van den Boogaerde, "The Composition and Distribution of Financial Assistance from Arab Countries and Arab Regional Institutions", *IMF Working Paper WP/90/67*, July 1990, at https://www.bookstore.imf.org/books/title/The-Composition-and-Distribution-of-Financial-Assistance-From-Arab-Countries-and-Arab-Regional-Institutions. See also Soliman Demir, *Arab Development Funds in the Middle East*, New York: Pergamon Press (for UNITAR), 1979. Demir provides a first-class discussion of the Kuwait Fund for Arab Economic Development that was established in 1961 and that literally lifted the Lower Gulf Shaykhdoms out of poverty before 1973 (pp. 1–24); and introduces the reader to the Arab Fund for Economic and Social Development, created in 1968, and that was led by Kuwait, Sa'udi Arabia and Libya (pp. 40–54).
33. "Brief History," Vienna, Austria: Organization of the Petroleum Exporting Countries, at https://www.opec.org/opec_web/en/abot_us/24.htm.
34. David P. Forsythe, "UNRWA, the Palestine Refugees, and World Politics: 1949–1969," *International Organization* 25:1, Winter 1971, pp. 26–45. See also Riccardo Bocco, "UNRWA and the Palestinian Refugees: A History within History," *Refugee Survey Quarterly* 28:2–3, 2009, pp. 229–252; and Asaf Romirowsky, "Arab-Palestinian Refugees," *Israel Studies* 24:2, Summer 2019, pp. 91–102.
35. "Forty Years of Development Assistance from Arab Countries," Washington, D.C.: The World Bank, 2 September 2010, at https://www.worldbank.org/en/news/feature/2010/09/02/forty-years-development-assistance-arab-countries.
36. Ragaei El Mallakh and Mihssen Kadhim, "Arab Institutionalized Development Aid: An Evaluation," *The Middle East Journal* 30:4, Autumn 1976, pp. 471–484. See also, Espen Villanger, *Arab Foreign Aid: Disbursement Patterns, Aid Policies and Motives* (CMI Report R 2007:2), Bergen, Germany: Chr. Michelsen Institute, at https://www.cmi.no/publications/2615-arab-foreign-aid-disbursement-patterns; Masood Hyder, "Humanitarianism and the Muslim World," *The Journal of Humanitarian Assistance*, August 2007, at https://sites.tufts.edu/jha/archives/52;

and Maurits S. Berger, *Religion and Development Aid: The Special Case of Islam*, The Hague: Netherlands Institute of International Relations, October 2006, at https://www.clingendael.org/sites/default/files/pdfs/20061000_cdsp_pap_berger.pdf.
37. *Arab Development Assistance: Four Decades of Cooperation*, Washington, D.C.: World Bank, June 2010, pp. 8–9.
38. *Ibid.*, p. 9.
39. *Ibid.*, pp. 26–27. Each of these funds maintain rich web-pages that incorporate valuable resources. See, for example, the OPEC Fund for International Development site at https://opecfund.org/who-we-are/at-a-glance; the Kuwait Fund For Arab Economic Development site at https://www.kuwait-fund.org/en/web/kfund; the Sa'udi Fund for Development site at

https://www.sfd.gov.sa; the Arab Fund for Economic and Social Development site at http://www.arabfund.org. See also *Islamic Development Bank Investor Presentation*, January 2021, at https://www.isdb.org/sites/default/files/media/documents/2021-01/IsDB%20Investor%20Presentation%20%28Jan%202021%29.pdf.

40 Sa'udi Fund for Development, *Annual Report 2019*, pp. 46–52, at https://www.sfd.gov.sa/en/web/guest/publications/-/asset_publisher/EkiAOIa5aWyu/content/2019-annual-report.

41 *Arab Development Assistance: Four Decades Of Cooperation*, Washington, D.C.: The World Bank, June 2010, at http://documents1.worldbank.org/curated/en/725931468277750849/pdf/568430WP0Arab010Box353738B01PUBLIC1.pdf. See also, Kishan Khoday, *Development at the Crossroads: Reflections from the Arab Region*, New York: United Nations Development Program, 10 June 2014 at https://www.undp.org/content/undp/en/home/blog/2014/6/10/development-at-the-crossroads-reflections-from-the-arab-region-1.html. See also Kingdom of Sa'udi Arabia, Ministry of Economy and Planning, and United Nations Development Program, *Millennium Development Goals: 1429 H/2008 G*, at http://www.undp.org/content/dam/undp/library/MDG/english/MDG%2520Country%2520Reports/Saudi%2520Arabia/KSA_MDG_Report_3_2008_English.pdf.

42 For additional details on the King Salman Center for Humanitarian Relief and Works, see its dedicated web-page at https://www.ksrelief.org.

43 "Saudi Arabia Provided $6bn in Aid to Palestinians Since 2000," *Saudi Gazette*, 28 May 2018, at http://saudigazette.com.sa/article/535741/World/Mena/Saudi-Arabia-provided-$6bn-in-aid-to-Palestinians-since-2000.

44 *Ibid.*

45 Rashid Hassan, "UN Lauds Saudi Arabia's 'Model' Refugee Aid Programs Around World," *Arab News*, 17 May 2019, at http://www.arabnews.com/node/1498151/saudi-arabia.

46 United Nations Relief and Works Agency for Palestine Refugees in the Near East, "King Salman Humanitarian Aid And Relief Centre (KSRelief) and UNRWA Sign US$1 Million Contribution for Covid-19 Response in Gaza," 1 May 2020, at https://www.unrwa.org/newsroom/press-releases/king-salman-humanitarian-aid-and-relief-centre-ksrelief-and-unrwa-sign-us1.

47 "Saudi Arabia Among Largest Global Donors of Aid: UN Report," *Arab News*, 3 October 2018, at https://www.arabnews.com/node/1382166/saudi-arabia.

48 For annual statistics, see The King Salman Humanitarian Aid and Relief Centre (KSRelief) site pages at https://www.ksrelief.org/Statistics/YearDetails/2019 and https://www.ksrelief.org/Statistics/YearDetails/2020.

49 "KSA's Aid Agency KSRelief Workshop on Humanitarian Aid, Relief," *Arab News*, 20 October 2018, at http://www.arabnews.com/node/1390701/saudi-arabia. See also UN-OCHA, "The Saudi Aid Platform—Technology to Track Foreign Contributions," *News and Press Release*, 12 June 2020 https://reliefweb.int/report/yemen/saudi-aid-platform-technology-track-foreign-contributions.

50 "Saudi Arabia Among Largest Global Donors of Aid: UN Report," *Arab News*, 3 October 2018, at http://www.arabnews.com/node/1382166/saudi-arabia. See also Table 4.5.

51 "Saudi Worldwide Relief Aid Nears $2 Bln, Yemen Top Beneficiary," *Al-Sharq Al-Awsat*, 5 August 2018, at https://aawsat.com/english/home/article/1353626/saudi-worldwide-relief-aid-nears-2-bln-yemen-top-beneficiary.

52 "Vital Work of Saudi Aid Agency Highlighted at UN Gathering," *Arab News*, 3 May 2019, at https://www.arabnews.com/node/1491681/saudi-arabia.

53 Bernard Lewis, "Khadim al-Haramayn," in, P. Bearman, Th. Bianquis, C.E. Bosworth, E. van Donzel, W.P. Heinrichs (eds.), *Encyclopaedia of Islam, Second Edition*, Leiden, The Netherlands: E. J. Brill, at http://dx.doi.org/10.1163/15733912_islam_SIM_4118.

54 Tufail Ahmad Qureshi, "Justice In Islam," *Islamic Studies* 21:2, Summer 1982, pp. 35–51. See also Hossein Askari and Abbas Mirakhor, *Conceptions of Justice from Islam to the Present*, New York: Palgrave, 2020; Lawrence Rosen, *Islam and the Rule of Justice: Image and Reality in Muslim Law and Culture*, Chicago and London: The University of Chicago Press, 2018; and Andrew Fallo, "Restoration as the Spirit of Islamic Justice," *Contemporary Justice Review* 23:4, 2020, pp. 430–443.

5 Pilgrimage and Migration Dilemmas: African Migrants in Sa'udi Arabia

1 For an assessment of how the annual pilgrimage strained Sa'udi authorities to provide safe and secure services, see Kheir Al-Kodmany, "Planning for the Hajj: Political Power, Pragmatism, and Participatory GIS," *Journal of Urban Technology* 16:1, April 2009, pp. 5–45. See also, Shaikh Safiur Rahman Mubarakpuri, *History of Makkah*, Riyadh: Darussalam, 2002; Asrar Qureshi, *My Pilgrimage to Makkah: Day to Day Recount of Hajj 2019*, n.c.: n. p., 2020; and Ulrike Freitag, *The History of the Hajj as Heritage: Asset or Burden to the Saudi State?*, Leiden, The Netherlands: Brill, 2019.

2 Although this research was conducted several years ago, and while circumstances have changed somewhat, it was difficult to secure access to individuals currently living illegally in the country, and to evaluate their views about a slew of topics. The original research was a unique opportunity that, regrettably, could not be duplicated.

3 William Ochsenwald, *The Hijaz Railroad*, Charlottesville: The University Press of Virginia, 1980, pp. 117–118.
4 Select Committee on Economic Affairs, *The Economic Impact of Immigration, Volume 1, HL Paper 82-I*, London: United Kingdom House of Lords, 1 April 2008, pp. 10 and 21.
5 Alice Bloch, Nando Sigona and Roger Zetter, *'No Right to Dream': The Social and Economic Lives of Young Undocumented Migrants in Britain*, Oxford: University of Oxford Refugee Studies Center, 2014, at https://www.phf.org.uk/wp-content/uploads/2014/10/Young-Undocumented-Migrants-report.pdf. See also, Ben Gidley and Hiranthi Jayaweera, *An Evidence Base on Migration and Integration in London*, ESRC Centre On Migration, Policy And Society, University of Oxford, July 2010, at https://www.london.gov.uk/sites/default/files/an_evidence_base_on_migration_and_integration_in_london.pdf.
6 Elaine Kamarck and Christine Stenglein, "How Many Undocumented Immigrants Are in the United States and Who Are They?," The Brookings Institution, 12 November 2019, at https://www.brookings.edu/policy2020/votervital/how-many-undocumented-immigrants-are-in-the-united-states-and-who-are-they/. See also Jens Manuel Krogstad, Jeffrey S. Passel and D'Vera Cohn, "5 Facts About Illegal Immigration in the U.S.," Washington, D.C.: Pew Research Center, 12 June 2019, at https://www.pewresearch.org/fact-tank/2019/06/12/5-facts-about-illegal-immigration-in-the-u-s/.
7 Relying on earlier research by Heckmann et al., and according to Jandl, the use of a ratio of 1:2 border apprehensions to undocumented entry in the case of the European Union was a reliable mechanism to determine relatively accurate statistics on the numbers of undocumented workers. In Germany, for example, Jandl noted that the ratio of Iraqis who managed to enter the country with no documents was as high as 1:5. An examination of the Yemeni undocumented migrants crossing the Sa'udi borders clandestinely was higher than 1:5 too, which meant that for each individual apprehended by immigration authorities, five managed to enter the country illegally. This further indicated that the number of undocumented migrants who managed to cross the Sa'udi borders from Yemen was several times higher than the number of people arrested while attempting to cross the Sa'udi border without proper documents. See Friedrich Heckmann, Tanja Wunderlich, Susan F. Martin and Kelly McGrath, "Transatlantic Workshop on Human Smuggling," *Georgetown Immigration Law Journal* 15:167, 2000–2001, pp. 167–182. See also Michael Jandl, "The Estimation of Illegal Migration in Europe," *Studi Emigrazione/Migration Studies* 41:153, March 2004, pp. 141–155.
8 "Saudi Arabia Builds Giant Yemen Border Fence," *BBC News*, 9 April 2013, at https://www.bbc.com/news/world-middle-east-22086231. See also Adam Bannister, "Plan for Saudi–Iraq Border Fence Demonstrates Strong

Role for Physical Security in Middle East," *IFSEC Global*, 17 October 2014, at https://www.ifsecglobal.com/security/five-layered-border-fence-saudi-iraq-border-signals-strong-role-physical-security-middle-east/.

9 Naturally, children born from illegal immigrants must also be accounted for, which was why the number of illegal migrants began to rise dramatically. Sudan and Yemen, on the one hand, were countries of emigration, mainly to the Arabian Peninsula, as well as transit and immigration countries for African migrants. Sa'udi Arabia, on the other hand, stood as one of the largest labor importers in the world. Of course, Yemen and Sudan [and all other African countries noted above with the exception of Nigeria] were among the least developed countries, heavily relying on foreign aid, whereas Sa'udi Arabia was a middle-income country. See Hélène Thiollet, *Refugees and Migrants from Eritrea to the Arab World, the Case of Sudan, Yemen and Saudi Arabia 1997–2007*, Cairo, Egypt: American University in Cairo Press, 2007.

10 This section of the chapter, which was first published in 2018, offers a summary of this research effort. For full details, see Fahad L. Alghalib Alsharif, "City of Dreams, Disappointment, and Optimism: The Case of Nine Communities of Undocumented African Migrants in the City of Jeddah," *Dirasat*, Number 35, Riyadh: King Faisal Center for Research and Islamic Studies, April 2018 [Hereafter Alsharif, "City of Dreams, Disappointment, and Optimism"].

11 "The sample size required to study any particular hidden population can be defined according to the 'saturation point' of data collection: [...] saturation—that is, stopping data collection when the results start to become redundant is the key determinant of sample size. In practice, this may mean specifying a range between 5 and 30 participants." See R. Josselson, Dan P. McAdams, and A. Lieblich, eds., *Up Close and Personal: The Teaching and Learning of Narrative Research*, Washington, D.C.: American Psychological Association Press, 2003, p. 37.

12 For full details, including demographic characteristics, gender and marital breakdowns, as well as religious affiliation, see Alsharif, "City of Dreams, Disappointment, and Optimism," pp. 14–18.

13 Alsharif, "City of Dreams, Disappointment, and Optimism," pp. 20–21.

14 Robert Worth, "Saudi Border With Yemen Is Still Inviting for Al Qaeda," *The New York Times*, 26 October 2010, at https://www.nytimes.com/2010/10/27/world/middleeast/27saudi.html. See also "Saudi Border Guards in the South Foil Drug Smuggling Attempt," *Arab News*, 12 August 2018, at http://www.arabnews.com/node/1355306/saudi-arabia.

15 Alsharif, "City of Dreams, Disappointment, and Optimism," p. 22.
16 Alsharif, "City of Dreams, Disappointment, and Optimism," p. 23.
17 Alsharif, "City of Dreams, Disappointment, and Optimism," p. 23.
18 Alsharif, "City of Dreams, Disappointment, and Optimism," pp. 23–24.
19 Alsharif, "City of Dreams, Disappointment, and Optimism," p. 24.

20 "Saudi Begins Changes to kafala Sponsorship System," *MEMO—Middle East Monitor*, 15 March 2021, at https://www.middleeastmonitor.com/20210315-saudi-begins-changes-to-kafala-sponsorship-system/. See also, "Saudi Expats Can Now Switch Jobs Without Permission," *Khaleej Times*, 14 March 2021, at https://www.khaleejtimes.com/region/mena/saudi-expats-can-now-switch-jobs-without-employers-permission.

21 Angus McDowall and Asma Alsharif, "Saudi's Illegal Immigrants Draw Fear of 'infiltrators'," *Reuters*, 27 March 2013, at https://www.reuters.com/article/us-saudi-immigrants-slum-idUSBRE92Q0MA20130327.

22 Of course, Eritrea was also at war with Ethiopia at the time, which caused enormous displacements. See Richard Reid, *Shallow Graves: A Memoir of the Ethiopia–Eritrea War*, London: Hurst, 2020, pp. 127–156.

23 Marie-Laurence Flahaux and Hein De Haas, "African Migration: Trends, Patterns, Drivers," *Comparative Migration Studies* 4:1, 2016, at https://comparativemigrationstudies.springeropen.com/track/pdf/10.1186/s40878-015-0015-6.pdf.

24 Fahad Alsharif, "Calculated Risks, Agonies, and Hopes: A Comparative Case Study of the Undocumented Yemeni and Filipino Migrant Communities in Jeddah," in Philippe Fargues and Nasra Shah, editors, *Skillful Survivals: Irregular Migration to the Gulf*, Jeddah, Geneva, Cambridge: Gulf Research Center, 2017, pp. 161–183 [Hereafter Alsharif, "Calculated Risks, Agonies, and Hopes"].

25 *World Development Indicators Database*, Washington, D.C.: World Bank, 19 March 2021, at https://data.worldbank.org/indicator/NY.GNP.MKTP.CD, and https://data.worldbank.org/indicator/NY.GNP.PCAP.CD?locations=SA.

26 "Shoura to Tackle Problem of 5 Million Illegals in Kingdom," *Arab News*, 11 November 2012, at http://www.arabnews.com/Shura-Tackle-Problem-5-Million-Illegals-Kingdom.

27 Saudi Arabia Builds Giant Border Fence, *op. cit.*

28 Michael W. Kelly, "Saudi Arabia: Oil and Saudi Development," *Harvard International Review* 8:4, March 1986, pp. 38–40.

29 Alsharif, "City of Dreams, Disappointment, and Optimism," p. 40.

30 Alsharif, "City of Dreams, Disappointment, and Optimism," p. 42.

31 Sophia Kagan, *Domestic Workers and Employers in the Arab States: Promising Practices and Innovative Models for a Productive Working Relationship*, ILO White Paper, International Labour Organization, Regional Office for Arab State, 2017, at https://www.ilo.org/wcmsp5/groups/public/—-arabstates/—-ro-beirut/documents/publication/wcms_619661.pdf.

32 Alsharif, "Calculated Risks, Agonies, and Hopes," pp. 161–183.

33 Alsharif, "City of Dreams, Disappointment, and Optimism," p. 47.

34 Alsharif, "City of Dreams, Disappointment, and Optimism," pp. 47–48.

35 Rosie Bsheer, "Kafala Politics and Domestic Labor in Saudi Arabia,"

Jadaliya, 17 September 2010, at https://www.jadaliyya.com/Details/23509.
36 Alsharif, "City of Dreams, Disappointment, and Optimism," pp. 47–48.
37 Republic of the Philippines, "A Guide to Saudi Labor and Immigration Rules," 15 April 2013, at https://dfa.gov.ph/dfa-news/statements-and-advisoriesupdate/164-a-guide-to-saudi-labor-and-immigration-rules.
38 Alsharif, "City of Dreams, Disappointment, and Optimism," p. 49.
39 Alsharif, "City of Dreams, Disappointment, and Optimism," p. 50.
40 See Alsharif, "Calculated Risks, Agonies, and Hopes," pp. 135–136.
41 Mohammed Al-Kinani and Jumana Khamis, "Saudi Arabia's Madinah Sets the Bar High for Welfare of Migrant Workers," *Arab News*, 1 August 2020, at https://www.arabnews.com/node/1665946/saudi-arabia.
42 Gaim Kibreab, Revisiting the Debate on People, Place, Identity and Displacement," *Journal of Refugee Studies* 12:4, 1999, pp. 384–410.
43 Reena Sehgal, "Nitaqat Law: Will it Solve Saudi Arabia's Unemployment Problems?," Delhi: Observer Research Foundation, 8 July 2013, at https://www.orfonline.org/research/nitaqat-law-will-it-solve-saudi-arabias-unemployment-problems/. See also Jennifer R. Peck, "Can Hiring Quotas Work? The Effect of the Nitaqat Program on the Saudi Private Sector," *American Economic Journal: Economic Policy* 9:2, May 2017, pp. 316–347.
44 "Saudi Sets $800 as Minimum Wage," *Trade Arabia: Business News Information*, 30 May 2011, at
http://www.tradearabia.com/news/MISC_199507.html.
45 "Saudi Jobs for Saudis is Crown Prince's Generational Challenge," *The Straits Times* [Singapore], 18 March 2021, at
https://www.straitstimes.com/world/middle-east/saudi-jobs-for-saudis-is-crown-princes-generational-challenge.
46 Françoise De Bel-Air, "Demography, Migration and Labour Market in Saudi Arabia," *Gulf Labour Markets and Migration GLMM*, Number 1, 2014, at
https://cadmus.eui.eu/bitstream/handle/1814/32151/GLMM%20 ExpNote_01-2014.pdf.
47 Adel Faqih, "Saudi Bolsters Campaign Against Illegal Expat Workers with Jail Terms," *The National*, 18 April 2013, at
https://www.thenational.ae/world/mena/saudi-bolsters-campaign-against-illegal-expat-workers-with-jail-terms-1.347130. See also, "Employers Hiring Illegal Workers Facing Prison, Ban in Saudi Arabia," *Arab News*, 6 February 2019, at https://www.arabnews.com/node/1447766/saudi-arabia.
48 Alsharif, "City of Dreams, Disappointment, and Optimism," pp. 50–51.
49 "Content" is actually the translation from Arabic of a word that indicates the lower level of satisfaction. It means that they are aware that this is the best deal they can get.
50 Katrin Marchand, Julia Reinold and Raphael Dias e Silva, *Study on Migration Routes in the East and Horn of Africa*, Maastricht Graduate School of Governance, August 2017, detailed at
https://migration.unu.edu/author/raphael-dias-e-silva

6 The Kingdom and Yemen: How Neighbors Became Refugees

1. The unified Republic of Yemen is the second-largest Arab state on the Arabian Peninsula after the Kingdom of Sa'udi Arabia, with a 2,000 kilometre (1,200 miles) coastline. Sana'a, the capital, was also the capital city of the Yemen Arab Republic (1962–1990) or North Yemen, while Aden was that of the People's Democratic Republic of Yemen (1967–1990), also known as South Yemen. For nearly a millennia, the Imams of Yemen and later the Kings of Yemen were religiously consecrated leaders belonging to the Zaydi branch of Shi'ah Islam, which differed from Twelver Shi'ah dogma by stressing the presence of an active and visible imam as leader. For Zaydis, the imam was expected to be knowledgeable in religious scholarship, and to prove himself as a worthy trailblazer, even in battle if necessary. Over time, but especially after 897, religious and political rule gained momentum as the "imamate" endured under varying circumstances until the 1962 revolution. Yemen was divided between the Ottoman and British empires in the 1800s, though a Zaydi Mutawakkilite Kingdom of Yemen was established after World War I, several decades before the creation of the republic in 1962.

   South Yemen remained a British protectorate until 1967 when it became an independent state and later a Marxist entity closely affiliated with the Soviet Union and the People's Republic of China. The two Yemeni states united in 1990 under 'Ali 'Abdallah Salih though the current war threatens it once again. For an introduction to these developments, see Paul Dresch, *A History of Modern Yemen*, Cambridge: Cambridge University Press, 2001.

2. F. Gregory Gause III, *Saudi–Yemeni Relations: Domestic Structures and Foreign Influence*, New York: Columbia University Press, 1990, pp. 2–5.

3. Resolution 2216 passed under the UN Charter's Chapter VII—expanded the sanctions regime through the creation of a targeted arms embargo against Huthi rebels and authorized states to "take the necessary measures to prevent the direct or indirect supply, sale or transfer to, or for the benefit of Ali Abdullah Saleh, Abdullah Yahya Al Hakim, Abd Al-Khaliq Al-Huthi, and the individuals and entities designated by the Committee established pursuant to paragraph 19 of resolution 2140 (2014)." See United Nations Security Council, Resolution 2216 (2015), 14 April 2015, at https://documents-dds-ny.un.org/doc/UNDOC/GEN/N15/103/72/PDF/N1510372.pdf.

4. Ibrahim Jalal, "Five years on, has the Arab coalition achieved its objectives in Yemen?," The Middle East Institute, 2 April 2020, at https://www.mei.edu/publications/five-years-has-arab-coalition-achieved-its-objectives-yemen. U.S. President Joe Biden terminated the American participation in the coalition's military activities in early February 2021, although most of the air activities—chiefly refueling fighters and bombers and the sharing of intelligence for precision aerial bombings of military targets with some degree of accuracy—were suspended several years ago.

See Ben Hubbard and Shuaib Almosawa, "Biden Ends Military Aid for Saudi War in Yemen. Ending the War Is Harder," *The New York Times*, 5 February 2021 [Updated on 10 February 2021], at https://www.nytimes.com/2021/02/05/world/middleeast/yemen-saudi-biden.html.

5. According to the UN Office for the Coordination of Humanitarian Affairs (OCHA), an estimated 233,000 deaths occurred in Yemen, including 131,000 from indirect causes such as lack of food, health services and infrastructure, by the end of 2020. See "UN Humanitarian Office Puts Yemen War Dead at 233,000, Mostly from 'Indirect Causes'," 1 December 2020, at https://news.un.org/en/story/2020/12/1078972.

6. It is not the purpose of this brief section to describe and assess the long and rich history between the two neighboring states but to highlight key developments that were followed by generous Sa'udi disbursements of sorely needed—and much welcomed—financial assistance. For background on ties, see Paul Dresch, *A History of Modern Yemen*, Cambridge: Cambridge University Press, 2000; and Robin Bidwell, *The Two Yemens*, Harlow, Essex, UK and Boulder, Colorado: Longman and Westview Press, 1983.

7. Gause, *Saudi–Yemeni Relations*, op. cit., pp. 57–59.

8. Dresch, *History of Modern Yemen*, op. cit., pp. 34–35.

9. Joseph Kostiner, *The Making of Saudi Arabia 1916–1936: From Chieftaincy to Monarchical State*, New York & Oxford: Oxford University Press, 1993, especially pp. 141–184.

10. Asher Orkaby, "Saudi Arabia's War with the Houthis: Old Borders, New Lines," *PolicyWatch 2404*, Washington, D.C.: The Washington Institute for Near East Policy, 9 April 2015, at https://www.washingtoninstitute.org/policy-analysis/view/saudi-arabias-war-with-the-houthis-old-borders-new-lines.

11. Gause, *Saudi–Yemeni Relations*, op. cit., pp. 58–59.

12. "Saudi Aid to Yemen Worth $11bn, Forum Told," *Arab News*, 2 May 2018, at http://www.arabnews.com/node/1295086/saudi-arabia. According to an Oxfam report, Sa'udi Arabia contributed US$ 297 million to the Yemen in 2020, which amounted to 666% of the 'fair share' contribution. See, OXFAM, Funding the Humanitarian Response in Yemen: Are Donors Doing Their Fair Share?, *Briefing Note*, October 2020, p. 7, at https://www.oxfam.org/en/research/funding-humanitarian-response-yemen.

13. The most prominent Yemeni who made it in the Kingdom was Muhammad bin Ladin who founded the Bin Ladin Conglomerate though other leading families benefitted from Sa'udi largesse. See Jason Burke, "Rags to Riches Story of the bin Laden Family is Woven with Tragedy, *The Guardian*, 1 August 2015, at https://www.theguardian.com/world/2015/aug/01/rags-to-riches-story-of-the-bin-laden-family-is-woven-with-tragedy. For the exceptional attention devoted to this issue, see Gwenn Okhrulik and Patrick Conge, "National

Autonomy, Labor Migration and Political Crisis: Yemen and Saudi Arabia," *The Middle East Journal* 51:4, Autumn 1997, pp. 554–565.

14 Bidwell, The Two Yemens, *op. cit.*, pp. 195–218. See also Dresch, *History of Modern Yemen, op. cit.*, pp. 89–99.

15 The Yemeni president was gunned down on 4 December 2017 by Huthi rebels. See "Ali Abdullah Saleh, Yemen's Former Leader, Killed in Sanaa," *BBC News*, 4 December 2017, at https://www.bbc.com/news/world-middle-east-42225574.

16 Peter Salisbury, *Yemen and the Saudi–Iranian 'Cold War'*, London: The Royal Institute of International Affairs [Chatham House], February 2015, p. 5, at https://www.chathamhouse.org/sites/default/files/field/field_document/20150218YemenIranSaudi.pdf.

17 "Yemen ex-Leader Saleh 'Amassed Up to $60bn'—UN Probe," *BBC News*, 25 February 2015, at https://www.bbc.com/news/world-middle-east-31632502.

18 Jamal S. al-Suwaidi, ed., *The Yemeni War of 1994: Causes and Consequences*, London: Saqi Books [for the Abu Dhabi-based Emirates Center for Strategic Studies and Research], 1995.

19 Michael Horton, "The Unseen Hand: Saudi Arabian Involvement in Yemen," *Terrorism Monitor* 9:12, 24 March 2011, at https://jamestown.org/program/the-unseen-hand-saudi-arabian-involvement-in-yemen/.

20 Barak A. Salmoni, Bryce Loidolt, and Madeleine Wells, *Regime and Periphery in Northern Yemen: The Huthi Phenomenon*, Santa Monica, California: RAND, 2010, pp. 1, 8, 64 and passim, at https://www.rand.org/content/dam/rand/pubs/monographs/2010/RAND_MG962.pdf.

21 Mai Yamani, "Saudi Arabia Goes to War," *The Guardian*, 23 November 2009, at https://www.theguardian.com/commentisfree/2009/nov/23/saudi-arabia-yemen-houthi-war. See also Christopher Boucek, *War in Saada: From Local Insurrection to National Challenge*, Middle East Program Number 110, Washington, D.C.: Carnegie Endowment for International Peace, April 2010, at https://carnegieendowment.org/files/war_in_saada.pdf.

22 Central Bureau of Statistics (Sana'a), and estimates from *Générations Arabes: l'Alchimie du Nombre,* Paris: Fayard, 2000, as quoted by Hélène Thiollet, "From Migration Hub to Asylum Crisis: The Changing Dynamics of Contemporary Migration in Yemen," in Helen Lackner, ed., *Why Yemen Matters*, London: Saqi Books, 2014, pp. 265–285.

23 'Abd al-Waahid al-Maytami Muhammad, "Le Marche du Travail Yemenite apres l'Unification," *Revue du Monde Musulman et de la Mediterranee*, Number 67, 1993, pp. 121–129 [the data is on p. 123].

24 Fred Halliday, *Revolution and Foreign Policy: The Case of South Yemen, 1967–1987*, Cambridge: Cambridge University Press, 1990, p. 162.

25 'Abd al-Waahid al-Maytami Muhammad, *op. cit.*

26 "Arab Versus Asian Migrant workers in the GCC countries," UN Expert Group Meeting on International Migration and Development in the Arab Region, Population Division Department of Economic and Social Affairs, United Nations, Beirut, 15–17 May 2006.

27 *Al-Mughtaribun: Al-Rafid al-Asasi lil-Tanmiyyah al-Mustadamah* [Emigrants: An Essential Contribution to Sustainable Development], Sana'a: Al-Majlis al-Istishari, Wizarat al-Shu'un al-Mughtaribin [Ministry for Expatriates], 1999.

28 *A Decade of Displacement in the Middle East and North Africa*, Geneva: Internal Displacement Monitoring Centre, 2021, pp. 3, 35–37, at https://www.internal-displacement.org/events/a-decade-of-displacement-in-the-middle-east-and-north-africa.

29 Matthew J. Gibney and Randall Hansen, eds., *Immigration and Asylum: From 1900 to the Present*, Santa Barbara, California: ABC-CLIO, 2005, p. 404.

30 Okruhlik and Conge, *op. cit.*, pp. 554–565, especially, 556.

31 Thiollet, "From Migration Hub to Asylum Crisis," *op. cit.*, p. 273.

32 *Ibid.*, p. 281.

33 Internal Displacement Monitoring Center, "Yemen: Internal displacement continues amid multiple crises," 17 December 2012, at http://www.internal-displacement.org/8025708F004BE3B1/(httpInfoFiles)/8D24A4E89B93B100C1257AD70052594B/$file/yemen-overview-dec2012.pdf.

34 Shabia Mantoo, "War Turns Yemen into Humanitarian Catastrophe," UNHCR, 20 December 2016, at https://www.unrefugees.org/news/what-is-happening-in-yemen-update-from-unhcr-representative/.

35 A Decade of Displacement in the Middle East and North Africa, p. 34.

36 "FairSquare Policy Brief #1: Migrant Workers In Saudi Arabia," October 2020, at https://fairsq.org/wp-content/uploads/2020/11/FS-Policy-Brief-1-Saudi-Arabia-1020.pdf.

37 "UN receives $1 billion contributions from Saudi Arabia and UAE to assist Humanitarian Crisis in Yemen," *Funds for NGOs*, 19 February 2021, at https://www2.fundsforngos.org/humanitarian-and-disaster-relief/un-receives-1-billion-contributions-from-saudi-arabia-and-uae-to-assist-humanitarian-crisis-in-yemen/. See also "UK Foreign Aid: Yemen Cut Condemned by Charities," *BBC News*, 6 March 2021, at https://www.bbc.com/news/uk-56301743.

38 "Smugglers See Thousands of migrants in Yemen as 'a Commodity', UN Agency Warns," *UN News*, 8 May 2018, at https://news.un.org/en/story/2018/05/1009122. See also *Protection Context For Migrants Passing Through Yemen: A Baseline*, Meraki Labs, 2019, at https://reliefweb.int/sites/reliefweb.int/files/resources/EN_Meraki_%20Yemen_%20Migration%20Report.pdf.

39 Martha Mundy, *The Strategies of the Coalition in the Yemen War: Aerial bombardment and food war*, Sommerville, Massachusetts: World Peace Foundation, 9 October 2018, at https://sites.tufts.edu/wpf/strategies-of-the-

coalition-in-the-yemen-war/. See also, "Yemen: Civilians Bombed, Shelled, Starved: War Crimes by Saudi-Led Coalition, Houthis Go Unaddressed," *World Report 2019*, New York: Human Rights Watch, 2019, at https://www.hrw.org/world-report/2019.

40 See the Human Rights Watch World Report 2019 introduction, *Ibid.*, at https://www.hrw.org/news/2019/01/17/yemen-civilians-bombed-shelled-

41 Mundy, *op. cit.*, p. 6.

42 For additional details, see the King Salman Humanitarian Air and Relief Center web-page at https://www.ksrelief.org/English/DataAndResult/Documents/Statistics%20for%20KSrelief%20Projects%20for%20Yemen%20(13%20March%202019).pdf.

43 Saeed Saleh Alghamdy, "Saudi Arabia's Worldwide Efforts to Support Refugees and the Forcibly Displaced," a paper presented at the International Conference on Forced Migration and Refugee Studies, Kuala Lumpur, Malaysia: Qulliyyah of Islamic Revealed Knowledge and Human Science, International Islamic University of Malaysia, 5–7 December 2017, issued as Report Number 17 by the Riyadh-based Center for Research and Intercommunication Knowledge, 2018, pp. 14–15. See also "KSA Gives $31 Billion Aid to 78 Countries, Yemen Tops List," *Arab News*, 22 June 2018, at http://www.arabnews.com/node/1325806/saudi-arabia.

44 It is interesting to note that circular migration occurred in many other locations around the world such as the case of seasonable migration of Mexicans to the United States of America.

45 Angus McDowall, "Foreign Workers Queue to Quit Saudi Arabia After Amnesty on Fines," *Reuters*, 28 May 2013, at https://www.reuters.com/article/saudi-expatriates-workers-amnesty/foreign-workers-queue-to-quit-saudi-arabia-after-amnesty-on-fines-idINDEE94R09D20130528; see also, Lulwa Shalhoub and Nada Hameed, "90 Day Amnesty Period Allows Illegal Workers to Return to Saudi Arabia," *Arab News*, 21 March 2017, at https://www.arabnews.com/node/1071511/saudi-arabia.

46 François Burgat, "Yémen: Les Ressorts d'un Conflict," *Questions Internationales*, Number 89, January-February 2018, pp. 121–127.

47 Thomas Juneau, "Iran's Policy Towards the Houthis in Yemen: A Limited Return on a Modest Investment," *International Affairs* 92:3, May 2016, pp. 647–663. See also Farzin Nadimi and Michael Knights, "Iran's Support to Houthi Air Defenses in Yemen," *POLICYWATCH 2953*, Washington, D.C.: he Washington Institute for Near East Policy, 4 April 2018, at https://www.washingtoninstitute.org/policy-analysis/view/irans-support-to-houthi-air-defenses-in-yemen; Gerald M. Feierstein, "Iran's Role in Yemen and Prospects for Peace," *The Iran Primer*, Washington, D.C.: The United States Institute of Peace, 6 December 2018, at https://iranprimer.usip.org/blog/2018/dec/05/iran's-role-yemen-and-prospects-peace; and Barbara A. Leaf and Elana Delozier, "It's Time for a

Serious Saudi–Houthi Back Channel," *War on the Rocks*, 9 January 2019, at https://warontherocks.com/2019/01/its-time-for-a-serious-saudi-houthi-back-channel/.

48 Tom Ruys and Luca Ferro, "Weathering the Storm: Legality and Legal Implications of the Saudi-Led Military Intervention In Yemen," *International and Comparative Law Quarterly* 65:1, January 2016, pp. 61–98.

49 This information is repeated here because it is so important and because it is so often ignored. See "Resolution 2216," S/RES/2216 (2015), Adopted by the Security Council at its 7426th meeting, 14 April 2015, New York: United Nations, 2015, at https://www.un.org/securitycouncil/s/res/2216-%282015%29-0.

50 "Saudi-led Coalition Announces End to Yemen Operation," *Reuters*, 21 April 2015, at https://www.reuters.com/article/us-yemen-security-saudi-idUSKBN0NC24T20150421.

51 These assaults were frequent and continued in early 2021. See for example, "Houthis Launch Air Attacks on Saudi Capital," *The Guardian*, 30 March 2020, at https://www.theguardian.com/world/2020/mar/30/yemen-houthis-launch-air-attacks-on-saudi-capital-riyadh;
Mohammed Benmansour, "Yemen's Houthis Reach Saudi Capital with Missiles for First Time since COVID Ceasefire," *Reuters*, 23 June 2020, at https://www.reuters.com/article/us-yemen-security-saudi-idUSKBN 23U0KA;
The Associated Press, "Saudis Say They Intercepted Houthi Missile Attack Over Capital," *The New York Times*, 27 February 2021, at https://www.nytimes.com/2021/02/27/world/middleeast/saudi-houthi-missile.html.

52 Sudarsan Raghavan, "Airstrike by Saudi-led Coalition Said to Hit Near Yemeni Hospital, Killing 8, including 5 children," *The Washington Post*, 27 March 2019, at
https://www.washingtonpost.com/world/middle_east/airstrike-by-saudi-led-coalition-said-to-hit-yemeni-hospital-killing-7-including-4-children/2019/03/27/7103b829-eda9-462a-aec1-be304044ac5e_story.html.

53 Reuters, "Aid Flights to Yemen Blocked after Saudi Arabian Jets Bomb Airport Runway," *The Guardian*, 28 April 2015, at
https://www.theguardian.com/world/2015/apr/28/aid-flights-to-yemen-blocked-after-saudi-arabia-bombs-airport-runway. See also Mohammad Hassan Al-Qadhi, *The Iranian Role in Yemen and its Implications on the Regional Security*, Riyadh: Arabian Gulf Centre for Iranian Studies (AGCIS), 2017, at
https://rasanah-iiis.org/english/wp-content/uploads/sites/2/2017/12/The-Iranian-Role-in-Yemen-and-its-Implications-on-the-Regional-Security.

54 Jeremy M. Sharp, "Yemen: Civil War and Regional Intervention," Washington, D.C.: Congressional Research Service [R43960], 21 March 2019, p. 15, available at
https://www.everycrsreport.com/files/20180824_R43960_71ff8842b861ec46d818c980e1b5cbaacd5c1799.pdf.

55 "Yemen War: Coalition Ceasefire to Help Combat Coronavirus Begins," *BBC News*, 9 April 2020, at https://www.bbc.com/news/world-middle-east-52224358. See also Bel Trew, "Saudi-Led Coalition Bombs Yemen 'Dozens' of Times Despite Declaring Ceasefire Last Week to Combat Coronavirus," *The Independent*, 17 April 2020, at https://www.independent.co.uk/news/world/middle-east/coronavirus-yemen-coalition-bombs-saudi-ceasefire-news-a9470801.html.
56 International Committee of the Red Cross, "More than 1,000 Former Detainees from Yemen Conflict Transported Home," 16 October 2020, at https://www.icrc.org/en/document/more-1000-former-detainees-yemen-conflict-transported-home.
57 Sharp, *op. cit.*
58 Julian Borger and Patrick Wintour, "Biden Announces End to US Support for Saudi-Led Offensive in Yemen, *The Guardian*, 5 February 2021, at https://www.theguardian.com/world/2021/feb/04/us-end-support-saudi-led-operations-yemen-humanitarian-crisis.

7 Syrian Refugees in Sa'udi Arabia: Integration Rather than Confinement

1 One of the world's most objective sources continued to raise doubts about Sa'udi Arabia, affirming and documenting (with graphics no less) that Riyadh did not "accept refugees," though "migrant workers drawn to domestic service and construction jobs [made] up nearly 40 percent of the population." See Paul Salopek, "Walking with Migrants," *National Geographic*, August 2019, pp. 40–63. Of course, even the percentage of migrants (40%) was inaccurate, assuming that there were approximately 34 million people living in the Kingdom, of whom about 20.7 million were Sa'udi citizens and 12.6 million were expatriate workers. The real percentage hovered about 50 percent, which raised significant national security concerns, though few contemplated the consequences of such lopsided figures.
For demographic figures, see Kingdom of Sa'udi Arabia, General Authority of Statistics, "Population by Nationality and Gender, 2019," at https://www.stats.gov.sa/en/5680. See also United States Central Intelligence Agency, "Saudi Arabia: People and Society," *The World Factbook 2020*, Washington, D.C.: Central Intelligence Agency, at https://www.cia.gov/the-world-factbook/countries/saudi-arabia/#people-and-society.
2 Global Media Insight, "Saudi Arabia's Population Statistics of 2021," 8 March 2021, at https://www.globalmediainsight.com/blog/saudi-arabia-population-statistics/.
3 For a useful overview, see "Syria: The story of the conflict," *BBC News*, 11 March 2016, at https://www.bbc.com/news/world-middle-east-26116868. See also Nikolaos van Dam, *Destroying a Nation: The Civil War*

in Syria, London and New York: I.B. Tauris, 2017; Steven A. Cook, "The Syrian War Is Over, and America Lost," *Foreign Policy*, 23 July 2018, at https://foreignpolicy.com/2018/07/23/the-syrian-war-is-over-and-america-lost/.

See also Mehmer Ozalp, "The Syrian War is Not Over, it's Just on a New Trajectory: Here's What You Need to Know," *The Conversation*, 5 February 2019, at https://theconversation.com/the-syrian-war-is-not-over-its-just-on-a-new-trajectory-heres-what-you-need-to-know-110292; Howard J. Shatz, "The Syrian Civil War Is Coming to an End," Santa Monica, CA: RAND, 8 April 2019, at https://www.rand.org/blog/2019/04/the-syrian-civil-war-is-coming-to-an-end.html; and "Why has the Syrian War Lasted 10 Years?," *BBC News*, 12 March 2021, at https://www.bbc.com/news/world-middle-east-35806229.

4 Jonathan Hassine, *Les Réfugiés et Déplacés de Syrie: Une Reconstruction Nationale en Question*, Paris: L'Harmattan, 2015, pp. 29–50.

5 Michael Slackman, "Syrian Troops Open Fire on Protesters in Several Cities," *The New York Times*, 25 March 2011, http://www.nytimes.com/2011/03/26/world/middleeast/26syria.html.

6 Peter Kellier, "Ghosts of Syria: Diehard Militias who Kill in the Name of Assad," *The Guardian*, 31 May 2012, at https://www.theguardian.com/world/2012/may/31/ghosts-syria-regime-shabiha-militias.

7 Nikolaos van Dam, *op. cit.*, p. 103. See also "Syria War: A Brief Guide to Who's Fighting Whom," *BBC News*, 7 April 2017, at https://www.bbc.com/news/world-middle-east-39528673; and Steven A. Cook, "Top Conflicts to Watch in 2021: What's Next for Syria," *Council on Foreign Relations*, 21 January 2021, at https://www.cfr.org/blog/top-conflicts-watch-2021-whats-next-syria.

8 Marisa Sullivan, *Hezbollah in Syria*, Middle East Security Report Number 19, Washington, D.C.: Institute for the Study of War, 1 April 2014, at https://www.jstor.org/stable/resrep07896?seq=1#metadata_info_tab_contents.

See also Seth G. Jones, "The Escalating Conflict with Hezbollah in Syria," Washington, D.C.: Center for Strategic and International Studies, 20 June 2018, at https://www.csis.org/analysis/escalating-conflict-hezbollah-syria; and Jeffrey White, "Hizb Allah at War in Syria: Forces, Operations, Effects and Implications," *CTC Sentinel* 7:1, January 2015, West Point Academy: Combating Terrorism Center, at https://www.ctc.usma.edu/hizb-allah-at-war-in-syria-forces-operations-effects-and-implications/.

9 Pavel K. Baev, "Russia Stumbles in the Fog of Syrian War," Brookings, 21 February 2018, at https://www.brookings.edu/blog/order-from-chaos/2018/02/21/russia-stumbles-in-the-fog-of-syrian-war/.

10 'Aqeel Mahfudh, *Syria and Turkey: A Turning Point or a Historical Bet?*, Doha, Qatar: Arab Center for Research & Policy Studies, 1 February 2012, at

https://www.jstor.org/stable/resrep12703?seq=1#metadata_info_tab_contents. See also Cengiz Çandar, "Erdoğan's War in Syria: A Path to Disaster," 6 March 2020, Stockholm, Sweden: Utrikespolitiska institutet, UI, at https://www.ui.se/utrikesmagasinet/analyser/2020/mars/erdogans-war-in-syria—a-path-to-disaster/.

11 Steven A. Cook, "Syria Is Turkey's Problem, Not America's," Council on Foreign Relations, 13 March 2020, at https://www.cfr.org/article/syria-turkeys-problem-not-americas.

12 For details, see Patrick Seale, *The Struggle for Syria: A Study of Post-War Arab Politics (1945–1958)*, New Haven, Connecticut: Yale University Press: 1987; Idem., *Asad: The Struggle for the Middle East*, Berkeley and Los Angeles: University of California Press, 1990; Mahmud Sadiq, *Hiwar Hawlah Suriyyah* [Dialogue About Syria], London: Dar 'Uqadh, 1993; and Faruq al-Shar', *Al-Riwayah al-Mafqudah* [The Missing Account], Beirut: al-Markaz al-'Arabi lil-Abhath wa-Dirasat al-Siyasat, 2015. For casualty statistics, see "More than 570 Thousand People were Killed on the Syrian Territory within 8 years of Revolution Demanding Freedom, Democracy, Justice, and Equality," Syrian Observatory for Human Rights, 15 March 2019, at http://www.syriahr.com/en/?p=120851. See also Priyanka Boghani, "A Staggering New Death Toll for Syria's War—470,000," *Frontline*, Boston: PBS [Corporation for Public Broadcasting], 11 February 2016, at https://www.pbs.org/wgbh/frontline/article/a-staggering-new-death-toll-for-syrias-war-470000/; and "On International Human Rights Day: Millions of Syrians Robbed of 'rights' and 593 Thousand killed in a Decade," Syrian Observatory for Human Rights, 9 December 2020, at https://www.syriahr.com/en/195385/.

13 "Massacre of Hama: Genocide and A crime against Humanity," Edgware, United Kingdom: The Syrian Human Rights Committee, February 1982, at https://web.archive.org/web/20130522172157/http://www.shrc.org/data/aspx/d5/2535.aspx. See also Kathrin Nina Wiedl, *The Hama Massacre: Reasons, Supporters of the Rebellion, Consequences*, Munich: Grin, 2007.

14 Nikolaos van Dam, *op. cit.*, pp. 74–84. See also Martin Chulov, "Assad Blames Conspirators for Syrian Protests," *The Guardian*, 30 March 2011, at https://www.theguardian.com/world/2011/mar/30/syrian-protests-assad-blames-conspirators. See also AP, "For Syrians, 8 Years of War Leaves Stories of Loss and Hope," *Arab News*, 16 March 2019, at https://www.arabnews.com/node/1467506/middle-east.

15 Nikolaos van Dam, *op. cit.*, pp. 96–118. See also Marwan Hisham and Molly Crabapple, *Brothers of the Gun: A Memoir of the Syrian War*, New York: Random House, 2018; and Rania Abouzeid, *No Turning Back: Life, Loss, and Hope in Wartime Syria*, New York: W. W. Norton & Company, 2018; and Sam Dagher, *Assad or We Burn the Country: How One Family's Lust for Power Destroyed* Syria, New York: Little, Brown and Company, 2019.

16 Alicia Sanders-Zakre, "What You Need to Know About Chemical Weapons

Use in Syria," Arms Control Association, 23 September 2018 [Updated on 14 March 2019], at https://www.armscontrol.org/blog/2018-09-23/what-you-need-know-about-chemical-weapons-use-syria.

17 James Ball, "Obama Issues Syria a 'Red Line' Warning on Chemical Weapons," *The Washington Post*, 20 August 2012, at https://www.washingtonpost.com/world/national-security/obama-issues-syria-red-line-warning-on-chemical-weapons/2012/08/20/ba5d26ec-eaf7-11e1-b811-09036bcb182b_story.html?noredirect=on&utm_term=.5ecb53bdfa74.

18 Bethan McKernan, "Ghouta Chemical Attack: Four Years Later, the World Looks on as Syria's People Continue to be Gassed," *The Independent*, 20 August 2017, at https://www.independent.co.uk/news/world/middle-east/ghouta-chemical-attack-syria-assad-anniversary-no-justice-for-survivors-a7903506.html.

19 "Syria War: What We Know About Douma 'Chemical Attack'," *BBC News*, 10 July 2018, at https://www.bbc.com/news/world-middle-east-43697084. See also Nawal al-Maghafi, "How Chemical Weapons Have Helped Bring Assad Close to Victory," *BBC Panorama*, 15 October 2018, at https://www.bbc.com/news/world-middle-east-45586903.

20 "Timeline of Syrian Chemical Weapons Activity, 2012–2018," Washington, D.C.: Arms Control Association, at https://www.armscontrol.org/factsheets/Timeline-of-Syrian-Chemical-Weapons-Activity. See also Rick Gladstone, "Syria Used Chlorine in Bombs Against Civilians, Report Says," *The New York Times*, 24 August 2016, at https://www.nytimes.com/2016/08/25/world/middleeast/syria-used-chlorine-in-bombs-against-civilians-report-says.html.

21 "Almost Half of Syria's Chemical Weapons Removed–OPCW," *BBC News*, 20 March 2014, at https://www.bbc.com/news/world-middle-east-26662801. See also "Last of Syria's Chemical Weapons Shipped Out," *BBC News*, 23 June 2014, at https://www.bbc.com/news/world-middle-east-27974379; and Scott Shane, "Weren't Syria's Chemical Weapons Destroyed? It's Complicated," *The New York Times*, 7 April 2017, at https://www.nytimes.com/2017/04/07/world/middleeast/werent-syrias-chemical-weapons-destroyed-its-complicated.html.

22 "OPCW Warns that Syria Must Speed Up Handover of Chemical Weapons," *Deutsche Welle*, 14 April 2014, at https://www.dw.com/en/opcw-warns-that-syria-must-speed-up-handover-of-chemical-weapons/a-17566900. See also Jane Dalston, "Syria Attack: Chemical Weapons Inspectors Retrieve Samples from Douma," *The Independent*, 21 April 2018, at https://www.independent.co.uk/news/world/middle-east/syria-douma-chemical-weapons-attack-latest-eastern-ghouta-russia-assad-a8315746.

23 Bob Woodward, *Fear: Trump in the White House*, New York: Simon & Schuster, 2018, p. 147. See also Ellen Francis, "Scores Reported Killed in Gas Attack on Syrian Rebel Area," *Reuters*, 4 April 2017, at https://www.reuters.com/article/us-mideast-crisis-syria-idlib-idUSKBN1760IB.

24 "U.S., Britain and France Strike Syria Over Suspected Chemical Weapons Attack," *The New York Times*, 13 April 2018, at https://www.nytimes.com/2018/04/13/world/middleeast/trump-strikes-syria-attack.html.

25 "Syria War: US Launches Missile Strikes in Response to 'Chemical Attack'," *BBC News*, 7 April 2017, at https://www.bbc.com/news/world-us-canada-39523654.

26 Phil Stewart and Suleiman Al-Khalidi, "U.S. Strikes Syria Militia Threatening U.S.-Backed Forces: Officials," *Reuters*, 18 May 2017, at https://www.reuters.com/article/us-mideast-crisis-syria-usa-idUSKCN18E2JU.

27 Robert Malley, The Unwanted Wars: Why the Middle East Is More Combustible Than Ever," *Foreign Affairs* 98:6, November-December 2019, pp. 38–46. See also, Kenneth Roth, "Syria: Events of 2019," Human Rights Watch, at
https://www.hrw.org/world-report/2020/country-chapters/syria#;
and Marko Valenta, Jo Jakobsen, Drago Župari -Ilji and Hariz Halilovich, "Syrian Refugee Migration, Transitions in Migrant Statuses and Future Scenarios of Syrian Mobility," *Refugee Survey Quarterly* 39:2, June 2020, pp. 153–176.

28 Khaled Yacoub Oweis and Tom Miles, "U.N. lifts Syria Death Toll to 'Truly Shocking' 60,000," *Reuters*, 1 January 2013, at https://www.reuters.com/article/us-syria-crisis/u-n-lifts-syria-death-toll-to-truly-shocking-60000-idUSBRE8AJ1FK20130102?feedType=RSS&feedName=topNews.

29 Patrick J. McDonnell, "U.N. Says Syria Death Toll Has Likely Surpassed 100,000," *Los Angeles Times*, 13 June 2013, at http://www.latimes.com/world/worldnow/la-fg-wn-un-syria-death-toll-20130613-story.html.

30 UN News, "More than 191,000 People Killed in Syria with 'No End in Sight'–UN," New York: United Nations, 22 August 2014, at https://news.un.org/en/story/2014/08/475652-more-191000-people-killed-syria-no-end-sight-un.

31 *Syria Confronting Fragmentation! Impact of Syrian Crisis Report, Quarterly based report (2015)*, n.p.: Syrian Centre for Policy Research, February 2016, p. 61, at http://scpr-syria.org/publications/confronting-fragmentation/.

32 Human Rights Watch, "Country Summary: Syria" January 2017, pp. 1–8 [the data is on p. 1]. See also *Amnesty International Report 2017/2018: The State of the World's Human Rights*, London: Amnesty International, 2018, pp. 349–353.

33 Syrian Network for Human Rights, at http://sn4hr.org accessed on 17 October 2018.

34 Syrian Network for Human Rights, at http://sn4hr.org accessed on 12 March 2021.

35 "During 7 Consecutive Years . . . about 511 Thousand People Killed Since

the Start of the Syrian Revolution in 2011," Coventry, United Kingdom: Syrian Observatory for Human Rights, 12 March 2018, at http://www.syriahr.com/en/?p=86573.
36 "On International Human Rights Day: Millions of Syrians Robbed of 'rights' and 593 Thousand killed in a Decade," Syrian Observatory for Human Rights, 9 December 2020, at https://www.syriahr.com/en/195385/.
37 Magnus Lundgren, "Mediation in Syria: Initiatives, Strategies, and Obstacles, 2011–2016," *Contemporary Security Policy* 37:2, April 2016, pp. 283–298.
38 Aron Lund, "Syria in Crisis: Exile Has No Religion," Beirut: Malcolm H. Kerr Carnegie Middle East Center, 15 December 2014, at https://carnegie-mec.org/diwan/57512.
39 United States Central Intelligence Agency, "Syria: People and Society," *CIA World Factbook*, at https://www.cia.gov/library/publications/the-world-factbook/geos/sy.html.
40 Hassine, *op. cit.*, pp. 107–125.
41 "Sunnis Struggle in Latakia, Says Citizen Journalist," *Syria Direct*, 24 November 2014, at https://syriadirect.org/sunnis-struggle-in-latakia-says-citizen-journalist/.
42 For useful examples, see Paolo Verme, Chiara Gigliarano, Christina Wieser, Kerren Hedlund, Marc Petzoldt, and Marco Santacroce, *The Welfare of Syrian Refugees: Evidence from Jordan and Lebanon*, Washington, D.C.: International Bank for Reconstruction and Development/The World Bank, 2016, and Dawn Chatty, *Syria: The Making and Unmaking of a Refuge State*, New York: Oxford University Press, 2017.
43 United Nations, *Syrian Regional Refugee Response*, 3 March 2021, Geneva: UNHCR, at https://data2.unhcr.org/en/situations/syria.
44 United Nations, *2018 Annual Report,* 3RP Regional, Refugee & Resilience Plan 2018–2019 in Response to the Syria Crisis, Geneva: UNHCR, at https://data2.unhcr.org/en/documents/download/68557.
45 Martin Chulow, "Iran Repopulates Syria with Shia Muslims to Help Tighten Regime's Control," *The Guardian*, 14 January 2017, at https://www.theguardian.com/world/2017/jan/13/irans-syria-project-pushing-population-shifts-to-increase-influence.
46 Francesco Guarascio and Tuvan Gumrukcu, "EU, Turkey in Stand-off Over Funds to Tackle New Migrant Crisis," *Reuters*, 6 March 2020, https://www.reuters.com/article/us-syria-security-turkey-eu-idUSKBN20T1RH.
47 The number of Palestinians in Lebanon is a tightly held secret for political reasons although one source claimed that there were 452,669 registered refugees in Lebanon as of January 2015. See "UNRWA In Figures as of 1 January 2015," Jerusalem: United Nations Relief and Works Agency, at https://www.unrwa.org/sites/default/files/unrwa_in_figures_2015.pdf.
When Amnesty International issued a highly critical study in 2007 that denounced the "appalling social and economic condition" of Palestinians in

Lebanon, Beirut relaxed some of its regulations that controlled employment opportunities. By 2010, Palestinians were granted the same rights to work as other foreigners in the country, which helped many find wage-earning jobs.

A mysterious census completed in January 2018 by the Lebanese Palestinian Dialogue Committee found that only around 175,000 Palestinian refugees lived in Lebanon, as opposed to previous UNRWA figures which put the number at between 400,000 and 500,000, but the lower end figures were dismissed as a horrible attempt to force the state to naturalize them to fit secret accords being reached by the Palestinian Authority to limit the number of Palestinians who might be allowed to return after a peace settlement with Israel. See Amnesty International, *Lebanon: Exiled and Suffering—Palestinian Refugees In Lebanon*, October 2007, at https://web.archive.org/web/20131211203636/http://www.amnesty.org/en/library/info/MDE18/010/2007; and "Palestinian refugees number 175,000," Lebanese Palestinian Dialogue Committee, *BusinessNews.com.lb*, 22 December 2017, at
http://www.businessnews.com.lb/cms/Story/StoryDetails.aspx?ItemID =6343.

48 Robert G. Rabil, *The Syrian Refugee Crisis in Lebanon: The Double Tragedy of Refugees and Impacted Host Communities*, Lanham, Maryland: Lexington Books, 2016.

49 John Knudsen "Syria's Refugees in Lebanon: Brothers, Burden, and Bone of Contention," in Rosita Di Peri and Daniel Meier, eds, *Lebanon Facing the Arab Uprisings: Constraints and Adaptation*, New York: Palgrave Macmillan, 2017, pp. 135–154.

50 Jordan Ingo Forum, *Syrian refugees in Jordan: A protection overview*, n.p., January 2018, at https://reliefweb.int/report/jordan/syrian-refugees-jordan-protection-overview-january-2018. See also UNHCR, Total Persons of Concern 2021, *op. cit.*

51 Ian Black, "Jordan Jitters Over Swelling Syrian Refugee Influx," *The Guardian*, 31 July 2012 at https://www.theguardian.com/world/on-the-middle-east/2012/jul/31/jordan-syria-refugees.

52 Josh Rogin, "U.S. and Jordan in a Dispute Over Syrian Refugees," *Bloomberg*, 6 October 2015, at
https://www.bloomberg.com/view/articles/2015-10-06/u-s-and-jordan-in-a-dispute-over-syrian-refugees. See also United Nations, *2018 Annual Report*, 3RP Regional, Refugee & Resilience Plan 2018–2019 in Response to the Syria Crisis, Geneva: UNHCR, at https://data2.unhcr.org/en/documents/download/68557.

53 Mohammad Ghazal, "Syrian Refugee Population Increases Slightly Last Year," *The Jordan Times*, 9 February 2018, at
http://www.jordantimes.com/news/local/syrian-refugee-population-increases-slightly-last-year.

54 "Syria Conflict: UN Says Refugee Crisis in Jordan 'Critical'," *BBC News*,

24 January 2013, at https://www.bbc.com/news/world-middle-east-21179835. See also Kathy Sullivan, "Water from a Stone: Jordanians Stretch Meager Resources to Sustain Syrian Refugees," *USAID Frontlines*, July 2013), at https://blog.usaid.gov/2013/04/water-from-a-stone-jordanians-stretch-meager-resources-to-sustain-syrian-refugees/; Nafez Ali and Saeb Farhan Al Ganideh, "Syrian Refugees in Jordan: Burden or Boon," *Research in World Economy* 11:1; Special Issue, 2020, pp. 180–194.

55 Taylor Luck, "In Jordan, Tensions Rise Between Syrian Refugees and Host Community," *The Washington Post*, 21 April 2013, at https://www.washingtonpost.com/world/middle_east/in-jordan-tensions-rise-between-syrian-refugees-and-host-community/2013/04/21/d4f5fa24-a762-11e2-a8e2-5b98cb59187f_story.html.

56 *Ibid*.

57 Ala' Alrababah and Scott Williamson, "Jordan Shut Out 60,000 Syrian Refugees—and Then Saw a Backlash. This is why," *The Washington Post*, 20 July 2018, at https://www.washingtonpost.com/news/monkey-cage/wp/2018/07/20/when-jordan-closed-its-border-to-refugees-the-public-protested-heres-why/?utm_term=.e5f1a8851283.

58 Jenna Krajeski, "The Fight for Kurdistan," *The New Yorker*, 22 September 2012, at

https://www.newyorker.com/news/news-desk/the-fight-for-kurdistan. See also "Information Kit: Syrian Refugees—Iraq, Humanitarian Inter-Agency Achievements," *3RP Regional, Refugee & Resilience Plan 2017–2018*, Number 17, May 2018, pp. 4 and 9, at https://data2.unhcr.org/en/documents/details/64021; and UNHCR, Total Persons of Concern 2021, *op. cit.*

59 Durable Solutions Platform, *Far From Home: Future Prospects for Syrian Refugees in Iraq*, Danish Refugee Council (DRC), International Rescue Committee (IRC) and Norwegian Refugee Council (NRC), January 2019, at https://drc.ngo/media/aatg3dkd/far-from-home-future-prospects-for-syrian-refugees-in-iraq_-january2019.pdf.

60 *Ibid.*, p. 9.

61 *Ibid.*, p. 10.

62 Kemal Kirişci, Jessica Brandt and M. Murat Erdoğan, "Syrian Refugees in Turkey: Beyond the Numbers," The Brookings Institution, 19 June 2018, at https://www.brookings.edu/blog/order-from-chaos/2018/06/19/syrian-refugees-in-turkey-beyond-the-numbers/.

63 "Turkey: Nearly 100,000 Unregistered Syrians Removed from Istanbul," *DW Deutsche Welle*, 4 January 2020, https://www.dw.com/en/turkey-nearly-100000-unregistered-syrians-removed-from-istanbul/a-51888092.

64 Kemal Kirişci, Jessica Brandt and M. Murat Erdoğan, *op. cit.*

65 M. Murat Erdoğan, "SYRIANS-BAROMETER-2017: A Framework for Achieving Social Cohesion with Syrians in Turkey," SB-2017, at https://mmuraterdogan.files.wordpress.com/2016/06/syrians-barometer-executive-summary.pdf. See also Ofra Bengio and Gencer Özcan, "Old Grievances, New Fears: Arab Perceptions of Turkey and Its Alignment with

Israel," *Middle Eastern Studies* 37:2, April 2001, pp. 50–92; and Tarek Osman, "Turks and Arabs," *The Cairo Review of Global Affairs*, Tahrir Forum, 17 September 2014, at https://www.thecairoreview.com/tahrir-forum/turks-and-arabs/.

66 *Turkey's Syrian Refugees: Defusing Metropolitan Tensions*, International Crisis Group, Europe Report Number 248, 29 January 2018, at https://d2071andvip0wj.cloudfront.net/248-turkey-s-syrian-refugees.pdf.

67 For an examination of these contradictory policies, see Christopher Phillips, *The Battle for Syria: International Rivalry in the New Middle East*, New Haven, Connecticut: Yale University Press, 2016 pp. 59–82; Raymond Hinnebusch and Özlem Tür, eds., *Turkey—Syria Relations: Between Enmity and Amity*, London and New York: Routledge, 2016; and Ali Askerov, ed., *Contemporary Russo–Turkish Relations: From Crisis to Cooperation*, Lanham, Maryland: Lexington Books, 2018.

68 Mehmet Cetingulec, "Turkey Removes Arabic Shop Signs as Refugee Problem Simmers," *Al-Moniror*, 17 July 2019, at https://www.al-monitor.com/pulse/originals/2019/07/turkey-syria-refugees-government-removes-arabic-shop-signs.html.

69 Jessica Elgot, "Father of Drowned Boy Aylan Kurdi Plans to Return to Syria: Abdullah Kurdi says he no longer wants to continue on to Europe and will take the bodies of his two sons and wife to be buried in home town of Kobani," *The Guardian*, 3 September 2015, at https://www.theguardian.com/world/2015/sep/03/father-drowned-boy-aylan-kurdi-return-syria.

70 "Most EU Countries Are Happy to Welcome Other Europeans: They are less keen on refugees from outside," *The Economist*, 25 March 2017, at https://www.economist.com/special-report/2017/03/25/most-eu-countries-are-happy-to-welcome-other-europeans.

71 United Nations Office for the Coordination of Humanitarian Affairs, Syrian Arab Republic, accessed on 28 May 2017, http://www.unocha.org/syria; see also "Syria Regional Refugee Response," *UNHCR Syria Regional Refugee*, accessed on 28 May 2017, at http://data.unhcr.org/syrianrefugees/regional.php;
and UNHCR, "Quarterly Regional Cash Assistance Monitoring Update," January to March 2020 (Q1), at https://data.unhcr.org/en/documents/details/77775.

72 United Nations Office for the Coordination of Humanitarian Affairs, "About OCHA Syria," New York: United Nations, June 2018, at http://www.unocha.org/syrian-arab-republic/about-ocha-syria.

73 United Nations Office for the Coordination of Humanitarian Affairs, "About OCHA Syria," New York: United Nations, March 2021, at https://www.unocha.org/syrian-arab-republic/about-ocha-syria.

74 It is critical to reiterate that Beirut refused to set up even temporary camps for Syrians because authorities feared repeating the fate that befell Palestinian refugees, who were sheltered in 12 official United Nations Relief

and Works Agency for Palestine Refugees in the Near East (UNRWA) camps, and whose numbers increased after every Arab–Israeli war since 1948. Although UNRWA claimed that 450,000 refugees were registered in Lebanon, the actual number was probably higher. See Sherifa Shafie, "Palestinian Refugees in Lebanon," *Forced Migration Online*, accessed on 28 May 2017, at

http://www.forcedmigration.org/research-resources/expert-guides/palestinian-refugees-in-lebanon/fmo018.pdf. An equally important detail about Syrians in Lebanon were the additional half-a million legally employed, most of whom carried work permits issued by the Ministry of Labor; a large percentage had been resident for several decades. For the Zaatari Camp, see Sally Hayden, "Inside the World's Largest Camp for Syrian Refugees," *The Irish Times*, 22 March 2017, at

http://www.irishtimes.com/news/world/middle-east/inside-the-world-s-largest-camp-for-syrian-refugees-1.3018821;

and UNHCR, "Jordan: Zaatari Refugee Camp," January 2021, at https://reliefweb.int/sites/reliefweb.int/files/resources/01%20Zaatari%20Fact%20Sheet%20January%202021.pdf.

75 Ishaan Tharoor, "The Arab World's Wealthiest Nations Are Doing Next To Nothing For Syria's Refugees," *The Washington Post*, 4 September 2015, at https://www.washingtonpost.com/news/worldviews/wp/2015/09/04/the-arab-worlds-wealthiest-nations-are-doing-next-to-nothing-for-syrias-refugees/?utm_term=.34b4014ce0d9.

76 The *Post* essay contains several tweets from Kenneth Roth, the executive director of *Human Rights Watch*, one of the world's leading international human rights organizations, which further affirmed the falsehoods cited here and which added presumed credibility to the assertions.

77 "How Many Muslim Refugees In Saudi Arabia?," *The Wall Street Journal*, 30 April 2017, at

https://www.wsj.com/articles/how-many-muslim-refugees-in-saudi-arabia-1493573797. See also Chase Winter, "Arab Monarchies Turn Down Syrian Refugees Over Security Threat," *DW Deutsche Welle*, 25 January 2016, https://www.dw.com/en/arab-monarchies-turn-down-syrian-refugees-over-security-threat/a-19002873.

78 Michael Stepehens, "Migrant Crisis: Why the Gulf States are not Letting Syrians in," *BBC News*, 7 September 2015, at https://www.bbc.com/news/world-middle-east-34173139.

79 Government of the Kingdom of Saudi Arabia, "Saudi Arabia Received 2.5 Million Syrians since Beginning of Conflict," 11 September 2015, Washington, D.C.: Royal Embassy of Saudi Arabia, at https://www.saudiembassy.net/saudi-arabia-received-25-million-syrians-beginning-conflict.

80 UNHCR Global Focus, 12 March 2021, at https://reporting.unhcr.org/middleeast.

81 For a good rebuttal see, Anhvinh Doanvo, "Western Media's Miscount of

Saudi Arabia's Syrian Refugees," *The Huffington Post*, 23 September 2015, at http://www.huffingtonpost.com/anhvinh-doanvo/europes-crisis-refugees_b_8175924.html. See also Government of the Kingdom of Sa'udi Arabia, "Saudi Arabia Pledges $75M More to Support Refugees," 21 September 2016, Washington, D.C.: Royal Embassy of Saudi Arabia, at https://www.saudiembassy.net/press-release/saudi-arabia-pledges-75m-more-support-refugees.

82 "Gulf States Response to Syrian Refugee Crisis—A Myth Debunked," *Open source Investigations*, at http://www.opensourceinvestigations.com/syria/gulf-states-response-to-syrian-refugee-crisis-a-myth-debunked/.

83 King Salman Humanitarian Aid and Relief Centre, at https://www.ksrelief.org/Statistics/ProjectStatistics.

84 "Arab Monarchies Turn Down Syrian Refugees Over Security Threat," *DW* [DeutscheWell], 25 January 2016, at http://www.dw.com/en/arab-monarchies-turn-down-syrian-refugees-over-security-threat/a-19002873.

85 Arab Monarchies, *DW* [DeutscheWell], 25 January 2016, *Ibid*.

86 Joshua Jacobs, "The Danger that Saudi Arabia Will Turn Syria into an Islamist Hotbed," *The Christian Science Monitor*, 12 April 2012, at http://www.csmonitor.com/Commentary/Opinion/2012/0412/The-danger-that-Saudi-Arabia-will-turn-Syria-into-an-Islamist-hotbed. See also Bilal Y. Saab, "How Saudi Arabia Can Contain Iran—and Other Benefits from Syria's Turmoil," *The Christian Science Monitor*, 31 August 2011, at http://www.csmonitor.com/Commentary/Opinion/2011/0831/How-Saudi-Arabia-can-contain-Iran-and-other-benefits-from-Syria-s-turmoil.

87 Julian Borger, "Saudi Arabia Says There Is 'No Future' for Assad in Syria," *The Guardian*, 30 September 2015, at https://www.theguardian.com/world/2015/sep/30/saudi-arabia-warns-there-is-no-future-for-assad-in-syria.

88 "Saudi Crown Prince Says Syria's Assad 'Is Staying'," *Sputnik News* (Quoting *Time Magazine*), 31 March 2018, at https://sputniknews.com/middleeast/201803311063093064-saudi-prince-assad-staying/.

89 Martin Chulov, Shawn Carrie, Asmaa Al Omar and Nadia Alfaour, "Syrian Refugees in Beirut and Istanbul Detained and Deported," *The Guardian*, 29 July 2019, at https://www.theguardian.com/world/2019/jul/29/syrian-refugees-in-beirut-and-istanbul-detained-and-deported.

90 United Nations, "Nearly 300,000 Syrians Displaced from Idlib since Mid-December, Security Council Hears," *UN News*, 3 January 2020, at https://news.un.org/en/story/2020/01/1054741.

91 A summary of the 185-page report, titled, "Summary by the Secretary-General of the report of the United Nations Headquarters Board of Inquiry into certain incidents in northwest Syria since 17 September 2018 involving

facilities on the United Nations deconfliction list and United Nations supported facilities," with important details was available at https://www.un.org/sg/sites/www.un.org.sg/files/atoms/files/NWS_ BOI_Summary_06_April_2020.pdf.
See also Bethan McKernan, "UN Inquiry Stops Short of Directly Blaming Russia Over Idlib Attacks, *The Guardian*, 7 April 2020, at https://www.theguardian.com/world/2020/apr/07/un-inquiry-stops-short-of-directly-blaming-russia-over-idlib-attacks-syria.

8 The Refugee Challenge for Saʻudi Arabia and the Muslim World

1. Several Western governments, including the United States and Hungary, devised specific audio-visual programs to discourage Mexican migration and Syrian refugee movements. The aim of these popular videos and songs, which were widely broadcast on social media outlets in advertisements in Lebanese newspapers in the case of Budapest, was to deter illegal travel. In addition to the United States and Hungary, Switzerland prepared videos destined for Cameroon to further restrain migration. Australia resorted to Facebook, Twitter and YouTube after 2014, showcasing videos in about 15 Asian languages, informing listeners that they should not make the continent their home. After 2015, even Norway—one of the most generous countries in terms of global assistance to refugees—got into the act, as it called on refugees not to risk their lives at the Russian border from where, it hammered, most if not all were bound to be denied admission. Brussels was blunt. It broadcast a simple message: "Do not come to Belgium." No similar campaigns were launched by any Arab country, including Saʻudi Arabia because, and simply stated, such efforts were ineffective. From an Arab as well as a Muslim perspective, they were also deemed to be breaches of religious obligations. See Antoine Pécoud and Julia Van Dessel, "Campagnes de Dissuasion Massive," *Le Monde Diplomatique*, Number 804, March 2021, p. 16.
2. Julie M. Norman, "Saudi Arabia Doesn't 'Do' Refugees—It's Time to Change That," *The Conversation*, 23 September 2015, at http://theconversation.com/saudi-arabia-doesnt-do-refugees-its-time-to-change-that-47307.
3. Professor Norman relied on flip language, "Saudi Arabia Doesn't 'Do' Refugees," which was unbecoming and, frankly, unprofessional. The evidence to what the Kingdom has done and continues to do is now amply provided in these pages that will, hopefully, avoid similar gratuitous remarks in the future.
4. Mashood A. Baderin, *International Human Rights and Islamic Law*, Oxford: Oxford University Press, 2005, p. 29.
5. Rashid Hassan and Sharif M. Taha, "Saudi Arabia's Fees on Expats' Dependents Draw Mixed Reactions," *Arab News*, 6 July 2017, at http://www.arabnews.com/node/1125051/saudi-arabia. See also "Saudi

Arabia: Tier 2 Watch List," in *Trafficking in Persons Report*, Washington, D.C.: United States Department of State, June 2018, pp. 369–372, at https://www.state.gov/documents/organization/282798.pdf.
6. Khadija Elmadmad, "Asylum in Islam and in Modern Refugee Law," *Refugee Survey Quarterly* 27:2, January 2008, pp. 51–63.
7. Musab Hayatli, "Islam, International Law and the Protection of Refugees and IDPs," *Forced Migration Review*, June 2012, at https://www.fmreview.org/sites/fmr/files/FMRdownloads/en/FMRpdfs/Human-Rights/human-rights.pdf.
8. In mid-2019, reports surfaced that Riyadh was contemplating drastic changes in its guardianship regulations, though it was too soon to know their impact if and when they were to pass. See Megan Specia and Hwaida Saad, "Saudi Guardianship Laws Could be Set to Change. Here's How Women Are Reacting," *The New York Times*, 21 July 2019, at https://www.nytimes.com/2019/07/21/world/middleeast/saudi-guardianship-women-react.html.
9. Hassen Altalhi, "Saudi Arabian Humanitarian Aid in Crises Management Periods," *Open Journal of Political Science* 7, 2017, pp. 380–393, at https://doi.org/10.4236/ojps.2017.73031.
10. *Ibid.*

Bibliography

Newspaper articles, wire reports, and essays published in non-academic journals that appear in the footnotes are not reproduced in this Bibliography. Entries are generally alphabetical by name, and alphabetical by title of the reference where the entry would be most likely sought.

A Decade of Displacement in the Middle East and North Africa, Geneva: Internal Displacement Monitoring Centre, 2021, at https://www.internal-displacement.org/events/a-decade-of-displacement-in-the-middle-east-and-north-africa.
Madeline-Sophie Abbas, "Conflating the Muslim Refugee and the Terror Suspect: Responses to the Syrian Refugee 'Crisis' in Brexit Britain," *Ethnic and Racial Studies* 42:14, 2019, pp. 2450–2469.
Engy Abdelkader, "The Rohingya Muslims in Myanmar: Past, Present, Future," *Oregon Review of International Law* 15:3, 2013, pp. 393–411.
Rania Abouzeid, *No Turning Back: Life, Loss, and Hope in Wartime Syria*, New York: W. W. Norton & Company, 2018.
Saeed Saleh Alghamdy, "Saudi Arabia's Worldwide Efforts to Support Refugees and the Forcibly Displaced," a paper presented at the International Conference on Forced Migration and Refugee Studies, Kuala Lumpur, Malaysia: Qulliyyah of Islamic Revealed Knowledge and Human Science, International Islamic University of Malaysia, 5–7 December 2017, issued as Report Number 17 by the Riyadh-based Center for Research and Intercommunication Knowledge, 2018, pp. 14–15.
Nafez Ali and Saeb Farhan Al Ganideh, "Syrian Refugees in Jordan: Burden or Boon," *Research in World Economy* 11:1; Special Issue, 2020, pp. 180–194.
Morad Alsahafi, "When Homeland Remains a Distant Dream: Language Attitudes and Heritage Language Maintenance Among Rohingya Refugees in Saudi Arabia," *International Journal of Bilingual Education and Bilingualism*, April 2020, pp. 1–12.
Fahad L. Alghalib Alsharif, "Calculated Risks, Agonies, and Hopes: A Comparative Case Study of the Undocumented Yemeni and Filipino Migrant Communities in Jeddah," in Philippe Fargues and Nasra Shah, editors, *Skillful Survivals: Irregular Migration to the Gulf*, Jeddah, Geneva, Cambridge (UK): Gulf Research Center, 2017, pp. 161–183.
———, "City of Dreams, Disappointment, and Optimism: The Case of Nine

Communities of Undocumented African Migrants in the City of Jeddah," *Dirasat*, Number 35, Riyadh: King Faisal Center for Research and Islamic Studies, April 2018.

———, "Kafala Reforms in Saudi Arabia: Converging Toward International Labor Standards," Riyadh: King Faisal Center for Research and Islamic Studies, February 2021, at
https://kfcris.com/pdf/130efbcff5567391146fc2bc9002efa4603b6b4891667.pdf.

———, *The Good, the Bad and the Ugly: Undocumented Labour in Saudi Arabia: The case of Jeddah*. Unpublished Doctoral Thesis, Exeter University, United Kingdom, 2015.

———, "Undocumented Migrants in Saudi Arabia: COVID 19 and Amnesty Reforms," *International Migration*, 19 March 2021, at
https://onlinelibrary.wiley.com/doi/epdf/10.1111/imig.12838.

Hassen Altalhi, "Saudi Arabian Humanitarian Aid in Crises Management Periods," *Open Journal of Political Science* 7, 2017, pp. 380–393, at https://doi.org/10.4236/ojps.2017.73031.

Rafat Y. Alwazna, "Islamic Law: Its Sources, Interpretation and the Translation of It into Laws Written in English," *International Journal for the Semiotics of Law* 29, June 2016, pp. 251–260.

Amnesty International Report 2017/2018: The State of the World's Human Rights, London: Amnesty International, 2018.

Arab Development Assistance: Four Decades of Cooperation, Washington, D.C.: World Bank, June 2010.

Joaquín Arango, "Explaining Migration: A Critical View," *International Social Science Journal* 52:165, September 2000, pp. 283–296.

Lisa Arrehag, Orjan Sjoberg and Mirja Sjoblom, "Cross-Border Migration and Remittances in a Post-Communist Society: Return Flows of Money and Goods in the Korçë District, Albania," *South-Eastern Europe Journal of Economics* 3:1, 2005, pp. 9–40.

Hossein Askari and Abbas Mirakhor, *Conceptions of Justice from Islam to the Present*, New York: Palgrave, 2020.

Ali Askerov, ed., *Contemporary Russo–Turkish Relations: From Crisis to Cooperation*, Lanham, Maryland: Lexington Books, 2018.

Mashood A. Baderin, *International Human Rights and Islamic Law*, Oxford: Oxford University Press, 2005.

Pavel K. Baev, "Russia Stumbles in the Fog of Syrian War," Brookings, 21 February 2018, at
https://www.brookings.edu/blog/order-from-chaos/2018/02/21/russia-stumbles-in-the-fog-of-syrian-war/.

Roland Bank, "Forced Migration in Europe," in Eleba Fiddian-Qasmiyeh, Gil Loescher, Katy Long and Nando Sigona, eds., *The Oxford Handbook of Refugee and Forced Migration Studies*, Oxford: Oxford University Press, 2014, pp. 690–702.

Adam Bannister, "Plan for Saudi–Iraq Border Fence Demonstrates Strong Role for Physical Security in Middle East," *IFSEC Global*, 17 October 2014, at https://www.ifsecglobal.com/security/five-layered-border-fence-saudi-iraq-border-signals-strong-role-physical-security-middle-east/.

Badriyyah al-Bashar, *Najd Qabla al-Naft: Dirasah Susyilujiyyah Tahliliyyah lil-Hikayat al-Sha'biyyah* [Najd Before Oil: Sociological and Analytical Studies of Popular Stories], Beirut: Jadawel, 2013.

Tanja Bastia and Ronald Skelton, *Routledge Handbook of Migration and Development*, Abingdon and New York: Routledge, 2020.

Françoise De Bel-Air, "Demography, Migration and Labor Market in Saudi Arabia," *Gulf Labor Markets and Migration GLMM*, Number 1, 2014, at https://cadmus.eui.eu/bitstream/handle/1814/32151/GLMM%20ExpNote_01-2014.pdf.

Ofra Bengio and Gencer Özcan, "Old Grievances, New Fears: Arab Perceptions of Turkey and Its Alignment with Israel," *Middle Eastern Studies* 37:2, April 2001, pp. 50–92.

Seyla Benhabib, "The End of the 1951 Refugee Convention? Dilemmas of Sovereignty, Territoriality, and Human Rights," *Jus Cogens* 2, July 2020, pp. 75–100.

Jonathan Benthall, *Islamic Charities and Islamic Humanism in Troubled Times*, Manchester, U.K.: Manchester University Press, 2016.

Maurits S. Berger, *Religion and Development Aid: The Special Case of Islam*, The Hague: Netherlands Institute of International Relations, October 2006, at https://www.clingendael.org/sites/default/files/pdfs/20061000_cdsp_pap_

———, "Understanding Sharia in the West," *Journal of Law, Religion and State* 6, 2018, pp. 236–273.

Tina Besley & Michael A. Peters, "Terrorism, Trauma, Tolerance: Bearing Witness to White Supremacist Attack on Muslims in Christchurch, New Zealand," *Educational Philosophy and Theory 52:2*, 2020, pp. 109–119.

Alexander Betts and Paul Collier, "Refuge: Transforming a Broken Refugee System," *International Journal of Refugee Law* 30:1, March 2018, pp. 173–178.

Abdalhaqq Bewley and Amal Abdalhakim Douglas, *Zakat: Raising a Fallen Pillar*, Dammam, Sa'udi Arabia: Diwan Press, 2020.

Robin Bidwell, *The Two Yemens*, Harlow, Essex, UK and Boulder, Colorado: Longman and Westview Press, 1983.

Yusuf Hamad al-Bissam, *Al-Zubayr Qabla Khamsin 'Aman ma' Nubdhah Tarikhiyyah 'an Najd wal-Kuwayt* [Zubayr Fifty Years Ago with a Historical Portion about Najd and Kuwait], London: Dar Al-Hikmah, 1971.

Richard Black, "Fifty Years of Refugee Studies: From Theory to Policy," *International Migration Review* 35:1, March 2001, pp. 57–78.

Alice Bloch, Nando Sigona and Roger Zetter, *'No Right to Dream': The Social and Economic Lives of Young Undocumented Migrants in Britain*, Oxford: University of Oxford Refugee Studies Center, 2014, at https://www.phf.org.uk/wp-content/uploads/2014/10/Young-Undocumented-Migrants-report.pdf.

Riccardo Bocco, "UNRWA and the Palestinian Refugees: A History within History," *Refugee Survey Quarterly* 28:2–3, 2009, pp. 229–252.

F. Kahan Bodur, *The Book of Alms: A Guide to Understanding Zakat and Wealth*, CreateSpace Independent Publishing Platform, 2020.

Pierre van den Boogaerde, "The Composition and Distribution of Financial Assistance from Arab Countries and Arab Regional Institutions", *IMF Working Paper WP/90/67*, July 1990, at https://www.bookstore.imf.org/books/title/The-Composition-and-Distribution-of-Financial-Assistance-From-Arab-Countries-and-Arab-Regional-Institutions.

Christopher Boucek, *War in Saada: From Local Insurrection to National Challenge*, Middle East Program Number 110, Washington, D.C.: Carnegie Endowment for International Peace, April 2010, at https://carnegieendowment.org/files/war_in_saada.pdf.

Caroline B. Brettell and James F. Hollifield, eds., *Migration Theory: Talking Across Disciplines*, New York and Abingdon, Oxon.: Routledge, 2015.

Rosie Bsheer, "Kafala Politics and Domestic Labor in Saudi Arabia," *Jadaliya*, 17 September 2010, at https://www.jadaliyya.com/Details/23509.

Ernest Alfred Wallis Budge, *A History of Ethiopia: Volume I—Nubia and Abyssinia*, New York: Routledge Revivals, 2014 [Originally published in 1928].

François Burgat, "Yémen: Les Ressorts d'un Conflict," *Questions Internationales*, Number 89, January-February 2018, pp. 121–127.

Shaykh Muhammad Hisham Burhani, translated by Amjad Mahmood, *A Believer's Guide To Zakat: A Treatise on its Rulings and Etiquette in the Hanafi School*, Heritage Press, 2014.

Peter Byers, *Rethinking Refugees: Beyond State of Emergency*, Abingdon, Oxon.: Routledge, 2013.

Dustin J. Byrd, *Islam in a Post-Secular Society: Religion, Secularity and the Antagonism of Recalcitrant Faith*, Leiden and Boston: Brill, 2016.

Cengiz Çandar, "Erdoğan's War in Syria: A Path to Disaster," 6 March 2020, Stockholm, Sweden: Utrikespolitiska institutet, UI, at https://www.ui.se/utrikesmagasinet/analyser/2020/mars/erdoans-war-in-syria-a-path-to-disaster/.

Tiziana Caponio, Peter Scholten and Ricard Zapata-Barrero, eds., *The Routledge Handbook of the Governance of Migration and Diversity in Cities*, Abingdon and New York: Routledge, 2020.

Dawn Chatty, *Displacement and Dispossession in the Modern Middle East*, Cambridge: Cambridge University Press, 2010.

———, *Syria: The Making and Unmaking of a Refuge State*, New York: Oxford University Press, 2017.

Aye Chan, "The Development of a Muslim Enclave in Arakan (Rakhine) State of Burma (Myanmar)," *SOAS Bulletin of Burma Research* 3:2, Autumn 2005, at https://www.soas.ac.uk/sbbr/editions/file64388.pdf.

Tuck Hoong Paul Chan, "A Review of Micro Migration Research in the Third World Context," in Gordon F. De Jong and Robert W. Gardner, eds,

Migration Decision Making: Multidisciplinary Approaches to Microlevel Studies in Developed and Developing Countries, New York: Pergamon, 1981, pp. 303–328.

Tianshe Chen, "Palestinian Refugees in Arab Countries and Their Impacts," *Journal of Middle Eastern and Islamic Studies (in Asia)* 3:3, 2009, pp. 42–56.

B. S. Chimni, "The Geopolitics of Refugee Studies: A View from the South," *Journal of Refugee Studies* 11:4, 1998, pp. 350–374.

David Collier and Colin Elman, "Qualitative and Multimethod Research: Organizations, Publication, and Reflections on Integration," in Janet M. Box-Steffensmeier, Henry E. Brady, and David Collier, eds., *The Oxford Handbook of Political Methodology*, Oxford: Oxford University Press, 2008, pp. 779–795.

Steven A. Cook, "Syria Is Turkey's Problem, Not America's," Council on Foreign Relations, 13 March 2020, at https://www.cfr.org/article/syria-turkeys-problem-not-americas.

———, "The Syrian War Is Over, and America Lost," *Foreign Policy*, 23 July 2018, at https://foreignpolicy.com/2018/07/23/the-syrian-war-is-over-and-america-lost/.

———, "Top Conflicts to Watch in 2021: What's Next for Syria," *Council on Foreign Relations*, 21 January 2021, at https://www.cfr.org/blog/top-conflicts-watch-2021-whats-next-syria.

Hannah Cooper, et al., *Funding The Humanitarian Response In Yemen: Are Donors Doing Their Fair Share?*, London: Oxfam, October 2020, at https://reliefweb.int/sites/reliefweb.int/files/resources/bn-funding-humanitarian-response-yemen-271020-en.pdf.

Heaven Crawley and Dimitris Skleparis, "Refugees, Migrants, Neither, Both: Categorical Fetishism and the Politics of Bounding in Europe's 'Migration Crisis'," *Journal of Ethnic and Migration Studies* 44:1, 2018, pp. 48–64.

"Country Summary: Syria," Human Rights Watch, January 2017, pp. 1–8.

Saleh Dabbakeh, "Iran: Saudi Airlift Vital Part of Bam Response," Geneva: *International Federation of Red Cross and Red Crescent Societies*, 23 January 2004, at https://reliefweb.int/report/iran-islamic-republic/iran-saudi-airlift-vital-part-bam-response.

Sam Dagher, *Assad or We Burn the Country: How One Family's Lust for Power Destroyed Syria*, New York: Little, Brown and Company, 2019.

Joyce Dalsheim, "On Demonized Muslims and Vilified Jews: Between Theory and Politics," *Comparative Studies in Society and History* 52:3, July 2010, pp. 581–603.

Uriel Dann, *Iraq under Qassem: A Political History, 1958–1963*, New York: Praeger, 1969.

Malin Delling, *Islam and Human Rights*, Goteborg University, Sweden, Department of Law, School of Economics and Commercial Law, 2004, at https://core.ac.uk/download/pdf/16310495.pdf.

Soliman Demir, *Arab Development Funds in the Middle East*, New York: Pergamon Press (for UNITAR), 1979.

Eliot Dickinson, *Globalization and Migration: A World in Motion*, London: Rowman and Littlefield, 2017.

Amy Doffegnies and Tamas Wells, "The Vernacularization of Human Rights Discourse in Myanmar: Rejection, Hybridization and Strategic Avoidance," *Journal of Contemporary Asia* 51:2, 2021, at https://www.tandfonline.com/doi/full/10.1080/00472336.2020.1865432?src=.

Antonio Donini, "Western Aid Agencies don't have a Humanitarian Monopoly," *Humanitarian Affairs Review*, Autumn 2004, pp.12–15, at http://www.humanitarian-review.org/upload/pdf/DoniniEnglishFinal.pdf.

Alan Dowty, *Closed Borders: The Contemporary Assault on Freedom of Movement*, New Haven and London: Yale University Press, 1987.

Paul Dresch, *A History of Modern Yemen*, Cambridge: Cambridge University Press, 2000.

Khadija Elmadmad, "Asylum in Islam and in Modern Refugee Law" *Refugee Survey Quarterly* 27:2, January 2008, pp. 51–63.

M. Murat Erdoğan, "SYRIANS-BAROMETER-2017: A Framework for Achieving Social Cohesion with Syrians in Turkey," SB-2017, at https://mmuraterdogan.files.wordpress.com/2016/06/syrians-barometer-executive-summary.pdf.

"Euro-African Dialogue on Migration and Development (Rabat Process)," *International Organization for Migration*, at https://www.iom.int/euro-african-dialogue-migration-and-development-rabat-process.

European Saudi Organization for Human Rights, *Deprivation of Nationality in Saudi Arabia: A Quarter of a Million People, and a Suffering for Nearly Half a Century*, Berlin: ESOHR, April 2016, at https://www.esohr.org/en/wp-content/uploads/2016/03/Deprivation-of-nationality-in-Saudi-Arabia.pdf.

Khaled Abou El Fadl, "Islamic Ethics, Human Rights and Migration," in Ray Jureidini and Said Fares Hassan, eds., *Migration and Islamic Ethics: Issues of Residence, Naturalisation and Citizenship*, Leiden and London: Brill, 2020, pp. 13–27.

Andrew Fallo, "Restoration as the Spirit of Islamic Justice," *Contemporary Justice Review* 23:4, 2020, pp. 430–443.

Far From Home: Future Prospects for Syrian Refugees in Iraq, Danish Refugee Council (DRC), International Rescue Committee (IRC) and Norwegian Refugee Council (NRC), Durable Solutions Platform, January 2019, at https://drc.ngo/media/aatg3dkd/far-from-home-future-prospects-for-syrian-refugees-in-iraq_-january2019.pdf.

Samih K. Farsoun, "Palestinian Diaspora," in Melvin Ember, Carol R. Ember, and Ian Skoggard, eds, *Encyclopedia of Diasporas*, Boston: Springer, 2005, at https://link.springer.com/referenceworkentry/10.1007%2F978-0-387-

Muhammad El Fasi and Ivan Hrbek, *Africa from the Seventh to the Eleventh Century*, Berkeley and Los Angeles: University of California Press, 1988.

Rick Fawn, "No Consensus with the Commonwealth, No Consensus with Itself? Canada and the Iraq War," *The Round Table* 97:397, 2008, pp. 519–533.

Ahmad Fawzi, *Twelve Prime Ministers*, Baghdad, n. p., 1984.

Gerald M. Feierstein, "Iran's Role in Yemen and Prospects for Peace," *The Iran Primer*, Washington, D.C.: The United States Institute of Peace, 6 December 2018, at

https://iranprimer.usip.org/blog/2018/dec/05/iran's-role-yemen-and-prospects-peace.

Erika Feller, "Refugees are Not mMigrants," *Refugee Survey Quarterly* 24:4, December 2005, pp. 27–35.

Niall Ferguson, *The War of the World: Twentieth-Century Conflict and the Descent of the West*, New York: Penguin Press, 2006.

Elena Fiddian-Qasmiyeh, "Introduction: Faith-Based Humanitarianism in Contexts of Forced Displacement," *Journal of Refugee Studies* 24:3, September 2011, pp. 429–439.

Elena Fiddian-Qasmiyeh, Gil Loescher, Katy Long, Nando Sigona, eds., *The Oxford Handbook of Refugee and Forced Migration Studies*, Oxford: Oxford University Press, 2014.

Marie-Laurence Flahaux and Hein De Haas, "African Migration: Trends, Patterns, Drivers," *Comparative Migration Studies* 4:1, 2016, at

https://comparativemigrationstudies.springeropen.com/track/pdf.

David P. Forsythe, "UNRWA, the Palestine Refugees, and World Politics: 1949–1969," *International Organization* 25:1, Winter 1971, pp. 26–45.

Ulrike Freitag, *The History of the Hajj as Heritage: Asset or Burden to the Saudi State?*, Leiden, The Netherlands: Brill, 2019.

Nanako Fujita, *Gunnar Myrdal's Theory of Cumulative Causation Revisited*, Nagoya, Japan: Nagoya University, Economic Research Center Discussion Paper, Number 147, April 2004, at

http://133.6.182.153/wp-content/uploads/2016/04/paper147.pdf.

Musa Furber, *UNHCR Zakat Collection And Distribution Report*, Abu Dhabi: Tabah Foundation, May 2017, at https://unhcrzakatfatwa.com/wp-content/uploads/2017/06/TR-1-UNHCR-Zakat-Collection-And-Distribution-English.pdf.

Elizabeth Fussell and Douglas S. Massey, "The Limits to Cumulative Causation: International Migration from Mexican Urban Areas," *Demography* 41:1, February 2004, pp. 151–171.

Habibu Umar Gado, *Al-Zakat: L'aumône*, Bassin, Mauritius: Éditions Notre Savoir, 2020.

Peter Gatrell, *The Making of the Modern Refugee*, Oxford: Oxford University Press, 2015.

F. Gregory Gause III, *Saudi–Yemeni Relations: Domestic Structures and Foreign Influence*, New York: Columbia University Press, 1990.

Matthew J. Gibney and Randall Hansen, eds., *Immigration and Asylum: From 1900 to the Present*, Santa Barbara, California: ABC-CLIO, 2005.

Ben Gidley and Hiranthi Jayaweera, *An Evidence Base On Migration And Integration In London*, ESRC Centre On Migration, Policy And Society, University of Oxford, July 2010, at https://www.london.gov.uk/sites/default/files/an_evidence_base_on_migration_and_integration_in_london.pdf.

Irial Glynn, "The Genesis and Development of Article 1 of the 1951 Refugee Convention," *Journal of Refugee Studies* 25:1, March 2012, pp. 134–148.

Steve J. Gold and Stephanie J. Nawyn, eds., *Routledge International Handbook of Migration Studies*, 2nd ed., Abingdon and New York: Routledge, 2020.

Elzbieta M. Gozdziak and Peter Marton, "Where the Wild Things Are: Fear of Islam and the Anti-Refugee Rhetoric in Hungary and in Poland," *Central and Eastern European Migration Review* 7:2, June 2018, pp. 1–27, at http://www.ceemr.uw.edu.pl/vol-7-no-2-2018/special-section/where-wild-things-are-fear-islam-and-anti-refugee-rhetoric-hungary.

"Gulf States Response to Syrian Refugee Crisis – A Myth Debunked," *Open source Investigations*, at http://www.opensourceinvestigations.com/syria/gulf-states-response-to-syrian-refugee-crisis-a-myth-debunked/.

António Guterres, "Millions Uprooted: Saving Refugees And The Displaced," *Foreign Affairs* 5:87, September/October 2008, pp. 90–99.

Hein De Haas, "Migration and Development: A Theoretical Perspective," *International Migration Review* 44:1, Spring 2010, pp. 227–264.

——, "The Internal Dynamics of Migration Processes: A Theoretical Inquiry," *Journal of Ethnic and Migration Studies* 36:10, 2010, pp. 1587–1617.

'Uthman Kamal Haddad, *Harakat Rashid 'Ali al-Kaylani Sanat 1941* [The Movement of Rashid 'Ali al-Kaylani in 1941], Sidon, Lebanon: Al-Maktabah al-'Asriyyah, ca. 1947–50.

Leen d'Haenens, Willem Joris, François Heinderyckx, eds., *Images of Immigrants and Refugees in Western Europe: Media Representations, Public Opinion and Refugees' Experiences*, Leuven, Belgium: Leuven University Press, 2019.

Ashraf Haidari, "Need to End Discrepancy Between Refugees and IDPs," *Raisina Debates*, Delhi: Observer Research Foundation, 5 November 2016, at https://www.orfonline.org/expert-speak/end-discrepancy-between-refugees-and-idps/.

Fred Halliday, *Revolution and Foreign Policy: The Case of South Yemen, 1967–1987*, Cambridge: Cambridge University Press, 1990.

Tomas Hammar, Grete Brochmann, Kristof Tamas, and Thomas Faist, *International Migration, Immobility and Development: Multidisciplinary Perspectives*, Abingdon, Oxon.: Routledge, 1997.

Badr-Edin El Hmidi, *Waqf and Zakat Institutions: The Socioeconomic Dimensions of Financial Accountability in Islam: A Theoretical and Practical Study*, Riga, Latvia: Noor [Shams] Publishing, 2019.

Sari Hanafi, "Gulf Response to the Syrian Refugee Crisis," *Sociology of Islam* 5 (2017), pp. 112–137.

John R. Harris and Michael P. Todaro, "Migration, Unemployment and Development: A Two-Sector Analysis," *The American Economic Review* 60:1, 1970, pp. 126–142.

Martin Harrow, "The Effect of the Iraq War on Islamist Terrorism in the West," *Cooperation and Conflict* 45:3, September 2010, pp. 274–293, at https://www.jstor.org/stable/45084609.

Jonathan Hassine, *Les Réfugiés et Déplacés de Syrie: Une Reconstruction Nationale en Question*, Paris: L'Harmattan, 2015.

James C. Hathaway and Michelle Foster, *The Law of Refugee Status*, Cambridge: Cambridge University Press, 2014.

Musab Hayatli, "Islam, International Law and the Protection of Refugees and IDPs," *Forced Migration Review*, June 2012, at https://www.fmreview.org/sites/fmr/files/FMRdownloads/en/FMRpdfs/Human-Rights/human-rights.pdf.

Friedrich Heckmann, Tanja Wunderlich, Susan F. Martin and Kelly McGrath, "Transatlantic Workshop on Human Smuggling," Georgetown Immigration Law Journal 15:167, 2000–2001, pp. 167–182.

Nicholas Van Hear, "Forcing the Issue: Migration Crises and the Uneasy Dialogue Between Refugee Research and Policy," *Journal of Refugee Studies* 25:1, March 2011, pp. 2–24.

David Held, Anthony McGrew, David Goldblatt and Jonathan Perraton, "Globalization," *Global Governance* 5:4, October-December 1999, pp. 483–496.

Lily Hindy, *Germany's Syrian Refugee Integration Experiment*, New York: The Century Foundation, 6 September 2018, at https://production-tcf.imgix.net/app/uploads/2018/09/03160422/germanys-syrian-refugee-integration-experiment.pdf.

Raymond Hinnebusch and Özlem Tür, eds., *Turkey–Syria Relations: Between Enmity and Amity*, London and New York: Routledge, 2016.

Marwan Hisham and Molly Crabapple, *Brothers of the Gun: A Memoir of the Syrian War*, New York: Random House, 2018.

Hans-henrik Holm and Georg Sorenson, eds., *Whose World Order? Uneven Globalization and the End of the Cold War*, Boulder: Westview Press, 1995.

Michael Horton, "The Unseen Hand: Saudi Arabian Involvement in Yemen," *Terrorism Monitor* 9:12, 24 March 2011, at https://jamestown.org/program/the-unseen-hand-saudi-arabian-.

Human Rights Watch, "Bangladesh: Halt Rohingya Relocations to Remote Island—Transfers Need Independent Assessment, Refugees' Informed Consent," New York: Human Rights Watch, 3 December 2020, at https://www.hrw.org/news/2020/12/03/bangladesh-halt-rohingya-relocations-remote-island.

———, *'Bangladesh Is Not My Country:' The Plight of Rohingya Refugees*, New York: Human Rights Watch, 5 August 2018, at https://www.hrw.org/sites/default/files/report_pdf/bangladesh0818_pdf.

Katalin Huzdik, *Migration Potential and Affecting Factors in Hungary in the First Decade of the 21st Century*, Godollo, Hungary: Szent István University Doctoral School of Management and Business Administration, 2014, at https://szie.hu/file/tti/archivum/Huzdik_ Katalin_thesis.pdf.

Masood Hyder, "Humanitarianism and the Muslim World," *The Journal of Humanitarian Assistance*, August 2007, at https://sites.tufts.edu/jha/archives/52.

International Bank for Reconstruction and Development, *Global Monitoring Report 2005: Millennium Development Goals—From Consensus to Momentum*, Washington D.C.: The World Bank, 2005.

International Committee of the Red Cross, "More than 1,000 Former Detainees from Yemen Conflict Transported Home," 16 October 2020, at https://www.icrc.org/en/document/more-1000-former-detainees-yemen-conflict-transported-home.

International Monetary Fund, *External Debt Statistics: Guide for Compilers and Users—Appendix III, Glossary*, Washington, D.C.: IMF, 28 August 2003, at https://stats.oecd.org/glossary/detail.asp?ID=6043.

"Iraqi Refugees, Asylum Seekers, and Displaced Persons: Current Conditions and Concerns in the Event of War," Human Rights Watch Briefing Paper, New York: Human Rights Watch, February 2003, at https://www.hrw.org/legacy/backgrounder/mena/iraq021203/iraq-bck021203.pdf.

Jaan Islam, *True Islam, Jihad, & Terrorism: Science of Islamic Foreign Policy*, New York: Nova Science Publishers, 2016.

Joseph G. Jabbra and Nancy W. Jabbra, "Consociational Democracy in Lebanon: A Flawed System of Governance," *Journal of Developing Societies* 17:2, January 2001, pp. 71–89.

Hosam al-Jablawi, "Syrian Refugees' Struggle with Temporary Status in Germany," *The Atlantic Council*, 26 February 2019, at https://www.atlantic-council.org/blogs/syriasource/syrian-refugees-struggle-with-temporary-status-in-germany/.

Ibrahim Jalal, "Five years on, has the Arab coalition achieved its objectives in Yemen?," Washington, D.C.: The Middle East Institute, 2 April 2020, at https://www.mei.edu/publications/five-years-has-arab-coalition-achieved-its-objectives-yemen.

Michael Jandl, "The Estimation of Illegal Migration in Europe," Studi Emigrazione/Migration Studies 41:153, March 2004, pp. 141–155.

Maja Janmyr, "No Country of Asylum: 'Legitimizing' Lebanon's Rejection of the 1951 Refugee Convention," *International Journal of Refugee Law* 29:3, 2017, pp. 438–465.

Sisira Jayasuriya and Peter McCawley, *The Asian Tsunami: Aid and Reconstruction after a Disaster*, Cheltenham, U.K.: Edward Edgar Publishing, 2010.

Roel Peter Wilhelmina Jennissen, *Macro-Economic Determinants of International Migration in Europe*, Amsterdam, Holland: Rozenberg Publishers, 2004, pp. 93–116.

Seth G. Jones, "The Escalating Conflict with Hezbollah in Syria," Washington, D.C.: Center for Strategic and International Studies, 20 June 2018, at https://www.csis.org/analysis/escalating-conflict-hezbollah-syria.

Jordan Ingo Forum, *Syrian Refugees in Jordan: A Protection Overview*, Jordan Ingo Forum, January 2018, at https://reliefweb.int/report/jordan/syrian-refugees-jordan-protection-overview-january-2018.

R. Josselson, Dan P. McAdams, and A. Lieblich, eds., *Up Close and Personal: The Teaching and Learning of Narrative Research*, Washington, D.C.: American Psychological Association Press, 2003.

Thomas Juneau, "Iran's Policy Towards the Houthis in Yemen: A Limited Return on a Modest Investment," *International Affairs* 92:3, May 2016, pp. 647–663.

Sophia Kagan, *Domestic Workers and Employers in the Arab States: Promising Practices and Innovative Models for a Productive Working Relationship*, ILO White Paper, International Labor Organization, Regional Office for Arab State, 2017, at https://www.ilo.org/wcmsp5/groups/public/—-arabstates/—-ro-beirut/documents/publication/wcms_619661.pdf.

Ivan Kalmar, "Islamophobia in the East of the European Union: An Introduction," *Patterns of Prejudice* 52:5, 2018, pp. 389–405.

Elaine Kamarck and Christine Stenglein, "How Many Undocumented Immigrants Are in the United States and Who Are They?," The Brookings Institution, 12 November 2019, at https://www.brookings.edu/policy2020/votervital/how-many-undocumented-immigrants-are-in-the-united-states-and-who-are-they/.

Michael W. Kelly, "Saudi Arabia: Oil and Saudi Development," *Harvard International Review* 8:4, March 1986, pp. 38–40.

Mohammad Tanzimuddin Khan and Saima Ahmed, "Dealing with the Rohingya Crisis: The Relevance of the General Assembly and R2P," *Asian Journal of Comparative Politics* 5:2, 2020, pp. 121–143.

Asma Shakir Khawaja, Asma Hussain Khan and Adnan Jamil, "An Insight Into Rohingya the Unwanted People," *Margalla Papers 2018*, Islamabad, Pakistan: National Defence University, 2018, pp. 53–62, at https://ndu.edu.pk/margalla-papers/doc/Margalla-Papers-2018.pdf.

Gaim Kibreab, Revisiting the Debate on People, Place, Identity and Displacement," *Journal of Refugee Studies* 12:4, 1999, pp. 384–410.

Joseph A. Kéchichian, *'Iffat Al Thunayan: An Arabian Queen*, Brighton, Chicago, Toronto: Sussex Academic Press, 2015.

———, *Power and Succession in Arab Monarchies*, Boulder, Colorado: Lynne Rienner Publishers, 2008.

Katelynn Kenworthy, "10 Important Facts About Refugees in Saudi Arabia," *The Borgen Project*, 15 June 2017, at https://borgenproject.org/refugees-in-saudi-arabia/.

Peter Kessler, "Iraqis Prepare to Leave Remote Desert Camp," *UNHCR News*, 28 July 2003, at https://www.unhcr.org/news/latest/2003/7/3f2560974/iraqis-

Hewa Haji Khedir, "IDPs in the Kurdistan Region of Iraq (KRI): Intractable Return and Absence of Social Integration Policy," *International Migration*, 2020, pp. 1–17, at https://onlinelibrary.wiley.com/doi/epdf/10.1111/imig.12716.

Kishan Khoday, *Development at the Crossroads: Reflections from the Arab Region*, New York: United Nations Development Program, 10 June 2014 at https://www.undp.org/content/undp/en/home/blog/2014/6/10/development-at-the-crossroads-reflections-from-the-arab-region-1.html.

Kelly Kimball, Robbie Gramer and Jack Detsch, "Beirut Explosion Imperils Lebanon's Refugee Population—and Aid Routes to Syria," *Foreign Policy*, 11 August 2020, at https://foreignpolicy.com/2020/08/11/lebanon-

King Salman Humanitarian and Relief Center, "Saudi Arabia Support to Rohingya Muslims," Rome, Italy: The Royal Embassy of Saudi Arabia in Rome, 2018, at

http://www.arabia-saudita.it/files/news/2018/07/rohingya_brochure_rev.pdf.

Nehginpao Kipgen, "Political Change in Burma: Transition from Democracy to Military Dictatorship (1948–62)," *Economic and Political Weekly* 46:20, 14–20 May 2011, pp. 48–55.

Kemal Kirişci, Jessica Brandt and M. Murat Erdoğan, "Syrian Refugees in Turkey: Beyond the Numbers," Washington, D.C.: The Brookings Institution, 19 June 2018, at https://www.brookings.edu/blog/order-from-chaos/2018/06/19/syrian-refugees-in-turkey-beyond-the-numbers/.

Johannes van der Klaauw, "Refugee Rights in Times of Mixed Migration: Evolving Status and Protection Issues," *Refugee Survey Quarterly* 28:4, 2009, pp. 59–86.

John Knudsen "Syria's Refugees in Lebanon: Brothers, Burden, and Bone of Contention," in Rosita Di Peri and Daniel Meier, eds, *Lebanon Facing The Arab Uprisings: Constraints and Adaptation*, New York: Palgrave Macmillan, 2017, pp. 135–154.

Kheir Al-Kodmany, "Planning for the Hajj: Political Power, Pragmatism, and Participatory GIS," *Journal of Urban Technology* 16:1, April 2009, pp. 5–45.

Joseph Kostiner, "Saudi Arabia and the Arab-Israeli Peace Process: The Fluctuation of Regional Coordination," *British Journal of Middle Eastern Studies* 36:4, December 2009, pp. 417–429.

———, *The Making of Saudi Arabia 1916–1936: From Chieftaincy to Monarchical State*, New York & Oxford: Oxford University Press, 1993.

Mary M. Kritz, Lin Lean Lim, Hania Zlotnik, *International Migration Systems: A Global Approach*, Oxford: Oxford Clarendon Press, 1992.

Daniel Krcmaric and Abel Escribà-Folch, "Dictators in Exile: Explaining the Destinations of Ex-Rulers," *The Journal of Politics* 79:2, April 2017, pp. 560–575.

Jens Manuel Krogstad, Jeffrey S. Passel and D'Vera Cohn, "5 Facts About Illegal Immigration in the U.S.," Washington, D.C.: Pew Research Center, 12 June 2019, at https://www.pewresearch.org/fact-tank/2019/06/12/5-facts-about-illegal-immigration-in-the-u-s/.

"Kurdistan Region of Iraq: Refugees' Movements Restricted—2 Miscarriages From Lack of Hospital Access," New York: Human Rights Watch, 27 November 2019, at https://www.hrw.org/news/2019/11/27/kurdistan-region-iraq-refugees-movements-restricted.

Lucia Kurekova, "Theories of Migration: Conceptual Review and Empirical Testing in the Context of the EU East-West Flows," Paper prepared for the Interdisciplinary Conference on Migration: Economic Change, Social Challenge, April 6–9, 2011, at University College London, pp. 8–9, at https://www.researchgate.net/profile/Lucia-Mytna-Kurekova-2/publication/268393052_Theories_of_migration_Conceptual_review_

Frank Laczko and Christine Aghazarm, eds., *Migration, Environment and Climate Change: Assessing the Evidence*, Geneva: International Organization for Migration, 2009, at https://environmentalmigration.iom.int/migration-environment-and-climate-change-assessing-evidence.

Barbara A. Leaf and Elana Delozier, "It's Time for a Serious Saudi–Houthi Back Channel," *War on the Rocks*, 9 January 2019, at https://warontherocks.com/2019/01/its-time-for-a-serious-saudi-houthi-back-channel/.

Lebanon: Exiled and Suffering—Palestinian Refugees In Lebanon, Amnesty International, October 2007, at https://web.archive.org/web/20131211203636/http://www.amnesty.org/en/library/info/MDE18/010/2007.

"Lebanon: There are More than 1.7 million Refugees in Lebanon. Most struggle to make ends meet," Anera (American Near East Refugee Aid), at https://www.anera.org/where-we-work/lebanon/.

Michiel Leezenberg, "Iraqi Kurdistan: A Porous Political Space," *Anatoli* 8, 2017, pp. 107–131.

Legal Status of Refugees: Egypt, Jordan, Lebanon, and Iraq, Washington, D.C.: The Law Library of Congress, Global Legal Research Center, December 2013, at https://www.loc.gov/law/help/refugees/2014-010156%20RPT.pdf.

Bernard Lewis, "Khadim al-Haramayn," in, P. Bearman, Th. Bianquis, C.E. Bosworth, E. van Donzel, W.P. Heinrichs, eds., *Encyclopaedia of Islam, Second Edition*, Leiden, The Netherlands: E. J. Brill, at http://dx.doi.org/10.1163/15733912_islam_SIM_4118.

Yi Li, "Saudi Arabia's Economic Diplomacy through Foreign Aid: Dynamics, Objectives and Mode," *Asian Journal of Middle Eastern and Islamic Studies* 13:1, March 2019, pp. 110–122.

Andrew Lipp, *The Muslim Brotherhood: Exploring divergent views in Saudi Arabia and Qatar*, Masters Thesis, Ames, Iowa: Iowa State University, 2019, at https://lib.dr.iastate.edu/cgi/viewcontent.cgi?article=8048&context=etd.

"List of OIC Member States Parties to the 1951 Convention Relating to the Status of Refugees and the 1967 Protocol," *Refugee Survey Quarterly* 27:2, 2008, p. 94.

Robert E. B. Lucas and Oded Stark, "Motivations to Remit: Evidence from Botswana," *Journal of Political Economy* 93:5, October 1985, pp. 901–918.

Aron Lund, "Syria in Crisis: Exile Has No Religion," Beirut: Malcolm H. Kerr Carnegie Middle East Center, 15 December 2014, at https://carnegie-mec.org/diwan/57512.

Magnus Lundgren, "Mediation in Syria: Initiatives, Strategies, and Obstacles,

2011–2016," *Contemporary Security Policy* 37:2, April 2016, pp. 283–298.

Charlotte Lysa, "A Recent History of Refugees in Saudi Arabia," *Ref-Arab Project*, 12 November 2020, at http://refugeehistory.org/blog/2020/11/12/a-recent-history-of-refugees-in-saudi-arabia.

Pardis Mahdavi, *Crossing the Gulf: Love and Family in Migrant Lives*, Stanford, California: Stanford University Press, 2016.

'Aqeel Mahfudh, *Syria and Turkey: A Turning Point or a Historical Bet?*, Doha, Qatar: Arab Center for Research and Policy Studies, 2012, at https://www.jstor.org/stable/resrep12703?seq=1#metadata_info_tab_contents.

Ragaei El Mallakh and Mihssen Kadhim, "Arab Institutionalized Development Aid: An Evaluation," *The Middle East Journal* 30:4, Autumn 1976, pp. 471–484.

Robert Malley, The Unwanted Wars: Why the Middle East Is More Combustible Than Ever," *Foreign Affairs* 98:6, November–December 2019, pp. 38–46.

Shabia Mantoo, "War Turns Yemen into Humanitarian Catastrophe," Geneva: UNHCR, 20 December 2016, at https://www.unrefugees.org/news/what-is-happening-in-yemen-update-from-unhcr-representative/.

Katrin Marchand, Julia Reinold and Raphael Dias e Silva, *Study on Migration Routes in the East and Horn of Africa*, Maastricht Graduate School of Governance, August 2017, at https://www.google.com/url?sa=t&rct=j&q=&esrc=s&source=web&cd=&ved=2ahUKEwiss8DvybzvAhWXQhUIHSH2BYUQFjAAegQIBhAD&url=https%3A%2F%2Fwww.merit.unu.edu%2Fpublications%2Fuploads%2F1517475164.pdf&usg=AOvVaw19xR6Fd59VOjPPlngl1iBk.

David Mathieson, *Perilous Plight: Burma's Rohingya Take to the Seas*, New York: Human Rights Watch 2009, p. 3, at https://www.hrw.org/report/2009/05/26/perilous-plight/burmas-rohingya-take-seas#.

"Massacre of Hama: Genocide and A crime against Humanity," Edgware, United Kingdom: The Syrian Human Rights Committee, February 1982, at https://web.archive.org/web/20130522172157/http://www.shrc.org/data/aspx/d5/2535.aspx.

Douglas S. Massey, Jorge Durand, Nolan J. Malone, "Principles of Operation: Theories of International Migration," in Carola Suarez-Orozco, Marcelo Suarez-Orozco, Desiree Baolian Qin-Hilliard, eds., *The New Immigration: An Interdisciplinary Reader*, New York: Routledge, 2004.

Douglas S. Massey, Joaquín Arango, Graeme Hugo, Ali Kouaouci, Adela Pellegrino and J. Edward Taylor, "Theories of International Migration: A Review and Appraisal," *Population and Development Review* 19:3, September 1993, pp. 431–466.

Eytan Meyers, "Theories of International Immigration Policy: A Comparative Analysis," *International Migration Review* 34:4, December 2000, pp. 1262–1263, at https://www.jstor.org/stable/2675981?read-now=1&refreqid=excelsior%3Afa41998e6c807f812550dcdfe2e85c11&seq=18#page_scan_tab_

"Migrant Workers In Saudi Arabia," FairsQuare Policy Brief #1, October 2020, at https://fairsq.org/wp-content/uploads/2020/11/FS-Policy-Brief-1-Saudi-Arabia-1020.pdf.

Claudio Minca, Danica Šanti , and Dragan Umek, "Managing the 'Refugee Crisis' Along the Balkan Route: Field Notes from Serbia," in Cecilia Menjivar, Marie Ruiz, and Immanuel Ness, eds., *The Oxford Handbook of Migration Crises*, Oxford: Oxford University Press 2019, pp. 445–464.

Ian Molho, "Theories of Migration: A Review," *Scottish Journal of Political Economy* 60:5, November 2013, pp. 526–556.

James Morrissey, "Environmental Change and Forced Migration: A State of the Art Review," Refugee Studies Centre, Oxford Department of International Development, Queen Elizabeth House, University of Oxford, January 2009, at
https://www.rsc.ox.ac.uk/files/files-1/dp-environmental-change-forced-migration-2009.pdf.

Shaikh Safiur Rahman Mubarakpuri, *History of Makkah*, Riyadh: Darussalam, 2002.

Al-Mughtaribun: Al-Rafid al-Asasi lil-Tanmiyyah al-Mustadamah [Emigrants: An Essential Contribution to Sustainable Development], Sana'a: Al-Majlis al-Istishari, Wizarat al-Shu'un al-Mughtaribin [Ministry for Expatriates], 1999.

'Abd al-Waahid al-Maytami Muhammad, "Le Marche du Travail Yemenite apres l'Unification," *Revue du Monde Musulman et de la Mediterranee*, Number 67, 1993, pp. 121–129.

Tobias Müller, "Constructing Cultural Borders: Depictions of Muslim Refugees in British and German Media," *Zeitschrift für Vergleichende Politikwissenschaft* [Comparative Governance and Politics] 12, March 2018, pp. 263–277.

Martha Mundy, *The Strategies of the Coalition in the Yemen War: Aerial bombardment and food war*, Sommerville, Massachusetts: World Peace Foundation, 9 October 2018, at https://sites.tufts.edu/wpf/strategies-of-the-coalition-in-the-yemen-war/.

Lilly Myat, "The Rohingya Refugee Crisis: Social, Economic and Environmental Implications for the Local Community in Bangladesh," Masters Thesis, College of Humanities, Arts and Social Sciences, Adelaide, Australia: Flinders University, 2018, at
https://flex.flinders.edu.au/file/20455f70-482e-480d-843e-288609037d12/1/thesis%20myat%202018.pdf.

Farzin Nadimi and Michael Knights, "Iran's Support to Houthi Air Defenses in Yemen," *POLICYWATCH 2953*, Washington, D.C.: The Washington Institute for Near East Policy, 4 April 2018, at https://www.washingtoninstitute.org/policy-analysis/view/irans-support-to-houthi-air-defenses-in-yemen.

Satoru Nakamura, "Saudi Arabian Diplomacy during the Syrian Humanitarian

Crisis: Domestic Pressure, Multilateralism, and Regional Rivalry for an Islamic State," Tokyo: IDE-JETRO [Institute of Developing Economics at the Japan External Trade Organization], 2013, at https://www.ide.go.jp/library/Japanese/Publish/Download/Seisaku/pdf/201307_mide_13.pdf.

"National Report Submitted in Accordance with Paragraph 5 of the Annex to Human Rights Council Resolution 16/21—Saudi Arabia," Human Rights Council, Working Group on the Universal Periodic Review Seventeenth session, Geneva: United Nations General Assembly, 21 October–1 November 2013, A/HRC/WG.6/17/SAU/1, pp. 14–15, at https://www.upr-info.org/sites/default/files/document/saudi_arabia/session_17_-_october_20 13/a_hrc_wg.6_17_sau_1_e.pdf.

Anagha Neelakantan, *New Attacks on Muslim Villagers in Myanmar's Rakhine State*, Brussels: International Crisis Group, 26 January 2014, at https://www.crisisgroup.org/asia/south-east-asia/myanmar/new-attacks-muslim-villagers-myanmar-s-rakhine-state.

Kassandra Neranjan and Sakshi Shetty, "From Encounter to Exodus: The Rohingya Muslims of Myanmar," Research Paper, 2018, at https://www.researchgate.net/publication/326922106_From_Encounter_to_Exodus_History_of_the_Rohingya_Muslims.

Kathleen Newland, The Iraqi Refugee Crisis: The Need for Action, Washington, D.C.: Migration Policy Institute, January 2008, at https://www.migrationpolicy.org/research/iraqi-refugee-crisis-need-action.

Julie M. Norman, "Saudi Arabia Doesn't 'Do' Refugees—It's Time to Change That," *The Conversation*, 23 September 2015, at http://theconversation.com/saudi-arabia-doesnt-do-refugees-its-time-to-change-that-47307.

William Ochsenwald, *The Hijaz Railroad*, Charlottesville: The University Press of Virginia, 1980, pp. 117–118.

"Official Development Assistance (ODA)," at http://www.oecd.org/dac/financing-sustainable-development/development-finance-standards/official-development-assistance.htm.

Gwenn Okhrulik and Patrick Conge, "National Autonomy, Labor Migration and Political Crisis: Yemen and Saudi Arabia," *The Middle East Journal* 51:4, Autumn 1997, pp. 554–565.

Abdul Azeez Maruf Olayemi, Abdul Majeed Hamzah Alabi, Ahmad Hidayah Buang, "Islamic Human Rights Law: A Critical Evaluation of UIDHR & CDHRI in Context of UDHR," *Journal of Islam, Law and Judiciary* 1:3, 2015, pp. 27–36.

Karen O'Reilly, *International Migration and Social Theory*, New York: Palgrave Macmillan, 2012.

Organization of the Petroleum Exporting Countries, "Brief History," Vienna, Austria: OPEC, at https://www.opec.org/opec_web/en/abot_us/24.htm.

Asher Orkaby, "Saudi Arabia's War with the Houthis: Old Borders, New Lines,"

PolicyWatch 2404, Washington, D.C.: The Washington Institute for Near East Policy, 9 April 2015, at https://www.washingtoninstitute.org/policy-analysis/view/saudi-arabias-war-with-the-houthis-old-borders-new-lines.

Tarek Osman, "Turks and Arabs," *The Cairo Review of Global Affairs*, Tahrir Forum, 17 September 2014, at https://www.thecairoreview.com/tahrir-forum/turks-and-arabs/.

OXFAM, Funding the Humanitarian Response in Yemen: Are Donors Doing Their Fair Share?, *Briefing Note*, October 2020, p. 7, at https://www.oxfam.org/en/research/funding-humanitarian-response-yemen.

Mehmer Ozalp, "The Syrian War is Not Over, it's Just on a New Trajectory: Here's What You Need to Know," *The Conversation*, 5 February 2019, at https://theconversation.com/the-syrian-war-is-not-over-its-just-on-a-new-trajectory-heres-what-you-need-to-know-110292.

Erlend Paasche, "Elites and Emulators: The Evolution of Iraqi Kurdish Asylum Migration to Europe," *Migration Studies* 8:2, 2020, pp. 189–208, at https://watermark.silverchair.com/mny036.pdf.

"Palestine and Saudi Arabia: Residence Status of Stateless Palestinians, including access to employment, education, health care and other services, and the ability to travel in and out of the country; requirements and procedures to renew residence status, including whether stateless Palestinians whose permits have expired face deportation and detention (2015–November 2017)," Ottawa, Canada: Immigration and Refugee Board of Canada, 14 November 2017, at https://www.refworld.org/docid/5afadfd94.html.

Serena Parekh, "Reframing the Refugee Crisis: From Rescue to Interconnection," *Ethics and Global Politics* 13, 2020, pp. 21–32.

Jennifer R. Peck, "Can Hiring Quotas Work? The Effect of the Nitaqat Program on the Saudi Private Sector," *American Economic Journal: Economic Policy* 9:2, May 2017, pp. 316–347.

Antoine Pécoud and Julia Van Dessel, "Campagnes de Dissuasion Massive," *Le Monde Diplomatique*, Number 804, March 2021, p. 16.

Christopher Phillips, *The Battle for Syria: International Rivalry in the New Middle East*, New Heaven, Connecticut: Yale University Press, 2016.

Philippines, Republic of the, "A Guide to Saudi Labor And Immigration Rules," 15 April 2013, at https://dfa.gov.ph/dfa-news/statements-and-advisoriesupdate/164-a-guide-to-saudi-labor-and-immigration-rules.

Michael, J. Piore, *Birds of Passage: Migrant Labor and Industrial Societies*, Cambridge: Cambridge University Press, 1979.

Nilesh Prakash, *The Development Impact of Workers' Remittances in Fiji*, a thesis presented in partial fulfilment of the requirements for the degree of Master of Arts at Massey University, Palmerston North, New Zealand, 2009, at https://mro.massey.ac.nz/xmlui/bitstream/handle/10179/1281/

Protection Context For Migrants Passing Through Yemen: A Baseline, Meraki Labs, 2019, at https://reliefweb.int/sites/reliefweb.int/files/resources/EN_Meraki_%20Yemen_%20Migration%20Report.pdf.

Mohammad Hassan Al-Qadhi, *The Iranian Role in Yemen and its Implications on the Regional Security*, Riyadh: Arabian Gulf Centre for Iranian Studies (AGCIS), 2017, at
https://rasanah-iiis.org/english/wp-content/uploads/sites/2/2017/12/The-Iranian-Role-in-Yemen-and-its-Implications-on-the-Regional-Security -.pdf.

Mohamed Mokhtar Qandil, *The Muslim Brotherhood and Saudi Arabia: From Then to Now*, Washington, D.C.: The Washington Institute for Near East Policy, 18 May 2018, at https://www.washingtoninstitute.org/policy-analysis/muslim-brotherhood-and-saudi-arabia-then-now.

Asrar Qureshi, *My Pilgrimage to Makkah: Day to Day Recount of Hajj 2019*, n.c.: n. p., 2020.

Tufail Ahmad Qureshi, "Justice In Islam," *Islamic Studies* 21:2, Summer 1982, pp. 35–51.

Amal Qutub, Nazir Khan, and Mahdi Qasqas, "Islam and Social Justice," in Norma Jean Profitt and Cyndy Baskin, eds., *Spirituality and Social Justice: Spirit in the Political Quest for a Just World*, Toronto: Canadian Scholars' Press, 2019, pp. 131–152.

Robert G. Rabil, *The Syrian Refugee Crisis in Lebanon: The Double Tragedy of Refugees and Impacted Host Communities*, Lanham, Maryland: Lexington Books, 2016.

"Refugee facts: What is a Refugee," Washington, D.C.: USA for UNHCR, at https://www.unrefugees.org/refugee-facts/what-is-a-refugee/.

Richard Reid, *Shallow Graves: A Memoir of the Ethiopia-Eritrea War*, London: Hurst, 2020.

Anthony H. Richmond, "Sociological Theories of International Migration: The Case of Refugees," *Current Sociology* 36:2, June 1988, pp. 7–25.

Asaf Romirowsky, "Arab-Palestinian Refugees," *Israel Studies* 24:2, Summer 2019, pp. 91–102.

Jeffrey Scott Rosen, *Remittances, Investment, and Portfolio Allocations: An Analysis of Remittance Usage and Risk-Tolerance*, doctoral dissertation, Ohio State University, 2007, at
https://etd.ohiolink.edu/apexprod/rws_etd/send_file/send?accession=osu1172936345&disposition=inline.

Lawrence Rosen, *Islam and the Rule of Justice: Image and Reality in Muslim Law and Culture*, Chicago and London: The University of Chicago Press, 2018.

Kenneth Roth, "Syria: Events of 2019," Human Rights Watch, at
https://www.hrw.org/world-report/2020/country-chapters/syria#.

Tom Ruys and Luca Ferro, "Weathering the Storm: Legality and Legal Implications of the Saudi-Led Military Intervention In Yemen," *International and Comparative Law Quarterly* 65:1, January 2016, pp. 61–98.

Senada Selo Sabic, "The Impact of the Refugee Crisis in the Balkans: A Drift Towards Security," *Journal of Regional Security*, 12:1, 2017, pp. 51–74.

Mahmud Sadiq, *Hiwar Hawlah Suriyyah* [Dialogue About Syria], London: Dar 'Uqadh, 1993.

Imad Salamey, "Failing Consociationalism in Lebanon and Integrative Options," *International Journal of Peace Studies* 14:2 (Autum/Winter 2009), pp. 83–105, at https://www.jstor.org/stable/41852994.

Issam M. Saliba, "Regulation of Foreign Aid: Saudi Arabia," Washington. D.C.: The Library of Congress, October 2011, at
https://www.loc.gov/law/help/foreign-aid/saudiarabia.php.

Yusuf Salih, *Al-Laji'un al-'Iraqiyyun fil-Sa'udiyyah* [Iraqi Refugees in Saudi Arabia], Riyadh: Maktabat al-'Arabi al-Hadith, 1993.

Peter Salisbury, *Yemen and the Saudi–Iranian 'Cold War'*, London: The Royal Institute of International Affairs [Chatham House], February 2015, p. 5, at https://www.chathamhouse.org/sites/default/files/field/field_document/20150218YemenIranSaudi.pdf.

Barak A. Salmoni, Bryce Loidolt, and Madeleine Wells, *Regime and Periphery in Northern Yemen: The Huthi Phenomenon*, Santa Monica, California: RAND, 2010, at
https://www.rand.org/content/dam/rand/pubs/monographs/2010/RAND_MG962.pdf.

Paul Salopek, "Walking with Migrants," *National Geographic*, August 2019, pp. 40–63.

Ben Sanders and Merrill Smith, "The Iraqi Refugee Disaster," *World Policy Journal* 24:3, Fall 2007, pp. 23–28.

Alicia Sanders-Zakre, "What You Need to Know About Chemical Weapons Use in Syria," Arms Control Association, 23 September 2018 [Updated on 14 March 2019], at https://www.armscontrol.org/blog/2018-09-23/what-you-need-know-about-chemical-weapons-use-syria.

"Saudi Arabia," Joint Submission to the Human Rights Council at the 31st Session of the United Nations Universal Periodic Review, New York: United Nations, 29 March 2018, at
http://www.institutesi.org/UPR31_SaudiArabia.pdf.

"Saudi Arabia's Population Statistics of 2021," Global Media Insight, 8 March 2021, at https://www.globalmediainsight.com/blog/saudi-arabia-population-statistics/.

"Saudi Arabia Sentences Loujain al-Hathloul to Prison: Human Rights Advocacy is not a Crime," Berlin: The European Saudi Organization for Human Rights (ESOHR), 29 December 2020, at
https://www.esohr.org/en/?p=3195.

"Saudi Arabia: Situation of Bidoons, including ability to obtain a passport; whether a person born to a Saudi mother and Bidoon father can obtain Saudi citizenship, and would be issued a Saudi passport as a minor (2014–June 2016)," Ottawa, Canada: Immigration and Refugee Board of Canada, 6 June 2016, at
https://www.refworld.org/docid/584406344.html.

Sa'udi Arabia, Kingdom of, Ministry of Economy and Planning, and United

Nations Development Program, *Millennium Development Goals: 1429 H/2008* at
http://www.undp.org/content/dam/undp/library/MDG/english/MDG%2520Country%2520Reports/Saudi%2520Arabia/KSA_MDG_Report_3_2008_English.pdf

———, "Population by Nationality and Gender, 2019," General Authority of Statistics, at https://www.stats.gov.sa/en/5680.

———, "Saudi Arabia: Amendment to the Income Tax & Zakat Regulations and Amnesty Extension," 8 October 2020, at
https://www.pwc.com/m1/en/services/tax/me-tax-legal-news/2020/saudi-arabia-amendment-income-tax-zakat-regulations-amnesty-extension.html.

———, "Saudi Arabia Citizenship System," Riyadh: Ministry of the Interior, available at http://www.refworld.org/pdfid/3fb9eb6d2.pdf.

———, "Saudi Arabia Pledges $75M More to Support Refugees," 21 September 2016, Washington, D.C.: Royal Embassy of Saudi Arabia, at https://www.saudiembassy.net/press-release/saudi-arabia-pledges-75m-more-support-refugees.

———, "Saudi Arabia Received 2.5 Million Syrians since Beginning of Conflict," 11 September 2015, Washington, D.C.: Royal Embassy of Saudi Arabia, at https://www.saudiembassy.net/saudi-arabia-received-25-million-syrians-beginning-conflict.

———, "The Governor's Message," Riyadh: The General Authority of Zakat and Tax, at https://gazt.gov.sa/en/AboutUs/Pages/Message.aspx.

"Saudi Arabia: Unwelcome 'Guests': The Plight of Iraqi Refugees," New York: Amnesty International, Index number: MDE 23/001/1994, 9 May 1994, at https://www.amnesty.org/download/Documents/184000/mde230011994en.pdf.

Sa'udi Fund for Development, *Annual Report 2019*, at
https://www.sfd.gov.sa/en/web/guest/publications/-/asset_publisher/EkiAOIa5aWyu/content/2019-annual-report.

Reena Sehgal, "Nitaqat Law: Will it Solve Saudi Arabia's Unemployment Problems?," Delhi: Observer Research Foundation, 8 July 2013, at https://www.orfonline.org/research/nitaqat-law-will-it-solve-saudi-arabias-unemployment-problems/.

Faruq al-Shar', *Al-Riwayah al-Mafqudah* [The Missing Account], Beirut: al-Markaz al-'Arabi lil-Abhath wa-Dirasat al-Siyasat, 2015.

Jeremy M. Sharp, "Yemen: Civil War and Regional Intervention," Washington, D.C.: Congressional Research Service [R43960], 21 March 2019, p. 15, available at
https://www.everycrsreport.com/files/20180824_R43960_71ff8842b861ec46d818c980e1b5cbaacd5c1799.pdf.

Howard J. Shatz, "The Syrian Civil War Is Coming to an End," Santa Monica, CA: RAND, 8 April 2019, at https://www.rand.org/blog/2019/04/the-syrian-civil-war-is-coming-to-an-end.html.

Michael Stephens, "Migrant Crisis: Why the Gulf States are not Letting Syrians in," *Royal United Services Institute* (RUSI), Doha, 7 September 2015, at https://www.bbc.com/news/world-middle-east-34173139.

Ayman Saleh, Serdar Aydin and Orhan Kocak, "A comparative Study of Syrian Refugees in Turkey, Lebanon, and Jordan: Healthcare Access and Delivery," *International Journal of Society Systems Science*, 8:14, April 2018, at https://dergipark.org.tr/tr/download/article-file/454654.

Issam M. Saliba, "Regulation of Foreign Aid: Saudi Arabia," Washington. D.C.: The Library of Congress, October 2011, at https://www.loc.gov/law/help/foreign-aid/saudiarabia.php.

Patrick Seale, *Asad: The Struggle for the Middle East*, Berkeley and Los Angeles: University of California Press, 1990.

———, *The Struggle for Syria: A Study of Post-War Arab Politics (1945–1958)*, New Heaven, Connecticut: Yale University Press, 1987.

Tom Segev, *1949: The First Israelis*, New York: The Free Press, 2018.

———, *One Palestine, Complete*, New York: Henry Holt and Company, 2001.

Andrew E. Shacknove, "Who is a Refugee?," *Ethics* 95:2, January 1985, pp. 274–284.

Sherifa Shafie, "Palestinian Refugees in Lebanon," *Forced Migration Online*, accessed on 28 May 2017, at http://www.forcedmigration.org/research-resources/expert-guides/palestinian-refugees-in-lebanon/fmo018.pdf

Abbas Shiblak, "The Lost Tribes of Arabia," *Forced Migration Review*, April 2009, at https://core.ac.uk/download/pdf/27063823.pdf.

———, "Stateless Palestinians," *Forced Migration Review* 26, August 2006, pp. 8–9, at http://www.fmreview.org/sites/fmr/files/FMRdownloads/en/palestine/shiblak.pdf.

Ahmad Ibrahim Shukri, *Education Manpower Needs and Socio-Economic Development in Saudi Arabia*, Doctoral Dissertation, University of London, United Kingdom, 1972.

Larry Sjaastad, "The Costs and Returns of Human Migration," *Journal of Political Economy* 70:5, Part 2: Investment in Human Beings, October 1962, pp. 80–93.

Claudena Skran, *Refugees in Inter-War Europe: The Emergence of a Regime*, Oxford: Clarendon Press, 1995.

Statista, "Largest Donors of Humanitarian Aid Worldwide in 2020 (in million U.S. dollars), by country," January 2021, at https://www.statista.com/statistics/275597/largers-donor-countries-of-aid-worldwide/.

Yvonne Stolz and Joerg Baten, "Brain Drain in the Age of Mass Migration: Does Relative Inequality Explain Migrant Selectivity?," *Explorations in Economic History* 49:2, 2012, pp. 205–220.

Kathy Sullivan, "Water from a Stone: Jordanians Stretch Meager Resources to Sustain Syrian Refugees," *USAID Frontlines*, July 2013, at https://blog.usaid.gov/2013/04/water-from-a-stone-jordanians-stretch-meager-resources-to-sustain-syrian-refugees/.

Marisa Sullivan, *Hezbollah in Syria*, Middle East Security Report Number 19,

Washington, D.C.: Institute for the Study of War, 1 April 2014, at https://www.jstor.org/stable/resrep07896?seq=1#metadata_info_tab_contents.

"Sunnis Struggle in Latakia, Says Citizen Journalist," *Syria Direct*, 24 November 2014, at https://syriadirect.org/sunnis-struggle-in-latakia-says-citizen-journalist/.

Jamal S. al-Suwaidi, ed., *The Yemeni War of 1994: Causes and Consequences*, London: Saqi Books [for the Abu Dhabi-based Emirates Center for Strategic Studies and Research], 1995.

Syria Confronting Fragmentation! Impact of Syrian Crisis Report, Quarterly based report (2015), n.p.: Syrian Centre for Policy Research, February 2016, p. 61, at http://scpr-syria.org/publications/confronting-fragmentation/.

Syrian Observatory for Human Rights, "During 7 Consecutive Years . . . about 511 Thousand People Killed Since the Start of the Syrian Revolution in 2011," Coventry, United Kingdom: Syrian Observatory for Human Rights, 12 March 2018, at http://www.syriahr.com/en/?p=86573.

Syrian Observatory for Human Rights, "On International Human Rights Day: Millions of Syrians Robbed of 'rights' and 593 Thousand killed in a Decade," Syrian Observatory for Human Rights, 9 December 2020, at https://www.syriahr.com/en/195385/.

Sherine El Taraboulsi-McCarthy, *A Kingdom of Humanity? Saudi Arabia's Values, Systems and Interests in Humanitarian Action*, Humanitarian Policy Group Working Paper, London: Overseas Development Institute, September 2017.

Edward J. Taylor, "The New Economics of Labor Migration and the Role of Remittances in the Migration Process," *International Migration* 37:1, March 1999, pp. 63–88.

John Telford and John Cosgrave, "The International Humanitarian System and the 2004 Indian Ocean Earthquake and Tsunamis," *Disasters* 31:1, 2007, pp. 1–28.

The Arab Refugee Paradox: An Overview of Refugee Legislations in the Arab Middle East, Baghdad: Al Nahrain Center for Strategic Studies, 2016, at https://www.kas.de/c/document_library/get_file?uuid=554c5e8e-7c06-a5a5-a73d-06023be2bd88&groupId=252038.

Hélène Thiollet, "From Migration Hub to Asylum Crisis: The Changing Dynamics of Contemporary Migration in Yemen," in Helen Lackner, ed., *Why Yemen Matters*, London: Saqi Books, 2014, pp. 265–285.

———, *Refugees and Migrants from Eritrea to the Arab World, the Case of Sudan, Yemen and Saudi Arabia 1997–2007*, Cairo, Egypt: American University in Cairo Press, 2007.

"Timeline of Syrian Chemical Weapons Activity, 2012–2018," Washington, D.C.: Arms Control Association, at https://www.armscontrol.org/factsheets/Timeline-of-Syrian-Chemical-Weapons-Activity.

Anna Triandafyllidou, *Routledge Handbook of Immigration and Refugee Studies*, 2nd ed., Abingdon and New York: Routledge, 2019.

Charles Tripp, *A History of Iraq*, 3rd ed., Cambridge: Cambridge University Press, 2007.

Turkey's Syrian Refugees: Defusing Metropolitan Tensions, International Crisis Group, Europe Report Number 248, 29 January 2018, at https://d2071andvip0wj.cloudfront.net/248-turkey-s-syrian-refugees.pdf.

Farouk Al-Umar, *Rashid al-kilani's Refuge to King Abdul-Aziz Between Arabic Tradition and Diplomacy: World Conference Researches on King Abdulaziz History*, Riyadh: King Faisal Center for Research and Islamic Studies, 1985.

United Kingdom, Select Committee on Economic Affairs, *The Economic Impact of Immigration, Volume 1, HL Paper 82-I*, London: United Kingdom House of Lords, 1 April 2008.

United Nations, "Arab Versus Asian Migrant workers in the GCC countries," UN Expert Group Meeting on International Migration and Development in the Arab Region, Population Division Department of Economic and Social Affairs, United Nations, Beirut, 15–17 May 2006.

———, Charter of the United Nations, "Chapter IX: International Economic and Social Co-Operation, Article 55c," San Francisco: United Nations, 26 June 1945, at
https://www.un.org/en/sections/un-charter/chapter-ix/index.html.

———, Development Programme, *Climate Change Vulnerability Index, 2017*, at https://reliefweb.int/report/world/climate-change-vulnerability-index-2017.

———, General Assembly, "Report of the United Nations High Commissioner for Refugees—Covering the period 1 July 2019–30 June 2020," A/75/12, New York: United Nations, at
https://www.unhcr.org/excom/bgares/5f69c6ca4/report-united-nations-high-commissioner-refugees-covering-period-1-july.html.

———, High Commissioner for Refugees, *2018 Annual Report*, 3RP Regional, Refugee & Resilience Plan 2018–2019 in Response to the Syria Crisis, Geneva: UNHCR, at
https://data2.unhcr.org/en/documents/download/68557.

———, High Commissioner for Refugees, *Desperate Journeys: Refugees and Migrants Arriving in Europe and at Europe's Borders (January–December 2018)*, Geneva: United Nations, January 2019, at https://www.unhcr.org/desperate-journeys/#.

———, High Commissioner for Refugees, *Global Trends: Forced Displacement 2019*, Geneva: UNHCR, 2020, at
https://www.unhcr.org/5ee200e37.pdf.

———, High Commissioner for Refugees, "*Handbook on Procedures and Criteria for Determining Refugee Status under the 1951 Convention and the 1967 Protocol Relating to the status of Refugees*, HCR/IP/4/Eng/REV.1, Geneva: United Nations High Commissioner for Refugees, 1992.

———, High Commissioner for Refugees, "Information Kit: Syrian Refugees—Iraq, Humanitarian Inter-Agency Achievements," *3RP Regional, Refugee & Resilience Plan 2017–2018*, Number 17, May 2018, at
https://data2.unhcr.org/en/documents/details/64021.

———, High Commissioner for Refugees, "Jordan: Zaatari Refugee Camp," January 2021, at https://reliefweb.int/sites/reliefweb.int/files/resources/01%20Zaatari%20Fact%20Sheet%20January%202021.pdf.

———, High Commissioner for Refugees, "Quarterly Regional Cash Assistance Monitoring Update," January to March 2020 (Q1), at https://data.unhcr.org/en/documents/details/77775.

———, High Commissioner for Refugees, *Syrian Regional Refugee Response*, 3 March 2021, Geneva: UNHCR, at https://data2.unhcr.org/en/situations/syria.

———, High Commissioner for Refugees, "Syria Regional Refugee Response," *UNHCR Syria Regional Refugee*, accessed on 28 May 2017, at http://data.unhcr.org/syrianrefugees/regional.php.

———, High Commissioner for Refugees, *The 1951 Refugee Convention and 1967 Protocols*, Geneva: United Nations, 2010, at https://www.unhcr.org/3b66c2aa10.

———, High Commissioner for Refugees, UNHCR Global Focus, 12 March 2021, at https://reporting.unhcr.org/middleeast.

———, Human Rights Council, "Joint Submission to the Human Rights Council at the 31st Session of the Universal Periodic Review: Saudi Arabia," Geneva: Universal Periodic Review, [Institute on Statelessness and Inclusion, the Global Campaign for Equal Nationality Rights and the European Saudi Organization for Human Rights], 29 March 2018, at https://files.institutesi.org/UPR31_SaudiArabia.pdf.

———, *International Migration 2020*, at https://www.un.org/development/desa/pd/news/international-migration-2020.

———, *International Migration 2020 Highlights*, at https://www.un.org/development/desa/pd/sites/www.un.org.development.desa.pd/files/international_migration_2020_highlights_ten_key_messages.pdf.

———, "More than 191,000 People Killed in Syria with 'No End in Sight'—UN," New York: United Nations, 22 August 2014, at https://news.un.org/en/story/2014/08/475652-more-191000-people-killed-syria-no-end-sight-un.

———, "Nearly 300,000 Syrians Displaced from Idlib since Mid-December, Security Council Hears," *UN News*, 3 January 2020, at https://news.un.org/en/story/2020/01/1054741.

———, Office for the Coordination of Humanitarian Affairs, "About OCHA Syria," New York: United Nations, June 2018, at http://www.unocha.org/syrian-arab-republic/about-ocha-syria.

———, Office for the Coordination of Humanitarian Affairs, Financial Tracking Services, at https://fts.unocha.org/donors/.

———, Office for the Coordination of Humanitarian Affairs, "Five Saudi Relief Planes Reach Iran," *News and Press Release*, 27 December 2003, at https://reliefweb.int/report/iran-islamic-republic/five-saudi-relief-planes-reach-iran.

———, Office for the Coordination of Humanitarian Affairs, "Sa'udi Arabia," at
https://www.unocha.org/middle-east-and-north-africa-romena/saudi-arabia.

———, Office for the Coordination of Humanitarian Affairs, "Saudi Arabia Joins Top Donors To The Haiti Appeal," *News and Press Release*, 28 January 2010, at https://reliefweb.int/report/haiti/saudi-arabia-joins-top-donors-haiti-appeal.

———, Office for the Coordination of Humanitarian Affairs, Syrian Arab Republic, accessed on 28 May 2017, http://www.unocha.org/syria.

———, Office for the Coordination of Humanitarian Affairs, "The Saudi Aid Platform—Technology to Track Foreign Contributions," *News and Press Release*, 12 June 2020, at https://reliefweb.int/report/yemen/saudi-aid-platform-technology-track-foreign-contributions.

———, Office for the Coordination of Humanitarian Affairs, "UN Humanitarian Office Puts Yemen War Dead at 233,000, Mostly from 'Indirect Causes'," 1 December 2020, at
https://news.un.org/en/story/2020/12/1078972.

———, United Nations Relief and Works Agency for Palestine Refugees in the Near East, "King Salman Humanitarian Aid And Relief Centre (KSRelief) and UNRWA Sign US$1 Million Contribution for Covid-19 Response in Gaza,"1 May 2020, at https://www.unrwa.org/newsroom/
press-releases/king-salman-humanitarian-aid-and-relief-centre-ksrelief-and-unrwa- sign-us1.

———, United Nations Relief and Works Agency, "UNRWA In Figures as of 1 January 2015," Jerusalem: United Nations Relief and Works Agency, at https://www.unrwa.org/sites/default/files/unrwa_in_figures_2015.pdf.

———, Security Council, Resolution 2216 (2015), 14 April 2015, at
https://documents-dds-ny.un.org/doc/UNDOC/GEN/N15/103/72/PDF/N1510372.pdf.

———, "Smugglers See Thousands of migrants in Yemen as 'a Commodity', UN Agency Warns," *UN News*, 8 May 2018, at
https://news.un.org/en/story/2018/05/1009122.

———, "Summary by the Secretary-General of the report of the United Nations Headquarters Board of Inquiry into certain incidents in northwest Syria since 17 September 2018 involving facilities on the United Nations deconfliction list and United Nations supported facilities," with important details was available at
https://www.un.org/sg/sites/www.un.org.sg/files/atoms/files/NWS_BOI_Summary_06_April_2020.pdf.

———, Treaty Collection, *Chapter V Refugees and Stateless Persons*, at https://treaties.un.org/doc/Publication/MTDSG/Volume%20I/Chapter%20V/V-2.en.pdf.

———, Treaty Collection, "Convention Relating to the Status of Refugees, Geneva, 28 July 1951", United Nations, *Treaty Series* 189:2, p. 7, at https://www.unhcr.org/5d9ed32b4.

―――, UN receives $1 billion contributions from Saudi Arabia and UAE to assist Humanitarian Crisis in Yemen, *Funds for NGOs*, 19 February 2021, at https://www2.fundsforngos.org/humanitarian-and-disaster-relief/un-receives-1-billion-contributions-from-saudi-arabia-and-uae-to-assist-humanitarian-crisis-in-yemen/.

United States of America, "Saudi Arabia: Tier 2 Watch List," in *Trafficking in Persons Report*, Washington, D.C.: United States Department of State, June 2018, pp. 369–372, at https://www.state.gov/documents/organization/282798.pdf.

United States of America, Central Intelligence Agency, "Saudi Arabia: People and Society," *The World Factbook 2020*, Washington, D.C.: Central Intelligence Agency, at https://www.cia.gov/the-world-factbook/countries/saudi-arabia/#people-and-society.

United States of America, Central Intelligence Agency, "Syria: People and Society," *CIA World Factbook*, at https://www.cia.gov/library/publications/the-world-factbook/geos/sy.html.

Marko Valenta, Jo Jakobsen, Drago Župari-Ilji and Hariz Halilovich, "Syrian Refugee Migration, Transitions in Migrant Statuses and Future Scenarios of Syrian Mobility," *Refugee Survey Quarterly* 39:2, June 2020, pp. 153–176.

Nikolaos van Dam, *Destroying a Nation: The Civil War in Syria*, London and New York: I. B. Tauris, 2017.

Paolo Verme, Chiara Gigliarano, Christina Wieser, Kerren Hedlund, Marc Petzoldt, and Marco Santacroce, *The Welfare of Syrian Refugees: Evidence from Jordan and Lebanon*, Washington, D.C.: International Bank for Reconstruction and Development/The World Bank, 2016.

Espen Villanger, *Arab Foreign Aid: Disbursement Patterns, Aid Policies and Motives*, (CMI Report R 2007:2), Bergen, Germany: Chr. Michelsen Institute, at https://www.cmi.no/publications/2615-arab-foreign-aid-disbursement-patterns.

Ahmed Abou-El-Wafa, *The Right to Asylum between Islamic Shari'ah and International Refugee Law: A Comparative Study*, Riyadh: Naif Arab University for Security Sciences, 2009, at https://www.unhcr.org/4a9645646.pdf.

Iain Watson, "Asian ODA, Assessing Emerging Donors in the Asian Region," in *Foreign Aid and Emerging Powers: Asian Perspectives on Official Development Assistance*, Abingdon and New York: Routledge, 2014, pp. 152–185.

William Montgomery Watt, *Muhammad: Prophet and Statesman*, New York: Oxford University Press, 1961.

Myron Weiner, "On International Migration and International Relations," *Population and Development Review* 11:3, September 1985, pp. 441–455.

Jeffrey White, "Hizb Allah at War in Syria: Forces, Operations, Effects and Implications," *CTC Sentinel* 7:1, January 2015, West Point Academy: Combating Terrorism Center, at https://www.ctc.usma.edu/hizb-allah-at-war-in-syria-forces-operations-effects-and-implications/.

Bibliography

A.A.I.N. Wickramasinghe and Wijitapure Wimalaratana, "International Migration and Migration Theories," *Social Affairs* 1:5, Fall 2016, pp. 13–32.

Kathrin Nina Wiedl, *The Hama Massacre: Reasons, Supporters of the Rebellion, Consequences*, Munich: Grin, 2007.

Catherine Wihtol de Wenden, *Atlas Mondial des Migrations*, Paris: Autrement, 2009.

Thomas G. Weiss and Larry Minear, "Do International Ethics Matter? Humanitarian Politics in the Sudan," *Ethics and International Affairs* 5:1, March 1991, pp. 197–214.

World Bank, *Arab Development Assistance: Four Decades of Cooperation*, Washington, D.C.: The World Bank, June 2010, at http://documents1.worldbank.org/curated/en/725931468277750849/pdf/568430WP0Arab010Box353738B01PUBLIC1.pdf.

———, "Forty Years of Development Assistance from Arab Countries," Washington, D.C.: The World Bank, 2 September 2010, at https://www.worldbank.org/en/news/feature/2010/09/02/forty-years-development-assistance-arab-countries.

———, The Kurdistan Region of Iraq: Assessing the Economic and Social Impact of the Syrian Conflict and ISIS, Washington, D.C.: World Bank, 2015, at http://documents.worldbank.org/curated/en/574421468253845198/pdf/940320REVISED0000Box391428BIQ0FINAL.pdf.

———, *World Development Indicators Database*, Washington, D.C.: World Bank, 19 March 2021, at https://data.worldbank.org/indicator/NY.GNP.MKTP.CD, and https://data.worldbank.org/indicator/NY.GNP.PCAP.CD?locations=SA.

Bob Woodward, *Fear: Trump in the White House*, New York: Simon & Schuster, 2018.

Robin Wright, "Saudi Arabia's Crown Prince Picks a Very Strange Fight with Canada," *The New Yorker*, 8 August 2018, at https://www.newyorker.com/news/news-desk/saudi-arabias-crown-prince-picks-a-very-strange-fight-with-canada.

Joshue Yaphe, *Saudi-Iraqi Relations, 1921–1958*, Doctoral Dissertation, Washington, D.C.: American University 2021.

"Yemen: Civilians Bombed, Shelled, Starved: War Crimes by Saudi-Led Coalition, Houthis Go Unaddressed," *World Report 2019*, New York: Human Rights Watch, 2019, at https://www.hrw.org/world-report/2019.

"Yemen: Internal displacement continues amid multiple crises," 17 December 2012, Internal Displacement Monitoring Center, at http://www.internal-displacement.org/8025708F004BE3B1/(httpInfoFiles)/8D24A4E89B93B100C1257AD70052594B/$file/yemen-overview-dec2012.pdf.

Kirsten Zaat, "The Protection of Forced Migrants in Islamic Law," Research Paper Number 146, Geneva: United Nations High Commissioner for Refugees, December 2007, at https://www.unhcr.org/research/working/476652cb2/protection-forced-migrants-islamic-law-kirsten-zaat.html.

Maysa Zahra, "Saudi Arabia's Legal Framework of Migration," Explanatory Note No. 4/2013, Gulf Labor Markets and Migration, European University Institute (EUI) and Gulf Research Center (GRC), 2013, available at http://www.gulfmigration.eu.

———, "Saudi Arabia's Legal Framework of Migration," Explanatory Note No. 3/2018, Gulf Labor Markets and Migration, European University Institute (EUI) and Gulf Research Center (GRC), 2018, available at http://www.gulfmigration.eu.

Olivier Zajec, *Frontières: Des Confins d'autrefois aux murs d'aujourd'hui*, Dourdan, France: Éditions Chronique, 2017.

Roger Zetter, *Protection in Crisis: Forced Migration and Protection in a Global Era*, Brussels, Belgium: Transatlantic Council on Migration and Migration Policy Institute, March 2015, at https://www.migrationpolicy.org/research/protection-crisis-forced-migration-and-protection-global-era.

Khayr al-Din al-Zirikli, *Shibh al-Jazirah fi 'Ahd al-Malik 'Abdul-'Aziz* [The Peninsula in the Era of King 'Abdul 'Aziz], Beirut: 1970.

Aristide R. Zolberg, Astri Suhrke and Sergio Aguayo, *Escape from Violence: Conflict and the Refugee Crisis in the Developing World*, Oxford: Oxford University Press, 1989.

Aristide R. Zolberg, Astri Suhrke and Sergio Aguayo, "International Factors in the Formation of Refugee Movements," *International Migration Review* 20:2, June 1986, pp. 151–169.

Index

9/11 tragedies, 5

'Abayas, 125, 135
'Abanmi, Suhail, 92
'Abdallah, King. *See* Al Sa'ud, 'Abdallah bin 'Abdul 'Aziz
'Abdul Nasir, Jamal [Gamal]. *See* Nasir
Abdullah, Waleed, 86
Abdurrahman, Rami, 174
Abhah (Sa'udi Arabia), xiii, 146
Abyan (Governorate), 154
Abou El-Wafa, Ahmed, 10, 61
Abu Dhabi Fund for Development (ADFD), 103
Aceh (Indonesia), 94, 96, 100, 202
Aden (Yemen), 148, 152, 153
Adubisi, Ali, 44
Afghanistan, xiv, 2, 5, 13, 69, 89, 106
African Charter on Human and People's Rights (1981), 8, 58, 216–230
Aguayo, Sergio, 33
Ahmed, Ali al-, 189–190
'Alawi (sect), 'Alawite, 168, 169, 175, 190
Albania, Albanians, 69, 85, 122, 192
Altahi, Hassen, 93–94, 97, 201–202
Aleppo (Syria), 170
Algeria, 69, 106, 184, 185, 239
'Ali, Zayn al-'Abidin bin [Zine al-Abidine Ben Ali], 48
'alim. See '*Ulamah*
American Red Cross, 96
Amir Idrissi (Yemen), 148
Amman, 110, 179, 180, 184
Amnesty International, 83, 84, 173, 184
'Anab Baladih (Syrian organization), 175
Ankara, 70, 169, 181–182, 189, 192
'Anizah (confederation), 49
Ansar al-Shari'ah, 154, 162
Ansar Allah. *See* Huthi(s)
Aoun, Michel, 192
Arab(s), 3, 4, 5, 7, 17, 32, 41, 42, 48, 51, *passim*

Arab Bank for Economic Development in Africa (BADEA), 102
Arab Charter on Human Rights (1994), 8, 58, 239–247, 268, 270
Arab Fund for Economic and Social Development (AFESD), 102
Arab Gulf Program for Development, 96–97
Arab Gulf Programme for United Nations Development Organizations (AGFUND), 102
Arab Monetary Fund (AMF), 102
Arab League. *See* League of Arab States
Arabian Gulf, 32, 148
Arabian Peninsula, 11, 32, 42, 145, 151
Arakan (region), 80, 81
Aramco, 96–97
Arango, Joaquin, 26
Armenia, Armenian(s), 47, 89, 175, 185
Armenian Genocide, 47
Arrukban, Abdulaziz bin Mohamed, 97
Arslan, Talal, 192
'Artawiyyah (camp), 83–84
Asir, 147, 148, 149, 150
Assad, Bashar al-, 168, 170, 172, 191–192
Assad, Hafiz al-, 169–170
Astana, 172
Assyrians, 175
Asylum, 2, 8, 9, 12–13, 17–18, 21, 22, 27, *passim*
Austria, 101, 184, 185
Australia, 2, 5, 120, 185, 189
'Awamiyyah, al-, 44
'Awlaki, Anwar al-, 162
Ayn al-Hilwih (Lebanon), 109
Azerbaijan, 69
Azraq Camp (Jordan), 178

Ba'ath, 168, 176
Baderin, Mashood, 58, 195
Badr, Imam Muhammad al- (Yemen), 150
Baghdad, 65, 75, 84, 101, 151, 169, 180

Bahrain, 69, 167, 184, 186, 188, 239
Balkan Wars (1912–1913), 34
Bam (Iran) earthquake, 100, 202
Bangladesh, 50, 51, 69, 78, 81, 82, 106, 110, 156
Banna, Hassan al-, 76
Basrah, 75
Bedouin, 148
Belgium, 184, 185
Benhabib, Seyla, 60
Benin, 69, 106
Berlin, 5, 44, 166, 190
Biden, Joe, 165, 304n4
bidun, 14, 41, 43, 48, 49–50, 53, 54, 197
Beirut, 3, 44, 57, 71, 72, 75, 177, 192
Bosnia, Bosnians, 176
Brazil, 185
Brookings Institution, 184
Brunei-Darussalam, 69
Bulgaria, 70, 71, 184, 185
Burkina Faso, Burkinabes, 17, 69, 106, 119, 122, 131, 136, 142
Burundi, 107

Cairo, 67, 68, 174
Cairo Declaration on Human Rights in Islam (1990), 8, 58, 231–238
Caliph, 112
Caliphate, 65, 91, 154
Cameroon, Cameroonians, 17, 69, 119, 122, 131, 136, 138, 321n1
Canada, 2, 5, 39, 82, 181, 183, 185, 189
Chad, Chadians, 17, 69, 106, 118, 122, 127, 131, 156
China, 106
Churchill, Winston, 75
Circassian (ethnicity), 175
Combatting Trafficking in Persons in Accordance with the Principles of Islamic Law, 261–271
Comoros, 69, 106, 239
Congo, 107
Convention on the Elimination of All Forms of Discrimination Against Women (CEDAW), 46, 60
Convention on the Rights of the Child (CRC), 15, 46, 52, 60
Cooperation Council for Arab Gulf States. *See* Gulf Cooperation Council
Çorabitir, Metin, 189
Croatia, 184, 185
Custodian of the Two Holy Mosques. *See* Khadim al-Haramayn al-Sharifayn

Côte d'Ivoire, 69
Cyprus, 185

Dacca, 81
Dada, Idi Amin (Uganda), 48
Daʿish [Daesh]. *See* Islamic State of Iraq and Syria (ISIS)
Damascus (Syria), 56, 75, 86, 168, 170–172, 176, 179, 191–192
Darʿah (Syria), 168, 170
Dawlah al-Islamiyyah fil-Iraq wal-Sham, Al-. *See* ISIS
Dayr al-Zur (Syria), 75, 175
Declaration of the Rights of Man and the Citizen (1879), 8
Denmark, 98, 184, 185
Developmewnt Cooperation Directorate (DAC), 97–98, 101–102
Djibouti, 69, 106, 125, 239
Doha (Qatar), 42, 184
Dohuk (Iraq), 65, 66
Donini, Antonia, 96, 97
Druze, 170, 192
Dubai, 146, 174
Duda, Andrzej Sebastian, 6
Dumah (Syria), 172

Egypt, 3, 4, 9, 16, 57, 59, 68, 69, 70, 71, 76–78, 82, 87, 100, 102, 110, 127, 145, 150, 159, 170, 176, 184, 185, 239
El Salvador, 33
Elmadmad, Khadija, 59
Erbil (Iraq), 65, 66
Erdoğan, Recep Tayyip, 172, 192
Eritrea, Eritreans, 17, 54, 107, 118, 122, 125–127, 130, 156
Ethiopia, Ethiopians, 16, 33, 106, 118, 122, 124, 137, 138, 156
Europe and refugees, 33–35
European Saudi Organization for Human Rights (ESOHR), 44

Faruk (Farouk), King, 76
fatwah, xiii, 264, 269
Faysal, King. *See* Al Saʿud, Faysal bin ʿAbdul ʿAziz
Filipinos, 119
Finland, 185
Foster, Michelle, 60
fuqara', 91, 201
France, 74, 75, 169, 184, 185, 189
Freeland, Chrystia, 39
Free Patriotic Movement, 192

Gabon, 69, 107
Gambia, 69, 106
Gaziantep (Turkey), 181
Gender Discrimination on Sa'udi Arabia's Nationality Law, 248–258
Georgians, 176
Germany, 5, 21, 75, 82, 111, 128, 166, 183, 184, 185, 189, 190
and Syrian refugees, 5–6
Ghamdi, Aqeel Al, 110–111
Ghomgham, Israa al-, 44
Ghana, Ghanaians, 17, 106, 119, 122, 131–132
Gharaibeh, Ayman, 155
Ghutah (Syria) chemical attack, 171
Greece, Greek(s), 58, 71, 176, 182, 184, 185, 196
Griffiths, Martin, 163
Guinea, 69, 107
Guinea-Bissau, 69
Gulf Cooperation Council (GCC), 4, 99, 184, 186, 188–190, 203, 259, *passim*
and financial aid to Syrians, 188–189
and Syrian refugees, 184–189
Guterres, António, 90
Guyana, 69

hadith(s), 267
Hadi, 'Abid Rabbu Mansur al-, 48, 146, 161, 164
Haiti, 93, 94, 97, 107
Haiti Emergency Response Fund, 97
hajj, 78, 91, 116, 117, 119, 122, 126–128, 131, 132, 134, 136, 139, 143–144, 190
Hakim, Abdullah Yahya Al, 162
Hama [Hamah] (Syria), 169, 170
Hammurabi, 58, 196
Hariri, Sa'ad, 192
Hasah Province (Sa'udi Arabia), xiii
Hathaway, James C., 60
Hathloul, Loujain al-, 44
Hayatli, Musab, 63
Held, David, 36
Hijaz [Hijazi] Province (Sa'udi Arabia), 119, 120, 144, 148, 254
hijrah [migration], 9, 56–60, 62, 143
and asylum, 57–61
Hindu, Hindus, Hinduism, 7, 51, 79, 80
Hizballah [Hezbollah], 169, 171, 174, 192
Homs [Hums] (Syria), 169
Honduras, 106

Hudaydah (Yemen), 149, 163, 164
Human Rights Watch, 157, 163, 173
Hungary, 6, 35, 184, 185
Husayn [Hussein], Saddam, 83, 145, 171
Huthi(s) [Yemeni rebels], 145–147, 151–152, 153, 154, 155, 156, 158–161, 165
Huthi, Abd Al-Khaliq al-, 162
Huthi, Husayn al-, 151
Horn of Africa, 124, 134, 156

Idlib (Syria), 172, 173, 192
ikhtilat, 135
India, Indians, 75, 94, 100, 107, 156, 189, 202
Indonesia, 69, 94, 100, 106, 119, 133, 134, 160, 202
Institute for Gulf Affairs (IGA), 189
Institute on Statelessness and Inclusion, 43
Internally Displaced Persons (IDPs), 9, 59, 60, 65–67, 89, 174
International Committee of the Red Cross (ICRC), 83
International Labor Organization, 177
International migration, 20–22, *passim*
and cumulative causation theory, 31
and dual labor market theory, 28–29
and globalization, 36
and institutional theory, 31
and migration system theory, 30–31
and neo-classical theory, 26–27
and network theory, 29–30
and new economic of labor migration theory (NELM), 27–28
and theories, 22–33
International Organization for Migration (IOM), 110
International Rescue Committee, 157
*iqamah, iqamah*s, 124, 127, 136, 138, 144
Iran, Iranians, 42, 69, 70, 71, 75, 82, 84, 100, 101, 146, 161–163, 164–165, 167, 168, 169, 171, 172, 173, 174, 176, 191
Iraq, Iraqis, 3, 4, 5, 11, 16, 27, 35, 47, 49, 54, 57, 65, 66, 67, 69, 74–76, 82–85, 87, 89, 101, 106, 110, 142, 145, 150, 151, 167–169, 174–176, 178, 180–181, 184, 185, 189, 239
Islah Party (Yemen), 161
Islam, 5, 6, 8, 9, 16, 16, 18, *passim*
and Five Pillars, 91
Islamic State (of Iraq and Syria)/ISIS, 42, 65, 66, 85, 168, 169, 171

Islamic Development Bank (IsDB), 102, 103
Istanbul, 181, 182
Israel, 15, 32, 52, 57, 100, 101, 168, 173, 178, 197
Italy, 75, 186, 189

Jabhat Fatah al-Sham (Syria), 168
Japan, 107, 189
Jiddah [Jeddah], xiii, 76, 86, 92, 117–120, 122–124, 126, 128–136, 138 139, 142–143, 159, 160
Jihad, Jihadist, 169, 170
Jizan (Sa'udi Arabia), 125, 146, 147, 148, 149, 150
Jordan, Jordanian(s), 3,4, 69, 75, 77–78, 82, 100, 102, 106, 110, 166–167, 174–180, 183–185, 189, 191, 239
Jubayr, 'Adil al-, 39, 191
Judaism, 9, 59

kafalah (sponsorship), 52, 54, 129, 264
kafil (sponsor), 126, 138
Katrina (Hurricane), 96
Kazakhstan, 69, 106
Kenworthy, Katelynn, 42
Kenya, 106, 230
Kerry, John, 171–172
Khadim al-Haramayn al-Sharifayn, 51, 79, 87–88, 101, 105, 112, 114, 118
Khalifa, Khaled, 109
Khan Shaykhun (Syria), 172
Khanneqin, 75
Khao Lak (Thailand), 94
Khatib, Hamzah al-, 170
Khattab, 'Umar ibn al-, 112
Khuli, Omar Al, 50
khums, 91
Kilani, Rashid 'Ali al-, 16, 27, 74–76, 87
Kilis (Turkey), 181
King Faysal [Faisal] Center for Research and Islamic Studies, ii, ix, x
King Faysal [Faisal] Foundation, ii
King Salman Center for Humanitarian Relief (KSRelief), 4, 105–111, 191, 202–203
Kosovo, 34
Krähenbühl, Pierre, 108
Kurd/Kurdish, 175, 180, 185
Kurdi, Aylan, 183
Kurdish Democratic Union Party (PYD), 169
Kurdish Regional Government, 65

Kurdish Syrian Democratic Forces (SDF), 168
Kurdistan Region in Iraq (KRI), 66
Kurdistan Workers' Party (PKK), 169
Kuwait, 3, 14, 49–50, 69, 83–84, 96, 99, 101–103, 145, 151, 167, 184–188, 197, 202, 239
Kyi, Aung San Suu, 81, 292n68
Kyrgyzstan, 69, 106

Latakiyyah (Syria), 175
Lavrov, Sergey, 171–172
League of Arab States, 4, 52, 100, 103, 245–247
League of Nations, 47, 48
Lebanon, 3, 4, 57, 69, 71, 72, 82, 100, 102, 106, 109–110, 128, 166–169, 174–178, 184–185, 189, 191, 192, 193
  and 1951 UN Convention, 3, 57, 72
  and Cedar Revolution (2005), 168
  and Palestinian refugees, 57–58
  and refugees, 71, 72
Lenderking, Timothy, 165
Lesbos (Greece), 182
Levant, Levantine, 5, 32, 57, 167, 168, 176, 178, 189
Libya, Libyan(s), 35, 48, 69, 184, 185, 239
Luxembourg, 98
Lysa, Charlotte, 55

Ma'abdi, Ahmad, 78, 79
Madagascar, 107
Madinah (Sa'udi Arabia), 9, 59, 60, 61, 63, 73, 112, 117–119, 123, 128, 129, *passim*
Mafraq (Jordan), 178
Magna Carta (1215), 8
Majlis al-Shurah, 207, 211, 248, 255, 256
Makkah (Sa'udi Arabia), 61, 73, 78, 91, 112, 117–119, 123, 128–129, 131–132, *passim*
Malaysia, 69, 110, 185
Malawi, 1
Maldives, 69, 106
Mali, 69, 107
Malik, Charles, 72
Malta, 186
Manchester, 1
Mari'ah (Syria), 171
masakin, al- (needy), 91, 201

Masjid al-Haram, 112, 210
Masjid al-Nabawih, 112
Mauritania, 69, 106, 131, 159, 239
Mauritius, 106
Mattis, Jim, 172
McGrew, Anthony, 36
Médecins Sans Frontières, 98
Merkel, Angela, 5
Migrations, 1, 3, 15, 19, 22, 23, 25, 36, 37, 47, 56, 57, 73, 78
  and undocumented workers, 127–129
Montenegro, 186
Morocco, 4, 69, 107, 239
Mozambique, 69, 107
muhajirun. See *hijrah*
Muhammad (Prophet), 59, 60, 62, 73, 114, 205, 206, 207, 266
Muslim, Muslims, x, 3, 7, 9, 10, 16, 18, 33, 35, 42, 48, 51–52, *passim*
Muslim Brotherhood, 16, 57, 76–78, 84, 87, 170, 178, 208, 240
Myanmar, ix, 2, 13, 14, 21, 50, 51, 78, 79, 90, 81, 106, 110, 197
  and religious sects, 78–82
Mutawakkilate Kingdom. See Yemen
Myrdal, Gunnar, 31

Nahr al-Barid (Lebanon), 109
Najd, Najdi (Saʿudi Arabia), 47, 48, 148, 254
Najran (Saʿudi Arabia), 147, 148, 149, 150
Nasir, Jamal ʿAbdul, xiv, 77, 150
Nepal, 82, 107
Netherlands, 43, 171, 184, 185
New Orleans, 96
Nicaragua, 106
Niger, 69, 106, 159
Nigeria, Nigerian(s), 17, 69, 106, 110, 119, 122, 123, 128, 130, 138
niqab, 125
North Macedonia, 186
Norway, 98, 184, 185, 321n1
Norman, Julie M., 40–42, 194–195
Nusrah, Jabhat al- (Sunni militia), 168

Obama, Barack H., 171
Official Development Assistance (ODA), 95, 97–98, 101–103, 105
Oman, Sultanate of, 69, 158, 167, 188, 239
OPEC Fund for International Development (OFID), 102–103
Orbán Victor, 6

O'Reilly, Karen, 29
Organization for Economic Co-operation and Development (OECD), 97–99, 101–102
Organization for the Prohibition of Chemical Weapons (OPCW), 171–172
Organization of Islamic Cooperation (OIC), 8, 10, 58, 68, 69, 70
Organization of Petroleum Exporting Countries (OPEC), 101
Othman, Nabil, 86
Ottoman Empire, 47, 145, 147–148, 249, 304n1
Operation Decisive [Firmness] Storm, 162

Pakistan, xiv, 48, 69, 78, 100, 106, 110, 156, 202
Palestine, 3, 15, 52, 68, 69, 106, 108, 110, 203, 239
Palestinian(s), 2, 3, 14, 15, 32, 41, 43, 49, 52–54, 56, 57, 72, 100, 101, 108, 109, 174, 177, 178, 197
Paris, 127, 206
Partiya Karkeren Kurdistane (Kurdistan Workers' Party, PKK), 169
Partiya Yekitiya Democrat (Kurdish Democratic Union Party, PYD), 169
Persia, Persian(s), 146, 176
Philippine(s), 106, 133, 137. See also Filipinos
Pillay, Navi, 173
Poland, 6, 107
Putin, Vladimir, 171, 172

Qaʿidah, al-, 168
Qaʿidah, on the Arabian Peninsula, al-, 146, 162
Qamishlih (Syria), 175
Qatar, 42, 69, 96, 99, 167, 184, 185, 186, 188, 189, 202, 239
Qur'an, Qur'anic [Holy Scriptures], 57, 61–63, 73–74, 82, 87, 91, 112–114, 124, 201, 205–207, 210, 215, 261, 263, 266, 269, *passim*
Quraysh tribe, 62

Rabiʿah, ʿAbdallah Al, 107–108
Rafhah (Camp), 4, 16, 54, 82–85, 87, 191
Rakhine (Province), 50, 79
Rangoon. See Yangoon

Refugees, 2–6, 8–18, 19, 22, 25, 28, 29, 30, 32, 34, 35, 36, *passim*
  and challenges to Sa'udi Arabia, 194–204
  and definitions, 12–14
  and discrimination and human rights violations, 43–45
  and Europe, 33–35
  and GCC States, 184–189
  and monotheistic faiths, 9
  and Muslim Brotherhood, 76–78
  and Shari'ah Law, 61–67
  and stateless persons, 13
  and Syrians, 85–87, 166–193
  and religious norms and obligations, 72–87
  and war for Iraq, 5
Research Center on Asylum and Migration in Ankara, 189
Riyadh, ii, xiii, 3, 4, 5, 7, 10, *passim*
Rohingya, 14–15, 21, 41, 43, 49, 50–55, 56, 78, 80–82, 87, 110, 197
Romania, 186
Roosevelt, Eleanor, 72
Royal United Services Institute (RUSI), 42
Russia, Russian(s), 21, 25, 97, 150, 167, 168, 179, 170–174, 176, 182, 185, 191, 192

Sa'adah (Yemen), 151, 152, 154
sadaqah, 91, 92, 113
Sa'id, Amin, 75
Sa'id, Nuri al-, 74, 290n49
Saladin, 112
salafih, 85
Salih, 'Ali 'Abdallah, 145, 150–152, 153, 154, 161
  and anti-Huthi actions, 150–152
Sallal, 'Abdallah, 150
Salman, King. *See* Al Sa'ud, Salman bin 'Abdul 'Aziz
Samta (Yemen), 125
Sana'a (Yemen), 99, 145, 147, 149, 151, 153, 163, 164
Sa'ud, Al, 48, *passim*
Sa'ud, 'Abdallah bin 'Abdul 'Aziz Al, (r. 2005–2015), xiv, 79, 140, 256
Sa'ud, 'Abdul 'Aziz bin 'Abdul Rahman Al (r. 1932–1954), 27, 47, 48, 75, 87, 147
  and refugees, 74–76, 87–88
Sa'ud, Fahd bin 'Abdul 'Aziz Al (r. 1982–2005), 151

Sa'ud, Faysal bin 'Abdul 'Aziz Al (r. 1964–1975), xiii, 76–78, 150
  and Muslim Brotherhood, 77–78
  and refugees, 76–78
Sa'ud, Khalid bin Faysal bin 'Abdul 'Aziz, Al, 79
Sa'ud, Sa'ud bin 'Abdul 'Aziz bin 'Abdul Rahman Al (r. 1953–1964), 77, 254, 255
Sa'udi Arabia, 1, 2, 3, *passim*
  and 8th largest donor in 2020, 99–100
  and 1951 UN Convention, 4–12, 47, 54–57
  and 1967 Protocol, 54–57
  and 1992 Basic Law, 53, 198
  and African migrants, 122–124, 129–132
  and amnesty initiatives, 138–140
  and amnesty policies 117, 122, 130, 137–140
  and amnesty policies towards Yemen, 155–156, 159–161
  and Anti-Trafficking in Persons Law, 53, 154–155, 198, 261–271
  and assistance to refugees in Yemen, 157–159
  and assistance to Syrian refugees in Jordan, 178–180
  and assistance to Syrian refugees in Lebanon, 177–178
  and breaking a work contract, 127
  and Burmese refugees, 14, 16, 78–82, 110
  and criticisms (on refugees), 41–43
  and expulson of Yemenis in 1990, 151
  and deportation laws, 134–138, 140–144, 198, 201
  and foreign aid, 97–111
  and foreign aid before and after 1973, 101–103
  and foreign aid as religious obligation, 111–115
  and gender discrimination, 45–47
  and General Authority of *Zakat* and Tax, 92
  and Jawazat (Office of Passports and Naturalization), 124, 137
  and impact of Syrian refugees in Kingdom, 183–184
  and integration of Syrians in the Kingdom, 189–191
  and international humanitarian assistance, 2000–2020, 95
  and Jordan Compact, 179

and judicial restrictions, 39, 84, 209, 242, 244
and Karantina (neighborhood), 123, 124, 142
and Kingdoms of Najd and Hijaz, 148
and labor laws, 52, 134–140, 198
and legal issues facing undocumented laborers, 134–135
and migrant working conditions, 132–134
and migration initiatives, 41–43
and migration plans for the future, 135–138
and Muslim Brotherhood refugees, 76–78
and nationality law, 45–47
and *nitaqat* [zoning], 117, 140–142
and ODA contributions, 2005–2020, 95
and Operation Restoring Hope, 162
and overstaying '*umrah* or *hajj* visas, 126–127
and pilgrimage dilemmas, 118–122, 142–144
and Red Crescent, 96, 111
and riyal diplomacy in Yemen, 149
and Rohingya, 51
and Royal Sa'udi Air Force, 85
and smuggling, 124–126
and spirit of 1951 UN Convention, 74, 90
and stateless communities, 47–52
and Syrian refugees, 166–167
and Ta'if Treaty (1934), 145, 148, 149, 150, 151, 152
and Third Monarchy (1932–), 47, 74, 147
and ties with Yemen, 147–152
and total foreign aid (1985–2020), 202
and United Nations, 2, 3, 5, 47, *passim*
and *Vision 2030*, 53, 92, 140, 156, 198
and Yemeni workers, 154–155
Sa'udi Fund for Development, ix, 18, 98, 103–105
Sa'udi Human Resources Development Fund, 141
Sa'udization, 45, 129
Serbia, 185
Senegal, 70, 106, 131
shahadah, 91
Shammar (tribe), 47
Shari'ah (Islamic) Law, xiii, 9, 10, 46, 52, 57, 60, *passim*
Sharif, Nawaz (Pakistan), 48

Shaykh(s), xiii, 86, 151
Shaykh, 'Abdul 'Aziz Al al-, 86
Shaykhdom, 50
Shayrat Air Base (Syria), 172
Shi'ah(s), 71, 83, 84, 192
Shi'ah dissidents, 44
Shumaysih (prison), 80
Shurah (consultation), xiii, 207, 211, 248, 255, 256
Sierra Leone, 70, 107
Singapore, 107, 185
Somalia, 70, 106, 110, 130–131, 138, 178, 186, 239
South Sudan, 2, 13, 107
Spain, 185
Sri Lanka, 94
Stephens, Michael, 42
Stockholm (talks on Yemen), 164
Sudan, Sudanese, 13, 17, 70, 106, 111, 118, 122, 123, 127, 128, 131, 138, 142, 156, 164, 178, 185, 239
Suhrke, Astri, 33
Sulaymaniyyah (Iraq), 65, 66
Sumatra (Indonesia), 94, 100, 202
Sunnah [traditions], 57, 206, 207, 215, 262
Sunni Islam, 16, 42, 43, 71, 85, 168, 170, 175, 176, 190
Suriname, 70
Sweden, 98
Switzerland, 111
Syria, Syrian(s), 2, 3, 4, 5, 6, 7, *passim*
  and 2011 uprisings, 170–173
  and appraisal of ongoing civil war, 5–7
  and army, 168
  and civil war casualties, 169
  and controversies over casualty figures, 173–174
  and demographic transformations, 174–183
  and Free Syrian Army, 168
  and Germany, 5–6
  and Hamah massacres, 170
  and refugees, 167–170
  and refugees in GCC States, 188
  and refugees in Iraq, 180–181
  and refugees in Jordan, 178–180
  and refugees in Lebanon, 177–178
  and refugees in Turkey, 181–183
  and Tomahawk missile attacks, 172

Tajikistan, 70, 106
Talminas (Syria), 171
Tamil Nadu (India), 94

Tanzania, 106
Tawiyyih, al-, 83
Thailand, 94, 106
Thiollet, Hélène, 174
Togo, 70
Trudeau, Justin, 39
Trump, Donald J., 172–173
Tunisia, 3, 48, 70, 170, 184, 185, 239
Turkawi, Mohammed al-, 86
Turkey, 2, 3, 4, 70, 71, 75, 82, 98, 100, 110, 167, 169, 172–180, 181–183, 184, 185, 189, 192
Turkmen, 175
Turkmenistan, 70, 175

Uganda, 70
'Ulamah, xiii, 91, 139
Umda(s) (community leader[s]), 121, 137
Ummah, 211–215, 231–232
'umrah, 78, 116, 117, 118, 119, 122–124, 126–128, 131, 132, 136, 139, 143
United Arab Emirates, 70, 85, 98, 99, 101, 111, 146, 164, 167, 179, 188, 202, 239
United Arab Emirates Air Force, 85
United Kingdom, 1, 5, 21, 74, 82, 98, 120, 181, 183, 184, 185
United Nations, x, 1, 2, 3, 4, 6, 11, 12, 15, 18, 20, 25, 32, 33, *passim*
  and 1951 Convention Relating to the Status of Refugees, 3, 33–36
  and 1967 Protocol, 3, *passim*
  and alternatives, 67–72
  and Egyptian reservations, 68–70
  and International Covenant on Civil and Political Rights (ICCPR), 47
  and International Covenant on Economic, Social and Cultural Rights (ICESCR), 47
  and Iranian reservations, 70
  and Optional Protocol to CAT (Convention Against Torture), 47
  and Security Council, 146
  and Security Council Resolution 2216 (2015), 162
  and Turkish reservations, 70–71
  and the United States of America, 71
  and Western values, 7–8
United Nations Children's Fund (UNICEF), 178
United Nations Development Program's Millennium Development Goals (MDGs), 105
United Nations Financial Tracking Service (FTS), x, 109, 203
United Nations High Commissioner for Refugees (UNHCR), 2, 10, 25, 39, 49, 67, 72, 82, 83, 86, 91, 92, 100, 109, 110, 155, 176, 177, 178, 180–184, 185, 188, 259
United Nations Human Rights Council (HCR), 43
United Nations Humanitarian Coordinators for Yemen, 163
United Nations Office for the Coordination of Humanitarian Affairs (OCHA), x, 93, 111, 155, 163
United Nations Organization for the Prohibition of Chemical Weapons (OPCW), 171–172
United Nations Relief and Works Agency for Palestine Refugees in the Near East (UNRWA), 108, 109, 203, 315n47
United Nations Universal Periodic Review (UPR), 43–44
United States, 2, 5, 21, 71, 82, 84, 96, 97, 98, 120, 127, 146, 162, 165, 171–172, 181–182, 185, 203
  and 1776 Declaration of Independence, 195
Universal Islamic Declaration on Human Rights (1981), 8, 72, 205–215
Uzbekistan, 70

Venezuela, 2, 13

War for Iraq and refugees, 5
Watan, al-, 92
Watson, Iain, 94
Wahhabism, 48
Whitson, Sarah Leah, 157
Win, U Ne, 15
Women's Refugees Commission, 44
World Food Program, 111, 159

Yahyah, Ahmad bin, 147, 148, 149
Yangoon, 50, 51
Yazidi(s), 175
Yekineyen Parastina Gel (People's Protection Units-YPG), 169
Yemen, Yemenis, 3, 4, 5, 7, 11, 15, 17, 48, *passim*
Yemen Arab Republic, 145, 150, 152, *passim*

Yemen, Mutawakkilite Kingdom of, 145, 304n1
Yemen, People's Democratic Republic of, 145, 152
Yemen, Republic of, 145, *passim*
  and consequences of Huthi takeover (2015–2018), 161–163
  and Egyptian troops, 150
  and expulsion of workers from Sa'udi Arabia, 145
  and free flow of migrants, 152–154
  and humanitarian assistance, 109–111
  and Imamate, 147
  and national dialogue conference (2013), 164
  and Operation Decisive [Firmness] Storm, 162
  and Sa'udi humanitarian assistance, 157–159
  and Tihamah region, 147
  and workers in Sa'udi Arabia, 154–155

Zaat, Kirsten, 62
Zaatari Camp (Jordan), 178, 184
Zambia, 106
zakat, 16, 56, 86, 89, 90, 103, 113, 201
  and foreign aid, 91–97
Zayidi(s), 151
Zolberg, Aristide R, 33

About the Authors

Joseph A. Kéchichian is a Senior Fellow at the King Faisal Center for Research and Islamic Studies (KFCRIS), in Riyadh, Saudi Arabia, and the CEO of Kechichian & Associates, LLC, a consulting partnership that provides analysis on the Arabian/Persian Gulf region, specializing in the domestic and regional concerns of Bahrain, Iran, Iraq, Kuwait, Oman, Qatar, Saudi Arabia, the United Arab Emirates and the Yemen. He was a Senior Writer with the Dubai-based *Gulf News* for two decades (1996–2017) and served as the Honorary Consul of the Sultanate of Oman in Los Angeles, California between 2006 and 2011.

Dr. Kéchichian is the author of fifteen published volumes, including *Saudi Arabia in 2030: The Emergence of a New Leadership* (Seoul, Korea: Asan Institute for Policy Studies, 2019); *From Alliance to Union: Challenges Facing Gulf Cooperation Council States in the Twenty-First Century* (Brighton, Chicago, Toronto: Sussex Academic Press [SAP], 2016); *The Attempt to Uproot Sunni-Arab Influence: A Geo-Strategic Analysis of the Western, Israeli and Iranian Quest for Domination*, which includes a translation of *Istihdaf Ahl al-Sunna* [Targeting Sunnis], by Nabil Khalife (SAP, 2017); *'Iffat Al Thunayan: An Arabian Queen* (SAP, 2015); *Power and Succession in Arab Monarchies* (Boulder, Colorado: Lynne Rienner Publishers; and Beirut: Riyad al-Rayyes Books, 2012)—in two volumes for the Arabic translation; *Faysal: Saudi Arabia's King for All Seasons* (Gainesville, Florida: University Press of Florida; and Beirut: Dar al-'Arabiyyah lil-Mawsu'at, 2012); *Legal and Political Reforms in Sa'udi Arabia* (London: Routledge, 2012; and Beirut: Riyad al-Rayyes Books, 2015, for the Arabic translation; co-authored with R. Hrair Dekmejian, *The Just Prince: A Manual of Leadership*, which includes a full translation of the *Sulwan al-Muta'* by Muhammad Ibn Zafar al-Siqilli (London: Saqi Books, 2003); *Political Participation and Stability in the Sultanate of Oman* (Dubai: Gulf Research Center, 2005); *Succession in Saudi Arabia* (New York: Palgrave, 2001: and Beirut and London: Dar Al Saqi, 2002, 2003 [2nd edition], for the Arabic translation); and *Oman and the World: The Emergence of an Independent Foreign Policy* (Santa Monica: RAND, 1995). A forthcoming volume, *The Nationalist Al Sa'ud Advisor: Yusuf Yassin of Sa'udi Arabia*, is under review.

About the Authors

Fahad Alsharif is a Senior Research Fellow at the King Faisal Center for Research and Islamic Studies (KFCRIS), in Riyadh, Saudi Arabia. He received his Ph.D. in Political Economy from the University of Exeter, UK. His dissertation, supervised by Professor Tim Niblock, was titled: *The Good, the Bad and the Ugly: Undocumented Labor in Saudi Arabia: The Case of Jeddah*. He received his M.Sc. in Administration specializing in Management from the Lindenwood University (Summa cum laude), and received his B.Sc. in Business Administration from the University of San Francisco, in the United States. Prior to joining the KFCRIS in 2017, he worked as an independent consultant and researcher at various public and private agencies in the fields of public policy (composing policy studies and briefs that were unpublished and confidential), and the political economy of labor migration. His previous experiences include working as an Adjunct Professor and Visiting Lecturer in Middle East Politics, International Studies, and Management.

At present, his research interests cover: Public policies, women empowerment, labor migration, education and the Saʻudi labor force. In 2017, representing KFCRIS, he received a research grant from Harvard University, School of Government for a project entitled "Skill Development and Job Creation in Saudi Arabia: An Assessment of the King Abdullah Scholarship Program (KASP)," in Light of the Saʻudi National Transformation Program. This project was supported by the Ministry of Labor and Social Development (MLSD) and funded by the Human Resource Development Fund (HRDF). The project produced several Briefs, including Alsharif and Mughal (2018), "Thirteen Years of Outbound Student Mobility of Saudi Women and Vision 2030: Does Gender Matter?", and "Outbound Student Mobility of Saudis and Government Sponsorship of Intensive English Language Studies Abroad."

He is the author of several publications, including "Undocumented Migrants in Saudi Arabia: COVID 19 and Amnesty Reforms," *International Migration Journal* [https://doi.org/10.1111/imig.12838 (2021)]; "Migration and the COVID-19 Pandemic in the Gulf: A Study of Foreign Expatriate Worker Communities' Coping Attitudes, Practices, and Future Prospects in Dubai and Jeddah," *Policy Report* No. 15, Konrad-Adenauer-Stiftung (co-authored with Froilan Malit, 2020); "Calculated Risks, Agonies, and Hopes: A Comparative Case Study of the Yemeni and Filipino Undocumented Migrant Communities in Jeddah," in Philippe Fargues and Nasra Shah, eds., *Migration to the Gulf: Policies in Sending and Receiving Countries* (Cambridge: Gulf Research Center, 2017); *City of Dreams, Disappointments and Optimism: The Case of Nine African Undocumented Migrants Communities in the City of Jeddah*, (Riyadh: KFCRIS, 2018); and *Empowering Women: Educational Programs and Reforms in the New Diversified Saudi Arabian Economy* (Riyadh: KFCRIS, 2019).